NEITHER WOLF
NOR DOG

NEITHER WOLF NOR DOG

American Indians, Environment, and Agrarian Change

DAVID RICH LEWIS

New York   Oxford
OXFORD UNIVERSITY PRESS
1994

Oxford University Press

Oxford   New York   Toronto
Delhi   Bombay   Calcutta   Madras   Karachi
Kuala Lumpur   Singapore   Hong Kong   Tokyo
Nairobi   Dar es Salaam   Cape Town
Melbourne   Auckland

and associated companies in
Berlin   Ibadan

Published by Oxford University Press, Inc.,
200 Madison Avenue, New York, New York 10016

Oxford is a registered trademark of Oxford University Press

Library of Congress Cataloging-in-Publication Data
Lewis, David Rich.
Neither wolf nor dog : American Indians, environment,
and agrarian change /
David Rich Lewis.
p.   cm.   Includes bibliographical references and index.
ISBN 0-19-506297-3
1. Indians of North America—West (U.S.)—Cultural assimilation.
2. Indians of North America—West (U.S.)—Agriculture.
3. Ute Indians—History.
4. Hupa Indians—History.
5. Tohono O'Odham Indians—History.
6. Social change—Case studies.
I. Title.   E78.W5L48   1994
978'.00497—dc20   93-40828

1 3 5 7 9 8 6 4 2
Printed in the United States of America
on acid free paper

"I do not wish to be shut up in a corral. It is bad for young men to be fed by an agent. It makes them lazy and drunken. All agency Indians I have seen were worthless. They are neither red warriors nor white farmers. They are neither wolf nor dog."

—Sitting Bull, Hunkpapa, 1881

"The Whites were always trying to make the Indians give up their life and live like white men—go to farming, work hard and do as they did—and the Indian did not know how to do that, and did not want to anyway. It seemed too sudden to make such a change. If the Indians had tried to make whites live like them, the whites would have resisted, and it was the same with many Indians."

—Big Eagle, Santee, 1862

PREFACE

Scholarly histories tend to grow out of and benefit from the questions generated by previous works and scholars. This study is no exception. In some ways this study is an elaboration of the themes set forward by Richard White in his path-breaking work *The Roots of Dependency*, for it takes up the issues of environment, subsistence, and social change where he leaves off—during the longer period of directed culture change and peripheral dependency. It is also a response to calls, by both anthropologists and historians, for comparative studies of the subsistence systems of Native Americans, of the processes and nature of subsistence change, and of the practical application of agrarian policies on the reservation level. As such, it is part of a small but growing body of scholarship on Native Americans and agriculture.[1] Finally, it is a work in ethnohistory, an interdisciplinary method combining the diachronic sources and perspectives of history with the synchronic sensitivity of ethnology and ethnography "to gain knowledge of the nature and causes of change in a culture defined by ethnological concepts and categories."[2]

Chapter One begins with an outline of the intellectual milieu that shaped the agrarian bent of American Indian policy, followed by a general description of how those policies took shape. Three case studies follow, each consisting of two chapters. The first provides ethnographic and environmental background for the second, which describes each group's experiences with and responses to settled reservation and allotted agriculture. Each of these chapters stands by itself, but they are better read as paired units. Ethnographic and environmental information discussed in the first will be referred to in the second without extended discussion. The chronological narrative of native culture and environmental change cannot be understood without a knowledge of the precontact status. This is particularly important for understanding native responses and the reproduction of cultural features.

Case studies can be subject-specific or stand as synedoche, the bit that reveals the universe, but there is always the question of typicality.

Comparative case studies mitigate this shortcoming to a degree by providing a wider base for analysis and generalization. I chose to study the Northern Utes, Hupas, and Tohono O'odhams for their mix of sameness and difference. First, all are western tribal groups. Each came under federal supervision at roughly the same time and experienced some form of imposed agrarian settlement in that sub-humid region beyond the hundredth meridian. Second, each group inhabited disparate environments and possessed different cultural and subsistence traditions. This diversity is important. Since cultural structures and environment delimit to some extent a people's response to change, each of these three groups become paradigmatic of a *range* of native behaviors and responses to the same directed change. Finally, I chose these peoples in hopes of broadening the representation of native groups in the literature. While all are well known, they have received less attention than some others. Each tribe's experience is exceptional but, I believe, broadly representative of the range of Native American experiences with agriculture. Ultimately the reader will determine just how representative.

Two final notes. First, the government compiled and continues to collect statistical information on Indian farming, making for what appears to be an excellent data base for quantification. But when one really digs into the narrative records, it becomes apparent how unreliable these statistics are. In the nineteenth century, agents regularly over-reported Indian farm production to impress the Bureau with their personal administrative success. Agents submitted annual reports with production figures prior to harvest. Discrepancies between estimates and actual harvests, and natural disasters between report and harvest, show up regularly in the correspondence. Also, the statistics do not always clearly identify variations in actual Indian farming—white agency farmers working land for Indians, whites leasing Indian fields, or "cultivated" versus actual "planted" acreage. Educated estimates on Indian farming can be made from the flow of correspondence and oral histories, but absolute reliance on government statistics is misleading. Therefore, I have used the most reliable statistics I could find, more as an indication of activity and the *direction* of change rather than as an absolute.[3]

Second, a word on the orthography used in this study. I am not a linguist, nor have I found a single orthographic system in which to render all of the native words I include in this study. Instead, I present native terms in italics as they appear in the ethnographic sources I consulted.

simple words of thanks are not enough to express my debt and gratitude. Finally, to Kim and Danica (who knows all good stories conclude with "The End") and that clan I proudly call my extended family, I dedicate this book.

ACKNOWLEDGMENTS

Many people and institutions need to be recognized for their contributions to this project—many more than I can remember or readily acknowledge. I would like to thank the D'Arcy McNickle Center for the History of the American Indian at the Newberry Library, Chicago, for a Pre-doctoral Fellowship (1985–86); Floyd A. O'Neil and the American West Center, University of Utah, for a year as a Visiting Scholar (1986–87); the Department of History, University of Wisconsin-Madison for a travel grant (1988); the office of the Vice President for Research, Utah State University, for a faculty research grant (1989–90); and the Department of History and College of Humanities, Arts, and Social Sciences, Utah State University, for subsidizing the cost of maps and photographs. Thanks also to the staff members of the numerous libraries and archives I visited for their help; to Winston P. Erickson for his work on the maps; to Fritz Scholder for his art and generosity; and to my editors at Oxford—Sheldon Meyer, Karen Wolny, and Joellyn M. Ausanka—for their interest and tremendous patience.

I want to thank just a few of the many people who shared their time, knowledge, and good humor with me: John Aubry, Steve Boyden, Richard H. Brown, Larry Burt, Anne M. Butler, Colin Calloway, Lester Chapoose, Carter Blue Clark, Wilfred Colegrove, Forest Cuch, Lee Davis, Eric Halpern and Beth Landau, Frederick E. Hoxie, Peter Iverson, Steve Kretzmann, Kathryn L. MacKay, Daniel J. McInerney, Jay Miller, Clyde A. Milner II, Josiah Moore, George Byron Nelson, Sr., Byron Nelson, Jr., and his family, Richard Sattler, Bernard Siquieros, Rose Summers, Helen H. Tanner, Gregory C. Thompson, Wilma Thompson, S. Lyman Tyler, Richard White, Patrick Wyaskett and his family, the UTOTs, and my colleagues in the Department of History, Utah State University. Robert Brightman deserves special recognition for helping a historian think like an ethnohistorian. Special thanks to Floyd A. O'Neil and Alan G. Bogue for their mentoring and continuing friendship. Anyone who knows these two men will understand why

CONTENTS

ILLUSTRATIONS

Maps

Photographs

NEITHER WOLF
NOR DOG

INTRODUCTION

Long before contact with Europeans, Native Americans developed elaborate cultural systems to help them order their physical and metaphysical world. They maintained diversified subsistence systems of their own design. They were hunters, gatherers, horticulturists. They inhabited varied environments and had different ways of explaining, using, regulating, and altering their surroundings as necessary or desirable. In turn the land shaped them, prescribing certain physical realities as well as opportunities for human action. It gave them a sense of place and identity. Euro-Americans, however, saw only wilderness and savagism and set about civilizing the land and people of the New World. Epidemic diseases, trade, the introduction of market values, and the appropriation of Indian land and resources all contributed to the transformation of native cultures. American policy makers sought to facilitate that evolutionary process through an agrarian-based program for Indian settlement and civilization. Indians were to become self-supporting yeomen farmers and farm families and then disappear into mainstream American society.

Reality is never as neat and clean as theory, and rarely meets simplistic expectations. The reality is that Native Americans did not disappear, culturally or biologically. They have persisted, in some cases against overwhelming odds, through adaptive change and a historical consciousness of their identity as separate peoples. This is a study about Native American responses to directed culture change, particularly the social and environmental consequences of directed subsistence change. Three western groups—the Northern Utes, Hupas, and Tohono O'odhams—serve as case studies. Each experienced and weighed the federal government's agrarian civilization program against its own cultural and environmental background. Each responded in culturally consistent ways to shape the nature of that change. And ultimately each found itself marginally incorporated or abandoned on the periphery of American society, a product of impractical theory and expectation. As Sitting Bull put it, they became neither warrior nor farmer, wolf nor dog.

Ethnohistorians studying culture change have been particularly interested in the relationships between society, subsistence, and environment. Cultural ecologists note that the greatest resistance to directed change generally centers on "core" structures, particularly systems of production. Subsistence is a fundamental structure of all cultures. It is a necessary activity and form of cultural expression that gives rise to custom. "As individuals express their life, so they are," wrote Marx and Engels. "What they are, therefore, coincides with their production, both with *what* they produce and with *how* they produce. The nature of individuals thus depends on the material conditions determining their production." However, some materialist explanations within cultural ecological theory stop there, focusing too narrowly on material constraints and cultures as simply functional adaptations to maximize production and environmental use.[1]

Taken to the extreme, this sort of environmental determinism denies the reciprocal nature of human creations and creativity. Marshall Sahlins points out that while humans live in a world of material constraints they do so "according to a definite symbolic scheme which is never the only one possible." A people's environment is both a biological sphere and a cultural creation. They determine and apply "use-values" for objects beyond mere function, in a "continuous process of social life in which men reciprocally define objects in terms of themselves and themselves in terms of objects." Subsistence production is therefore "something more and other than a practical logic of material effectiveness. It is a cultural intention." Culture constitutes or defines utility. Cultural symbols influence the choice and application of productive or adaptive options, and in turn are constantly tested, reinterpreted, or discarded in the wake of the cumulative environmental and material consequences of those choices. Production is tied to both material aspects and symbolic meanings. Symbols modify and are modified by production in the reciprocal processes of subsistence, environmental, and social change. Ultimately, cultural or ecological change is explained, is given *meaning* by material and symbolic structures.[2]

Societies and their attendant subsistence systems have never been static. Change is a natural component of biological and social organisms, but is not necessarily a unilateral or unilinear process. It is rarely a zero-sum equation—one group does not necessarily lose cultural elements in direct proportion to the elements they adopt. Change can come from within in the form of internal innovation, or change can come exogenously through the diffusion of innovative or contradictory ideas, techniques, or materials. Such elements of change themselves undergo a process of initial acceptance, dissemination and testing, modification or reinterpretation, and integration or rejection. Exogenous change can be nondirective and permissive, or directed and acculturative. While total acculturation is an extreme and infrequent end result, acculturation itself can be an adaptive and bilateral process affecting all parties involved in continuous contact.[3]

Change is not just something that happens *to* someone or something, it is a negotiated *response* to the situation. Culture change is best described as a process of adaptation, cultural reproduction, and structured transformation. Adaptation is "a means of maintaining conditions of existence in the face of change." It involves "any cultural response, or an open-ended process of modification, which copes with the conditions for existence by selectively reproducing and extending them." Adaptations can be cultural or biological, group or individual, short- or long-term strategies that coexist with conflicting or contradictory adaptations.[4]

Adaptation itself is an ongoing process of reproduction and transformation, inseparable from its consequences. "One may question," Sahlins writes, "whether the continuity of a system ever occurs without its alteration, or alteration without continuity."[5] In the process of adapting, people continue to interpret and give value to objects and actions based on existing cultural understandings, reproducing that understanding even as the objects and actions themselves change. At the same time, it is possible for people to "creatively reconsider" their cultural understandings when actions for those schemes are no longer significant. The synthesis of these processes is historical alteration or "structural transformation"—the reproduction of values and meanings as a culture is altered in action over extended periods of time. "The same kind of cultural change," Sahlins continues, "externally induced yet indigenously orchestrated, has been going on for millennia."[6]

Put another way, history does not necessarily equal absolute change because "culture functions as a *synthesis* of stability and change, past and present, diachrony and synchrony." According to Sahlins, "Every practical change is also a cultural reproduction," an attempt to keep things the same. Yet "every such reproduction of the categories is not the same. Every reproduction of culture is an alteration, insofar as in action, the categories by which a present world is orchestrated pick up some novel empirical content." The result is historic change or transformation—the more things seem to stay the same, the more they change.[7]

According to this view of change as cultural reproduction and transformation the following pattern develops. In directive contact situations, native populations consciously or unconsciously attempt to reproduce their system by applying old cultural categories to new structures to make them culturally understandable or acceptable. These new elements and functional values are fitted into traditional categories and resumed within the cultural structure. Even though such adopted elements may be redefined and used in ways unintended by the directive group, the continual incorporation of new elements invariably leads to subtle changes in basic categories of thought or action. Therefore, what starts as a conservative attempt to retain and reproduce cultural structures ultimately becomes a process of transformation and culture change.

Change is not just an internally arbitrated process. Part of the variability in the pace and scale of directed culture change relates to the level of influence the core group has on peripheral groups, and the reciprocal impact of the periphery on the core. Thomas D. Hall explains this process in terms of a continuum of incorporation—social, political, and economic. Demands for change are weakest on the contact peripheries, "areas external to the world-economy and areas where contact has barely occurred." Towards the middle of the continuum are the absorbed but ineffectively incorporated "regions of refuge." This "marginal periphery" retains older forms of social relations and is frozen in regional development, reserved by the core for later use. While marginals have little access to or impact on core markets, they are expected to intensify existing production and generate new goods for sale. At the far end of the continuum is the incorporated dependent periphery, the emergence of an economic peasantry involved in some form of cash crop production with a significant impact on the core. Groups move back and forth along this continuum at different times, but the longer and more directed incorporation becomes, the less chance there is of retreating to older ways of life. This reciprocal interaction of core and periphery along the incorporation continuum helps define the physical and temporal process of culture change.[8]

Native Americans on the "external arenas" of contact continued to operate much as they always had. They became integrated on the periphery of American society with the loss of land and subsistence resources and implementation of the government's agrarian Indian policy. Most Indian groups responded by selectively adopting aspects of white society and economy as necessary or desirable. They resisted—passively or actively—other structural and ideational elements requiring more radical changes. The elements they adopted and adapted most readily paralleled existing cultural structures and values. Indians adopted some white material goods on a replacement level—substituting white for native items to perform preexisting tasks more easily—without immediately giving up those pursuits or the cultural meanings attached to them. They reintegrated those items into existing beliefs or practices, a reproduction that tempered the immediate or potential upheaval of unmitigated directed change. By the late nineteenth century, as choices narrowed and the transformation became more pronounced, native groups experienced their complete incorporation as dependents on the periphery of American society. Even then, the process of reproduction continued as natives actively searched for ways to maintain their identities and survive on the periphery.[9] That is the story told here.

1

AGRICULTURE, CIVILIZATION, AND AMERICAN INDIAN POLICY

A consistent theme in United States Indian policy has been the attempt to civilize and assimilate Native Americans along agrarian lines. The federal government, religious organizations, and interested "friends of the Indians" saw settled western-style agriculture as the most appropriate means of making the Indian over again in their own image. They believed that the only way to save Indians from certain extinction, to incorporate them, to ensure their self-sufficiency and right to the land was to transform them into individualistic yeoman farmers and farm families, the backbone of American democracy. This belief, based in American agrarian idealism and the social-scientific view of unilinear social evolution, persisted into the twentieth century, influencing each major policy trend. Yet the success of agrarian-based policy directives rarely matched the desires or rhetoric of policy makers who refused to consider seriously the land and peoples they were so confident they could remake.

The Idea

In the history of Western Civilization, ancient Greeks and Romans were among the first to idealize agriculture as a productive pursuit and lifestyle. Aristotle, Xenophon, Socrates, Plato, and Hesiod sang the praises of the husbandman. Cicero, Virgil, Horace, Pliny, and Cato praised the agrarian tradition and sturdy yeoman farmer. They deemed agriculture "the mother of all arts," and "the only employment essential to man's needs and happiness." This tradition became part of Renaissance literature, which borrowed much of its philosophy from the classics. It reinforced teachings from the Bible demonstrating divine approbation for the farmer. Agricultural panegyrics persisted in eighteenth-century European romantic thought and literature as elite landholders, recognizing their position as genteel agriculturalists, played up the importance, dignity, and virtues of country life in an increasingly commercial age.[1]

European economists and political theorists praised agriculture as well. The French "Physiocrats" argued that agriculture embodied natural law, constituted the source of all wealth for nations, and should therefore dictate the sociopolitical order. In 1758, Swiss jurist Emmerich de Vattel praised agriculture for its social and economic value. "Of all the arts," he wrote, "tillage, or agriculture, is doubtless the most useful and necessary, as being the source whence the nation derives its subsistence. . . . [I]t forms the surest resource and the most solid fund of riches and commerce, for a nation that enjoys a happy climate." Nowhere was that physical and intellectual climate more "happy" than in the predominantly agricultural society of colonial North America.[2]

In revolutionary America, the independent yeoman farmer and landowner became symbols of egalitarian American democracy, blessed by God and a "virgin" American environment. "We are a people of cultivators," wrote Hector St. John de Crèvecœur, the independent farmer's most vocal advocate, ". . . the most perfect society now existing in the world." John Taylor, president of the Agricultural Society of Virginia, described the agricultural state as a paradise chosen by the "divine intelligence," who would ultimately judge those seeking to enter heaven by their "agricultural virtues." Agricultural clubs flourished in the early nineteenth century, spreading the gospel of agrarianism through metaphors of fertility, growth, increase, and Christian civilization, "all centering about the heroic figure of the idealized frontier farmer armed with that supreme agrarian weapon, the sacred plow."[3]

Among American Enlightenment thinkers and agrarian spokesmen, Thomas Jefferson voiced the moral virtues of small freeholding farmers in language at once classical and mythopoeic. In his *Notes on the State of Virginia*, Jefferson wrote, "Those who labor in the earth are the chosen people of God, if ever He had a chosen people, whose breasts He has made His peculiar deposit for substantial and genuine virtue." In letters to John Jay and James Madison, he called farmers "the most valuable citizens . . . tied to their country, and wedded to its liberty and interests, by the most lasting bonds." Jefferson viewed the self-sufficient farm and farm family as an idealized model for a open and democratic American society, expanding in a seemingly uninhabited and limitless environment.[4]

The Theory

In a development paralleling this rising agrarian idealism, European "social science" theorists confronted the differences between their society and those of Africa and the New World. They sought to explain the disparity in terms of preexisting paradigms—biblical creationism, declension, and the Great Chain of Being. By the mid-eighteenth century, these scholars developed models of "natural law" that explained social diversity without sacrificing European cultural hegemony. Most models stressed the relationship between subsistence systems and social development, that over time society naturally progressed through three or four distinct and consecutive stages, each corresponding roughly to a different subsistence mode—hunting (savage), herding (barbarian), agriculture, and commerce. Agriculture usually marked the beginning of true "civilization," with commerce distinguishing European civilization from others. Euro-Americans accepted this progressive development model as representing natural law and used it to define not only differential social development, but natural rights to and the proper use of land.[5]

This stage theory of progressive development from savage to barbarian to civilized society found fertile ground in the American atmosphere of agrarian idealism and revolutionary egalitarianism. It offered American leaders a powerful intellectual tool in the debate over Indian policy. Thomas Jefferson, Benjamin Rush, and Albert Gallatin placed American Indians in this teleological hierarchy and canonized the belief that they must advance toward civilization through these stages or become extinct. Lewis Cass and William Clark, superintendents of Indian affairs on the western frontiers of an expanding United States, echoed this developmental framework in their reports and writings, as did Thomas McKenney, the first commissioner of Indian affairs and architect of early American Indian policy.[6]

From the 1830s on, government officials, missionaries, and reformers emphasized the possibility of Indian development and assimilation—"through the stages of the hunter, the herdsman, the agriculturalist, and finally reaching those of commerce, mechanics, and the higher arts"—as part of "Nature's laws." Henry Rowe Schoolcraft, long associated with Indian affairs in the Old Northwest, concluded, "Civilization . . . cannot permanently exist without the cultivation of the soil. It seems to have been the fundamental principle on which the species were originally created, that they should derive their sustenance and means of perpetuation from this industrial labor." The popular pervasiveness of this progressive theory is apparent in the seal designed for the Territory of Wisconsin in 1838, which contained the Latin motto *Civilitas Successit Barbarum* surrounding an appropriate agrarian backdrop.[7]

Between 1850 and the 1870s, the stage theory of human development merged easily with a growing body of evolutionary thought in the biological and social sciences. Lewis Henry Morgan, working in the same intellectual milieu as Herbert Spencer, Charles Darwin, and Edward Tylor, proposed a familiar yet elaborate evolutionary paradigm of universal cultural stages. All societies, he argued, followed the same evolutionary path—savagism to barbarism to civilization—differentiated by "ethnical" breaks. According to Morgan, "the successive arts of sub-

sistence [hunting, pasturage, and agriculture] . . . afford the most satisfactory bases for these divisions." Applying this theory to the problem of
civilizing American Indians in 1878, Morgan stressed that Indians
would have to develop slowly through pastoralism to agriculture on
their way to civilization and assimilation—that societies were unable to
jump such "ethnical periods" of subsistence development without grave
consequences. Morgan's evolutionary paradigm influenced a generation
of policy makers and scholars, for he put into print, in systematic social
science terms, a blueprint for Indian policy.[8]

The Reality

The application of this stage theory and common portrayal of Indians
as "savages" in the process of development required white society to
ignore the realities of native subsistence systems. To justify Indian dispossession from the land, Euro-Americans denigrated indigenous agricultural systems and set their own systems of cultivation as the standard
for judgement.

Evidence suggests that Indian cultivation in the New World dates to
7000 B.C. Domesticated crops appeared in the Southwest by 2000 B.C.,
in the Mississippi drainage and Southeast between 1000 B.C. and A.D.
700, in the Plains Woodlands between 250 B.C. and A.D. 1000, in the
Great Basin by A.D. 400, and in the Northeast by A.D. 700. Settled or
shifting cultivation was a well established part of native subsistence and
ceremonial systems prior to white contact. Nearly 50 percent of native
groups cultivated domesticants at contact, producing 25 to 75 percent
of their total subsistence needs. Peoples living in the Connecticut River
valley of Massachusetts described six of the thirteen phases of their
lunar calendar in terms of horticultural product schedules, and estimates for the area show that corn alone provided 50 to 60 percent of
subsistence.[9]

Generally, native groups practiced a shifting cultivation with various
levels of sedentism. Individuals, families, or clans held usufruct rights to
certain cleared plots within a communally controlled band or tribal territory. In the Northeast and Southeast, Indian males participated in
clearing fields by girdling trees and burning heavy ground cover, leaving
women to plant and cultivate the gardens until harvest. Likewise, in the
riverine Plains environments women tended garden plots around semi-
sedentary villages, while in the Southwest men carried on the extensive
irrigated, flood-plain, and dry farming operations from their pueblos or
seasonal camps. Most groups intercropped their plants in mounded, un-
tilled fields. They applied little additional fertilizer, extending the natural fertility of the soil by burning, periodic fallowing, and the symbiotic
relations of plant intercropping. Digging sticks, antler rakes, and wood,
shell, or scapula hoes were the primary tools of cultivation. Native
peoples cared for at least eighty-six cultigens in North America, in-

cluding corn, beans and peas, tobacco, squash and gourds, melons, sunflowers, Jerusalem artichokes, flax, hemp, and cotton. When added to a long list of specifically gathered cultivars—roots, greens, berries, seeds, and herbs—their horticultural produce was substantial.[10]

Early European explorers duly noted the extensive fields and grain reserves of eastern Indian farmers, and early colonists in Virginia and New England appropriated Indian crops, fields, and methods to their advantage and salvation. Prior to the total disruption of native subsistence systems through loss of land, infectious disease, and war, Native Americans enjoyed a much more dependable subsistence from the American environment than did Euro-American settlers. Nevertheless, Euro-American settlers chose to ignore the gulf between the reality of Indian farming and their own conceptions of Indians as wandering "savages" suffering the hardships and periodic starvation of hunters. They continued to believe in the superiority of their own subsistence strategy which was agrarian, sedentary, and intensive, relying upon domesticated animals for protein, fertilizer, and power. They looked down on native systems, which were seasonally variable and diverse, which included non-domesticants, and balanced labor with leisure, accumulation with subsistence. From their perspective, native agriculture did not conform to civilized standards, for Indians raised only a limited number of plants in poorly cultivated, intercropped fields, cared for by women.[11]

In the Euro-American view, this division of labor firmly discredited Indian cultivation. Women were to occupy themselves with the domestic arts of homemaking while men tended the fields. Whites viewed hunting as inimical to a stable family life and freely condemned it as a uncivilized occupation that contributed to male idleness and female slavery. Even with his studied understanding of Indian societies and subsistence systems, Albert Gallatin disparaged this arrangement: ". . . that the labor necessary to support a man's family is, on the part of the man, a moral duty, and that to impose on woman that portion, which can be properly performed only by man, is a deviation from the laws of nature."[12]

This denigration of Indian agricultural accomplishments provided added justification for the confiscation of native lands. Both biblical and European legal traditions spoke to the natural and proper use of land. John Winthrop, first governor of Massachusetts Bay Colony, argued that by ignoring God's dictum to "improve the land," Indians left the country a virtual *vacuum domicilium*, a wilderness, open to those who would properly possess and settle it. Swiss jurist Emmerich de Vattel concurred that it was "the law of nature to cultivate the land," so that civilized European nations might legally appropriate a just amount of territory from those "who, to avoid labour, choose to live only by hunting, and their flocks."[13]

Colonial powers came to rely on these justifications when purchase or conquest of land through "just war" failed. In calling for Indian removal from Pennsylvania in 1792, Hugh Henry Brackenridge argued that they did not cultivate the soil, and "I pay little regard, therefore, to any right which is not founded in agricultural occupancy." Alexis De Tocqueville supported the colonist's claim to the land, for "it is by agriculture that man wins the soil, and the first inhabitants of North America lived by hunting." In justifying Indian removal, Lewis Cass, governor of Michigan and Secretary of War under Andrew Jackson, simply summarized agrarian and natural-rights philosophy.[14]

In the final analysis, Euro-Americans believed that when civil and savage society met, natural law required the savage to yield, accommodate, take up farming, or face certain extinction. They used this doctrine of proper land use throughout the nineteenth century as both a weapon against and a plan for American Indians. Once ensconced in the American tradition, prophets of Manifest Destiny utilized it against the British in Oregon Territory, against Mexico and the Philippines, until eventually American capitalists turned it on end to argue the dispossession of increasingly "marginal" agriculturalists.[15]

The Policy

In America, equating "civilization" with agriculture and viewing Indians as "savages" in the human hierarchy effectively spelled out the relationship between whites and Indians. It justified the dispossession of Indians from land and provided a framework for their eventual civilization or a rationale for their extinction. It required their involvement with the soil in a direct and settled subsistence system, the acquisition of domestic arts, and their conversion to Christianity. From rude attempts by missionaries in colonial America to more concerted efforts by church and state in the nineteenth century, Euro-Americans attempted to force a settled agrarian subsistence system on Native Americans. These efforts culminated in the creation of the Office of Indian Affairs, in the appointment of Indian agents, agency farmers, field matrons, and manual labor instructors, and ultimately in the policy of allotment.

In colonial America, Euro-Americans did little directly to convert Indians to an agricultural existence. While John Eliot made some attempt to settle Indians in "praying towns" where they might learn the "civilized arts," most early missionaries worried about the salvation of Indian souls rather than lives. Others experimented with educational approaches linking Christianity and agrarian civilization. Most prominent was Eleazer Wheelock, who established Moor's Charity School in Connecticut, and later Dartmouth College in New Hampshire, to train Indian missionaries and instruct them in the agricultural and the domestic arts. British colonial officials, however, felt that Indians were more valuable as actors in the fur trade and intercolonial struggles and discouraged such settlement. Sir William Johnson, superintendent of Indian affairs in the northern department (1755–74), consistently opposed plans by religious societies to establish schools or Indian farming communities. He feared losing the fur trade and believed Indians could be Christianized without altering their subsistence economy.[16]

While following many of the practical and diplomatic aspects of British Indian policy, leaders of the newly independent American government argued that instead of lavish gifts in the British style, "tools of husbandry" be distributed to tribes "who may be disposed to live by agriculture." George Washington and his secretary of war, Henry Knox, carried out this policy first with the Seneca, convincing Cornplanter to have agents teach his nation to farm so they might keep their land.[17]

Beginning with the Creeks in 1790, the government put into formal treaty its commitment to encourage a settled agrarian lifestyle by promising to provide domestic animals, agricultural implements, and instructors. The Indian Trade and Intercourse Act of 1793 affirmed this resolve by allowing the appointment of "temporary" agents to regulate trade and encourage "the Arts of husbandry and domestic manufactures, as means of producing, and diffusing the blessings attached to a well regulated civil Society." Agents like Benjamin Hawkins became unflagging advocates of this approach, which he believed would make Creeks "useful to themselves and to mankind; happy in their condition, and independent of the world." While not always happy with the rate of change, he firmly believed in the ultimate direction.[18]

During the next eighty years of formal treaty making, federal negotiators received explicit instructions to attach articles devised to introduce Indians to private property and a settled agrarian lifestyle. Negotiators promised eastern groups seed and domestic animals, tools of husbandry, and "suitable persons . . . to teach them to make fences, cultivate the earth, and such of the domestic arts as are adapted to their situation." Removal treaties included provisions for relocation on "good tillable land" and aid in breaking and fencing those lands. Negotiators encouraged tribes to take their cash annuities in agricultural implements and made indefinite agreements with western tribes that when they "eventually" settled down they would receive agricultural instructors. Even the peace medals distributed at these negotiations symbolized the government's commitment to agrarian civilization with their images of Indians trading tomahawks for plows, tepees for cabins.[19]

Thomas Jefferson expanded the government's campaign for Indian civilization. Reassured by moderate successes in the program, Jefferson signed the second Indian Trade and Intercourse Act (1802), which provided fifteen thousand dollars per annum for materials and instruction. Jefferson liberally endorsed the agrarian lifestyle he believed would provide Indians a more bountiful and stable subsistence, and, at the same time, free up land desired by white settlers. He called for the expansion of trading houses to encourage Indian sedentism and agriculture, to foster acquisitiveness and debt, and to tie them to an American market economy. Through this double-edged agrarian and trade policy he believed a "coincidence of interests" could be reached between Indians who desired goods and had a "surplus" of land, and whites who desired land and had a surplus of goods.[20]

In his second inaugural message, Jefferson summarized his Indian policy, noting that

> humanity enjoins us to teach them agriculture and the domestic arts; to encourage them to that industry which alone can enable them to maintain their place in existence, and to prepare them in time for that state of society, which, to bodily comforts, adds the improvement of the mind and morals. We have therefore liberally furnished them with the implements of husbandry and household use; we have placed among them instructors in the arts of first necessity; and they are covered with the aegis of the law against aggressors from among ourselves.[21]

Jefferson expected his "instructors in the arts of first necessity"—his agents and farmers—to facilitate the eventual merger of Indians into white society, but he remained painfully aware of the slow progress and the potential realities of removal or extinction.

Thomas L. McKenney, superintendent of Indian trade (1816–22) and the first commissioner of Indian affairs (1824–30), carried on the agrarian bent of Jefferson's policy. In 1818, Congress formalized the position of Indian agent, and McKenney ordered agents to spread the "gospel of agriculture and domestic arts" by cultivating garden plots at their factories. "This is the way," wrote McKenney, "you will most effectively promote the *great object of the Govt.* towards these unenlightened people." The House Committee on Indian Affairs concurred:

> Put into the hands of their children the primer and the hoe, and they will naturally, in time, take hold of the plough; and, as their minds become enlightened and expand, the Bible will be their book, and they will grow up in habits of morality and industry, leave the chase to those whose minds are less cultivated, and become useful members of society.

In 1819, Congress passed a Indian civilization act that provided an annual fund of ten thousand dollars, "to employ capable persons of good moral character, to instruct them in the mode of agriculture suited to their situation; and for teaching their children in reading, writing, and arithmetic."[22]

Long before this act, Christian missionaries had maintained a number of Indian schools and model farms, but this new source of funding and a corresponding wave of religious revivalism stimulated an explosion of missionary activity. The American Board of Commissioners for Foreign Missions, the Society of Friends, the Society for Propagating the Gospel, the Catholic, Moravian, Baptist, Methodist, and Episcopal churches, all took advantage of federal funds and established mission stations or manual labor schools with "pattern" farms staffed by white farmers and domestic instructors.[23] Indian boys received instruction in farming and the mechanical arts, while girls received a full domestic education. Books, such as *The Osage First Book* compiled by the American Board, contained basic literacy lessons with sentences stressing the importance of farming, proper female roles, uses of tools, the importance of cabins, private property, and the general benefits of civilization. Americus L. Hay, a Methodist missionary, recalled, "In school and in field, as well as in kitchen, our aim was to teach the Indians to live like white people." By 1848, the Indian Bureau outlined its own educational program stressing agriculture for boys and "housewifery" for girls attending some 110 boarding and manual labor schools.[24]

Despite the rhetorical emphasis on agrarian civilization, federal Indian policy was implicitly one of removal and the extinguishment of Indian land rights. In the 1820s and 1830s, officials formulating removal spoke in terms of the inevitable displacement of "savages" by advanced agrarian societies yet stressed their commitment to assisting tribes in new homelands, "happily adapted" to agriculture.[25] Rationales for removing successful agricultural tribes like the Cherokees were twisted and full of self-interest. The Georgia Assembly went so far as to argue that Cherokees "had no right to alter their condition and become husbandmen" after they had concluded treaties reserving their right to use the land as hunters. In practice, removal placed Indians in alien environments and disrupted established social and subsistence systems, forcing some tribes to rely solely on the hunt until materials arrived for clearing and fencing new fields. The haphazard direction of removal, the marginal lands assigned to Indians, and even the rational choice of tracts suited to hunting by groups resisting forced subsistence change made the rhetoric of removal ring hollow.[26]

Removal and the continued westward expansion of white settlement necessitated the creation of a system of discrete reservations to serve as the locus for directed culture change. In 1850, Indian Commissioner Luke Lea outlined the basic reservation policy in which each tribe would receive "a country adapted to agriculture" for a permanent home. Restricted there until deemed "civilized," Indians would be forced by necessity to take up farming as traditional subsistence resources disappeared. Agency farmers, blacksmiths, mechanics, and teachers would assist them in this transition to a settled agrarian lifestyle. For an annual salary of about six hundred dollars, agency farmers were to care for agency livestock, distribute seed and equipment, and open a "model" or "pattern" farm. There they would show their charges how to farm, supply the agency with food, and, it was hoped, induce Indians to open their own farms.[27]

As the number of reservations and the size of the Indian bureaucracy increased in the 1860s, so did charges of corruption, fraud, and mismanagement. After studying the problems and balancing the goal of "changing the wild hunter into a cultivator of the soil . . . the savage into a civilized man," the Senate's Doolittle Committee recommended in

1867 the appointment of missionary agents of "good character" to lead the civilization program. Responding to that report and the appeals of Christian reformers, President Ulysses S. Grant invited religious groups to nominate their own members as agents and agency personnel.[28]

The Grant Peace Policy emphasized Christian civilization and assimilation over military force and extinction while addressing criticisms of graft and corruption in the Indian Service. It also served, as Interior Secretary Carl Schurz stated, "To set the Indians to work as agriculturalists or herders, thus to break up their habits of savage life and make them self-supporting." Christian reformers stressed that missionaries be "*practical business men* who can instruct them how to live by the cultivation of the soil, and the teachings of God's Word," but in practice missionary agents did not always live up to such expectations. The continued difficulties of attracting and keeping qualified people, incompetence, and outright corruption plagued churchmen's efforts and good intentions. As missionaries they worked for Indian salvation but measured their success or failure against Indian progress toward agrarian civilization.[29]

Despite a doubling in the number of agency farmers between 1869 and 1881, and some evidence of an increase in Indian participation, the advancements of Indians toward "civilization" did not meet the ethnocentric expectations of most reformers. Indians lacked adequate agricultural implements, seed, and instruction or resisted farming altogether. The curtailment of rations and cash annuities along with other measures designed to coerce Indians to farm did not seem to be working. Reformers looked for new ways to force Indians to take up the plow.[30]

Allotment, Farmers, and Instruction

Over the years a general attitude developed within the Indian Bureau that "the common field is the seat of barbarism; the separate farm the door to civilization." Recognizing the benefits of individual property ownership and having experimented with voluntary allotment on several reservations, federal officials moved toward breaking up the collectivism of reservation life.[31]

Fundamentally, allotment was an agrarian policy for imparting civilization, carried out with horse-plow agriculture in mind. It accommodated philanthropic desires to transform Indians into independent yeomen farmers in the best Jeffersonian tradition and served the narrow self-interest of those desiring additional land for white settlement. Reformers, including Massachusetts Senator Henry L. Dawes, believed that giving each Indian a separate plot of land would break up communal farming practices, secure Indians' individual titles to land, encourage industry, hard work, and thrift, halt nomadism, instill a sense of property and pride, end Indian dependency, and ultimately promote civilization and assimilation. On 8 February 1887 the Dawes General

Allotment Act became law—fulfilling, ironically enough, the nation's commitment to the agrarian myth as it moved into an urban-industrial age where farmers were forced to take collective action to address political and economic inequality and the environmental realities of farming small homesteads.[32]

Between 1887 and the 1920s, agricultural instruction took on a new purpose as government officials and reformers reconsidered their assumptions about the nature of social development and Indian assimilation. America was increasingly urban and industrial, no longer a nation of simple yeoman farmers. The persistent heterogeneity of immigrant identity and the failure of one hundred years of civilization programs to eradicate Indian cultures flew in the face of the American "melting pot" ideal. As Indians ceased being "romantic" figures and became farmers, the public lost interest in them. Policy rhetoric strayed from the long-held goal of assimilating Indians into mainstream American society toward a less optimistic program of merely incorporating them on the margins—of encouraging local agrarian self-sufficiency, then withdrawing federal assistance, leaving Indian families to cope on marginal lands with little access to national markets or society.[33]

Intent on the success of allotment and the ultimate end of Indian dependency, the government appropriated funds to hire more and better-trained agency farmers and farmer's assistants "to superintend and direct farming among such Indians as are making effort for self-support." Between 1881 and 1905 the number of agencies reporting farmers topped 80 percent and the total number of farmers more than doubled. The Indian Bureau directed farmers to demonstrate practical techniques on the agency farm. Following allotment, these were to be phased out and demonstrations carried out on individual allotments by farmers living in "district stations." "District" farmers were to be local administrators, keeping records and enforcing agency rules in addition to caring for agency equipment and encouraging Indians to farm and accumulate productive livestock. Farmers received technical assistance from other government agencies, including the bureaus of Reclamation, Plant Industry, Animal Industry, and Entomology, and the Agricultural Extension Service. Commissioner Thomas J. Morgan made it clear that "the employment by the government of white farmers is a temporary expedient," and that Indian peoples must learn to work their own allotments, but agency farms and farmers remained important resources into the 1930s.[34]

While the government emphasized agricultural training for Indian males, it did not neglect the other half of the farm family equation. Field matrons were the white farmers' female counterparts, instructing Indian women in all aspects of domestic arts and home economics in order to provide a stable home for their model agrarian families. Their broadly defined duties included teaching food storage and other home manufactures, sewing, cooking, cleaning, keeping domestic livestock and a kitchen garden, and encouraging industry, Christianity, and a civilized appearance.[35] On the allotted reservations, farmers and matrons organized agricultural fairs to stimulate production and healthy competition among the Indians, interest their non-farming tribesmen, and disseminate information. They followed up by organizing agricultural associations or homemaking clubs, creating a mutual support group for their "progressive" Indian farm families.[36]

The emphasis on agricultural instruction and self-sufficiency spilled over into the curriculum of government Indian schools. Indian Bureau officials stressed practical, manual labor education, with just enough of the "3 R's" for basic literacy. "I much prefer to know that he can plow, sow, and harvest," wrote Secretary of the Interior Henry Teller in 1884, "than to know that he has made great attainments in a literary way." Following the lead set by Hampton and Carlisle, later Indian schools maintained fields, shops, and domestic quarters where male and female students labored at least half of each day under the direction of "industrial teachers." This, educators believed, would contribute to the self-sufficiency of the school and teach Indians skills appropriate to life on an allotment.[37]

What book learning Indian children received reinforced the agrarian and domestic bent of their practical training. During the early twentieth century, government publications, course study guides, and directives for Indian schoolteachers stressed the domestic and agricultural lessons Indians should learn in school. Textbooks contained practical math applications for farm and household, readings extolling agrarian values, and written and oral presentations on industrial themes. Commencement addresses by visiting dignitaries and graduating students stressed the benefits of agricultural education and labor. Indian school periodicals were full of stories about "successful" Indian farmers and homemakers—role models for students returning to wrest a living from allotted reservations.[38]

The increased number of agency farmers, field matrons, and teachers, and the emphasis on agrarian civilization, did not magically transform Indian peoples or solve the real problems of allotted reservations. Complaints about the uneven quality and work of Indian Bureau employees (particularly farmers) continued, despite stricter hiring standards and work rules.[39] The emphasis on field agriculture worked against other economic possibilities and environmental realities. The Indian Bureau hesitated to promote livestock ranching over farming on western reservations because of the emphasis on individual allotment and fear that herding reinforced nomadic tendencies.[40] On the other hand, the bureau did approve less restrictive leasing and land patenting policies, "sink or swim" measures intended to end Indian dependency and satisfy the land hunger of western interests.[41] Despite the recognition that most reservation lands west of the hundredth meridian were too arid for unirrigated farming, the bureau continued to pursue its agrarian goals. Extensive irrigation projects, built in the early twentieth century with Indian monies, generally came too late to save Indian farmers and ended up benefiting neighboring whites who bought up or leased allotments along the ditches.[42]

As the hollow promises and unpleasant realities of allotment became increasingly apparent, the Indian Bureau created a pageant to mask the increasing dependency and marginalization of Indian people. The ceremony commemorated the final act of allotment, in which individuals received full title to their land and became citizens, symbolizing their progress from Indian savagery to agrarian civilization. In 1916 at Santee Agency, each Sioux male receiving a patent to his allotment emerged from a tent, shot a last arrow into the air to symbolize the end of his "Indian" life, and took hold of a plow to symbolize his new life. The agent administered a solemn oath of citizenship and gave each man a flag, a badge, and a purse to signify his new status. Women took a special oath as homemaker and received a flag, badge, workbag, and purse.[43] In this final act, government officials and reformers created a tableau of policy success quite at variance with the larger reality of allotment.

By 1930, it became clear that allotment and, by extension, the agrarian program for Indian civilization, had failed in its promise of incorporating Indians or turning them into self-sufficient yeoman farmers. The 1928 Meriam Report blasted allotment and detailed desperate reservation conditions. Investigators enumerated the weaknesses of the agricultural program—inadequate equipment and instructions, environmental limitations, market isolation, and native resistance. Despite this the report concluded that agriculture remained "the chief economic possibility for the great majority of Indians," although the effort should be directed away from competitive market agriculture to the development of self-sufficient family farms.[44]

The Meriam Report's recommendation came as small farmers, both Indian and non-Indian, began suffering the effects of a deepening economic and environmental nightmare. Commissioner John Collier and the Indian Reorganization Act of 1934 put an end to allotment as depression put a virtual end to Indian farming. Under Collier, the Indian Bureau recognized the national trend away from small family farms to larger corporate operations and retreated from attempts to transform Indians into self-sufficient or even individual market farmers. Collier's bureau encouraged corporate tribal farming and ranching operations by supporting the reacquisition and consolidation of tribal lands and arranging reimbursable loans and stock programs, but few of these proved as successful over time as did other tribal economic ventures. Environmental limitations, the lack of capital, technical knowledge, and markets, the advantages of leasing, and Indian disillusionment with farming hindered such operations.[45]

Indian participation in and Indian Bureau emphasis on agriculture faded during the 1940s and 1950s as attention shifted to livestock ranching. But slowly, both farming and ranching were replaced by Bureau and tribal schemes for wage work, resource development, relocation, and termination. Tribal trust land status and complicated heirship cases further limited Indian operations. By the 1960s Indian Bureau programs discounted agriculture as a viable source for reservation economic development. Recent intertribal attempts to reinvigorate Indian agricultural activities have emerged, but their proposals have been blocked by the Indian Bureau's concern for individual over tribal land rights. While many Indian people continue to live in rural areas and spend part of their time working land or livestock, few make a living at it. Today, land leasing, water sales, and resource mining turn more profit for tribal peoples than eking out an existence as the idealized yeomen farmers and farm families of a bygone era and policy vision.[46]

Conclusion

The blanket application of this agrarian program with little regard to cultural and environmental variations between tribes and reservations proved the greatest weakness of American Indian policy. With their ethnocentric values and "good intentions," Anglo reformers and officials attempted to assimilate Indians and, failing that, reduced them to the lowest Euro-American denominator, the poor farmer. They rarely questioned why Indians should abandon their own customs to adopt those of their white adversaries. They were too busy trying to instill notions of private property and awaken accumulative desires—"to get the Indian out of the blanket and into trousers—and trousers with a pocket in them, and with a *pocket that aches to be filled with dollars!*"[47] Reformers believed that Indians' landed inheritance naturally suited them to farm, even when their remaining lands dictated a marginal farming economy on the periphery of American society. Overlooking the fact that even non-Indian farmers were struggling to make a living in sub-humid areas, they forged ahead, secure in their agrarian idealism and faith in progressive social development.

The agrarian bent of American Indian policy did not continue on faith and theory alone, but in part because government officials and reformers could point to a number of notable "success stories." Prior to allotment, certain Native American leaders and groups requested agricultural implements and training in response to the collapse of all or part of their older subsistence strategies. Traditional agrarian peoples provided the most visible examples of adaptation and success. Officials believed that allotment simply reinforced this trend. Yet studies indicate that following allotment, Indian farming actually declined—that by the early twentieth century the breakup of tribal farming projects, restrictions on property rights and access to credit, and inducements to lease and sell lands ultimately discouraged Indian farming.[48]

While true, this assessment provides only a partial explanation for the problems of Indian farming in the twentieth century. Like all generalizations about the nature of government programs and Indian agriculture, it tends to conceal the complexity and diversity of the experience. It quantifies success and failure in terms of Euro-American values. It tells us more about American society than native societies. What needs to be addressed just as seriously is the response of Native Americans as rational actors, living in known environments, with their own scales of value and their own cultural reactions to farming and directed changes entailed in American Indian policy.

2

NÚČIU, THE NORTHERN UTE PEOPLE

The Utes (*Núčiu*) are a culturally self-identifying group of affiliated
bands which inhabited the eastern Great Basin and Rocky Mountain
parks of Colorado, Utah, and northwestern New Mexico. They are
Southern Numic speakers of the Numic (Shoshonean) family within the
Uto-Aztecan language stock.[1] Once ranging widely throughout this
region in search of food, trade, and resources, the modern Utes retain
only a vestige of their extensive estate: the Uintah-Ouray Reservation in
northeastern Utah, Southern Ute in southwestern Colorado, and Ute
Mountain along the western Colorado-New Mexico border.

According to their mythology, Utes are descendants of a myth-time
world family composed of beings sharing both human and animal
characteristics. Among the Southern Numic, "Earth Diver" myths account for the creation of land from Ocean Woman and explain how
these myth-time animal beings (particularly Wolf and Coyote) shared in
the final process of creation. Ute ancestors learned how to live and
behave from this family until the animal beings became parts of the
cosmic environment or took their present form. Animals observed in
nature today are considered collateral relatives descended from these
spirit ancestors. From the Ute point of view, their stories explain the
natural order of the world and serve to instruct each new generation in
the proper behavior toward that world and each other.[2]

One Southern Ute story tells how *Sinawaf* (Wolf, the Ute culture
hero/trickster) and Coyote (the trickster) populated the world. In the beginning there were no people. One day *Sinawaf* made his knife sharp
and, without telling Coyote, went off to the hills to cut some nice straight
branches from a *tü'va* bush (serviceberry). He brought back several bun-

dles of these sticks, cut them into pieces about the same length, and tied them up in a sack. He repeated this until the sack was nearly full. Coyote was curious, so when *Sinawaf* went out the sixth and last time, Coyote untied the sack. People rushed out of the sack, shouting loudly in different languages, and scared Coyote away. Whites came out first and fled east; the rest who went north and south were Indians. They scattered over the country, raising quite a cloud of dust. When *Sinawaf* saw this, he cursed his brother for being too nosy. "I was going to divide all by hundreds, but most of them are gone," said *Sinawaf*. Only ten were left in the sack, so *Sinawaf* made one group Apache, one each Pueblo, Mescalero, Navajo, and Paiute, and one Ute. "This small tribe shall be Ute," said *Sinawaf*, "but they will be very brave and able to defeat the rest." To Coyote he said, "You spoiled it, now the other Indians are going to attack us. You must look out carefully now. Those who speak different languages will be our enemies; they will fight and kill us and one another."[3]

Archaeologists suggest a longstanding human occupation of the Great Basin area and the more recent appearance of Numic peoples. Desert Archaic hunter-gatherers inhabited the area between 10,000 B.C. and A.D. 400, hunting small game and gathering seeds and roots in a slightly cooler and moister environment than the present Basin offers. About A.D. 400 the Anasazi with their Basketmaker-Pueblo culture traditions moved across the Colorado River into southern Utah. At about the same time the Fremont Culture emerged in northeastern Utah, possibly as Desert Archaic peoples settled down and borrowed Anasazi traits. Both the Fremont and Anasazi were relatively sedentary peoples with a developed maize-bean-squash horticultural complex. Both lived in rectangular, wetlaid masonry dwellings constructed in cliff faces or on the valley floors. They constructed pit house granaries and made coiled and twined basketry, gray-black pottery, and clay figurines. Both prospered until A.D. 1200–1400, when changing climate and the intrusion of Numic hunter-gatherers forced their withdrawal.

Lexico-statistical analysis indicates that these Numic groups developed in southern California about the time of Christ and fanned out to the north and east. Southern Numic ancestors of the Utes arrived in the eastern Basin by A.D. 1200 and in western Colorado by A.D. 1300. After a period of coexistence they displaced or absorbed marginal Fremont and Anasazi agriculturalists by their superior hunting-gathering adaptation. Over time autonomous "bands" emerged, reciprocally identified as *Núčiu*. Early-nineteenth-century observers identified at least eleven major Ute bands representing numerous local residency groups, each inhabiting a particular subsistence territory. They include the Tumpanuwac, Pahvant, San Pitch, Sheberetch, and Uinta-ats (now Uintah), the Yamparka and Parianuc (now White River), the Taviwac (now Uncompahgre), the Wiminuc, Kapota, and Muwac (now Southern Ute and Ute Mountain Ute). A twelfth band, the Cumumba or Weber Utes, were probably Shoshones who moved to the Uintah Reservation.[4]

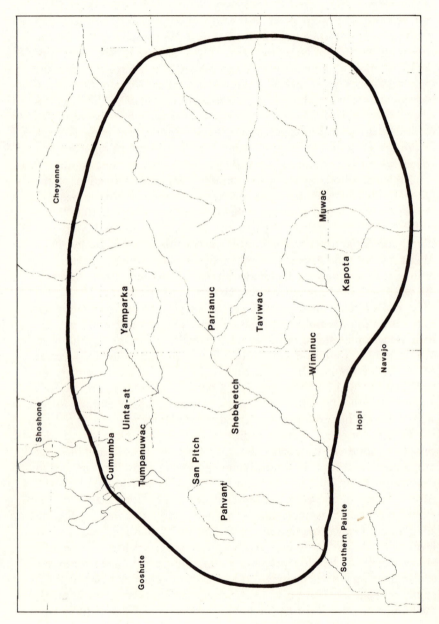

1. Ute Hunting Territory and Band Distributions

Environments

Ute legends tell of when the earth was flat and smooth everywhere and the animals lived together as people do now. One day *Sinawaf* told Hawk (*Kuesuvf*) to set up his quiver as a target. *Sinawaf* shot an arrow that glanced off the quiver and plowed up the face of the land, moving in every direction, pushing up mountains and hills, digging canyons, and creating river valleys. In councils that followed, the animals argued over the length of seasons. After much debate they decided there should be three winter months, but the trickster Coyote added an additional month (March) called "buckskin end," when all stored food would be gone and people would stew their grease-soaked rawhide bags for food. After this council, each nation chose a new home particularly suited to their needs—Hawk and Eagle (*Kwanutch*) took the rocks and craggy peaks, while Duck (*Cheeguch*) chose the marshes; Badger (*Oonahpooch*) chose a warm burrow and Bear (*Kweeyagu:t*) a sheltered cave; Wolf and Buffalo (*Tawooch*) took the open plains and Deer (*Tee-etch*) the forests. As they separated they began to speak different languages, and their children soon forgot that all nations once spoke the same language. They fought and quarreled and slowly became as they are today.[5]

The topographic and biotic environment of Ute territory is extremely diverse, incorporating the dry expanses of the Great Basin and the high alpine reaches of the Rocky Mountains. The land is both stark and lush, monotonous and breathtaking. The ecological wealth of this region lies in its diversity of species, which, given the recurrent pattern of basin and range, results in numerous biotic communities of similar resources scattered irregularly throughout the region. Latitude, elevation, and exposure influence the local biota, but water—plentiful in some areas, seasonally scarce in others—is the key to life in this arid landscape. Floral and faunal species tend to be more abundant in the north and east, where higher elevations capture more moisture.[6]

In the west, steep, sparsely wooded mountains sweep down into broad arid valleys, then rise again, repeating a basin and range topography. Elevations in the region vary from 4,000 to 10,000 feet, and annual precipitation averages less than ten inches. Piñon pine (*Pinus edilus*) and juniper (*Juniperus utahensis*) dominate the hillsides, while mountain mahogany, willow, cottonwood, and oak brush hug the moister canyons and foothills. These north-south fault-block ranges produce ephemeral streams that generally drain westward, causing most flora and fauna—and therefore human populations—to cluster along the lower benches. In this area, serviceberry, elderberry, wild rose, and raspberry appear, as well as sagebrush (*Artemisia*) and valuable roots and seed grasses. These western-draining streams feed two large freshwater lakes—Utah and Sevier—as well as the Great Salt Lake. Moving away from ephemeral canyon streams, the vegetation becomes increasingly sparse, turning dusty green, yellow, and dry over the course of the summer. In the arid valley bottoms, sagebrush, rabbitbrush, shadscale, saltbrush, and greasewood predominate, along with various grasses, cacti, yucca, and food plants like amaranth, Indian ricegrass, gray molly, sunflower, and lamb's-quarter.[7]

In eastern Utah the land rises to the Colorado Plateau and adjacent Yampa and Uncompahgre plateaus, high broken tablelands dissected by north-south hogbacks and deep canyons created by tributaries of the Green and Colorado rivers. Erosion of the soft red and white sandstone and gray limestone has created a series of cliffs and rock benches, arches and spectacular canyons set off against the dark green background of piñon-juniper covered plateaus and distant lavender mountains. The region is high (5,000–11,000 feet) and semi-arid, with five to nine inches of annual precipitation and over thirty inches of snow. Seed grasses, root plants, and sagebrush grow in the plateau valleys, merging with piñon and juniper forests that give way in the higher elevations to mountain mahogany, aspen, ponderosa pine, and Douglas fir. Willow and cottonwood mark the watercourses, while serviceberry, chokecherry, elderberry, and buffalo berry grow in protected areas.[8]

North of the plateau is the Uintah Basin, an asymmetric synclinal basin extending roughly 100 miles east to west and 125 miles north to south. From the Uinta Mountains (13,000 feet) on the north the land slopes southward to the valley floor (5,000 feet) and then rises again across the Tavaputs Plateau to the Roan and Book Cliffs (11,000 feet). The basin is composed of a number of different biotic zones and a relative cross-section of flora and fauna found in the rest of Ute territory. Ecozones vary from the Subalpine pine and fir-forested Uinta Mountains, to dissected plateau and canyonlands with their piñon-juniper cover, to the broad dry benchlands and narrow flood plains of the Uinta drainage. The basin averages less than eight inches of annual precipitation, yet heavier rainfall (over forty inches) and snowpacks in the Uinta Mountains create heavy runoff through the valley. In the south, thin soil and sparse vegetation contribute to erosion and areas of badlands terrain.[9]

The eastern half of Ute territory lies in the Colorado Rockies, with numerous 13,000- to 14,000-foot snow-capped peaks and high mountain passes of the Arctic-Alpine zone. Pine, fir, and spruce forests give way to narrow alpine valleys, hemmed in by a lush deciduous growth. Numerous alpine flowers and herbs, seed grasses, berries, and root plants make this an ideal summer habitat for game animals and humans. Three large interior valleys or "parks" provide respites in this rugged terrain. Annual precipitation increases dramatically with elevation from twenty to over forty inches, and snowpacks in the higher elevations can exceed two hundred inches. In the far eastern reaches of Ute territory, mountains give way to the grass- and sagebrush-covered high plains of eastern Colorado.[10]

Faunal species usually maintain a predictable range between certain life zones yet migrate widely on a seasonal cycle. Some of the more important large mammals of the region include the mountain sheep, deer, elk, moose, antelope, bear, coyote, wolf, mountain lion, and, in early historic times, buffalo. Smaller mammals include the fox, muskrat, marmot, badger, beaver, porcupine, skunk, rabbit, squirrel, weasel, gopher, prairie dog, and other rodents and reptiles. Ute territory is rich with avian species, including assorted raptors and migratory waterfowl, sage hen, grouse, mourning dove, quail, and pigeon. In lakes and streams, trout, whitefish, chub, and suckers are most common.

Subsistence

The Utes practiced a flexible subsistence system elegantly adapted to both the harshness and abundance of their environment. The basic unit of Ute production was the bilateral extended family, composed of a married couple, children, and a few attached relatives. Ute bilaterality made for extensive kin networks, but functional families and allied family groups remained small to exploit the thinly spread resources during the season of their precipitous maturation. Each family group followed a circuitous seasonal movement within a known territory to take advantage of local resource abundance. Depending on band location, Utes might travel to the mountains in the summer and fall to hunt, to the piñon forests and plateau valleys to hunt and gather nuts, seeds, and roots in the fall, to the lower foothills and valleys where game could be found and food caches used during the winter, and to streams or lakes to catch fish in the spring. Experience taught them that to rely on one resource or to remain in one place too long meant death.[11]

Ute hunting and gathering territories were never formal or exclusive but were the familiar subsistence range of extended families, mutually recognized between groups and theirs by right of habitual use and seasonal occupancy. Such territoriality was emotional on a certain level, yet practical in that it spread family groups out in familiar areas to maximize subsistence within the numerous biotic communities of the region. The practice of rotating use within each hunting territory or of sharing another's territory for one season allowed "fallow" periods for the regeneration of floral and faunal resources.[12]

Ute subsistence activities were largely individualistic and gender-specific, yet at peak times both sexes worked together. Men aided in the gathering of piñon nuts, and women participated in fishing and animal drives. Ute family groups did band together to live and hunt at certain times out of necessity, but they were not communalistic in the full sense of the word. Utes owned material property individually, even within extended families. Likewise, food resources belonged to the person who obtained them, even in communal operations. Informal and reciprocal sharing facilitated the redistribution of resources among family groups.[13]

Ute men did most of their hunting individually or in small groups. Prior to the hunt, Ute men made prayers for success but did not formally dance, sing, or practice animal shamanism (animal spirit charming and capturing) to aid them in their hunts as did Numic groups in the western Basin. Since the animals they killed were descendants of myth-time figures and therefore related, Ute hunters ritually butchered and offered certain body parts to appease the supernatural animal beings or "bosses." They considered women to be antagonistic to the hunt, especially during menstruation or shortly after childbirth. Occasionally, extended families congregated to take part in communal hunts for plentiful rabbit, antelope, buffalo, fish, or insect populations in a particular area. For such hunts, a shaman or chief, specifically designated by his dreams and "power" (*puwa*) or chosen for his leadership ability, directed the proceedings.[14]

Ute men hunted most of the large mammals in their territory. They used animal disguises and game calls to attract their prey, and bows and arrows to make the kill. They stalked, ambushed, or used fire to drive deer, elk, buffalo, and mountain sheep. Ute hunters feared and respected bears for their human traits, ritually addressing them with the kin term "Father's Sister" before taking them during hibernation. In the eastern Basin, Ute encampments held communal rabbit and antelope drives, using fire or drivers to force their game into long woven-fiber rabbit nets or into brush corrals. Utes hunted or snared most small mammals for food and fur, yet valued wolves, mountain lions, coyotes, and foxes for their skins only. Women broiled or stone-boiled fresh meat or smoked and pounded it into pemmican for storage in parfleche bags or coil-woven baskets. They boiled large bones for their marrow and prepared animal skins for clothing, accoutrements, and dwellings.

Around lakes and streams, Ute men and women caught fish by hand, in willow baskets or weirs, and shot them with barbed arrows from shore or from rush rafts. Women broiled fresh fish or split and dried them, storing them whole or powdered in baskets for winter use. Individual Utes stalked waterfowl that gathered at these lakes, or worked communally to drive them into ambushes or nets. They ate a variety of birds and their eggs, including sage hen, mourning dove, grouse, and quail, and captured others like owls, hawks, and eagles for their feathers. In the drier eastern Basin, Utes ate snakes and other reptiles when necessary, as well as cicadas, crickets, and grasshoppers, which they roasted and ground into a protein-rich meal.[15]

Ute women gathered and utilized many edible seeds, plants, and roots in their physical environment. Pine nuts were a staple, parched in baskets with hot coals and stored whole or as ground meal for winter use. The women mixed the meal with water to form small meal balls or boiled it into mush. Women gathered wheat grass (*Agropyron*), bentgrass (*Agrostis*), bluegrass (*Poa*), needle grass (*Stipa*), and June grass (*Koeleria*), and seeds from lamb's-quarter (*Chenopodium*), sunflowers, and amaranth, among others, which they stored whole or parched and ground into flour. The people ate raspberries, strawberries, gooseberries, serviceberries, currants, buffalo berries, rose and juniper berries in season or dried and cached them in baskets underground. Chokecherries (*Prunus*), molded and dried into round cakes for winter use, were a particularly important fruit resource. Women gathered numerous roots, including yampa (*Perideridia*), camas (*Camassia*), sego lily (*Calochortus*), tule, valerian, and yucca, as well as seasonal greens and thistles, cactus leaves and fruit, and some acorns. Women also collected and processed vegetal fibers for baskets, cordage, and clothing. Ute men gathered native tobacco (*Nicotiana*) and numerous other plants valued for their medicinal or ceremonial power.[16]

While Utes consumed a broad range of flora and fauna, they did not domesticate these species nor did they eat everything available to them. Utes encouraged the growth of preferred plant species through burning, broadcast sowing, and selective gathering, which in turn encouraged some animal species. They acquired what maize they desired from raiding and trading with the pueblo peoples well into the nineteenth century.[17] Utes observed specific food taboos and preferences. Dietary rules and taboos applied to women and their husbands during menstruation, pregnancy, and post-parturition. Taboos on consuming first kills and specific organs surrounded the hunter and his family. Colorado Utes considered porcupines, grasshoppers, horses, snakes, and other reptiles and insects inedible, while the southern and western Ute used all of these. They all considered the flesh of dogs, wolves, coyotes, foxes, weasels, wolverines, and mountain lions to be inedible. But in times of scarcity and starvation, the people ate many less-desirable foods for their nutritive value, including stewed rawhide or parfleche bags and rabbit-skin robes.[18]

There were significant differences in subsistence strategies between the Ute bands, given the biotic communities they exploited. In the western areas, Utes placed more emphasis on plant foods, fish, and insects, which were more abundant and often more reliable than large mammals. Ute women became more important as economic providers and buffers against starvation when the hunt failed. This enhanced position increased the matrilocal tendency of most Utah Ute. In the mountains and parks of northeastern Utah and western Colorado, Utes were much more dependent on large game mammals and the materials derived from these animals. Such differences became more marked in historic times as Colorado Utes acquired horses and adopted some Plains cultural trappings well before their Basin neighbors.[19]

The horse both reinforced and modified previous Ute subsistence strategies. It did not change the *variety* of resources utilized, but it did allow for more *selectivity* and concentration on those previously valued. Utes hunted buffalo on the high plains of Colorado and in the Great Basin region prior to acquiring horses. The horse merely reinforced this patterned preference for big game, even among the Utah Ute. It increased their range and hunting efficiency, improved the transportation of food and material goods over greater distances, and made larger and longer "band" congregations more feasible, but it did not induce Utes to relinquish the security of their diversified subsistence strategy for the vagaries of any single resource.[20]

Society

Ute society centered around the extended bilateral family, and periodic congregations of related or affinal kindreds to form local residence groups of from twenty to one hundred persons. These groups frequently traced relations through the matriline and resided matrilocally, but membership was fluid and flexible enough to adjust to personal and local environmental realities. Local leaders were older men who, through persuasion, influence, and proven ability, achieved a level of consensus for their plans. Most groups recognized specialized leaders who directed specific activities (hunting, moving camp, dances, or raiding) and had little or no authority over the group in other matters.

Larger "band" organization was limited to periodic congregations for defense, for spring Bear dances, or for summer hunting or fishing camps. Such summer congregations, especially around Utah Lake, could number a thousand people. Bands consisted of local residence groups linked by bilateral kinship networks and their common territorial range—specific features usually reflected in their band name. Local groups and even extended family groups remained relatively autonomous, because most bands lacked formal political organization. Local leaders in band councils (which could include women) decided necessary matters subject to community approval. Dominant groups often provided the most influential leaders—leaders who ultimately came to the attention of white officials looking to negotiate with a single "chief." Ute bands recognized their larger group identity in custom, language, and territory, and remained united through kinship, trade, and defense against common enemies, but there was no larger Ute "nation" with long-lasting political allegiances or tribal councils.[21]

The appearance of horses in the late seventeenth century and their differential diffusion to western bands touched off certain changes in Ute society. Ute bands in Colorado obtained horses by 1640 and were more influenced by Plains cultural traits than were some western bands that acquired horses as late as 1830. Horses facilitated the accumulation of more material goods and sparked an elaboration of Ute material culture. Decorated skins replaced fiber and brush for clothing and lodgings. Horses themselves became symbols of wealth, success, and social status, thereby influencing the selection and tenure of Ute leaders. Utes expanded their territory, becoming important middlemen in the intertribal horse trade and noted raiders. They sold Goshute and Southern Paiute slaves to the Spanish and then raided Spanish trade routes and settlements. They clashed more frequently with the Cheyenne, Arapaho, Lakota, and Comanche. The horse and Plains cultural influences sparked incipient warrior societies and more formal leadership structures among some eastern Ute bands, but Ute warriors emphasized material gain in horses or slaves and never adopted the ritualized features of Plains warfare. Utes remained practical and flexible in their responses to Plains influences, selectively incorporating and interpreting adaptive items and ideas in terms of their own cultural matrix while rejecting others.[22]

Ute cosmology revolves around stories of the myth-time activities of their ancestors. Rituals are pragmatic and individualistic, emphasizing specific acts to achieve specific ends, rather than a single philosophy that binds all observances together in a system. Ute religion mirrors the broader cultural emphasis on practicality and efficiency in systems that must sustain them in a strenuous environment.[23]

The central concept is *puwa* ("power"), "a universal kinetic energy that flows through the universe as the source and summary of existence." *Puwa* is animistic, residing in a plethora of personalized spiritual beings, objects, and phenomena. It can be harnessed, stored, controlled, and used for good or evil. Throughout the Great Basin, water (*pa*) and *puwa* are closely associated and sought after, for both sustain life, both are thinly distributed with local sources of concentration, and both are associated with sacred locations.[24]

Both men and women could gain *puwa* and become shamans (*puwarat*, "one who has power") through inheritance or repeated dreams and visions of power animals who instructed them in the songs, techniques, and paraphernalia they should use. Some used their *puwa* to lead hunting or raiding parties, to control the weather, or to direct group relocations, while others used their *puwa* to heal or cure a certain range of illnesses with herbs (*bowa'gant*, "medicine man") or through supernatural powers (*mutusukwi'gant*, "Indian doctor"). In Ute cosmology, ghosts, witchcraft, the violation of taboos, evil dreams, or intrusive objects caused disease. Utes judged a person's *puwa* by his or her record of success and guarded against those who turned their *puwa* to evil purposes (*awu puwarat*).[25]

Utes practiced relatively few rituals outside life cycle observances. Birth, puberty, menstruation, marriage, pregnancy, and death were accompanied by prescriptive rather than proscriptive rituals and taboos, emphasizing health, group well-being, and future success. Utes disposed of their dead quickly, burying them in rock crevices, giving away their possessions or burning them with the deceased. Families burned or abandoned their skin tepees or brush dwellings and went into mourning to avoid being troubled by ghosts (*nusakwu=ci* or *anipic*) and "ghost sickness."[26]

The most significant group ritual was the annual Bear Dance or *mama'qunikap'*, referring to the back-and-forth shuffle step of the dance. The dance took place in March as local residence groups began to congregate in spring camps. Utes describe the ritual as originally being taught to a hunter by a bear who had just emerged from hibernation and was dancing back and forth on its hind legs. Utes danced to appease this myth-time ancestor and speed its recovery, to charm themselves against attack, to cure illness, and to promote the general welfare of the group. These dances were important social events, uniting local groups afer their winter isolation and providing a forum for courtship and marriage between groups.[27]

In the late nineteenth century, Northern Utes tried or adopted several new religious ceremonies—Christianity, the Ghost Dance, Peyotism, and the Sun Dance. Most nominally accepted Christianity in a syncretic blend with their own beliefs. Their negative experience with the Ghost Dance movement of the 1870s and their cultural fear of ghosts made the movement of the late 1880s unpopular. Peyotism and the Sun Dance made the greatest impact, coming in response to the real and perceived deprivation of reservation life and the threat of allotment. Although Utes adopted both of these religions from other Indian groups, they interpreted, adapted, and applied them in terms of their own cultural understanding as a means of ensuring the health, well-being, and solidarity of the Ute people. Through the Sun Dance (*taku-nikai*, "thirsty dance"), individuals danced for three or four days and nights without food or water to gain *puwa* for the health and benefit of the collective group. Ute Peyotism likewise stressed those aspects of health, healing, and group unity so central to Ute religious concerns.[28]

Ute social and subsistence solutions to survival in an environment incorporating periodic abundance and scarcity were characteristically lean and resilient. Their practical approach allowed them to take advantage of changing resources in their environment and to utilize new technologies, whether internally generated or imported. Their adaptations proved efficient and effective, and while life was never easy, Utes managed to live and maintain a cultural balance with their environment.

For nearly five hundred years the Ute people lived and prospered in their territory. They periodically skirmished with surrounding tribes and gained a respected reputation as powerful adversaries. Seventeenth-century Spanish contact was minimal, reaching only the southern boundaries of Ute territory, with the notable exceptions of the transient expeditions of discovery by Rivera (1765), Dominguez and Escalante (1776), Anza (1779), and the Arze-Garcia party (1813). Utes acquired horses and trade goods from the Spanish, raided their pueblos and supply lines, and even aided them in wars against the Comanche, but they fiercely resisted Spanish administration.

In 1800 there were at least eight thousand Ute people, living in one or another of the eleven major Ute bands. Intercultural contacts increased in the nineteenth century as Euro-American fur trappers moved into Northern Ute territory. Etienne Provost, the Chouteau-De Mun party, Antoine Robidoux, William Henry Ashley, Peter Skene Ogden, Jedediah Smith, Kit Carson, and Miles Goodyear all brought parties through Ute territory or established temporary trading posts to serve the area before 1847. With this contact came increased trade in fur, hides, and horses for white trade goods and guns, but the Northern Utes continued aloof and independent in this "middle ground" contact situation. Only after settlement of the Salt Lake and Utah valleys by Mormons did they experience the full impact of white intrusion on their subsistence economies and the beginnings of economic and political dependence.[29]

3

AGRICULTURE AND THE NORTHERN UTES

In 1847, the first wave of Mormon settlers entered Ute territory and began to build their Kingdom of God on earth—a kingdom that did not include the native residents of Utah. Utes were slowly removed from the best lands and subjected to a series of policies designed to transform them into settled and self-sufficient agrarians. Reservation farming and ranching represented a fundamental change in their social and subsistence organization. Utes responded on both individual and group levels to this cultural assault, selectively adopting, adapting, and reproducing Ute ways within an ever-changing environment. Ultimately Ute resistance, both passive and active, and the economic and physical realities of agriculture in a tenuous environment left them economically dependent and incorporated on the periphery of American society.

Mormons, Utes, and Indian Farms

When members of the Church of Jesus Christ of Latter-day Saints arrived in the Salt Lake Valley, they appropriated land lying in a buffer occupancy zone between Ute and Shoshone peoples. Having dealt with transient trappers and traders before, Tumpanuwac Utes worried little about allowing Mormons into that contested region. The Mormons, hard-pressed and almost destitute, discarded earlier church policy of purchasing or renting land from Indian owners and claimed the area based on divine donation and their own "beneficial use." Settlers plowed and planted crops that first short season but had to rely on stored foods and what they could hunt and gather in the surrounding area to see them through the winter. As more settlers entered the

valley in 1848, competition with Utes for relatively scarce natural resources increased.[1]

In the spring of 1849, Mormon president Brigham Young sent
"missionary" settlers south into Utah Valley, a crossroads for Indian
trade and a crucial Ute resource area. The settlers constructed Fort
Utah with its adjacent fields on an annual Tumpanuwac Ute campsite—
a strategic location with fresh water, abundant grass, and forage for Ute
horses. Indian agent John Wilson reported that the settlement "has not
only greatly diminished their formerly very great resource of obtaining
fish out of Utah Lake and its sources," but "has already driven away all
the game." As the settlers appropriated the grass and game, plowed and
fenced the land, and deprived Utes of access to their rich valley, the
Tumpanuwac turned to an alternate yet categorically parallel food
resource—Mormon livestock. Unwilling to compensate the Utes or lose
their livestock, the settlers retaliated and drove the Tumpanuwacs from
the valley in February 1850.[2]

An uneasy peace reigned for the next few years, but as Mormon
settlers expanded south into Millard and San Pete counties, they disrupted the finely balanced Tumpanuwac, San Pitch, and Pahvant subsistence strategies and precipitated the recurring patterns of Ute
starvation, begging, and depredation on Mormon livestock and fields.
In 1851, Utah Indian superintendent J. H. Holeman warned that Mormons had settled "on all the most valuable lands." "The Indians have
been driven from their lands and their hunting grounds destroyed without compensation wherefore they are in many instances reduced to a
state of suffering, bordering on starvation," he wrote. "In this situation
some of the most daring and desperate approach the settlements and
demand compensation for their lands, where upon the slightest pretexts,
they are shot down or driven to the mountains."[3]

Brigham Young denied the charges but realized some truth in them.
Publicly he reiterated his stance that it was "cheaper to feed Indians
than to fight them" and moved to quiet the growing resentment of his
followers, who had to do the actual feeding. In 1851, Young called several church members to serve as "Indian farmers," and set aside three
farm reserves in Millard, San Pete, and Iron counties. Young's aim was
to "institute among them the means of procuring the subsistence necessary to prolong life" as the "fast diminishing" products of their "kilsome
chase" proved insufficient. The farms became mere feeding stations,
providing food but little instruction. Utes continued to compete with
expansive Mormon settlers for valley and foothill resources. As settlers
changed the ecology of the region by plowing up native plants, planting
domesticates, and killing wildlife "pests" to protect their crops and livestock, Utes found themselves forced to beg or raid for the transformed
floral and faunal resources.[4]

The Walker War of 1853–54 culminated years of tensions between
Utes and Mormons over territorial and subsistence displacement. Tum-

panuwac chief Wakara led a series of effective but unsystematic raids on isolated Mormon communities to procure food and livestock. Recognizing the motivation and objectives, Brigham Young ordered his people to "fort up," retaliate swiftly when possible, and trust in Mormon numbers and Ute starvation to end the war. Young's assessment proved correct but not his hopes that Wakara would lead his people into peaceful agrarian settlement. At the treaty meeting in 1854, Agent Edward A. Bedell asked Wakara "if he or his men desired to raised wheat and potatoes etc." Wakara answered as a Ute leader would, without binding others by his word—that "he would much prefer to trade and hunt himself, but he would be glad to have the Indians work and raise wheat and corn." He held out the hope that *other* Indians *might* agree to farm and that the produce of that labor would be welcome, but that *he* would not participate.[5]

By 1855 the Tumpanuwac subsistence complex was in disarray. Mormon fields and pastures completely blocked Ute access to gathering grounds in Utah Valley, and game became scarce. Seining had already depleted the once prodigious fishery of Utah Lake, and Indian agents had to ask Mormon fishermen to assist Utes in obtaining a winter supply of fish. All along the line of Mormon settlement, similar instances of competition, displacement, and environmental change occurred. "The fertile valleys along the base of the mountains, from which they ever derive their subsistence are now usurped by the whites," wrote Agent Garland Hurt, "and they are left to starve or steal, or to infringe upon the Territories of other bands." Epidemic diseases ravaged Ute populations. Grasshoppers and drought reduced Mormon crops and their willingness to continue sharing their hard-won produce. As fear of renewed raiding increased, Indian agents revived the idea of agrarian self-sufficiency and Indian farms.[6]

In the spring of 1855, Agent Garland Hurt announced his intention to create three Ute farms, each staffed by a white farmer who would distribute supplies and provide practical instruction. Hurt's idea was to get those Indians who "have expressed a willingness to do so" to settle permanently at the farm and become self-supporting. Other Utes would see this, he believed, and follow suit. Without official approval, Hurt reserved farms at Corn Creek in Millard County (36 square miles), Twelve Mile Creek in San Pete County (144 square miles), and on the Spanish Fork River in Utah County (640 acres) for Tumpanuwac and Pahvant Utes.[7]

Brigham Young seconded Hurt's efforts but defined the problems. "The idea of cultivating the earth for a subsistence gains slowly among them, for it is very adverse to there [*sic*] habit of idleness." Young reported that Pahvants under Kanosh were perhaps the most willing, but "many of the Old warriors of his tribe do not like the idea of labor, hence he meets with more or less difficulty." Arapeen, a Tumpanuwac leader, desired livestock that could "travel with him in his meanderings" but was "careless about Agriculture." Like his brother Wakara, Arapeen preferred to have local whites farm for him. In council, Ute leaders did not openly oppose the farms but universally questioned Hurt as to how they would survive, saying that "they were very poor, and had to hunt most all the time to keep from starving, and if they laid down their bows to work in the fields they would soon be obliged to pick them up again." Believing that to remain in one place too long meant death, they refused to abandon their mobile and diversified subsistence strategy—as weak as it was becoming—for the vagaries of a single, sedentary mode of production like farming.[8]

Work on the farms went forward despite difficulties clearing and irrigating the land and attracting permanent Ute residents. Most Utes continued their seasonal rounds. Those unable to keep up remained near the farms, drawing rations until band members returned to claim what white farmers had produced. Many lingered through the fall and winter, camping and hunting in the nearby foothills as they had before Mormon occupation. Overall farm production was erratic, forcing agents to purchase rations and encourage Utes to leave the farms to hunt. In 1857, white farmers cultivated just over 700 acres planted to wheat, oats, corn, potatoes, barley, and garden vegetables. Hurt reported 60 Utes working at Spanish Fork, 50 Pahvants at Corn Creek, and 25 to 30 at Twelve Mile Creek farm. Arapeen and 720 Utes arrived at Twelve Mile Creek that summer, but most left after the very disappointing harvest. Hurt blamed consistently poor farm yields on short growing seasons, drought, grasshoppers, and inadequate farm equipment. He also complained that those who did not work in the fields were "lavished profusely" with farm produce by those who did—likely part of a reciprocal exchange of foodstuffs that he interpreted as wasteful and uncivilized.[9]

Hopes for the Indian farms dimmed further when federal troops marched on Utah in 1857—58 to subdue the "rebellious fraternity" of Mormonism. During this Utah War, Agent Hurt fled the territory, fearing Mormon reprisals on non-Mormons. In the aftermath, Alfred Cummings replaced Brigham Young as governor, and Jacob Forney became Indian superintendent. Forney insisted that Utes "perform all the work" on the farms. He explained, "Indians are proverbially lazy, and only the pinchings of hunger will drive them to work; so much white labor has heretofore been employed to do the work for them, and they have not been sufficiently taught that their subsistence depends upon their own labor." Despite his expectations, white farmers continued to operate the farms. In 1859, farm labor costs and subsistence provisions necessitated by widespread crop failures exceeded federal appropriations. Governor Cummings dismissed Forney and closed the farms, convinced that Utes would never be farmers.[10]

In the first ten years of Mormon expansion into the oasis environments along the Utah front range, Utes were displaced from their most productive hunting and gathering habitats. Indian farms offered some supplement, but consecutive crop failures and severe winters between 1858 and 1860 forced Utes to travel further east and south into the territories of neighboring bands. Those who stayed near the farms faced death by starvation and disease. By 1862 those farms had been stripped and their improvements sold to purchase meager relief rations. If they failed as a way to promote agrarian civilization and self-sufficiency, they did introduce Utes to agency rations and crops, new resources in an ever-diminishing subsistence environment.[11]

Uintah Reservation

By 1861 plans were underway to consolidate Utah Utes in eastern Utah. Not wanting to lose valuable land that his own people might use, Brigham Young ordered a survey of the Uintah Basin, but his scouts found the area "one vast 'contiguity of waste,' and measurably valueless, excepting for nomadic purposes, hunting grounds for Indians and to hold the world together." Since Mormons did not want it and Utes showed no disposition to farm anyway, officials deemed the valley suited to their condition and set aside over two million acres as the Uintah Valley Reservation.[12]

Setting aside a reservation and getting Utes to accept it were two different matters. The Uintah Basin was not the waste that Young's scouts claimed, but neither was it an ideal year-round environment. The agency itself was poorly planned and underfunded by a government preoccupied with civil war. Utes who ventured into the valley did so to receive food and clothing before continuing their hunts. Congress finally appropriated $30,000 in 1864 to prepare the reservation and aid Utes "in becoming self-supporting, by means of agriculture," but that came only after renewed hostilities threatened the territory.[13]

The Black Hawk War (1863–68) was little more than an intensification of Ute raiding that had been going on for years. During this period of increasing subsistence deprivation and resistance to removal, a war leader named Autenquer ("Black Hawk") emerged among the San Pitch. He formed alliances between Utah and Colorado Ute bands, Southern Paiutes, and even Navajos, leading some one hundred followers in deadly raids to obtain supplies from Mormon communities. Warriors interviewed in 1872 stated "that hunger often caused them to go on raids to get cattle to eat" because agents stole what Washington had sent them. They blamed the Mormons who "had stolen their country and fenced it up. The lands that their fathers had given them had been taken for wheat fields. When they asked the Mormons for some of the bread raised on their lands, and beef fed on their grass, the Mormons insulted them, calling them dogs and other bad names."[14]

At a peace council in 1865, Brigham Young and Utah Indian superintendent O. H. Irish tried to convince Ute leaders to cease raiding and move to their reservation. Irish explained that the "Great Spirit" and the "great Father at Washington" wanted their lands to produce "grain, corn and such things as go to make his children comfortable, happy and prosperous." Irish continued, "We want to make little farms for them all. We do not want to make a great big farm and have the Government work it, but to make little farms and have you work them and that the produce and everything on them will then be yours, and you will have it." If they would remove to the Uintah Reservation, Irish promised, they would receive farms and cattle, schools for their children, gifts of clothing, food, and implements amounting to $1.2 million over sixty years. All they had to do was sign the treaty ceding their "possessory right" to all other lands and move within one year.

In their speeches, Ute leaders like San-pitch told Irish that "I do not want to trade the land nor the title to the land." Tabby-to-kwana added that "they never thought of such a thing." Kanosh challenged the government's plans and offers of assistance with his own experience. "I have worked at Corn Creek a long time and I have got nothing. President [Brigham] Young gave me five cows, and when the grasshoppers came and eat up my grain I had to sell them to get something to eat." They generally opposed removal, saying that "they wanted to live around the graves of their fathers," but realized that option was disappearing in the wake of settlers' plows. Assured that they could continue to hunt and gather on all public lands, all but one of the Ute leaders present signed the Spanish Fork Treaty. Little did they know as they moved toward the reservation that the Senate would reject the treaty and its promised benefits would never materialize.[15]

The Uintah Valley Reservation offered little for the arriving Ute bands. The agency changed location four times between 1864 and 1868 in search of reasonable farm land. Late frosts and swarms of grasshoppers devastated first and even second grain plantings, and early frosts limited vegetable crops. Agents spent their limited funds for subsistence provisions, while Ute families continued to travel widely in search of food. Hounded by starvation and Mormon militias in central Utah, Black Hawk's followers finally turned to an older civil leader, Tabby-to-kwana, who led them onto the reservation in 1869. There they found 110 cultivated acres awaiting them, spread out in small plots for each band across the reservation. "Quite a number of Indians have a patch of ground, of two or three acres, on which they are raising wheat, potatoes, turnips, pumpkins, melons, and other vegetables," observed John Wesley Powell as he passed through. He also noted their continued preference for skin lodges over cabins which were unnatural and impractical given their migratory patterns and mortuary customs.[16]

While Agent Pardon Dodds induced some families to settle and work on the farms, Superintendent F. H. Head admitted that there existed a "great antipathy to work on the part of the men, the greater part of what was done being by the squaws and children" while the men went hunting. White laborers performed nearly all of the plowing and planting, trying to illustrate to Ute males "the dignity of labor," but the

reproduction of cultural patterns dividing labor along gender lines precluded male farming—digging in the earth was the subsistence province
of women. Government surveyor Almon H. Thompson likewise observed that "the employees at the Agency plough the land, furnish seed,
dig the irrigating ditches, cut the grains; in fact do all the work that re-
quires the use of tools. The Indians irrigate a little," he admitted, but
"the 'bucks' make the squaws do the work while they race horses or loaf
around the Agency." "The Indians do not make good agriculturalists,"
he wrote; their grain crops were a failure, and "something ought to be
done in the way of stock raising." As conducted, the agency was "a
cheat, a swindle," and "the white man could better afford to board him
in Illionis [*sic*] than to keep up a reservation here."[17]

That was the situation Agent John J. Critchlow discovered when he
arrived at Uintah Valley in 1871. Critchlow, the best of a rather sad lot
of Grant Peace Policy agents, charged his predecessor with a "fertile
imagination" in falsifying reports on the actual agricultural accomplishments of the agency. Critchlow reported only 85 cultivated acres, including 15 broken that very year; crop values of $30,000 in 1869 were
more realistically $2,310 in 1871. "There seems never to have been
anything more done for them than to keep them quiet and peaceable
by partially feeding and clothing them and amusing them with trin-
kets." Critchlow decried the quality of employees and lack of supplies
and requested additional appropriations to improve the agency.[18]

Critchlow's administration marks a period of intense effort to
improve the condition of Uintah Utes and transform them into self-
sufficient farmers, but the effort met with little success. Agency
farmers struggled with environmental problems—climate, lack of
readily available water, and physical isolation. "The broken character of
the land, by streams, slough, rocky and alkaline patches," Critchlow
wrote, "makes it discouraging, even to skilled laborers; much more is it
so to those [Utes] unaccustomed to habits of industry." Critchlow
recognized that both the Ute people and Uintah Basin were better
suited to a herding economy, but his proposals to start such an industry went unheeded.[19]

Between 1873 and 1875, Critchlow estimated fifty to eighty families
had small fields or gardens, providing up to three-eighths of their subsistence. "Of course," he wrote in 1873, "their farming was not done in
the most approved manner." Agency laborers plowed, planted, cultivated, cut, and threshed Indian hay and grains. When Ute families returned from their summer travels, the women harvested what garden
produce managed to grow during their absence. A majority of families
refused to settle near the agency and continued this kind of modified
subsistence round, incorporating traditional resources with crops and
rations. While hunting in Colorado, Uintahs would pass themselves off
as White River Utes in order to collect additional rations, reciprocating
when White Rivers visited Utah.[20]

Critchlow also had to deal with Ute factionalism and changing leadership patterns. Once at Uintah, the different bands grew fearful of each other, believing that evil shamans (*awu puwarat*), either white or Ute, were destroying their resources and causing the illnesses ravaging their families—reproducing cultural disease theory and cures to explain these epidemics. This fear of evil shamans coupled with Ute individualism precluded attempts to interest Utes in collectively operating larger agricultural fields. Factions emerged around leaders. Tabby held a small following willing to try a mixed agrarian life, while Captain Joe, a San Pitch chief, attracted those less disposed to farming.[21]

Critchlow's biggest problem was a passive but persistent resistance to farming. He reported a telling incident in 1872.

> Douglas, the White River chief, with quite a number of his band, came to the agency and succeeded in persuading our Indians, who had up to that time intended to farm, to give it up and let the white men farm for the Indians, telling them that Washington did not intend that they should work; also ridiculing those that farmed, calling them squaws, and finally succeeded, toward the later part of April, in inducing our Indians to leave with him for a visit and council at some point south. Thus it has occurred that all the farming operations have been performed by the employees.[22]

Utes used this formulaic explanation repeatedly to justify their reluctance to farm, until, over the years, it became myth-like in its retelling. Joseph Jorgensen traces this formula from a 1867 Southern Ute explanation:

> . . . the Great Spirit created the first man an Indian. . . . when the Indian tribes increased, they made a ladder to get to the place where the Great Spirit was, and the Great Spirit scattered them, and made them speak several languages; and some of them became white from fear, and the Great Spirit then said that it was now the wish of the Great Spirit to have the white man work and plant for the Indian.

While biblically influenced, the story was told for strictly Ute purposes. "Washington" replaced the "Great Spirit" in a 1872 White River Ute version, which was retold in two variations by Colorado Utes in 1877 and 1878. As late as 1908, Utes related the same story, "and [were] rather literally adhering to its doctrine, that is, they refused to work." In this way, Ute men symbolically relegated whites to the status of useful food providers, reinforcing their own cultural categories concerning the proper type and division of labor.[23]

By 1880, most Utah Utes resided within the bounds of the Uintah Reservation. They continued to hunt and visit off-reservation, but that pattern became more difficult as white ranchers and miners moved into eastern Utah and western Colorado. Even those who tried farming did not change their lifestyle overnight. In the aftermath of the Little Big Horn, Critchlow lamented that twenty to thirty Utes left to fight Lakotas, or perhaps just to hunt. "Most of those that went were our best farmers," he reported—farmers who were still Ute warriors.[24] While Utah Utes managed to dodge government plans to consolidate Paiutes and Shoshones on the Uintah Reservation, they could not avoid the arrival of Taviwac (Uncompahgre) and Yamparka and Parianuc (White River) Ute bands from Colorado.

Uintah and Ouray Reservations

Although Colorado Ute bands experienced an earlier and more direct contact history with Euro-Americans, the wholesale invasion of their heartland came later than with Utah Utes. Few Spanish or Mexican land grants seriously impinged on Ute territory, and Ute raiding and trading continued largely undisturbed. After the United States acquired the Southwest in 1848, officials conducted negotiations at Santa Fe with the regional Indian peoples. The 1849 Ute treaty provided for a vague reservation where Utes were to cease their "roving and rambling habits," settle in pueblos, and cultivate the soil. The agreements had little impact on the majority of Utes living far to the north. In 1853, settlers moving into the San Luis Valley of southern Colorado sparked Muwach and Kapota Ute raiding known as the Ute War of 1854–55, leading to another round of treaties and Ute land cessions.[25]

The discovery of gold in 1859 prompted a population explosion and the organization of Colorado Territory by 1861. Miners flooded into the mountain parks of central Colorado, and confrontations with Parianuc and Taviwac Utes ensued. To maintain peace and control Utes, the government established agencies at Conejos for the Taviwac and Hot Sulphur Springs for the Parianuc and Yamparka. In an 1863 treaty council at Conejos, federal negotiators coerced a Taviwac majority into ceding disputed mineral lands—most of which was not Taviwac territory—in return for guaranteeing Ute hunting rights, protection against further white intrusions, and presents, including livestock and agricultural instruction.[26] Utes continued their subsistence rounds, ranging as far as the high plains of eastern Colorado, but competition for land and resources increased steadily in 1865 as another rush brought miners to the western slope of Colorado. Some Taviwac settled in at Conejos Agency and tried their hand at farming, although, as a local cavalry officer noted, "The women do all the work; the warrior considers work a disgrace to manhood." The men seemed to spend their time hunting and gambling, especially on their horses, which they raised in large numbers.[27]

After a particularly bad winter of subsistence shortfalls, federal officials tried to get Colorado Utes to agree to a limited reservation. In that council, Ouray of the Taviwac Ute explained the problems his people faced:

> Long time ago, Utes always had plenty. On the prairie, antelope and buffalo, so many Ooray can't count. In the mountains, deer and bear, everywhere. In the streams, trout, duck, beaver, everything. Good

Manitou gave all to red man; Utes happy all the year. White man came, and now Utes go hungry a heap. Game much go every year—hard to shoot now. Old man often weak for want of food. Squaw and papoose cry. Only strong brave live. White man grow a heap; Red man no grow—soon die all.

He rejected reservation talk, saying, "Utes stop not in one place, and Comanches no find. But Utes settle down; then Comanches come and kill. Tell Great Father, Cheyennes and Comanches go on Reservation *first*; then Utes will." Experience taught them that they must remain mobile to elude their enemies and to maintain a diversified subsistence strategy, but this fundamental cultural logic was lost on council commissioner General William Sherman, who gave up, saying, "They will have to freeze and starve a little more, I reckon, before they will listen to common sense."[28]

Continued mineral exploration and white settlement prompted another treaty meeting in March 1868 at which Ute leaders ceded all lands east of the 107th meridian, leaving them a 15-million-acre reservation. Ouray and others signed with the understanding that the government would "strike out all that relates to mills, machinery, farming, schools & going onto a reservation"—basically gutting the "civilizing" intent of the treaty. The government opened new agencies at Los Pinos for the Taviwac and at White River for the Yamparka, Parianuc, and Uinta-ats.[29] Agency farms, established to both feed and encourage Utes to work, proved unsuccessful without irrigation in the high, dry environment. At White River, agents struggled to maintain a tribal herd of five hundred Texas cattle and a 10-acre farm against Ute indifference. The Taviwac adopted sheep and cattle but declined to keep or use milk cows. Despite official hopes and the example of Ouray, who pacified agents by accepting a small farm and adobe house, Colorado Utes continued their subsistence round. In 1871 officials opened a Denver agency to accommodate Utes traveling to and from the buffalo grounds, deciding it was cheaper to let them hunt than to keep them on the reservations as farmers.[30]

By 1873, American miners pouring onto the reservation prompted officials to renegotiate the 1868 treaty with angry Utes. In the Brunot Agreement—the product of official threats, bribes, and signature fraud—Utes relinquished the rich gold fields of the San Juan Mountains but refused to cede their hunting rights or valley lands. Ouray, a pivotal Taviwac leader and the focus of government "gifts," explained, "Perhaps some of the [white] people will not like it because we did not want to sell some of our valley and farming land. We expect to occupy it ourselves before long for farming and stock raising. About 80 of our tribe are raising corn and wheat now, and we know not how soon we shall have to depend on ourselves for our bread." In the meantime, he knew that those lands would continue to provide his people a minimum subsistence. Despite Ouray's acquiescence, White River leaders denied the

validity of the agreement and continued their strong resistance to both
territorial cessions and farming.[31]

Ute insistence on hunting rights did not pass unnoticed by the
government. John Wesley Powell reported that Utes still had an abundance of game "and can live by hunting, and as long as that condition
of affairs exists they will never desire to cultivate the soil, and no substantial progress can be made in their civilization." Only nineteen families out of 2,900 White River and Uncompahgre Utes made any attempt
to farm by 1875. The rest held "superstitious prejudices against the performance of manual labor." Powell's answer was not to remove them to
Utah as some suggested, but to open more land for settlement. "The
sooner this country is entered by white people and the game destroyed
so that the Indians will be compelled to gain a subsistence by some
other means than hunting, the better it will be for them."[32]

That kind of subsistence hunting was becoming increasingly difficult, especially for Utes at White River Agency who refused to recognize
the treaties signed by Uncompahgre leaders without their consent.
Miners encroached on Ute lands, and conflicts between hunting parties
and settlers increased. Hard winters, dry summers, and restrictions on
the sale of weapons and ammunition to Indians after 1876 hindered
Ute hunts. In 1877, White River Utes grew more restive when rations
and annuity goods failed to reach their agency for the third year
running. Forest fires raged throughout western Colorado in 1878 and
1879, some set by Utes to clear underbrush, improve game animal
habitats, and, as one put it, "to make heap grass next spring for ponies."
Utes actually set few fires that burned out of control, but Colorado
newspaper editors, politicians, and settlers used the fires to demand,
"The Utes Must Go!"[33]

Into this explosive situation marched Nathan C. Meeker, poet,
newspaperman, and unrequited idealist. During his life he participated
in a Fourierist utopian phalanx in Ohio, joined a Campbellite common-
wealth, and became the agricultural editor for Horace Greeley's New
York *Tribune*. He was an outspoken agrarian socialist who embraced the
ideals of Jeffersonian agrarian democracy. With Greeley's help, Meeker
founded Union Colony, Greeley, Colorado, in 1870, his own agrarian
utopia. Never truly successful in any of his business or communal ventures, Meeker took the agency job at White River in order to pay off
debts and keep his colony alive. Besides, what better place to test his
agrarian principles and expertise than among the Indians. Meeker renewed his old phalangist zeal by rereading Charles Fourier's works
before leaving for White River in May 1878.[34]

Meeker's first act as agent was to move the agency 15 miles downstream to Powell Valley, a superior agricultural site containing 3,500
acres of "good" land. White River Utes opposed the move. The valley
was prime winter pasturage for their horses and contained dancing and
gaming grounds, including a race track. Some Indians had already

planted potatoes that spring, including a Ute named Johnson (Poowa-gudt), "who takes the lead in progress and enterprise." Johnson and his wife Susan (Ouray's sister) kept three cows, goats, and poultry, and maintained a permanent house. His farming method, however, out-raged Meeker. Johnson used "his retainers"—about fifteen to twenty women and children—to care for his potatoes, supervising them "like a first-class business man." Johnson's personal dislike for farming seemed general among males. Women, however, showed more interest, es-pecially in potatoes, which were similar to yampa root in consistency and taste when cooked or eaten raw. As yampa declined in importance, Utes integrated the potato into existing food and production categories, making it part of the subsistence domain of women.[35]

At the end of the first season, Meeker assessed the situation at White River. "Their chief pursuit," he wrote, "is hunting, the breeding and care of horses and horse racing, or in other words, gambling, which is carried on daily more than six months in a year." Utes were naturally lazy, he complained, made worse by inept employees unequipped to teach them how to farm. "Their only idea of an agency is that it shall be a place where they get supplies." Meeker aimed to change that.[36]

Next spring, Meeker began work in earnest on the new agency fields. He brought in several practical farmers from the Union Colony and reported that they fenced 80 acres, with 20 planted to wheat and 20 more partially cleared for potatoes. Meeker's work was made more difficult by Captain Jack (Nicaagat) and his followers, who opposed fencing and clearing the valley. On the other hand, Meeker reported that over thirty followers of Douglas (Quinkent) worked on the farm. Meeker won Douglas over by promising him extra rations and money to buy ammunition so his followers could hunt. In effect, Douglas's men worked on the farm not for the produce, but in order to earn money for weapons to reproduce their hunting activities. Jack's followers ridiculed and threatened Douglas's men until they eventually quit. Then, in a purely political move, Jack accepted a farm near the old agency in order to placate Meeker and to solidify his opposition to Douglas.[37]

As work on the farm progressed, Meeker turned his attention to Ute horses. "The practice of these Indians in keeping and holding horses on an extensive scale is not only discouraging to farm industry," he wrote, "but is working most serious inconvenience, if not loss, to the cattle interest." He estimated Utes owned 4,000 horses, with 2,000 in Powell Valley using up feed and forcing agency cattle into the hills. Meeker recognized that Ute wealth and prestige were dependent on horses and set out to change that relationship. He saw his hopes taking shape when Johnson brought him two horses, asking that they be broken for plowing. Meeker's employees began training the horses, feeding them grain to put them in working condition. Later, he dis-covered that Johnson had been racing these horses and that the entire purpose of his request had been "to get them in good heart so that he could beat his brethren of the turf." Meeker was furious, and relations with Johnson cooled.[38]

As Ute opposition stiffened, Meeker became more dogmatic in his efforts to force Utes to farm, threatening to cut off rations to those who would not work. Jack and a Ute delegation complained to Colorado Governor Frederick W. Pitkin about Meeker's plowing and threats, telling him "they thought their civilization much superior to that of the white man, and said that they much preferred that the Agent would give them their food and leave them to live their own lives." Upon returning from a trip to Washington, D.C., Piah, a Taviwac/Parianuc leader, was reputed to have said, "White father at Washington said Indian must make potato, cabbage, and work. I tell white father no make potato, cabbage, no work; Indian hunt, fish. No hunt, no fish, Indian fight and die. Me great warrior. Warriors no plow." Through the summer, tensions mounted on both sides as Utes left the agency to hunt deer and trade hides for weapons, as forest fires blazed, and as Meeker continued to plow Ute pastures.[39]

In September 1879, after years of broken promises, subsistence displacement, and passive resistance, White River Utes pushed back. The incident began when Meeker found out that Johnson was only pasturing horses on his field and ordered 50 acres plowed, including part of a race track. In Johnson's absence, his wife Susan objected, but the plowing went on until two of Johnson's relatives fired shots over the plowmen's heads. Meeker called a council with Jack and Douglas, who told him "that he had plowed enough land, that they must have feed for their horses." Meeker replied, "You have got too many horses; you had better kill them." After a lengthy talk, Jack acquiesced, and the plowing continued the next day. About this time Johnson returned, found his field being plowed, and argued that Meeker should plow an adjacent sagebrush field instead. Meeker again suggested that Johnson shoot some of his horses. Outraged at the suggestion, Johnson forced Meeker from the office and publicly knocked him to the ground. Realizing the danger he was in, Meeker wired for troops to protect the agency.

Between 10 and 28 September tensions remained high. The White Rivers feared the approaching troops from Fort Steele, Wyoming, and prepared to defend themselves. On 29 September 1879, Jack's warriors ambushed Major Thomas Thornburgh's command at Milk Creek after Thornburgh ignored warnings from Meeker and the Utes not to enter the reservation. The next day, while the soldiers were pinned down, Douglas's men attacked the agency, killing Meeker and eleven men before fleeing south to the Grand River with three women and a child as hostages. By mid-October, when it became clear that the Uintahs and Uncompahgres would not join their struggle and that more soldiers were nearing their camp, the White Rivers negotiated a surrender through Chief Ouray.[40]

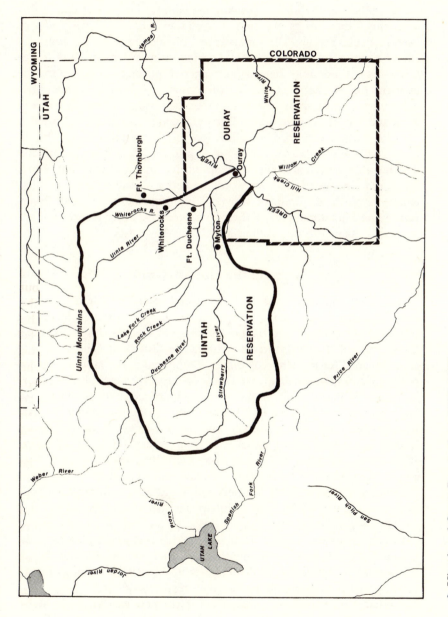

2. Uintah and Ouray Reservations, 1868–1896

The incident predictably increased agitation for the removal of all Utes from Colorado, even the Uncompahgre and southern bands that were not involved. In an effort to avoid relocation, Ute leaders—particularly Ouray, who mediated the final peace—stressed that Utes did not object to the idea of plowing the land for farms, but that in this case, the White Rivers objected to the *location* of the plowing. Ouray used this subtle, politically sophisticated distinction to reassure investigating commissioners that peaceful agricultural settlement *on their own lands* was still possible. Investigators agreed, placing the blame for the incident on Meeker's aggressive agrarianism. "He was a great agriculturalist, and he thought he could succeed in forcing the Indians to work and accept the situation as farmers," said General Charles Adams, "but he did not take into consideration that it is almost impossible to force Indians into that sort of labor all at once." Still, the commission decided that better agricultural land existed in Utah and that White River and Uncompahgre Utes would be better off there. Between 1881 and 1882 the Army forcibly removed White Rivers to the Uintah Reservation and Uncompahgres to their own executive order reservation adjoining Uintah—the two-million-acre Ouray Reservation.[41]

Farming the Uintah-Ouray

White River and Uncompahgre Utes faced several problems in Utah. Neither group found much prepared for them, and they faced the problems of replacing material possessions and altering lifestyles to meet the realities of an ever-limited subsistence environment. The shock was especially bad for the Uncompahgres. Compared to the mountain parks of their Colorado homeland, the Ouray Reservation was a bleak and arid wasteland. White Rivers, on the other hand, arrived uninvited in an area already inhabited by Uintah Utes who were none too happy to share their limited resources, especially when they discovered the differences in rations and annuity payments each group received. Ultimately, White Rivers settled on land in the east along the Whiterocks River, and both groups agreed to pool their combined allowances—reinforcing a growing communal attitude. While Uintahs and White Rivers worked out their differences in the 1880s, both maintained a distrust and enmity towards the Uncompahgres for their part in earlier land cessions, for their apparent wealth in livestock, and for their use of the best grazing lands on the Uintah Reservation. Despite their differences, however, the three bands maintained a broader cultural solidarity in opposition to the common threat posed by Indian policy and white trespassers.[42]

Whatever improvement Agent J. J. Critchlow saw in the Uintahs' participation in agriculture before 1881 faded when the White Rivers arrived. Never truly defeated, they were "indolent and know nothing of farming or caring for themselves by civilized pursuits, and what is worse, many of them have no desire to learn. . . . they laugh at the

Uintahs for farming, and say they ought to fight and then Washington would furnish them plenty to eat." Reports circulated of a band of 190 led by Captain Jack and Colorow, two White River Utes who refused to come to the new agency. Likewise, the Uncompahgres were unhappy about their removal and resisted opening new farms. Their agent reported that farming the Ouray Reservation was pointless anyway without an expensive irrigation system. Given this situation, Critchlow saw an opportunity for Uintah farmers to expand production and trade surplus wheat and hay to the newcomers in exchange for agricultural labor or cut firewood, but the local market economy he envisioned never materialized. While Uintahs farmed 250 acres in 1882, smut and grub worms destroyed any surplus wheat they might have made. Aside from those few who farmed or worked as agency freighters and laborers, the majority of Utes refused such work and turned to agency rations. In this two-reservation setting of nearly four million acres, the 2,825 Northern Utes were a politically and economically dependent people.[43]

Through the rest of the nineteenth century, Utes passively resisted wholesale agrarian settlement, incorporating farming as only one of several subsistence alternatives. Special Agent Paris H. Folsom gives the best description of the type of farming conducted on the Uintah Reservation throughout this period:

> Dotted here and there are their little farms and homes, blending so quietly with nature itself, that the line of separation seems really blurred and lost. Here "a farm" as they call it—a few acres fenced, right in the open meadow, closely surrounded and heamed in by a rich green sward—the whole family at work or play in the corn, potatoes, peas and beans, children, babies and all. . . . Their greatest happiness is in the complete domestic circle that is their greatest comfort—often the only one—their ambition is limited to, and satisfied with a low order of livlihood, and united, undisturbed families.

Folsom's description of Uintah farms as hardly more than garden plots by white standards, their satisfaction with what little these fields produced, and their retention of "wigwams" and the scattered, family circle settlement is indicative of the limited accommodation made by Uintahs even after years of contact. Folsom blamed the lack of incentives—there was no market for their produce aside from traders who bought low, charged high prices for goods, and resold Indian produce to the agency at inflated prices. He recommended that instruction given on the agency farms "should be applied and given to the Indians upon *their own* farms, and that the Government should purchase its needed supplies for the required agency stock from the Indians," thus encouraging a healthy market economy.[44]

Folsom saw the outward manifestations of a troubled agricultural economy but missed the meaning of cultural resistance. At Uintah Agency, agents noted that Uintahs showed more promise than the White Rivers, who "have never taken kindly to agriculture," and even burned the agency farm fence in an act of defiance. With 243 acres planted in wheat, oats, potatoes, and vegetables in 1885, the agent admitted that Utes raised only one-third of their subsistence, with rations and hunting each accounting for one-third. As for ranching, two Uintahs owned nearly half of the 1,600 Ute cattle. Optimistic estimates in 1888 put the number of individuals farming or ranching at 70 out of a population of over 1,000, and even then white laborers did the majority of the work.[45]

Conditions were similar or worse at Ouray Agency. In 1886, Uncompahgres cultivated 70 acres in "about 45 *Patches* rather than *farms*" of from one to four acres each, scattered for thirty miles along the bottoms of the Duchesne and White rivers. Spring flooding had washed out these farms for two years running, while those above the flood plain suffered from drought and alkaline soil. Agents complained that their scattered camps made them difficult to supervise and that the environment was "not very inviting . . . and it is doubtful at present if all the tribe can find enough arable land in the reservation to subsist upon." To top it off, Uncompahgre factions emerged. "One party is in favor of farming and trying to learn something of civilization; the other party cannot be induced to change their methods of life." They stayed away from the agency except to collect rations and annuities and subsisted by herding sheep and cattle and hunting in the southern recesses of the rugged Taviputs Plateau.[46]

While Utes resisted farming, Ute agents discovered their continuing attachment to horses. In 1885, agents estimated the Uintah-White River herd at 7,000 horses and the Uncompahgre herd at 5,300, well beyond any practical agricultural need. Their attempts to encourage ranching attracted a few families from each band who amassed several hundred cattle and several thousand sheep, but it remained a rather narrow and a highly mobile enterprise. Uintah agent Elisha W. Davis was quick to note that "in the matter of stock raising the Indians have a decided preference to ponies over cattle. Four or five Indians of the Uintah tribe own nearly all the Indian cattle on this reserve. Their influence among the tribe is measured by the number of ponies they possess, and as long as this custom obtains among them they will raise horses in preference to cattle." Worse yet, they trained the best horses for racing, not plowing. Ouray agent J. F. Minniss concurred, estimating that "they spend three-fourths of their time gambling, horse racing, and hunting."[47]

Ute attempts to maintain that mobile, hunting lifestyle proved increasingly difficult. Throughout the 1880s and 1890s, Utes left the reservation to hunt in Colorado for much-needed meat and hides, a right guaranteed them in the 1880 removal agreement. But increasingly they ran into hostile citizen militias and state game wardens called "deer police," who attacked them, confiscated their possessions, and drove them back to Utah, claiming that they were indiscriminately killing and wasting deer and livestock. Ute agents investigated, disproved the worst allegations, yet dutifully ordered Utes back to the reservation. After one confrontation, agency employee George K. Burnett noted that "the loss of their jerk meat was a particularly severe one," since they relied on it for winter use, rations at the agency "being at the best of times nearly a starvation allowance." When told in council that their off-reservation hunting rights had been superseded by state game laws, Ute leaders argued that their rights and needs remained constant. "There are no brands on the deer and to whom do they belong? We were raised to hunt them for their meat and skins," they said. "If Washington wants us to farm he must send things to farm with to each Indian, not a few things, then maybe we can live at home." Utes continued to hunt in Utah, Colorado, and Wyoming into the twentieth century, but between restrictions and depletion, game was never again the subsistence staple it had been for so many generations.[48]

Given Ute resistance to farming, their preference for horses over cattle, and their increasing dependence on rations, agents decided to disband the tribal herd in the 1880s in order to generate revenue by leasing Ute grazing lands. White ranchers accustomed to running their livestock in the underutilized Strawberry Valley for free ignored the new policies, and run-ins between Utes and trespassing cowboys kept tensions high. In 1890, things got so bad that a Ute council requested the removal of all non-Indian stock from the reservation, but the trespass and damage to their range continued. Two years later, under mounting political and economic pressure, the council reconsidered and approved five-year leases with bonded ranchers. Through the rest of the 1890s, Utes leased most of the Strawberry Valley at $7,100 per year, the money being divided per capita and deposited in Individual Indian Money accounts. In the late 1890s, some Uintahs went one step further and leased their unallotted fields to whites. Agents accepted leasing because it put Indian land under cultivation, but the Indian commissioner rejected the idea of a profitable Indian landlord system, believing that Indians should be farming themselves. Overall, leasing became an viable cultural and economic alternative to actually farming or ranching for land-rich–cash-poor Utes.[49]

In an environment admittedly better suited for grazing than farming, bureau officials continued to pursue the agrarian ideal for a rapidly declining Northern Ute population. In 1895, Agent James F. Randlett reported that the 925 Uncompahgres had 850 acres cultivated or broken, while the 442 Uintahs and 403 White Rivers had 2,600 acres cultivated or broken on the combined four million-acre Uintah-Ouray Reservation. Approximately 60 percent of Ute families lived within a 15-mile radius of the agency at Whiterocks, while the rest were scattered up to 60 miles to the south and west. With the help of agency employees who did the majority of the heavy farm labor, Utes raised wheat, oats, grass and alfalfa hay, and garden vegetables. Randlett, however, estimated that Utes obtained only 30 percent of their total subsistence from their own labor in "civilized pursuits," 10 percent from hunting, and 60 percent from government rations.[50]

While the statistics of Northern Ute farming improved in the 1890s, Ute cultural practices and attitudes towards agricultural labor remained little changed. Agent Robert Waugh reported their "dogged pertinacity" in horse racing, dancing, and mortuary customs resulting in the destruction of cabins and valuable personal property. They complied with orders for their "civilization" but returned to their old habits once officials were out of sight. Waugh candidly noted that Ute males were "the most practical & least theoretical of any beings I ever came across. He wants the least & enjoys the most with the least care or effort. He views with a jealous eye any & all efforts to intrude the White Mans ways & wants upon him, & would resist them by force only that he thinks that would be harder." Part of that passive resistance took the form of complaints that agency farmers were not doing enough of the work for them—plowing, fencing, building houses, and digging irrigation ditches—and should therefore be "sent away," suspending farm progress. By continuing to equate white farmers with personal laborers, the product of a culturally constructed race-role hierarchy, Utes attempted to deflect directed agrarian change.[51]

Not all Northern Utes resisted such change. Sent out to investigate

Uintah Basin near Whiterocks. Edward Sapir, 1909. Special Collections, Marriott Library, University of Utah.

the situation, Special Agent George W. Parker concluded that on the whole, Utes "do not appear to be making any advancement in agriculture . . . although I find individual indians displaying considerable thrift." These, he noted, were generally Uintahs, living west of the agency along the Duchesne River. Ute agents deemed them more "progressive" than Uncompahgres and White Rivers when it came to farming, leasing, and schools. At times agents tried to exploit the factionalism that developed between so-called progressives and traditionalists to force through their own agenda but could never completely grasp what remained a fluid, issue-oriented process of individual response and negotiated decision-making between and among the Ute people. Whether it was hunting or farming, ranching or leasing, horses or cattle, Utes continued to adapt and to reproduce cultural values and behaviors in this reservation context, even as their economic and political choices narrowed and dependence on government rations increased.[52]

Northern Ute Allotment

Government officials established the legal framework for dividing Ute lands in severalty in the 1880 Ute Agreement and the 1887 General Allotment Act but did not pursue that option until trespassing miners discovered valuable Gilsonite (asphaltum) deposits on the Uintah and Ouray reservations in 1886 and 1888. Interior department officials released 7,040 acres from Uintah in 1888 to appease mining interests but resisted calls for altering the Ouray boundary. Six years later, Congress caved in to mining lobbyists and created a commission to allot Uncompahgres and open the Ouray Reservation.[53] Ute agent James F. Randlett protested the plan, charging that the reservation had never contained enough farmland and had been a fraud from the beginning. As Randlett expected, the commission confirmed that there was insufficient agricultural land for allotment, but Congress forged ahead, ordering Uncompahgres allotted on either the Ouray or Uintah reservations by 1 April 1898, with or without the consent of any of the three bands. Uintah and White River Utes would simply be reimbursed $1.25 per acre for lands assigned to Uncompahgres.[54]

In council, White River leaders Sowawick, Maricisco, and Catoomp realized they would be next and voiced their opposition to allotment and to selling land to the Uncompahgres. They understood the connection between severalty and farming and in their speeches rejected allotment through metaphorical attacks on the things that would separate their lands (fences), that would tie them to a specific plot (log houses), make their land agriculturally viable (irrigation), and undercut their land use patterns and resistance to farming. They opposed opening the reservations to whites whom they feared would settle among them. All of these things threatened a more collective lifestyle and identity that developed out of the deprivation of the reservation experience as Ute elders died, as paths to leadership evolved, and as individual families found fewer opportunities to live without help from the larger group. Having witnessed the disastrous consequences of individualistic action when dealing with the federal government, these White River leaders voiced the collective opposition of all three bands. For their actions, Agent William Beck requested that these "incendiary" leaders be imprisoned in Florida.[55]

Uncompahgres likewise opposed allotment, but, realizing they could not halt it, they attempted to sabotage the plan. Instructed to allot 160 acres to each head of household and 80 acres to each member over eighteen years of age, allotting commissioners worked slowly in the face of bad weather and uncooperative Utes. They reported that 42 Uncompahgres, including leaders like Ouray's widow Chipita and her brother Andrew McCook, demanded the lands they already inhabited. Commissioners noted that most of these sites were "ranches" rather than farms, situated in narrow canyons remote from the agency. Others declined to choose an allotment and were simply assigned lands. By 1904, 384 Uncompahgres held allotments, including 101 on the Ouray Reservation that were judged "entirely valueless, even for grazing purposes." One Utah attorney claimed that the Indians made their selections knowing "absolutely nothing about the value of land," when in fact they chose them specifically to avoid being removed to Uintah and to reproduce a hunting and herding lifestyle, thus subverting the settled agrarian intent of allotment. Allotting agents reported their failure to get even a single Uncompahgre to accept or visit allotments on the Uintah Reservation, while those without allotments "roam at will over a vast extent of 'bad land' territory, like the deer or coyote, totally without the reach of civilizing influences."[56]

While allotment went forward at Ouray in 1898, Congress ordered the Uintah Reservation allotted in severalty "by the consent of a majority of the adult male Indians." The Uintahs, White Rivers, and remaining Uncompahgres were to select lands for themselves or be assigned lands "in their best interest." Agent Howell P. Myton, one of the allotting commissioners, replied, "If the consent of the Indians is necessary to be obtained in order to open the Uintah Reservation, it will be useless for Congress to pass any more laws or spend any more money for that purpose, for I do not believe there is an Indian on the reservation who is willing or favors selling any part of their land."[57]

Over the next four years, Myton and the other commissioners surveyed the Uintah Reservation and found little fit for farming or even grazing due to climate, soils, and the interspersion of "waste lands" within productive areas. They held numerous councils to gain the required Ute approval but met consistent opposition. While Uintahs and White Rivers agreed to supply land to Uncompahgres who were "their friends and neighbors," they refused to allow anyone else to hold allotments. Even Tabby-to-kwana, long a participant farmer, feared allotment as an attack on the integrity of Ute lands and people. The commissioners were strongly impressed that "they did not want to be disturbed in the quiet and peaceable possession of their lands."[58] Congress, however, was not impressed and granted the Interior secretary authority to allot the reservation without Ute consent. Ute family heads were to receive 80 acres and family members 40 acres each, half of what was offered them in 1899 and half of what the Uncompahgres accepted in 1898. With the exception of a tribal grazing reserve, the rest of the reservation would be opened for sale at $1.25 per acre. Bureau officials sent Special Agent James McLaughlin to inform the Utes and coerce their consent before proceeding anyway.[59]

McLaughlin was a seasoned bureau veteran, known among the Indians for his hard line but straight talk. In May 1903, McLaughlin met in council with Uintah and White River Utes and explained the recent Supreme Court decision of *Lone Wolf* v. *Hitchcock*, which gave Congress plenary power to abrogate Indian treaty stipulations. He told them that their consent was no longer necessary, that Congress had already decided allotment was in their best interest. McLaughlin continued:

> The reservations were made large in days gone by when you could make a living by hunting and large reservations were then necessary and possible, but with the tide of immigration coming into the country, game has become scarce and you can no longer live by hunting: and therefore you must take to agriculture to make a living for yourselves and families.

Over and over again he told them that the only way to protect themselves from the inevitable wave of white settlers approaching the Uintah Basin was to secure the best agricultural lands now and settle down as farmers.[60]

Led by Tim Johnson, a White River spokesmen, individual Utes explained their connection with the land and adamantly denied the government's right to open their reservation. Captain Joe (WR) told McLaughlin:

> The Indian reservation was not put down for nothing. It is held down by something heavy. . . . There is only one land here and that is the Indian's land and it belongs to the Indians. . . . Here are the Uncompahgre Indians here and the White River Indians, and the Uinta Indians and we want to hold our reservation. There is a line from here on the top of these mountains where the Indians living on the reservation can go any place, and that is good. We have these mountains, and streams and don't want anybody coming on this reservation.

Red Cap (WR) reiterated, "This reservation is heavy. The Indians have grown here and their bones are under the ground, covered over with earth. That is the reason it is so heavy." John Star (WR) told McLaughlin, "You see me and I see you. My flesh is black: you have good flesh, you are white like this paper here. My flesh looks like the ground. That's the reason I like this land: my flesh is like the ground. That's the reason I am going to keep it." Warren (Uintah) argued simply, "It is not buckskin or deer's hide, and I do not want to sell it."

Other Utes took different approaches calculated to raise legitimate questions. Sowsonocutt (WR) said, "The Indians have lots of cattle and horses. When we take the Government's little pieces of land, how are we to run our horses inside on little pieces of land?" Grant (Uintah) added, "What are my horses going to do when I have only a little piece of land? Must I tie my horses in that little field?" Appah (WR) agreed, summarizing that "when you tell us that we must take farms, we do not like that on account of our horses." Wandrodes, a major Uintah cattle owner, argued that 80 acres was not enough, and he would sign only if he could keep his extensive range land around Rock Creek. Black Hawk (Uintah) raised the issue of their readiness and the threat of land alien-ation. "I have no sense, and I know it," he told his listeners. "I just play with this land [farming], but when I had money, I threw it away. I am here on this land. That is what holds me up. I do not want you to steal it from me." Above all, Utes worried about neighboring Mormons, who were already encroaching on their land and water, and the flood of new settlers who would destroy their communality. Charley Mack con-cluded, "What are the Indians going to do? It is like sand. You throw water upon sand and it will cave in and wash off: so with Indians, after a while there will be none left."[61]

For six days the Utes talked to McLaughlin, as Little Jim (WR) put it, "even if you have no ears." Appah likened him to "a storm coming down from the mountains when the flood is coming down the stream and we can't stop it," but, he asserted, "I have this reservation line fixed and you can't throw it aside." In the end, McLaughlin proceeded with his job. Of the 159 Uintah and 122 White River adult males, only 82 (75 and 7 respectively) signed the allotment document, and those mainly to show good will in the face of what they now understood to be inevitable. In a show of defiance, Sowawick and 25 White River Utes fled toward the Black Hills of South Dakota but were quickly returned by Indian police—presaging the active resistance yet to come.[62]

In preparation for allotment, government employees made compre-hensive surveys of the Uintah Reservation. They concluded that the broken nature of the country would make even the best agricultural lands along the river bottoms and low benches extremely difficult and expensive to clear and irrigate. Irrigation itself was uncertain since whites had been diverting water for years from the upper Strawberry drainage to irrigate Wasatch County farms. Agents worried that Utes would rapidly lose more water rights once the reservation was opened. Throughout the process, White Rivers remained very antagonistic toward the survey crews and destroyed survey markers to stop the work. Reports circulated that Utes were stockpiling firearms and ammunition to resist allotment, but the work continued.[63]

Between April and July 1905, the Ute Allotting Commission made 591 Uncompahgre and 774 Uintah and White River allotments totaling 103,265 acres on the Uintah reserve. The commissioners tried to allot land individuals requested or had previously improved. They set aside the best agricultural lands along the major streams in order to protect Ute water rights by limiting white access. However, irrigation engineer and allotting commissioner W. H. Code noted that Utes frequently chose non-arable lands or allotments "interspersed with areas and ridges of rocky soil which would discourage any New England farmer." He also complained that White River Utes "are always rounding up bands of wild ponies and branding their colts, an occupation which they have more interest by far than the selection of allotments." Those who refused to select their own allotments were assigned lands. In addition to allotments Utes received a 250,000-acre tribal grazing reserve—a narrow strip running 60 miles long the foothills of the Uinta Mountains. Of their remaining lands, the president withdrew the Uinta National Forest and Strawberry Valley before opening the rest to settler entry.[64]

Allotment represented a fundamental threat to an evolving Ute society. Utes lost control of land as white settlers flooded the opened reservation. "From the very nature of the Country," wrote Agent C. G. Hall, "the allotments made to the Indians were so located that the Indians are considerably mixed in with white settlers, and, as a result, many conflicts between the Indians and settlers have occurred." Disputes broke out over boundaries, the use of water and timber, Indian burial sites, trespassing livestock, and problems associated with an increased access to alcohol. Beyond that, allotment represented an attempt to re-individualize Utes after years of collectivist policies and informal cooperation necessitated by a dependent reservation economy. Utes responded by selectively adapting to or resisting directed change, and, like other groups, they adopted new rituals intended to change the social order or revitalize their culture. There is no indication that Utes adopted Wovoka's Ghost Dance in the late 1880s—their experience with the dance in the 1870s was a pragmatic failure and their uneasiness about ghosts kept the religion unpopular—but the Sun Dance was another matter.[65]

Introduced during the allotment crisis of the 1890s by General Grant or Grant Bullethead, a Uintah who learned it from Wind River Shoshones, the Sun Dance echoed the individualistic tenor of Ute beliefs. Utes seized the model and reinterpreted it, reproducing their religious system with its health component within the framework of that single dance. Spurred by a sense of real and perceived deprivation, Northern Utes adopted the Sun Dance as a social movement to effect change, to redeem the individual rather than to transform the total social or natural order. In practice, the Sun Dance mirrored the contradictions between collectivism and individualism facing Utes under

Northern Ute Sun Dance lodge at Whiterocks, ca. 1900. Mr. Merriman, Whiterocks Trading Post. Special Collections, Marriott Library, University of Utah.

the seesaw federal policies of reservation and allotment. Utes danced in a collective effort to gain and benefit from *puwa* (power) derived through individual participation in the dance. That power would then be used for the benefit, cohesion, and health of the sanctioning group (good power) rather than become individualized (bad) power. Along with Peyotism, which gained Ute followers in the 1910s as the problems of allotment, irrigation, farming, and leasing increased, the Sun Dance offered Northern Utes a way to bind the people together.[66]

While the Sun Dance offered one way to deal with the changes of allotment, White River Utes once again took direct action. Nine months after allotment, a band of nearly four hundred Utes, mainly White Rivers led by Appah and Red Cap, left the reservation and marched to South Dakota, where they planned to settle among the Lakotas. This group, made up of those most opposed to agriculture, allotment, and the opening of their reservation, received little help from the Lakotas. Necessity soon forced them to work for the railroad or in nearby Rapid City. In 1908 they agreed to return to their allotments, under guard and little honored by their fellow Utes.[67]

Irrigation

With allotment completed, government officials turned their attention to protecting Indian water rights and making the land more hospitable for agriculture. For years, Ute agents had complained that farming was impossible on more that a handful of acres without irrigation. In 1906, Congress approved the 80,000-acre Uintah Irrigation Project and appropriated $600,000, to be reimbursed through the sale of unallotted Ute lands. As irrigation officials moved forward with the project, they met Ute opposition to the costs of further dividing their lands into an agrarian system. Many Utes refused to work on the ditches or prepare their allotments for water, while those who took the wage labor jobs had little time to farm. But perhaps more serious, officials realized that the reservation had been opened under state law, thereby forfeiting federal protection of Indian water rights as affirmed in *Winters v. U.S.* (1908). Utah required the filer of primary water rights to show "beneficial use" within fourteen years or else forfeit those rights. In effect, all allotments not cleared, leveled, planted, and using one second-foot of water per 80 acres before 1919 would lose their primary water rights to white homesteaders with secondary or tertiary rights. With those primary rights would go the productive capability and resale value of Ute allotments and any hope of the people becoming self-sufficient farmers.[68]

Beginning in the eastern districts, where there were more allotments, irrigation work went forward as quickly as possible, but officials soon realized that Utes would hardly be able to prove use on 10 percent of their lands by the 1919 deadline. In an effort to save Ute water rights, Agent C. G. Hall received permission to arrange five-year leases at twenty-five cents per acre, with or without the consent of Utes who could not or would not make the necessary improvements. Explaining to a Ute council, Hall suggested that they continue to live on a corner of their allotment and perform wage labor for the white lessee, or that perhaps they should consider selling part of their allotment to raise capital for improving their remaining land or for buying cattle. Despite Ute opposition to further land sales, agents encouraged older and incompetent Indians to sell their land with the primary water rights intact so they could gain some immediate benefit. In 1911 alone, Ute agents arranged the sale of 67 (5 percent) of 1,365 total Ute allotments. Agency farmer Charles L. Davis noted that older White River Utes, particularly those who returned from South Dakota, "are clamoring against any of their members selling any lands of any kind, yet we are unable to get them to put forth effort to develop these lands." While head men intimidated band members to keep them from signing away heirship lands, the sales and leasing continued.[69]

Between 1915 and 1917, Superintendent Albert H. Kneale redoubled efforts to save the water, despite his observation that "no one connected with the Bureau had the slightest expectation of any successful outcome." The year before his arrival, Utes held 6,147 improved acres and leased another 7,113 acres, leaving the remaining 68,869 allotted acres (84 percent) idle. Kneale arranged more liberal leases at no or low cost and distributed promotional literature across the country to attract white lessees. Closer to home, he used Utes' Individual Indian Money accounts to defray the costs of fencing and plowing and permitted lessees access to the Ute grazing reserve. By 1917, Kneale had arranged 1,764 leases totaling 54,000 allotted acres and had nearly 20,000 allotted acres sold or pending sale.[70]

Critics, however, charged that Utes were losing some of their best agricultural lands and that white settlers and lessees were benefiting disproportionately from the Indian-financed irrigation system. Those who purchased Ute allotments escaped having to pay for the construction of the system. Agents complained that settlers frequently took more than their legal share of water or siphoned off water through illegal spur ditches built across unoccupied allotments. After trying to make the land pay quick returns, a number of settlers defaulted on their unsecured government loans, while lessees used Ute lands without making adequate improvements or abused the land for short-term profits, leaving it barren and alkaline. On top of that, critics charged that errors in canal construction left thousands of acres without adequate water to meet primary user needs.[71]

In January 1921, after an 18-month extension, the Indian Irrigation Service managed to perfect primary water rights on 77,195 allotted acres—23,108 acres now in white hands and the majority of the rest leased to whites. The Uintah Irrigation Project itself covered 93,000 acres (80,306 acres fit for cultivation) at $13 per acre reclaimed, double the original $600,000 appropriation. But the costs to the Ute people went well beyond that: the sale and leasing of some of the best agricultural lands to non-Utes; faulty construction and improper irrigation techniques that increased erosion and brought up alkali patches rendering other lands worthless; and charges against each individual allotment that amounted to as much as $1,200 beyond the tribal

Father and son on ration day, Ft. Duchesne, ca. 1899–1902. Mrs. Howell P. Myton. Myton Collection, Box 1. Special Collections, Marriott Library, University of Utah.

construction costs and annual water fees, payable whether used or not. The irrigation project proved to be an expensive benefit to those Utes who actually used the water and a federal gift to those who bought Ute allotments or used their canals. Its legacy was one of tribal and individual indebtedness and further land sales far outweighing, in Ute terms, the economic or cultural worth of the project.[72]

Ute Farming in the Twentieth Century

In the first three decades of the twentieth century, Utes faced a rapidly changing political and economic reality. Their old leaders, treaties, and lifestyles disappeared, and their numbers plummeted from 1,660 in 1900 to a low of 917 in 1930. Allotment left them divided on small farms, besieged by an array of new neighbors, indebted, dependent, yet defiant. During the same period Ute agricultural statistics increased steadily, revealing the extent of leasing and attempts to save Ute water rights, as well as a small but growing number of Ute families earning a modest living by running livestock and working the land.

In 1905, agents counted 131 Ute farms with 4,572 tilled acres, not all of it planted and most worked by agency employees or lessees. Indian farming, one extension agent noted, "has been of the indifferent, unscientific and unprofitable kind. The present prevailing custom is for the Indian owner to employ a white man to run the farm, paying him a definite share of the products." This tendency became more pronounced after allotment, and, despite frequent disagreements between landlord and tenant, many Utes found this a comfortable way to earn a living, please agents concerned with statistics, and avoid the routine of agricultural labor.[73]

Ute attitudes towards agricultural labor evolved more slowly than bureau officials wished. White River and Uncompahgre Utes lagged behind Uintahs and a growing mixed-blood population in working their own land. In 1907, Arrive, an Uncompahgre, defended his people's habits against the agent's critique: "They work a while and then rest a while and then work again. . . . We like to smoke cigarettes on ditch work. Work little while then smoke." "It's pretty hard to get an Indian to farm," recalled Hal Daniels, Sr. "The Indians worked, but some of them didn't do nothing. They just sit and watch." This reproduction of Ute values frustrated Superintendent Kneale. He noted that they showed "little desire to please those in authority" and got by on rations, lease payments, and interest from a claims case settlement. "For the most part," he recalled, "the Utes were wholly content to make their living expenses conform to this income, so there was little occasion to perform manual labor." They had good grazing lands but ran mostly horses. They had primary water rights that their white neighbors valued "only slightly less than life itself," but seemed not to care. According to Kneale, they were set to practice "a subsistence form of farming, with a minimum of effort," but instead chose to do "practically nothing" but gamble, visit, and draw rations.[74]

Resistance to an agrarian lifestyle manifested itself in other areas as well. After 1905, few Utes actually lived on their own allotments, preferring to reproduce extended family residences on a single plot. A 1909 census indicated that only 78 of 443 Uintahs, 8 of 469 Uncompahgres, and 16 of 296 White Rivers lived on and cultivated their allotments. Into the 1930s, a majority of Utes continued to inhabit tepees pitched next to the log and frame cabins built for them. If they did not bury their dead under the floor or burn the house down according to mortuary practices, they frustrated their agents by stabling horses in the structures. Utes perpetuated marriage customs that complicated agency heirship cases, and maintained an indifference toward the agency schools. Ordered to round up students, Ute policemen effectively mediated the differences in white and Indian expectations by being less than vigorous in pursuing truants.[75]

In this period of directed agrarian change, native religions offered Utes alternatives to incorporation, ways to assert their cultural identity and "Indianness." While Utes adopted the outward trappings of Christianity—becoming nominal Mormons, Episcopalians, or both—they continued to Bear Dance, to recognize native shamans, and to experiment with the Sun Dance and Peyote religions. Government officials charged that the dances took children away from school and families away from their farms at crucial periods and that they encouraged gambling, immorality, and the spread of disease. When the Indian Bureau banned the Sun Dance in 1913, Utes cloaked it in agrarian imagery to appease their agents, calling it a "Harvest" or "Thanksgiving" dance. Again, Indian police protected their people by failing to enforce the ban. Likewise, the Indian Bureau charged that peyote was addictive and drove people crazy. Ute agents moved to suppress the religion when it appeared at Uintah-Ouray in 1914, but by 1919 more than half followed the Peyote Way. Uintahs and Uncompahgres readily adopted Peyote, while conservative White Rivers rejected it as an introduced cult. Over the next decade, official suppression, internal Ute criticism, and religious pragmatism reduced the Peyote following and drove the religion underground.[76]

While government officials tried to change Ute attitudes and ban native religions, they recognized the existence of far more serious structural problems. First, the quality of allotted lands selected, assigned, or retained by Utes after the sales and leasing hindered later agricultural efforts. Some Utes consciously chose nonarable lands. A number of Uncompahgres picked isolated areas in the Hill Creek country suited to hunting and running sheep and refused to be reallotted. Other allottees claimed that agents assigned then side-hills and cobblestoned areas, leaving better adjacent lands open for white homesteaders. Inspector E. E. Paine berated the allotting commission, noting, "Several of the allotments on which I was could not have been plowed except, possibly, by a battery of artillery, could not be seeded except with shot-guns, and, if the seed germinated by any chance, the crops could not be harvested except by the use of Zeppelins." Not all were so bad, but over time and given poor water management, alkali and erosion plagued even the best allotments.[77]

Second, in an age of steam- and gas-powered equipment, Utes farmed with horse-drawn implements into the late 1920s. Selling land to buy modern equipment was an undesirable option, yet few qualified for or were willing to risk reimbursable government loans given the scale of their farms. Instead Utes borrowed agency machinery or col-lectively purchased and shared what equipment they could. Even then Utes lacked instruction in the use of that equipment and practical agri-cultural techniques. The Indian Bureau had trouble attracting and keeping quality farm personnel given the low pay and isolation. Ute agents complained that their farmers were too busy patrolling the reser-vation against trespassers or plowing fields for individual Indians. In 1912, Agent Martin assigned each of his farmers a specific district to supervise through in-field demonstrations. Until they were replaced in 1937 by county extension agents, these district farmers were the most direct link between the people, their agent, and federal policy.[78]

Northern Utes interviewed in the 1960s recalled that most of the district farmers did a fair job. "You know, we used to have a few good crops when he was here, but now you don't see them now," recalled Hal Daniels, Sr., about his district farmer L. H. Mitchell. Daniels and others remembered the farmers coming by buggy and team to visit, sharing seed and information, passing along local news, and staying for dinner. A certain cultural understanding that Utes valued developed in those visits. Conner Chapoose recalled:

> Old Indians, they talk a little English. They understood their farmer, and the farmer understood them. They come in and sat down. They tongues loose; more often they had their meals to cook. But they'd give it to these men. They used to always have Indian meal. . . .

But that personal relationship changed over time. By 1932, Ute leaders criticized district farmers for doing too much clerical work and not enough field demonstration, and one farmer admitted that they had become more like subagents than practical farmers. Even then, Cha-poose contrasted the stable relations Utes had with district farmers to their dealings with transient extension agents who established little cultural rapport and reordered agricultural policies with no apparent consistency.[79]

Finally, the biggest structural obstacle to Ute farming success was the lack of markets. Reservations in general were isolated environments, physically and economically removed from American market capitalism. The Uintah-Ouray Agency specifically was 120 miles from the railroad in Salt Lake City and 110 miles up and over the Uinta Mountains from Fort Bridger and the transcontinental line. In the early twentieth century, a narrow-gauge spur of the Denver and Rio Grande Railroad and a standard-gauge line of the Denver and Rio Grande Western pushed to within 60 and 80 miles respectively of Fort Duchesne. But since all crops had to be freighted to the railroad and then shipped by rail to even more distant markets, officials noted as late as 1920 that "it practically limits farming operations to the production of forage and grain crops and such produce as can be consumed locally."[80]

Before allotment, local market demands more than covered what little surplus the dozen or so Uintah and mixed-blood Ute farmers managed to produce. Utes sold oats, hay, straw, wheat, and garden produce to the agency staff and troops at Fort Duchesne, bartered with local traders, or distributed produce informally within their kin groups. But in 1912 the fort closed, just as the irrigation project allowed more Utes, white lessees, and homesteaders to bring more land under more intensive cultivation. Agency farmer Charles Davis warned the Indian Bureau that "the market for farm products is now about overdone, and many settlers are having trouble to dispose of their crops for much needed cash." He cautioned that if all Ute allotments were cultivated, "over-production" would destroy the local market. H. W. Dick, superintendent of irrigation, concurred: "At the present time everything produced on the reservation is consumed within the territory but it is but a short time until an outside market must be sought."[81]

Despite cultural resistance and these structural problems, the period between 1912 and 1928 was actually the high point for farming and ranching at Uintah-Ouray. In 1912, of 267 able-bodied adult Ute males, 176 (66 percent) possessed farms averaging 32 cultivated acres. By 1920, 79 percent of the 275 able adult males owned cultivated fields averaging 41 acres, although agency employees or white tenants actually worked most of that in an effort to save Ute water. While nearly every family maintained a home vegetable garden, after 1920 alfalfa, grass hay, and hardy grain crops for livestock feed comprised 95 percent of cultivated Ute acreage. "The Indians were more settled on their farms," recalled Conner Chapoose. "They . . . look forward to hay cropping and gardening." Oran Curry remembered people living near each other in clusters "all along the river bottom from Randlett down to Ouray. . . . Alot of the Indians done a little farming in there—nice little homes. . . . they raise little gardens, vegetables, great for watermelon." At the height of Ute farming in 1928, Utes controlled 15,243 irrigated acres and leased another 28,819 acres to area farmers. Irrigation advisers Preston J. Porter and Charles A. Engle boasted that the Utes did "more farming . . . than the Indians of any other reservation."[82]

Ute ranching also increased. Despite the loss of prime grazing land to the Strawberry Valley Reclamation Project, in 1911 Utes ran 3,500 cattle, 2,554 sheep, and 3,695 horses on the grazing reserve, in the Uinta

National Forest, or on the isolated opened lands of the southern Ouray Reservation. Most families owned horses and a few cows for meat, selling them only when necessary, while 15 Uintah and Uncompahgre ranchers controlled the majority of livestock. During the 1910s, Ute agents continued leasing large areas of the grazing reserve and tried to convince Utes to round up and sell their "wild" horses to improve the range for "productive" livestock but met with a persistent, if passive, resistance. Ute ranchers countered with the idea of creating a tribal herd to prevent white stockmen from gaining control of the range through leasing, but they were defeated by those (particularly White Rivers) who desired the continued distribution of lease income. Leasing and the growth of Ute herds continued apace despite worries about overgrazing. Livestock ownership had broadened considerably by 1922, when Utes organized their first grazing association, and by 1925 the total numbers of animals had steadily increased to 6,663 cattle, 6,400 sheep, and 3,712 horses.[83]

This overall agricultural expansion resulted in part from the emergence of a nationally marketable cash crop, alfalfa seed. In the 1910s, the Uintah Basin's relative isolation made it an ideal place for developing new genetic seed stocks. Between 1922 and 1930, Ute and white farmers alike benefited from this lucrative trade in alfalfa seed, producing $4.1 million worth of seed as well as winter feed for livestock. Agricultural fairs sponsored by the agency in the 1910s encouraged Utes to expand their garden plots into fields, and a Farm Chapter Club organized in 1925 by Henry Harris served as a support network for forty Ute members. Harris, a Uintah farmer, cleared $3,000 in alfalfa seed sales that year, but 1925 proved to be the peak of the boom. "That spoiled men," recalled Harris.

> I went in too heavy the following year. I wanted to double what I made the next year. I was getting into the white man's way, the more money I made the more I wanted, and I made a failure of it.

As seed market prices declined, Basin farmers watched heavy water assessments and damage from weather and insects eat up what little profit remained. The boom responsible for involving more Utes in commercial farming went bust as the nation slid into depression.[84]

Even at its peak, farming for a majority of Utes was never much more than a subsistence enterprise—home gardening, cutting grass hay for their livestock, and perhaps raising some hay or alfalfa seed for sale. Annual farm income during the 1920s ranged between two and three hundred dollars per Ute family. Given those numbers, it is not surprising that the depression affected Utes relatively less than other people, but they too suffered the market economy collapse. Ute families maintained their vegetable gardens and, as one district farmer noted in 1932, were "making a living" by simply "existing" on their farms. Uintah farmer Jasper Pike recalled:

It was just root hog or die [laughs]. . . . Pretty rough. . . . I think the only reason we made it was that my wife could make more gravy with a sack of flour and a barrel of water than any other woman. . . . It was pretty slim; pretty slim.

In the Uintah Basin, 50 to 70 percent of the population received general relief in 1936 or benefited from the handful of FERA and WPA jobs available. Utes received small per capita distributions from the tribe, and nearly all worked for or received rations. By 1936, Utes cultivated only 8,887 acres, 58 percent of their predepression total. Alfalfa continued to make up two-thirds of that cropped acreage, but yields dropped to 50 percent of the 1926–31 state average.[85]

As the alfalfa boom peaked, Utes shifted production from cattle to sheep. Sheep offered more rapid annual returns in the form of both wool and meat and seemed able to survive on increasingly overgrazed ranges. Ute herds peaked in 1932–33 at 3,576 cattle, 14,200 sheep, and 762 horses, and then declined in numbers as overgrazed ranges and depressed markets took their toll on both the number of animals and owners. Ute ranchers switched back to cattle, which they felt were less detrimental to the range, organizing three livestock associations to manage the grazing reserve and oversee much-needed stock reduction sales. The associations themselves were primarily large kinship networks designed to pool labor and assets. In the 1940s, association ranchers took advantage of revolving cattle pool programs to improve the quality of their livestock and were able to secure the return of 726,000 acres from the old Ouray Reservation known as the Hill Creek Extension. But by the early 1950s, unable to generate capital or maintain their cooperative kinship focus in the face of the termination of mixed-blood Utes and renewed tribal per capita payments, the associations collapsed.[86]

This agricultural expansion and contraction had a number of environmental consequences. The alfalfa boom encouraged open speculation in marginal lands. Inefficient irrigation practices on a large number of relatively small farms stressed land that was already susceptible to alkali. Mono-cropping alfalfa reduced the diversity of fields and increased the prevalence of related insects and diseases. Demand for irrigation water strained an already weak system and finally outstripped supply during the state-wide droughts of 1931–34. Even then, agents failed to get Utes to switch from alfalfa to less water-hungry crops like corn because they were more labor intensive. Although production and profits fell, water assessments and reimbursable loan payments continued, forcing Utes to sell their land to the newly formed Uintah and Ouray Ute Tribe. Both white and Ute farmers abandoned overcropped fields to grow up in weeds. Ranchers replaced cattle with sheep on increasingly marginal range. Both precipitated a cycle of erosion from broken lands and overgrazed watersheds that choked irrigation ditches with silt. Following a heavy rainstorm on 3 September 1936, agricultural experiment station personnel measured 17,500 tons of solid matter passing a single point on the Duchesne River in one hour—enough to bury one acre of land 10 feet deep. The loss of water and top soil to erosion and alkali left parts of the Uintah Basin agriculturally sterile for years afterward.[87]

The boom and bust experience of the 1930s turned Utes from farming. Those who continued found it hard going. Between 1945 and 1950, Utes cultivated fewer than 4,000 acres, less than they had in 1905. By 1951 heirship status complicated title to 80 percent of remaining allotments. In one case, thirty-three claimants vied for a single heirship plot. At the same time, mechanization reduced both the number of Utes needed to run a farm as well as the number who could afford to. Costs, like water assessments, aggravated individual farmers. "I am pleading for my people," one Ute told the business council in 1949. "This water charge should be cut down. Farmers can't go out to earn money for water and still buy seed. I guess children will have to eat water this winter." As assessments continued to rise, irrigation structures fell into disuse and disrepair.[88]

Unable to compete with white farmers who outproduced them on the same acreage, Utes leased a majority of their irrigable land—as much as 78 percent in 1950—just as the government phased out its agricultural extension program. "And I think," said Conner Chapoose, an extension aide, "that's just about the time we needed the supervision." After the cooperative livestock associations collapsed in the 1950s, the tribe established its own herd and farm to produce winter feed, but those operations employed relatively few people. By 1956 there were only thirty-seven Ute farmers, and between 1958 and 1964, Joseph Jorgensen observed only eleven men doing much farming. Today, only a handful of Ute families grow alfalfa and grass hay for their livestock, but none depends entirely on farming or ranching for a living.[89]

Utes interviewed during the 1960s recalled the heyday of Indian farming at Uintah-Ouray with some fondness. Uncompahgre Lulu Brock grew up on a 160-acre farm in Randlett.

> When I was small I used to, you know, travel through there and I see houses and got gardens and haystacks and cattle and horses and everything there, you know. Everything just look fine, you know, nice and everything. But nowadays you go down there and you just see the houses, the barest kind. They don't have no hay, nothing.

Conner Chapoose noted that Utes always had hay fields and gardens, "but today there is quite a sad story for me to go back over the farm lands that we had and ways that I've seen them when they was in productive. . . . They had nice homes and a lot of weeds and brush is all over there which wasn't there at the time when I first seen it. Just seen bountiful hay stacks." He added that "there might be a few of them that do have gardens. . . . But it's something they're not doing it. For some reason or other they're not gardening." "The People are too lazy I guess," lamented Lulu Brock. "They don't have anything to work with." "Oh, I think they're getting more like whites, majority of whites at least," joked Jasper Pike with a laugh. "They know how to steal and they won't pay their bills." Hal Daniels, Sr., summed up years of Ute experience when he said, "I don't know. It don't seem [they] like it too much. I done it all my life but I worked hard."[90]

Núčiu

The history of farming on the Uintah-Ouray Reservation is one example of how federal policies, economic and environmental realities, and Northern Ute cultural responses to those changes swept Utes from cultural self-sufficiency to dependency and enforced marginality. While the government singlemindedly pushed its agrarian assimilation programs, environmental changes mounted and reservation subsistence alternatives narrowed without Utes being incorporated, socially or economically. In this situation, Utes attempted to reproduce their social and subsistence system with its mixed resource use, gender division of labor, balance of work and leisure, and animal valuations within the framework of reservation agriculture. They made token efforts to please and appease paternal white officials, adopting what they found useful or least painful or ultimately necessary. But as the environmental bounds of their world closed in, Utes became increasingly dependent on rations and then later on leasing as subsistence alternatives to actual agricultural labor.

Allotment and irrigation projects like the one at Uintah-Ouray marked a renewed effort to incorporate Indians more fully but, failing that, left them abandoned on the periphery of American society. Despite contemporary acknowledgment that the land and people of the Uintah Basin were better suited for pastoral rather than agricultural pursuits, the government pressed forward, dividing the land into unworkably small units. Allotment separated families from their kin groups and interspersed them with white settlers, limited the usable land for a ranching economy, and accelerated the pace of environmental change and land alienation. Northern Ute landholdings fell from nearly four million acres in the 1880s to 360,000 acres in 1905, a 91 percent reduction. By 1934, 26 percent of all allotments had been alienated, 64 percent were tied up in heirship status, and nearly 22,000 irrigated acres were leased to whites.[91]

While the three bands differed in their responses and experiences, they all resisted the subjugation of their culture. Passive and active resistance to allotment and farming strengthened Ute cultural identity, but as strategy it also generated increased dependence and marginality. Some accepted allotment and adopted a modified agricultural lifestyle. Others, when given a choice of lands, chose areas conducive to traditional lifestyles or to grazing and not agriculture. They maintained

their horse herds as sources of native wealth and prestige despite pressure to use the land for market animals. When directed change for agriculture grew too intense, Utes resorted to violent opposition and
withdrawal. When that failed, they turned inward to find strength in
group-oriented, pan-Indian religions like the Sun Dance and Peyotism,
which fortified their cultural identity as *Núciu* and "Indian." But even
that identity changed over time with increasing intermarriage. Tension
between full and mixed-blood peoples over control and direction of the
tribe precipitated a social and economic partition in 1954 with the
termination of those of less than 50 percent Ute blood.[92]

Pushed and pulled by policies encouraging collectivism then individualism then collectivism again, Utes searched for a balance between
self and group, needs and wants. Ute families adapted to the changing
environment and transformed subsistence economy of the allotted
reservation, tending gardens and livestock for home use. But when Ute
farmers finally ventured into market production, those markets were
swept away in an economic collapse beyond their control. Full incorporation and dependency followed in 1937, when Northern Utes accepted
the Indian Reorganization Act and an economy based on per-capita
income from claims cases, leases, and natural resource royalties. Since
then Utes have ridden the political and economic dependency roller
coaster of federal and state programs, multinational corporation balance
sheets, and world energy markets.[93]

In the last fifty years the Northern Ute Tribe has attempted to re-
capture alienated reservation lands, protect their water rights, and establish political jurisdiction over the region. Yet much of their land
remains leased or idle and generates little directly in the way of agricultural produce or jobs for Ute peoples. Like other rural peoples in the
West, the Northern Utes are caught in a shrinking agricultural economy,
forced to depend on wage work and lease and royalty payments from
natural resource extraction. As one Ute said of this trade-off,

> The dividends and royalties have made people dependent. They don't
> have any incentive or ambition anymore. Before 1950, everyone had a
> small piece of ground, a few cows, a garden, and shared tractors. They
> could at least support their families. They were more self-sufficient.
> Now only about ten people in the tribe own their own farm, the land,
> and work it. So people are worse off now than before. They are better
> off in that they have money, but they are worse off for their own
> betterment.[94]

A renewed agricultural economy is probably inadvisable given national
realities, but there is always the possibility of something in between.
Both land and water are in place but will remain separate until Northern
Utes choose to create their own market for social and economic change.

4

HUPA, THE PEOPLE OF NATINOOK

In 1851, Treaty Commissioner Redick McKee learned about a people his Yurok informants called "Hoopah," a geopolitical name for the people living "where there is water" along the *hupa-sr* or Trinity River in northwest California. The people called themselves *Natinook-wā*, "the people of *Natinook*"—"the place by the river to which the trails lead back." Federal officials adopted variations of the Yurok appellation, designating these people the Hupa and their residence Hoopa Valley. Linguistically Hupas are members of the Athapaskan language family of the Na-Dene stock. Historically they inhabited twenty-five villages along the Trinity from its junction with the Klamath River on the north to where the South Fork of the Trinity meets Grouse Creek on the south. Their hunting and gathering territories extended from the divide between Pine and Redwood creeks on the west to the Trinity Alps and Red Cap Creek on the east. Today Hupas control a 12-mile-square reservation centered around the thirteen villages of Hoopa Valley.[1]

In Hupa cosmology there are six universes, each containing a complete physical world. Then there is *Deddeh Ninnisan*, "This Earth," at the center of which is Hoopa Valley. This Earth has always existed except in certain details. In the first of three epochs, *Yīmantūwiñyai* ("the one lost across [the ocean]" or "old man over across"), the Creator and Hupa culture hero, sprang from the earth in the entryway of a *xonta* (a semisubterranean split cedar plank house). Following his emergence came the *Kīxûnai*, a race of Immortals who preceded humans on This Earth. *Yīmantūwiñyai* traveled throughout the world establishing its order and condition. He obtained fire, procured and gave life to deer, salmon, and eels, and provided edible herbs and roots for the *Kīxûnai* who had no food. He punished those who practiced cannibalism, molded the landscape, and established ritual medicines, ceremonial dances, and dance grounds for the Immortals.

The end of this myth-time epoch came when *Yīmantūwiñyai*'s wives grew jealous of his philandering and ruined the world by burying his children alive. Mortal Indians called *Kyuwinyanyan* ("those who eat acorns") began to emerge where *Yīmantūwiñyai* had paused in his travels. In order to avoid contamination by mortals, the *Kīxûnai* prepared to leave This Earth and journey to "the world across the ocean northward." Smoke hanging low on the mountains signaled the emergence of the Hupa people at the center of This Earth, along the Trinity River where *Yīmantūwiñyai*'s trails to and from sacred spots converged. Hupas adopted the subsistence and ceremonial patterns established by *Yīmantūwiñyai* and inherited all that the Immortals left behind, including the original sacred house (*xonta nikyao*) and sacred sweat house (*taikyuw nikyao*) at the village of *Takimildiñ*. They lived according to the old ways at the center of This Earth until the appearance of whites heralded the present epoch.[2]

Archaeological surveys of Hoopa Valley suggest many parallels with tribal tradition—an older nonmaritime people supplanted by a riverine-equipped Northwest Coast-type culture, which in turn was absorbed or displaced by the Athapaskan Hupas. While lexico-statistical analysis posits a low time depth for Athapaskan arrival in the region (A.D. 900–1300), radiocarbon dating of the fire pit in the sacred *xonta* at *Takimildiñ* indicates continuous use for five to seven thousand years. These proto-Hupans possessed an adaptive hunting and gathering tradition, enabling them to move into underutilized territories. After arriving, they underwent rapid acculturation, first to the resident Hokan- and Penutian-speaking peoples with their established acorn gathering economies, and then to the Algic-speaking Yuroks and Wiyots whose innovative, coastal-oriented adaptations exposed them to Northwest Coast cultural traits and fishing technologies.[3]

Environments

The heart of Hupa territory is Hoopa Valley, Humboldt County, California, located 180 miles south of the Oregon border and 30 airline miles from the Pacific Coast, but over 60 miles by twisting mountain road from coastal Eureka, California. The valley itself is a beautiful alluvial flood plain of 3,500 acres, about seven miles long and averaging less than one mile wide. It dips with the northwesterly drainage of the river, falling from 450 to 250 feet above sea level. The turbulent, turquoise-colored Trinity River splits the valley into irregular east and west sides or "fields" as it snakes its way to the Klamath River and the Pacific Ocean. Broad gravel and sand bars mark the Trinity's seasonal flood plain, giving way to the verdant valley floor and open parks of deciduous trees and shrubs. Valley soils are fairly shallow and porous sandy loams overlaying up to 50 feet of alluvial sand and gravel resting on a pre-Tertiary sedementary formation. The valley climate is mild "Mediterranean," with dry warm summers and cool rainy winters, averaging a 230-day growing season and annual precipitation in excess of 50 inches, most of which falls between November and March.

Hoopa Valley is isolated from the coast by steep and heavily forested mountains of the Klamath and Coastal ranges. From the valley floor the mountain walls rise sharply for 1,500 feet on both sides and then ascend more gradually to over 4,000 feet on the west side separating Redwood Creek and the Trinity River. On the east side the mountains climb to over 6,000 feet in the spectacular Trinity Alps. Precipitation ranges between 50 and 80 inches annually in this moderately cool forest zone, creating the low misty clouds that hang on the slopes like the phantom smoke of creation. Snow frequently blankets the mountain peaks, further isolating the valley, but rarely accumulates on the valley floor. Six major drainages within Hoopa Valley feed the Trinity River before it disappears into the rugged lower gorge.[4]

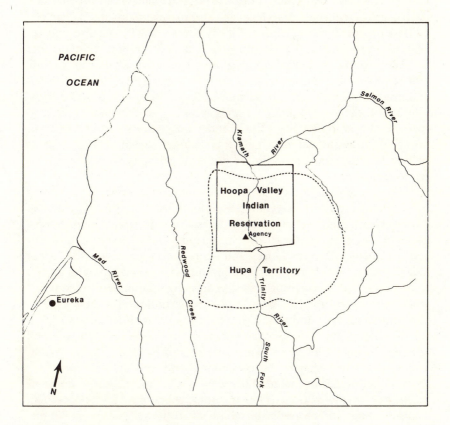

3. Hupa Territory and Hoopa Valley Indian Reservation

There are three broadly defined biotic zones in Hupa territory, each offering a particular combination of habitats and desirable resources.[5] Only a very small part of Hupa territory lies in the Woodland-Grass belt—valley floors and some lower foothills supporting intermittent stands of trees and brush within larger grassy meadows. These areas produce an abundance of seed grass species used by both humans and game animals. Groves of oak trees (*Quercus*) litter the ground with acorns. Willows, alder, cottonwood, sycamore, and hazel grow along the water courses while manzanita, deer brush, and digger pines hug the cooler valley margins. Only a few redwoods (*Sequoia sempervirens*) ever grew in Hoopa Valley, it being too dry and far from the coast—making it necessary for Hupas to buy their redwood canoes from the Yuroks. Periodic fires shaped this parkland environment the Hupas called *xontehtl* ("fire spreads out"). Fire-controlled brush cover stimulated seed grass and acorn production, creating a better wintering area for game animals and a better subsistence environment for humans.

In the foothills, deeply rooted broad-leaf shrubs form a dense cover which is nearly impenetrable. This woody Chaparral community consists of chamise, ceanothus, poison oak, and manzanita, mixing with deer brush, scrub oak, laurel, toyon, and mahogany in the higher elevations or northern exposures. Fire was essential in shaping and reshaping this Chaparral zone, making it useful for both humans and browsing game animals. Burning destroyed the chaparral canopy and toxic leaf compost, allowing oak saplings to become established and grass and forb species to germinate from dormant seeds. Brodiaea, soap plant, camas, and mariposa lilies sprouted quickly and proliferated for several years following a fire. Tender new shoots and lighter cover attracted browsing animals and their hunters to the opened areas before the chaparral re-established itself, crowding out lower-lying herbaceous growth.[6]

Above the Chaparral zone are the coniferous forests which cover most of Hupa territory. Ascending from foothills to mountains, groves of oak, yew, and madrone give way to forests of digger, sugar, and yellow pine (*Pinus*), cedar (*Libocedrus*), chinquapin, and Douglas fir (*Pseudotsuga menziestii*). Red fir, Jeffrey and white pine grow below the higher jagged peaks. Fire, both natural and human-set, was an integral part of this forest ecology—opening park meadows by thinning out trees, deadwood, and chaparral growth, stimulating germination of new growth, and improving the hunting and gathering potential of the forests.

The Hupa environment was wealthy in faunal as well as floral species. Deer and elk roamed the forests and foothills. Black, brown, and grizzly bears shared the mountains with bobcats and mountain lions. Other predators included the wolf, coyote, gray fox, and domesticated dog. Smaller mammals like the otter, fisher, mink, weasel, racoon, badger, rabbit, and ground squirrel inhabited the valley area, as did turtles, rattlesnakes, and other reptiles. Assorted raptors and scavengers kept watch on the migratory waterfowl, ruffed grouse, pheasant, quail, and pileated woodpeckers that made the valley their home. In the Trinity River, trout, sturgeon, and suckers shared the water with migratory salmon, steelhead trout, and lamprey eel.[7]

Subsistence

The Hupa people lived in an environment of abundance, one that they actively modified with fire to increase its productive potential. Their diet "varied with the season of the year," reported the Hoopa Valley Agency physician in 1865: "Each successive month furnished its own peculiar staple articles." Theirs was a harvest economy based on periods of intensive gathering, preparation, and storage of foods and materials as each came into season, leaving time for periods of rest and public ceremony. Although diverse and balanced, this subsistence system did not rule out the possibility of cyclical resource failure and starvation. Cautionary tales warned against eating too much or wasting food lest it run out and *Yīnûkatsisdai* ("in the south [upstream] he lives"), the "boss" of the vegetal world, become angry and withhold his bounty.[8]

The basic unit of Hupa subsistence production was the extended family, which divided labor by gender. Men were responsible for hunting and fishing while women and children gathered vegetal materials and processed all foodstuffs for storage. Periodically, related family groups within the patrilocal village joined in communal hunts, and intervillage cooperation marked construction of the annual fish weir, but most economic and subsistence pursuits were individual undertakings. Even the produce from communal efforts remained individually owned. In times of scarcity, village headmen redistributed stored food to needy families.

Hupa subsistence pursuits were very place specific, emanating from the stable, geolocal Hupa villages along the Trinity River. The climate and relative abundance of Hoopa Valley and the surrounding mountain environment made extended seasonal out-migrations unnecessary, and hunting parties seldom ventured from the safety of the valley into the physically and supernaturally "dangerous" hills for more than several days at a time. Individual Hupas held the rights to specific hunting, fishing, and gathering grounds as privately owned property. These rights gave them the privilege of controlling use, rental, alienation, and inheritance, as well as liability for damages incurred on the property. Trespassers were subject to litigation and fines. Not all Hupa families owned each type of subsistence property, and not all properties were individually owned. Village headmen set aside some communal land for general public use. Individuals without land rights rented their use from others or helped landowners in communal hunts as dependents.[9]

Hupas utilized the abundance of their biotic environment but focused on three major subsistence resources, each corresponding roughly with one of their three environments and ultimately with their "world renewal" ceremonies. First, Hupa men fished for anadromous salmon, eel, and steelhead trout in the Trinity River. In the early spring, lamprey eels (*Lampetra tridentata*) appeared in the Klamath and Trinity rivers, and Hupa men caught them at night with dip nets. In May, Chinook or king salmon (*Oncorhynchus tschawytscha*) made their way up the Trinity to spawn. Following ritual observances for the first salmon taken, men fished from frame platforms along portions of privately owned shoreline, using dip nets, spears, funnel traps, and gill nets. Women could own fishing properties but were not allowed to fish or come into contact with men's equipment lest they "spoil" the fishing. Women prepared both salmon and eel by broiling the flesh or smoke-drying and storing it for winter use.

A second run of Chinook and Coho or silver salmon (*O. kisutch*) began in September, followed in the late fall by steelhead trout (*Salmo gairdneri*). Hupas anticipated the fall salmon run by constructing a fish dam or weir extending across the entire river. Originally the weirs were said to have been constructed exclusively at *Takimildiñ* until the headman there became too old and "loaned" his authority to the village of *Medildiñ*; thereafter, the location of the weir alternated annually between the two most sacred towns in the upper and lower halves of the valley. The construction of the weir was an elaborate ritual and physical undertaking, presided over by a chief formulist. Men from all villages helped

Fishing from a northern California fish dam. E. S. Curtis, 1923. Special Collections, Marriott Library, University of Utah.

in the communal construction of this pole-and-lattice-work dam in order to fish from platforms built on the downstream side. Women were forbidden from even coming near the dam. Dam construction allowed enough salmon to escape and spawn while affording the people an adequate supply of winter meat. The first high waters of the new year washed away the fish weir, opening the river and renewing the cycle.[10]

The second major subsistence pursuit—for acorns, a Hupa staple—took place in the valley margins and foothills of Hoopa Valley. Following the First Acorn Ceremony, Hupa families gathered acorns from privately owned and tended groves of tanbark oaks. While the tanbark acorns were lower in protein and higher in fiber content than others, Hupas preferred them for their thicker shells and resistance to rot and insects. When these failed, Hupas gathered acorns from Pacific, black, and maul oaks. Depending on species wild oaks are extremely productive, yielding from 500 to 1,000 pounds of acorns per large tree. Yet they produce such abundance cyclically—once every two to four years. Hupas interpreted this biological fact as the work of *Yīnûkatsisdai*, the Immortal "boss" of plant life, who passed unseen through the valley with a burden basket of acorns. If he saw waste or the improper use of his gifts he withheld them, creating a shortage or even a famine. The next year he would provide bounteously. Hupas respectfully observed the rules and formulas but also gathered enough acorns to last two years.

Hupa women took charge of the acorns, transporting them back to the villages in large conical burden baskets. There they shelled and split the acorns, sun-drying them on their *irxonta* roof. They stored the acorns in tightly woven hampers until needed, then ground them into flour. Women leached the acorn flour of its bitter tannic acid by placing it a sand basin and repeatedly soaking it with hot water. They stone-boiled the meal into an acorn mush or baked it into cakes.[11]

In addition to acorns, women gathered the bulk of the vegetal food, fiber, and medicine used by the Hupa household. They collected nuts from the chinquapin, hazel, California laurel, sugar and digger pines, dug roots from the lily family (*Lilium*), and gathered fresh shoots from the wyethia, cow parsnip, balsam, and angelica plants. They harvested the fruit of the madrone and manzanita and a variety of berries and grass seeds, especially wild oats (*Avena*) and madia, which they collected from charred plants after men burned the fields. Hupa women dried and stored their plant foods in finely woven baskets decorated with geometric designs. Plants gathered for their medicinal or ritual value included angelica root, yarrow, wild ginger, sage, deer brush, sorrel, and California poppies. Tobacco (*Nicotiana*) was by far the most important medicinal, ritual, and social herb. Individual men planted and harvested plots to avoid being contaminated by wild tobacco which, they believed, could become poisonous from growing on a forgotten grave.[12]

The third subsistence pursuit took place in the foothills and mountains surrounding Hoopa Valley. Individual men stalked deer with bow

and arrows, wearing disguises of full deer skins with head and simu-
lating the movements of the animal to get a close shot. Hupa hunters
also used noose snares of twined iris fiber rope along trails to catch deer
or drove them with dogs or fire into ambushes. Occasionally elk wan-
dered into the valley, where they were driven into the river and shot.
Groups of Hupa hunters killed hibernating bears for food and skin but
valued panthers, wolves, bobcats, foxes, and coyotes for their fur alone.
Hupas also hunted a variety of small mammals and birds, including
pileated woodpeckers for their decorative red scalps.

Prior to and during the hunt, Hupa men followed certain ritual and
practical observances to ensure their immediate and future success.
They abstained from female contact, took sweat baths, and smoked
themselves and their weapons with aromatic herbs. Since the deer's soul
was thought to be immortal, ritual treatment and butchering was important lest the *Tan*, the Immortal deer "boss," withhold future deer
and spoil the hunter's luck. Hupa men passed deer meat into the *xonta*
through a special opening in the wall at the back of the house, where it
became the women's property. Women broiled or roasted meat on
stones or over coals, or stone-boiled it in soup in watertight baskets.
Excess meat was smoked and stored. Men saved deer sinew for bow
string and lacing, shaped antlers and bones into tools, and used the
hooves for ceremonial rattles. They carefully disposed of all waste and
animal bones by hiding them in trees out of the reach of dogs. Men also
processed the animal skins used for clothing, bags, and ceremonial regalia, particularly for their main world renewal ceremony, the White
Deerskin Dance.[13]

Given such relative subsistence abundance, it is not surprising that
Hupas observed numerous food restrictions and taboos. In general they
avoided reptiles, insects, bird eggs, and the flesh of scavenging mammals. They did not eat quail or meadowlarks since they believed these
spent the day in the underground regions of the dead gambling for the
souls of living men. The people did not eat dogs and were shocked
when they saw the first white men do so, for *Yīmantūwiñyai* created
dogs out of his own feces as a companions for mortals. During significant events in the life course fresh meat and fish were taboo for prescribed periods. Certain parts of the deer were specifically taboo to
women (eyes, ears, tongue, head, and fetus), while other parts (liver and
floating ribs) were generally taboo. Fresh seafood had to be dried before
being brought into Hoopa Valley. Combining fresh salmon and meat at
a single meal was forbidden, for mixing flesh from two separate domains
was sure to upset each animal spirit and ruin the hunter's luck.[14]

The Hupa subsistence system was eminently adapted to the variety
and bounty in their environment. The mild climate and their emphasis
on salmon, acorns, and deer allowed them to remain year round in
Hoopa Valley. What they could not produce locally they obtained
regionally in an elaborate trade network. Their harvest economy and

active management of that environment—burning, selective sowing, fruit and nut horticulture—amounted to a quasi-agricultural subsistence system that made possible an elaborate Northwest Coast material culture and political and religious organization. What hindered the development of a full-blown agricultural complex like that found throughout the Southwest may have been the very natural abundance of their environment, access to trade, and balanced cultural choices.[15]

Society

The basic unit of Hupa society was the extended family tracing descent through the patriline. Such families consisted of a man and his wife, their children, and possibly some grandchildren, unattached relatives, or slaves. Female exogamy and patrilocal residence were the norm. Women and children lived in the family *xonta*, while men came there mainly to eat. Men and older boys from several families worked and slept in a nearby *taikyuw*, or sweat house. Conjugal relations occurred during summer in the privacy of brush shelters built along the river.

Villages consisted of between 6 and 28 related kin households, or 50 to 200 people. At the time of white contact, 1,000 Hupas lived in 12 of 13 village sites in Hoopa Valley. Another 500 to 1,000 closely related people known as South Fork Hupas (*Hleluhwe*, "people who live where two streams converge") inhabited 12 villages further up the Trinity River, but were not included in the social or ceremonial life of Hoopa Valley. Kinship networks were the foundation of village solidarity, and wealth and birth determined social status in this hierarchical society. With no formal chiefs or councils, village leadership fell to the individual with the most wealth in possessions, property rights, and kindred. Villagers followed this headman because he was able to distribute food or the rights to use his private properties in times of scarcity. His wealth allowed him to settle disputes between villagers or villages with money—tusk shells, clam shell disks, pileated woodpecker scalps, and strings of dentalium shells, which men measured and valuated against standardized tattoos on their forearms.[16]

The meandering Trinity River created a natural division of the valley floor into eight discrete "fields," called *tlah ninnisan*, "one world," by the Hupa people, marking local associations and separations between villages. Two districts or religious associations partitioned the villages of Hoopa Valley. The southern district (*Tinuheneu*) included the villages of *Xaslindiñ*, *Djictanadiñ* ("where two rivers meet," Tish-tang-a-tang ranch), *Xōwûñkut* (Kentuck ranch), *Medildiñ* ("the place of boats," Matilton ranch, the largest of all Hupa villages), and *Tōltsasdiñ* (abandoned). The northern district (*Natinuwhe*) included the villages of *Tsewenaldiñ* (Senalton ranch), *Takimildiñ* ("place of the acorn feast," Hostler ranch, the spiritual center and second largest village), *Miskût* ("bluff upon," Meskut ranch), *Tceïndeqotdiñ* ("place where he was dug up," referring to a mythic Hupa figure), *Kintcūwhwikût* ("on the nose"), *Xonsadiñ* ("deep water place"), and the deserted villages of *Tsemeta* and *Dakisxankût*. The richest men in the southern and northern districts acted as ceremonial leaders for the whole tribe.[17]

With no formal tribal council, Hupa villages maintained their group identity through language, geographic proximity, collective religious observances, and intermarriage. They maintained social order through a conceptually precise legal system based on fiscal compensation. Any crime, personal injury, or insult, whether intentional or accidental, could be exactly valued in terms of money or property. Individuals settled legal claims by using neutral go-betweens to negotiate mutually acceptable terms, and fulfilled them with payments in the form of money, personal property, or even personal service (slavery). Headmen were responsible for settling intravillage or intratribal disputes since individuals, not the community, controlled wealth. Settlement extinguished all hostilities and further liabilities. This system of compensation and settlement rested on the fear of such squabbles escalating into feuds that could lead to further property destruction or bloodshed and even split the group. As in most "proto-capitalistic" systems, power, wealth, and prestige gave individuals a distinct advantage in settling legal cases.[18]

The Hupa people avoided feuds and intertribal warfare when possible because, according to their legal code, it was expensive and destructive of material goods. Yet they were an expansive people who did not back away from conflict with their neighbors. Hupas were respected combatants yet maintained no warrior class or honors. They often hired warriors or shamans from neighboring tribes to do battle for them. Wars or, more commonly, feuds broke out over cases of murder, witchcraft, insult, or injury that were not quickly settled. Only very wealthy men could lead war parties, for all damages and killings had to be compensated afterword or else reciprocal revenge would continue. War parties of five to ten men staged surprise raids and then withdrew. Leaders discouraged excessive looting and killing because of the settlement costs, but Hupas did take slaves.[19]

The most important Hupa social customs centered around notable events in the life course of an individual—birth, maturation, marriage, childbirth, and death. Most life-course events required both women and men to observe food and activity taboos and to recite ritual formulas to insure the health and future of the individuals involved. From birth to death, Hupas greeted each new day by bathing in the river. After a permissive childhood, boys entered adult society by moving into the *taik-yuws* while girls underwent a ten-day Flower Dance and received the first in a series of colored basket caps and facial tattoos. Thereafter women observed a monthly menstrual segregation of ten days until menopause. Marriage required payment of a bride price to the woman's family, usually in dentalium shells or woodpecker scalps, and determined the status of the children. Both polygyny and divorce were possible and acceptable. Hupas dealt with death quickly. Relatives prepared the body and removed it from the *xonta* feet-first through a side wall so its ghost could not get back in. They buried the body, head upstream, in a shallow grave lined with wood planks and decorated with personal belongings. Mourning family members underwent a ritual purification to keep the ghost away and never spoke the person's name again.[20]

In Hupa cosmology, place is all important. At the center of This Earth was Hoopa Valley, former residence of the Hupa culture hero and Immortals. Here they established sacred dwellings and place-specific ceremonies. They left trails and sacred spots in the mountains that required ritual observance, for they remained passageways between worlds through which Immortals and mortals could communicate. Hupas anthropomorphized many objects and phenomena in their natural world and used them as signals indicating the condition of life and wishes of their deities. In almost all ceremonies or undertakings, Hupa men and women recited ritual formulas—stories of the successful actions of the Immortals in similar situations—to ensure the success of the event at hand. They believed that the performance of a formula compelled the aid of certain deities.[21]

Hupas believed that aside from inflicted wounds, diseases occurred when some foreign object lodged in the body and carried on a type of warfare. Diseases resulted from breaking some rule or ignoring the warnings of supernatural spirits that inhabited sacred places. Likewise, evil "shamans" (*kitdoñxoi*) with proper formulas could obtain and use power objects (especially human remains) to sicken and kill a victim. Hupas recognized three types of professional shamans or "doctors" who specialized in curing a specific range of illnesses. The *kĭmautciltcwe* were usually men, herbalists who learned the verbal formulas which gave the herbs their power. The *tintatcinwûnawa* ("soul-loss" doctors) were usually women who danced, sang, and recited ritual formulas in order to diagnose disease through clairvoyance or dreams. Few of these doctors attempted to extract "pains," leaving that to the *kitētau*, or "sucking doctors," usually women, who performed ritual formulas to locate, identify, and then press or suck out the offending object. All cures were public and required payment, which doctors returned should their patients fail to recover.[22]

Several other public ceremonies focused on ritual health maintenance and bolstered collective identity. The people held two Jump Dances each year, one in the spring (*xaitcitdilya*, or "Winter Dance") in the corral-style dance pit at *Miskût*, and the other in the fall (*tuñktcitdilya*, or "Fall Dance") at *Takimildiñ*. The people wore their finest ceremonial clothes and danced for ten days to ward off sickness as *Yĭmantûwiñyai* did before humans appeared on This Earth. The Brush Dance (*xonnawe*), performed for an individual, involved ritual ministrations accompanied by three nights of public singing and dancing.[23]

Three major "first fruit" ceremonies marked the Hupa subsistence calendar—events ritually celebrated to thank the resource "bosses" and to insure future success. The First Eel Ceremony (*luwxan*) belonged to the villagers of *Takimildiñ*. On a March night, a priest-formulist fished for eels while repeating the eel formula. After he ritually prepared and consumed his catch, the people were free to fish for eels. The First Salmon Ceremony (*nokingxan*) was a similar ritual owned by the people of *Medildiñ*. Each spring as the first salmon appeared, a single priest-formulist proceeded to the falls at Sugar Bowl (in Willow Valley, south of Hoopa) where he caught, ritually prepared, and consumed the first salmon before opening fishing to the people. The third group subsistence ritual was the Acorn Ceremony (*nokyinxan*), held in the fall at *Takimildiñ* to ensure food, health, and success. The chief formulist prepared a feast of new acorn soup for the villagers and recited the proper formulas thanking the acorn "boss," *Yĩnûkatsisdai*, for his gifts.[24]

The most important Hupa ritual was the White Deerskin Dance (*xonsiltcitdilya*, "summer" or "along the river dance"), a world renewal ceremony that involved all the Hupa villages. Each year in August, the people gathered together to symbolically remake the world by re-creating the departure of the Immortals from This Earth. Led by a priest-formulist, the ten-day dance began at *Takimildiñ* and proceeded in stages upstream by canoe and then back downstream to Bald Hill (*Nitûkalai*) at the north end of the valley. The dance leaders landed at various dancing grounds and villages along the river, where they were met by the people. Men and women wore their finest shell jewelry over decorated skin and woven fiber costumes. Men brought out their valued stuffed white deerskins, ceremonial obsidian blades, and woodpecker-scalp headbands. Many individuals owned or could borrow the necessary dance regalia, but only the headmen at *Takimildiñ* and *Medildiñ* owned the legal right, regalia, and wealth necessary to stage the ceremony properly. The dance culminated Hupa efforts to ensure the continuation of life—to prevent natural disasters and the failure of their subsistence resources, to clean out all evil and sickness in the world, and to reaffirm their group identity as *Natinook-wā*, "the people of where trails return."[25]

For hundreds of years Hupas inhabited their isolated valley along the lower Trinity River, taking from their environment the necessities of life and accumulating the wealth and property that brought status and power. They actively modified their environment with fire, and their environment repaid them with more abundance. Their riverine adaptation and harvest economy allowed them the physical and economic stability to build an elaborate legal system and material culture. They danced and recited formulas to remake the world and to protect themselves, their neighbors, and This Earth.

In the eighteenth century Hupas heard of Spanish settlements far to the south and probably saw metal objects and trade goods circulating in advance of that settlement. In 1775, Spanish ships under the command of Don Bruno de Hezeta and Don Francisco de la Bodega y Quadra landed at Trinidad Bay to trade with the coastal Indians. Other Spanish, British, Russian, and American ships followed, landing at Trinidad, Point St. George, and Humboldt Bay, chasing sea otters and seeking to trade for furs. They remained close to the shore, but their trade goods reached Hoopa Valley.

In April 1828, Jedediah Smith passed through Hoopa Valley on his way north. He found the people friendly and helpful and willing to trade deerskins, manzanita flour, and dogs for blue trade beads, knives, and axes. The Hupa themselves feared these white men who rode tame deerlike beasts and ate dogs. Hupas called them *yimandil* ("across they go around")—beings who could circle the world and cross oceans like the Immortals. In 1833, more trappers (now called *kiwamil*, "creatures with fur") passed through Hoopa Valley and began working the surrounding area, beginning the cycle of violence that engulfed the Hupas' neighbors. Little violence reached the isolated Hoopa Valley until the era of the California gold rush and the appearance of miners and white settlers. Hupas called them *misah kititlut* ("their mouths flap"), marking the white descent from supernatural beings to ill-mannered persons with whom they struggled for control of their land and resources.[26]

5

FARMING AND THE CHANGING HARVEST ECONOMY IN HOOPA VALLEY

The California gold rush of 1849 brought an increasing number of foreigners into the foothills and mountains of northern California—a relatively abundant environment supporting concentrated native populations like the Hupa Indians. Ultimately epidemic disease, subsistence displacement, and intentional genocide decimated California Indian populations. Whole groups disappeared, not simply or cleanly, but ever so quickly. The Hupa themselves managed to avoid the worst of that early contact and eventually obtained their beautiful mountain valley as a reservation. American plans to transform the people into subsistence and, ultimately, market agriculturalists went forward much as they did elsewhere, but while the abundance of their natural environment remained the Hupa people did little to cooperate with their "transformation." Over time and given their cultural predisposition to fixed habitations, a traditional "harvest" economy, private usufruct property rights, and an acquisitive nature, Hupas adopted the outward practices and methods of settled agriculture. They desired and accepted allotment, livestock, and agricultural implements. But in the end the environmental parameters of their valley limited this socioeconomic transformation, forcing them to look elsewhere for sources of economic development.

Treaties, Warfare, and a Reservation

The gold rush came early to the upper reaches of the Trinity River when Major P. B. Reading found gold there shortly after the discovery at Sutter's Mill. Prospectors moving up the Sacramento Valley kept looking for an easier way to supply themselves from the ocean. In November 1849, eight men led by Josiah Gregg set out along the South Fork of the Trinity River in the belief that it flowed into Trinidad Bay, where they hoped to obtain supplies for their burgeoning mining community. Their trip in the dead of winter took them through Hoopa Valley, where the exhausted miners helped themselves to dried salmon after the inhabitants of one village fled. Confronted later that night by eighty Hupa warriors, the miners made amends with gifts and awed the people with demonstrations of their firearms. In turn Hupas warned them not to continue down the Trinity, but to cross the mountains westward as the quickest and safest route to the coast. Following this advice the miners made their way to the coast, found nothing at Trinidad or Humboldt bays, and continued southward until they reached San Francisco in February 1850.[1]

News of Gregg's trip sparked an expansion of supply cities up the coast in 1850—Trinidad, Humboldt City, Eureka, Bucksport, and Union (Arcata)—and miners invaded the surrounding hills in search of golden wealth. They brought cholera, small pox, and other diseases to the coastal and riverine Indians and nourished the prevalent attitude that an Indian's life was worthless. Conflict increased as new trails opened up the interior. Miners blamed Indians for pilfering horses and supplies; Indians blamed miners for trespassing in their territory, killing game, and bringing famine, strange diseases, and violence to their land. Most of the new trails bypassed the isolated Hoopa Valley, but the people felt the effects of the invasion around them. In 1850, miners attacked and burned the South Fork Hupa village at Burnt Ranch, killing fourteen Indians suspected of stealing horses. Miners attacked other Indian villages along the Salmon, Redwood, and Eel rivers, and Indian warriors retaliated against isolated mining groups. War had come to borders of Hoopa Valley.[2]

When California joined the Union in September 1850, whites outnumbered the rapidly declining native population. State and federal officials recognized the impact of white expansion and moved to quiet the violence through treaties with the remaining Indian groups. Between 1850 and 1852, federal treaty commissioners George Barbour, O. M. Wozencraft, and Redick McKee made 18 treaties with 139 tribal groups. In October of 1851, McKee met in council at the junction of the Trinity and Klamath rivers with the Karoks, Yuroks, and a delegation from Hoopa Valley. He promised the assembly a protected reservation and gifts if they would agree to cease hostilities, wear clothes, live in houses, and "learn to draw their subsistence from the soil, and not be dependent upon game and fish for food." The treaty signed, McKee continued on his way, but the piece of paper did little to change either Indian or white attitudes and actions. Californians opposed the treaties, which they felt reserved too much valuable land, and on 8 June 1852 the Senate rejected all 18 treaties.[3]

In the meantime, Congress established the California Indian Superintendency, headed by Edward F. Beale. Beale recommended the establishment of self-sufficient reservations, each with a military post supported by Indian crops. The reservations were to be impermanent, movable when necessary in order to protect both Indian and white interests, but nothing came of Beale's plan in the north. Miners and settlers continued to trespass on Indian lands, displacing and killing the native inhabitants. By 1855, two-thirds of the California Indians surviving Spanish colonization succumbed to this American invasion.[4]

While isolated from the worst of the invasion, Hoopa Valley did not escape. Between 1853 and 1855, Captain David Snyder persuaded settlers around Humboldt Bay that the peaceful Hupa had "proved themselves trustworthy," and he established a permanent farming community in Hoopa Valley. Settlers moved onto lands underutilized in the wake of epidemics that reduced Hupa populations and disrupted subsistence activities. It is unclear why Hupas allowed these intruders to stay, but in their own way they tolerated this agricultural—as opposed to mining—invasion and managed to live in relative peace with the settlers for nearly a decade. Hupas worked for, traded, and intermarried with these settlers, obtaining desired goods and foodstuffs while keeping the horrors of genocidal warfare from their own valley.[5]

But the conflict continued to escalate around them. The 1855 Red Cap War raged between neighboring Yuroks, Karoks, and white miners until the government established the Klamath Reservation. Indian wars of resistance along the Mad and Klamath rivers, Redwood Creek, and Pacific coast kept state and local militias busy in northern California. In 1860, local whites massacred over three hundred peaceful natives living on Indian Island and around Humboldt Bay in one night. These "wars" were nothing more than campaigns of extermination against the Hupas' neighbors—the Karok, Yurok, Wiyot, Wintun, Chimariko, Chilula, Whilkut, Nongatl, and South Fork peoples—what Hubert Howe Bancroft deemed "one of the last human hunts of civilization and the basest and most brutal of them all." The brutality of the conquest mirrored the rapacity with which whites went after natural resources—gold, fish, timber, and arable land—and continued through disease and starvation until few native peoples remained. Hupa isolation, peaceful demeanor, and astute political actions kept them from being removed to the Klamath Reservation but did not keep war from their valley.[6]

As early as 1858, the Klamath agent warned that white volunteers gathering in Weaverville planned to march on Hoopa Valley, "with the intention of exterminating the Indians in that valley." Area whites suspected that Hupas supplied and directed allied Indian groups in their raids on Redwood Creek settlers, so the government established Fort Gaston in Hoopa Valley to keep an eye on Hupa activities. It appears that Hupa leaders chose the political strategy of hiring mercenaries to fight their wars, reproducing tactics used in intertribal conflicts. Their traditional political and military influence in the region and their subsistence and material wealth gave them ample means and opportunities to carry on such a covert war of resistance without bringing the conflict to Hoopa Valley. Hupa leaders astutely denied any knowledge of or participation in the hostilities and resisted furnishing the army with guides. As part of an 1862 peace treaty Hupa headmen relented, but the guides seemed unable to locate any "hostiles" for the troops, whose orders were to kill all but women and children in what one officer termed "this Indian war, or rather hunt." In fact, the Hupa guides acted to warn and protect their neighbors.[7]

Volunteer militia officers in the area doubted the Hupas' professed friendship and innocence, noting that they were the "most influential tribe in this portion of the state," capable of directing and supplying other tribes in a guerrilla war in order to avoid suspicion and violence. The fact that soldiers found and killed several Hupa men running with hostile Redwood Indians, that Hupas were able to surrender their weapons yet quickly obtain more, and that major Indian ambushes occurred in proximity to Hoopa Valley kept white suspicions alive. In September 1863, whites had their hunches confirmed when three Hupa renegades turned up in the Hupa village of *Medildiñ*. Troops from Fort Gaston surrounded the village and, after a three day stand-off, took 116 prisoners, including 41 warriors. The military forced the entire village to relocate nearer the fort for supervision, thereby changing the location of *Medildiñ's* biennial fish dam and Jump Dance pit and upsetting the cultural and cosmological geography of Hoopa Valley.[8]

This military action brought the Hupa conflict into the open, but not under control. Before the Fort Gaston dragnet closed on *Medildiñ* village, Big Jim of *Medildiñ* left the valley with 30 warriors, including the three suspect renegades, to carry on a war of resistance in the hills. By December of that year, Tseweñaldiñ John joined Big Jim, and the resistance swelled to over 125 Hupa, Redwood, and South Fork warriors. They carried on a two-part guerrilla war from their mountain retreats— one against whites and one as part of an existing intervillage feud.

The feud began in 1859 after a *Tseweñaldiñ* woman killed a white soldier in self-defense. The next year, soldiers from Fort Gaston wantonly killed a *Takimildiñ* man who failed to procure Hupa women for them. *Takimildiñ* villagers interpreted this as a reprisal killing and blamed the village of *Tseweñaldiñ* for starting the killing with the soldiers. They demanded financial restitution, but the people of *Tseweñaldiñ* refused and a bloody feud ensued. The commanders of Fort Gaston did nothing to halt the intervillage violence, hoping the villagers would eradicate each other. The feud merged with the resistance movement when Tseweñaldiñ John attacked *Takimildiñ* villagers, killing Bill Hostler, the brother of headman Charley Hostler, who led the movement for peaceful cooperation with whites. Joining the causes of resistance and feud in one movement expanded the size of the rebel Hupa force, but it also increased the eagerness of other Hupas to aid the soldiers in tracking down the renegades.[9]

Despite having 10 to 15 Hupa scouts from the *Takimildiñ* faction, Karok mercenaries, and about 50 white "adventurers," Fort Gaston soldiers could not catch the renegades or protect the valley. John and Big Jim's raids forced white settlers in Hoopa Valley to band together or flee for safety. This so-called Bald Hills War (1858–64) exposed the subtle, decade-long Hupa policy of hiring mercenary Indians to do their fighting. Fort Gaston officers now openly condemned Hupas as the "cunning scoundrels" who had been "the prime movers in most of the outrages for years," preventing "other Indians from committing deeds of violence in their territory," while orchestrating raids "at a distance for revenge and plunder and to draw troops away from here." By May 1864, open resistance began to crumble as the renegades had trouble obtaining food and supplies from a captive and economically pressed valley population, or in the hills filling up with soldiers and local militia men. Hupa renegades sued for peace and most returned to *Medildiñ* that spring.[10]

In the wake of the Bald Hills War, California Indian superintendent Austin Wiley considered requests that Hupas be removed to the new Round Valley Reservation but observed realistically that "it would take a soldier for every Indian to keep them there." In August 1864, Wiley met a group of Hupa leaders, still armed and defiant, who told him they would "prefer death or starvation in the mountains to removal." Instead of pressing removal, Wiley negotiated a treaty setting aside the "whole of Hoopa valley," about 38,400 acres, as a reservation. It allowed Hupas to hunt, fish, and gather on their land and promised that the government would provide them with clothing and blankets, an agent, physician, teachers, and "a sufficient number of employees to instruct the Indians in farming and harvesting." White settlers were to be moved off the land and compensated. Although not officially established until 1876 by executive order, the Hoopa Valley Indian Reservation received its first agent and began operations in October of 1864.[11]

Farming the Unofficial Reservation, 1864–76

Hupas survived the California Indian wars in better shape than most groups, in part due to their relative isolation, subsistence diversity, and political strategies, but the costs were still frightful. Between 1850 and 1865, disease, starvation, and war reduced their population from an estimated 1,500–2,000 people to 650 survivors. Years of conflict broke the Hupas' political alliances in the region and curtailed their harvest economy. Deer and elk seemed to disappear from mountains crowded with armed men, and valley oaks failed to produce adequate acorn crops for several years running. Upstream placer mining ruined spawning beds and choked the Trinity and Klamath with silt. Salmon "almost deserted" the rivers as whites began commercial fishing operations. Religious discouragement grew as Hupa harvest and world renewal ceremonies seemed to fail them. The continuing feud disrupted Hupa society, making group ceremonies impossible without restitution and the return of harmony. While Hupas managed to retain their homeland, reservation status entailed a new political and economic dependency.[12]

Agent Robert Stockton arrived in Hoopa Valley in late 1864 and established an agency and farm near Fort Gaston on Agency Field. He also oversaw the departure of white settlers in March 1865 and arranged the transfer of some twelve white farms, orchards, and a flour mill to agency control. Indian subsistence remained a major problem that first spring, but the Army "generously" gave Stockton 7,800 pounds of "condemned" flour stored at Fort Gaston in exchange for the promise of an equal quantity of "good flour" from the agency harvest. The Army might have made good on this fast deal, but late planting and drought left little to be harvested that year. This crop failure made life difficult, but Stockton was heartened by an initial expression of Hupa interest. Agency personnel demonstrated farming techniques to a few Hupa men and women who worked in the fields, but most remained too busy "gathering wild seeds and acorns in the season of them."[13]

The poor crop showing gave ammunition to citizens of Eureka in calling for Hupa removal. They argued that "it is bad policy to give them arable lands that they will not work, when the hill or mountainous country does them better." But during the 1866 season, Stockton and agency employees put 325 acres into production using the labor of Indians who "learned willingly." Stockton reported an expected harvest of 4,000 bushels of wheat as well as oats, corn, potatoes, and other vegetables. He planned to reward those who worked on the farm with clothing and food, but expectations outstripped the actual harvest. With annual salmon catches down, Stockton distributed beef and food rations to most Hupa families. Nevertheless, California Superintendent Charles Maltby assured his superiors that the 1,200 acres of arable valley land "can supply all demands in the way of subsistence, and produce a surplus which would go far towards making the reservation self-sustaining."[14]

Progress at the agency farm might have continued in 1867, but that spring Stockton and three others died in an attempt to arrest an ex-renegade and suspected Hupa thief named Frank. Fearful employees fled the agency, and farm operations virtually ceased. Little but volunteer grains and vegetables grew in the agency fields that summer. Hupa guides helped the soldiers capture and kill Frank in November, but the breach in agency authority and the subsequent murder of several other prominent Hupa leaders—including Tseweñaldiñ John and Charley Hostler—refueled the feud between *Tseweñaldiñ* and *Takimildiñ*.

In addition to physical attacks, *Takimildiñ* leaders hired Redwood Creek shamans to work slow deadly magic on *Tseweñaldiñ* villagers.

According to Hupa belief, this evil sorcery worked, but it also boome-
ranged and took its toll on *Takimildiñ* leaders who ordered and paid for
its use. Fear and suspicion of outside sorcery increased as the government moved remnant neighboring bands through Hoopa Valley on their
way to other reservations. Over the next thirty years, perhaps twenty

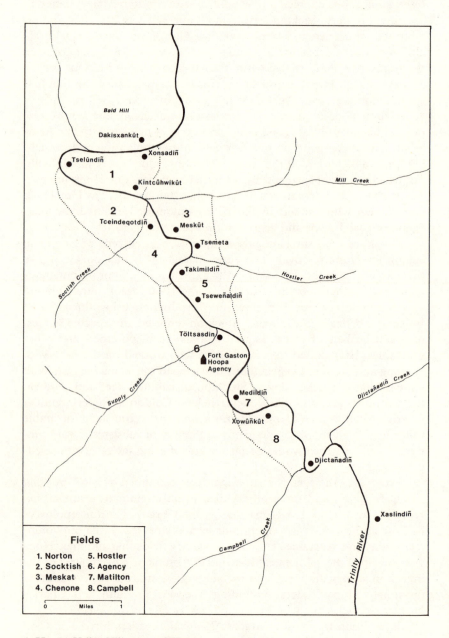

4. Hoopa Valley Villages and Fields

people from both villages died in attacks directly attributable to the feud. *Tseweñaldiñ* descendants blamed sorcery for the deaths and mysterious diseases that left only two survivors by 1924—reproducing older categories of disease theory to explain their lineal demise. Again, Fort Gaston soldiers did little to stop the killing and, in fact, introduced the diseases and contributed to the violence that plagued every Hupa village into the twentieth century.[15]

Between 1864 and 1877, Hoopa Agency lacked consistency in personnel and administration as well as money and supplies to carry on the government's agrarian civilization program. Hupas watched eight agents come and go, with the commanders of Fort Gaston filling in between. Civilian agents and army officers lost little love in the debate over Indian policy and who should control it, nationally or in Hoopa Valley. Politically astute Hupa leaders took advantage of the antagonism arising from this dual jurisdiction by playing off agent against army commander to get what they wanted or to remedy problems originating from either jurisdiction. If one pressed the people too hard, they would appeal to the other for relief. Their system worked very well in mitigating both the arbitrary authority of a single individual and the intensity of early directed culture change.

In one such incident, soldiers cut down oak trees for fuel on Campbell Field, 1.5 miles from Fort Gaston. After hearing Hupa complaints, Agent W. H. Pratt wrote the commander, "The grove of oak timber in question produces annually large quantities of acorns of *great value* to the Reservation, as food for the Indians, also [live]stock, of which both are very fond." He suggested the soldiers cut the "hillside pine forests." Major Henry R. Mizner agreed, noting that while some Hupas worked the fields, "These Indians are chiefly fed and clothed by the Government," and continue to "gather Acorns, Roots, and Salmon in considerable quantity for subsistence." Hupa men remained uninterested and even unwilling to farm the agency fields, but they used agency rations to supplement dwindling dietary staples. Some performed wage work for the army as scouts or supplied the fort with building materials, while others worked as agency laborers and freighters. But an agriculturally self-sufficient economy continued to elude Hupa agents, many of whom proved inexperienced and uncaring.[16]

Environmentally, successful field agriculture in Hoopa Valley was difficult to begin with. The valley was isolated. It took pack mules two to five days to traverse the 54 miles from Eureka or 83 miles from Crescent City over difficult mountain trails. Freight rates of $2.80 per hundred pounds raised the price of all imported supplies considerably. Winter rains and snow frequently isolated the valley for weeks, and accompanying mountain run-off caused the Trinity River to jump its banks periodically and scour the valley floor, depositing thick layers of silt and gravel. Lumbering on nearby slopes for agency, fort, and native needs increased these flooding and erosion problems.

The Trinity River itself divided the roughly 1,200 acres of arable land into eight isolated fields—four on each side of the river, the extremes being seven miles apart. Since the river was passable only by canoe ferry and a single government foot bridge, travel and movement of agricultural equipment between fields was difficult. Agents had to request and maintain more agricultural implements than normal for a reservation that size. Stands of trees and rocky flood-plain sections made some fields hard to cultivate, and the alluvial valley soils retained little moisture and wore out quickly. Variable spring weather made early planting a gamble, while lack of rain during the critical summer growing season limited the success of unirrigated fields. Hupa social and economic structures took these environmental realities into account, but they proved a formidable barrier to western-style market agriculture.[17]

In 1870, acting agent Captain S. G. Whipple finally voiced the cultural reason why Hupa men were so reluctant to farm the agency fields when they proved such good wage workers. "Acquisitiveness," he observed, "is a prominent trait in the character of these people, and may lead them to great efforts, but they do not appreciate communism." He explained that it had "always been their custom to pay each other for services rendered," and that individual control and ownership of land were traditional values. Those who did work in the fields found no incentive since those who did not received the same rations. Furthermore, it became clear that certain people were reluctant to work together, especially since it might bring feuding families or villagers together in the same field. Later agents noted the same tendency—that "[they] are not disposed to labor on the reservation in common, but will work industriously when allowed to do so on their own individual account." To get around this, Whipple instituted a work-for-pay scheme on top of weekly ration distributions. When Hupa men learned that they would be paid extra, they readily accepted reservation jobs.[18]

In 1871, Hupa men planted 785 acres in grain and cereal crops before the Indian Bureau replaced Whipple with Reverend David Lowry of the Methodist-Episcopal Church. Lowry was more missionary than farmer and more interested in reaping souls than wheat. He ignored Whipple's wage work policy and replaced the entire agency staff with "Christians," including the farmer who was "co-habiting" with an Indian woman. Hupa men quit working and the farm fell apart. Lowry managed to save only 350 acres of wheat and oats and 100 acres of hay that year and decided to let the land lie fallow the following season in order to more fully proselytize the Hupa. Under Lowry and the following three missionary agents, agency farm size and production fell over 50 percent. Agent E. K. Dodge blamed his poor crop showing on fields deemed second rate, worn and exhausted from over-cropping. In fact they probably were, for these Christian agents used the same acreage each year without breaking new land or systematically rotating nutrient-draining grain crops. While dairy and beef cattle might have been a viable industry, Dodge reduced the tribal herd from 135 cattle to just 20 head because, in his opinion, they were too difficult to maintain.[19]

Watching from Fort Gaston, Major Henry Mizner voiced Hupa complaints that they were approaching the point of starvation from the "*incompetency* and *neglect*" of these civilian agents. Rations had been cut and were being distributed only to those who worked. Mizner pointed out that wheat grown in the valley was insufficient to provide both flour and seed necessary for self-sufficiency. Moreover, Campbell Field, "the best farm in the valley," was not even planted. While most Hupas wore "citizen" dress, knew some English, and desired white-style houses, Mizner knew of "none having embraced Christianity" despite missionary efforts. He warned that they were returning to their traditional subsistence rounds in increasing numbers and that if things did not improve they would "take to the hills and give us trouble."[20]

The Christian agents had plenty to complain of themselves, and most of it centered on the negative influence of Fort Gaston soldiers and neighboring white miners who trespassed on the reservation. Despite post orders prohibiting soldiers from visiting the villages or bringing alcohol into the valley, there were numerous reports of drunken soldiers assaulting Hupa women, breaking into *xontas*, fighting with and even murdering Hupa men, aiding and abetting feuding parties, and generally disturbing the peace in Hoopa Valley. One complaint noted that a drunken soldier entered a *xonta* against the wishes of the occupants and "spent the night there vomiting and by his conduct causing much excitement among them." Alcohol, a problem among Hupas as well as soldiers and area whites, exacerbated internal social discord. Liaisons with soldiers spread venereal and other communicable diseases through the valley population, reducing Hupa numbers to a low of 414 by 1880.[21]

When Agent J. L. Broaddus reached Hoopa Valley in 1875, he found a hopeless situation and proceeded to make it even worse. Instead of breaking and planting new ground, Broaddus focused on breaking Hupa native beliefs, dances, and their spirit. In his mind the surest way to accomplish that was to remove them from their valley. "By sending them away from here," he argued, "you break up their old associations to a very great extent, and open up new avenues for improvement." His rationale for removal centered on the dilapidated condition of the agency buildings, mills, and equipment, the poor quality and limited extent of agricultural lands, and his own inability to eradicate Hupa culture—all of which were relatively true. Between 1875 and 1877, Broaddus helped his argument by reducing rations and planting less than 200 acres of worn land in grains which did not even produce enough seed for the next season. Broaddus dismissed both military and local white opponents of removal as self-interested profiteers—part of the corrupt "Indian Ring."[22]

Even the suggestion of removal was impossible for Hupas to entertain. Their social and ceremonial world was inextricably linked to

Hoopa Valley, and to abandon this cultural and natural environment meant death, an end to "the people of where trails return" and This Earth. As rumors spread through the valley, Hupa leaders began to play-off agency against military. A Hupa delegation told post commander Rich G. Parker:

> They are all violently opposed to leaving this valley, say that the Government gave it to them, and if it now wants to take it away, and sell it to the Whites, they will be satisfied, that they will remain here and work for the Whites, as they did before the valley was made a Reserve, that they want to live peaceably, but if they are to be forced from their homes without having Committed any Depredations, they will go to the Mountains.

Parker believed that the Hupas would fight if forced to move to Round Valley or Indian Territory as proposed. Several groups of men had already left the valley in January 1876, and their families were preparing to join them. Broaddus tried to induce a Hupa delegation to visit Round Valley, but, sensing a trap, they backed out. Leaders organized an uncustomary spring White Deerskin Dance lasting six weeks rather than ten days to renew their world and connection to place. Privately, Hupa individuals threatened to kill anyone who even visited Round Valley with agency staff.[23]

In the wake of the Little Big Horn incident, Bureau officials approved Broaddus's removal plan. That September, Broaddus called a council to announce the closing of the reservation—a reservation roughly 12 miles square (89,572 acres), given official status by executive order only three months earlier. Lieutenant James Halloran of Fort Gaston sat in on the proceedings and recorded the Hupa outrage. "Buck Billy" Beckwith, "an industrious and certainly the most intelligent Indian on the Reservation," spoke for the people. He refused to leave the valley, criticized the lack of rations, and expressed their collective desire to farm. He blamed the agency employees for the crop failures, saying, "White men were employed to work, and the Indians were anxious to learn, but the white men would not work and how could the Indians learn?" Halloran agreed with Billy's assessment and charged Broaddus with mismanagement, nepotism, and with retaining "a worthless set of employees," including an agency farmer whom Broaddus acknowledged "knew very little about his business." Halloran feared for the safety of area whites should Hupas take to the hills. He also worried about Hupa subsistence since, for the second straight year, "the acorn crop upon which they mostly depend is very small."[24]

After holding a Jump (or perhaps a Calamity) Dance that October to ward off evil, Hupa leaders gave their final refusal to leave Hoopa Valley. Despite this resistance, Broaddus forged ahead, selling off movable property or transferring it to Round Valley Agency. Even after being notified that the agency would close, Fort Gaston soldiers received no orders to forcibly relocate the Hupa people. In January 1877, the secretary of war accepted jurisdiction over Hoopa Valley until such time as the interior secretary decided to open another civilian agency. Hupas were left in possession of their valley and their rights, but this time under exclusive military supervision.[25]

Hoopa Valley Agriculture in the Military Years, 1877–90

In May 1877, Captain Rich G. Parker assessed what was left of Hoopa Agency after Broaddus's sales—namely the dilapidated grist and saw mills, agency buildings and records. "The removal and sale of this property has left the Indians without any means of cultivating the land," wrote Parker, "and while there is on the Reservation from 800 to 900 acres of good wheat land, not one acre is under Cultivation." He reported many sick and destitute Indians, blaming the "misrepresentation, mismanagement, and inefficiency of the [civilian] agents who have been in charge for the past six years." Unable to do anything with the agency farm in 1877, Parker distributed rations to supplement traditional subsistence staples of salmon and acorns, which formed an estimated 63 percent of the Hupa diet. Over the next several years, military agents slowly restored the fenced fields, mills, and buildings of Hoopa Valley Agency and ultimately the confidence of the Hupa people.[26]

Hupa interest in farming reemerged when military agents simply reinstituted the "wage for labor" plan so effective in the 1860s. In 1880, 27 families farmed while others operated the agency sawmill, selling 50,000 board feet of lumber to the army at $20 per thousand. In 1881, agent Lieutenant Gordon Winslow reported a 418-acre agency farm "worked by the Indians with perfect willingness," producing wheat, oats, potatoes, and hay. About fifty Hupas cultivated another 100 acres for themselves in "small and large patches," while others showed interest in the nine neglected orchards planted by early white settlers. Encouraged by this general interest, Winslow instituted practical agricultural instruction at the agency day school and set aside a six-acre garden plot.

Despite these improvements, Hupas continued to give "their chief attention" to salmon fishing, "as upon it depends, on an average, one-third of their subsistence." Deer and acorns likewise remained important foodstuffs, leading Winslow to complain that "it is only through an Indian's stomach that work to amount to anything can be got out of him." Agent Captain Charles Porter noted the Hupa dependence on rations and farm wages, and that their own garden patches, while numerous, "are on a scale of total insignificance when compared with the wants of the cultivators." "In fact," Porter wrote, "their cultivation seems to be regarded as a pastime and as a concession to the wishes of the agent rather than as a means of contributing to their self-support." Hupas were "accommodating themselves to the changed conditions," he wrote, "but none of them really believe in the propriety, advantages, or justice of their compulsory change of life," especially not the elders who held to their rituals, shamans, feuds, subsistence activities, and foods. Once again, Porter suspended the payment of wages for work on the agency farm, and Hupa participation declined accordingly.[27]

Agents could see but not fully understand that Hupa farming at this time was more a subsistence reproduction than a linear transformation. Hupa garden agriculture, often carried out by women, did not disrupt the cultural categories or natural rhythms of persistent hunting-gathering-fishing activities. Hupas accepted farming, along with rations and wage labor, as functional but nonexclusive subsistence pursuits. Their disinclination to abandon a diversified subsistence strategy with its own internal cosmology and proven layers of safety nets for the vagaries of a single form of production subject to ever-changing agency policies seemed reasonable, especially while their natural environment made that preference possible.

Porter's disgust with Hupa farming, with the continuing influence of Hupa shamans and native religious beliefs, with the problems of alcohol, venereal disease, and violence associated with the ongoing feud, led him to recommend abandoning the reservation in favor of homesteads. Instead, the army replaced him in 1886. Captain William E. Dougherty understood the situation in Hoopa Valley better than most and set out to improve the agricultural economy. He increased the practical manual labor content of the Hoopa School curriculum to 50 percent and sponsored agricultural fairs to stimulate interest and competition among adults. He reinstituted wage work on the agency farm and at the agency sawmill, where Hupa men cut over 220,000 board feet of lumber each year for new frame houses. Instead of stressing an agency farm alone, Dougherty made assignments of 10 to 20 acres to individual Hupa families. This individualized and competitive approach struck a responsive chord approximating older Hupa social and subsistence norms. Between 1886 and 1889, the amount of cultivated land doubled to over 900 acres, with Hupas working 85 percent of that area. By 1890, Hupa families owned 148 horses and mules, 110 cattle, 1,000 fowl, and over 100 hogs.[28]

If there were pull factors for Hupa men to begin farming, there were also push factors. Commercial fishing and canneries at the mouth of the Klamath River in the 1880s reduced the number of salmon and steelhead trout making their way up the Klamath and Trinity rivers to spawn, reducing both the Hupas' relative catch and the absolute number of those species each year. Furthermore, the articles for California statehood did not exempt Indian reservations from state legal jurisdiction. The state designated the Klamath as a "navigable" river (although, in fact, it was not), thus giving them jurisdiction over the river bed and the right to regulate commercial and subsistence fishing. The California legislature passed fish and game laws prohibiting groups like the Hupa from constructing weirs to take game fish. Confrontations between state game wardens and Hupas occurred periodically, but the people resisted orders to pull down their annual dam. Despite the establishment of a state fish hatchery in Hoopa Valley in 1889, Hupa catches steadily declined. Fewer people participated in weir construction or gathered the valley acorns, and by 1890 subsistence derived from such sources dropped to 13 percent of total.[29]

As Hupa farming participation increased in the late 1880s, Dougherty and the Hupa people ran into environmental and economic problems. Wild mustard, Canadian thistle, blackberry, and other invasive plant species began to move into fields and disturbed hillsides. Hogs, a favorite among the people because they "multiply enormously without requiring any care or attention on the part of the proprietors," wreaked havoc in poorly fenced fields and gardens. Finally, the isolation of Hoopa Valley limited valley farmers' ability to market their growing surplus production. While a military telegraph joined valley with coast in 1885, mule trails remained the main transportation link, leaving Fort Gaston and the agency as the only real markets for valley crops.[30]

In 1887, Hupas petitioned Dougherty and the Indian Bureau for a valley wagon road, "for they fully realize," wrote Dougherty, "that while they remain shut up in this valley, without access to a market, except over a mule trail, they can have no hope of escaping the miserable hand to mouth existence they have endured heretofore." Dougherty described $2,500 worth of surplus fruit rotting in the orchards each year and announced that valley grain production would soon double that needed for local consumption and seed. "Without a road to market where the Indians may enjoy the advantages of competition in selling and buying," wrote Dougherty, "it will not be possible to give effect to the policy of the Interior Department to make the Indians self sustaining and independent of the Government, or to advance their condition much beyond what it is at present." Bureau officials agreed and approved construction of the road with Indian labor.[31]

Concurrent with this growing Hupa interest in market agriculture came the first rumblings of allotment. Less than two months after passage of the Dawes General Allotment Act (1887), Commissioner John D. C. Atkins recommended that Hoopa Valley Reservation be allotted in severalty. Dougherty worried that limited arable valley land "makes it impossible to provide each family and adult male with a sufficient amount of land to enable each to live singly by agriculture alone," but he hoped to expand that base by inducing some of the 442 Hupas to open new places on the 1,500-acre, brush-covered Bald Hill. His own experience with simple land assignments made clear the continuing "disaffection" between feuding Hupa villages. Dougherty believed that moving close-knit family groups away from each other and mixing village fields would facilitate the breakup of traditional villages and their corresponding political and religious divisions. "Undoubtedly contro-

versies will arise between those who will find themselves joint occupants
of the same subdivisions where the lines are run," he wrote, "but these
may as well be settled first as last." The potential for profound cultural
change outweighed any temporary problems, and in 1889 General Land
Office surveyors began dividing the valley into equitable units.[32]

Hupa responses to allotment varied, but in general the people ap-
preciated the idea of individual landownership. In meetings with Bureau
inspectors, Hupa spokesmen expressed their desire for lands in severalty—fields of their own which they could improve and be secure in
those improvements. Byron Nelson, Jr., writes of his people, "They
wanted allotments, not because having individual farms would make
them more like white men, but because Hupa families had always held
rights to particular areas in the valley. Just as each family had had a
place to hunt and fish and gather plants, each wanted a place to farm."
They desired to reproduce cultural landholding structures within an
alien reservation framework. They accepted agriculture and allotment,
white clothing, tools, money, and houses while maintaining their village
identity, religious practices, and economic patterns. New foods comple-
mented rather than supplanted native staples. Men farmed, but took
time off to hunt and fish in season. Women prepared foods from wheat
flour mixed with acorn meal, and gathered native plants to supplement
garden produce. The selective adoption of items from what white officials considered a superior cultural whole, and the incorporation and
reproduction of those items in Hupa cultural terms, remained a source
of constant frustration.[33]

So, too, were the soldiers of Fort Gaston. As allotment and road
surveys went forward in 1889, perennial complaints about the soldiers'
negative influence gained force. National progressive reform groups
blamed the military and post trader for subjecting Hupas to prosti-
tution, venereal disease, drunkenness, violence, and blatant profiteering.
Calls mounted to close Fort Gaston and administer Hoopa Valley from
the California Mission Agency, but inspectors cleared the military of the
worst charges and recommended against agency consolidation. Inspectors pointed out that Fort Gaston was the only market open to
Hupas, and should it be closed they would have "no market for their
grain and forage, and there will be neither inducement or encourage-
ment for them to advance or improve their farms." A petition signed by
43 Hupa males requested that troops remain until the valley was allotted in order to protect Indian interests and provide a "market for sale
of our surplus produce." Otherwise, they agreed, "it will be useless to
increase our efforts to farm."[34]

Under fire from reformers, Commissioner Thomas J. Morgan decided to re-establish a civilian agency. Late in 1890, Dougherty turned
over Hoopa Agency to his civilian replacement, Isaac A. Beers, and the
period of military administration came to a close. Troops remained at
Fort Gaston for two more years to protect regional Indians from white

trespassers and to ensure the peaceful completion of allotment. By all accounts the economic situation of Hoopa Valley was much improved by thirteen years of military control, yet the social problems complained of by reformers and Hupas themselves were very real. If Hupas learned some adaptive skills during this period, they also acquired the problems and vices of their teachers' civilization.

Allotment Dreams

When Agent Isaac A. Beers arrived in November 1890, he found the Hoopa Valley Reservation in a state of flux. Earlier that year the Trinity River, fueled by runoff from unusually heavy winter snows and rain, boiled over its banks and flooded a large part of the valley. It destroyed the grist and saw mills, washed rock and gravel onto Indian fields, and covered two houses and the main valley road. Agency personnel and Indians spent most of that year trying to reconstruct damaged fields, property, and the wagon road. Fort Gaston's status remained unresolved, but rumors presaged its closing. Finally, the Hupa people anxiously awaited word of the allotment surveys. Beers himself doubted there was enough arable land in the valley, but from what he saw of Hupa interest in farming, he supported the plan.[35]

In 1891, almost every Hupa family had a garden plot, tended by the women, while men worked in the fields in what Beers considered an irregular manner. "The Indian prefers farming to all other occupations, as he has only to put his seed in the ground and wait at his leisure for the harvest," wrote Beers. "Any pursuit that would keep him busy most of the time, though he might receive more profit from it, he does not like." Beers's objection to this arrangement was in its apparent reproduction of Hupa cultural norms. Women "gathered" from gardens while men pursued resources farther afield. The laziness Beers inferred balanced intense periods of male labor—once hunting and fishing, now farming—with leisure time for personal or cultural elaboration. Profit or accumulation in the traditional Hupa sense was important, but only when it could be used in ways that brought power and status to the owner. And during this period when white agents usurped most of the political power from traditional leaders, that outlet became the group activities and rituals which, in themselves, required wealth and time away from the fields.[36]

Beers's job became complicated by the executive order addition of the Klamath River Extension to Hoopa Valley in 1891. The Extension, formerly part of the Klamath Reservation established for Yuroks in 1855, consisted of a strip one mile wide on each side of the Klamath from its junction with the Trinity River to the Pacific Ocean. Beers had to supervise the welfare of the relatively scattered Yuroks, who lived chiefly by commercial fishing and traditional resource use, who held little if any arable land, and who had lived in relative freedom for years under military control. Furthermore, since agency police could patrol the area,

Washington officials believed there was no more need for soldiers. In January 1892, the secretary of war ordered Fort Gaston closed and all post buildings and nonmovable property sold to the Indian Bureau.[37]

Realizing the economic impact of the closing, Hupas petitioned to keep it open. Beers argued that the military's demand for hay and grain was the motivating factor behind Hupa farming and that "the post has been and now is their *only market.*" Closing Fort Gaston would slam the door on market agriculture and wage labor in the valley. While Hupas sold some grain to pack trains and to Yuroks and Karoks, they could not compete against Arcata farmers and grain merchants for regional markets because of prohibitive freight rates. Despite a second petition signed by 100 Hupa men, the last soldiers left Hoopa Valley in June 1892. The Indian Bureau quickly converted the post barracks into a boarding school and completed the Hoopa Valley wagon road that year—both creating markets for labor and produce—but neither the school nor the road provided access to a cash market capable of handling Hupa production. Likewise, slackened demand and lower lumber prices reduced production and earnings at the agency saw mill. Lacking ready markets, and with the uncertainty of land tenure caused by the slow progress of allotment, Hupa farmers cut back cultivation from 900 acres in 1889 to 600 acres in 1894.[38]

During the post-closing episode, Beers made a telling assessment of Hupa agriculture. "The success of a few who first adopted this work encouraged the others," wrote Beers, "so that at present time the question is not, how shall I induce others to cultivate land, but where shall I find land for them to cultivate."[39] Not only was Hoopa Valley isolated, making its produce and timber uncompetitive in the coastal commercial markets, but it was physically limited. Allotment plats created from the 1889 survey indicated 2,475.5 acres of valley land, of which 65 percent (about 1,600 acres) was actually arable or potentially reclaimable. The survey merely confirmed what agents already knew—that there was not enough land to give each of the roughly 450 Hupas a sustainable farmstead.

In 1894 and 1895, special agents commenced allotting Hoopa Valley after completing work on the Klamath River and Extension reservations. William Dougherty, recently returned to Hoopa Valley to replace Beers as agent, argued that the allotment plat ignored the realities of valley settlement. Most families already had assigned plots on their home field, "laid off on lines perpendicular to the course of the Trinity River," thereby reproducing in part the nature of aboriginal land and resource ownership. Each had access to the river, space to garden, and room for a frame house. Despite slight variations over time as more aggressive families expanded at the expense of less successful ones, the system worked well. Culturally and ecologically this division made more sense than the official surveyor's arbitrary lines intended to create sufficient and more manageable units for field agriculture.[40]

Houses rising above the *xonta* and *taikyuw* at *Takimildin* village. Pliny Earle
Goddard, 1906. Phoebe A. Hearst Museum of Anthropology, The University
of California at Berkeley.

Hupas happily participated in the allotment process, putting forward claims to previously worked family fields. Three hundred sixty-two
Hupas received small valley allotments averaging 6.5 acres, of which no
more than four acres were arable. Of these allottees, 63 received supple-
mental or grazing allotments on Bald Hill or in the surrounding forests,
while 87 Hupas received no land at all, preferring to wait for lands as
yet unsurveyed. Allotting agent Charles Turpin promised all individuals
more land once the government surveyed the surrounding forested
mountains. Turpin forwarded the allotment schedule to the interior
secretary for the issuance of trust-patents, but the need for further surveys and the number of unresolved allotment requests delayed official
approval until that approval was no longer possible.[41]

While there were some disputes over field boundaries as Hupa
families settled into this new pattern of land use, the false sense of security allotment gave sparked a resurgence in Hupa farming. By 1900
the amount of Indian-cultivated land rebounded past its previous high
to 1,100 acres, nearly all of it planted in wheat, oats, barley, corn, and
hay. At the same time, a small but growing number of families raised
cattle for personal consumption or sale. Hupas owned 307 horses

and mules, 450 cattle, and 846 swine, which, unlike the hay or sacks of grain they consumed, could transport themselves to outside markets. In turn, Hupa dependence on native and nonagricultural subsistence resources dropped to its lowest point ever. Even wage labor in the Hupa timber industry continued to decline for want of markets as production fell from over 220,000 board feet in the late 1880s to 28,000 in 1900.[42]

Hupa field agriculture began to reach its environmental limits in the first decade of the twentieth century given the existing farm technologies and techniques. Cultivation leveled off at about 1,200 acres by the 412 to 453 Hupas, fully 25 percent of them products of Hupa marriages with Anglo miners, traders, and soldiers. Superintendent William B. Freer reported that "the Hupa Indians are farmers. Every family sows and reaps its crops each year, depending thereon for a portion of the year's supply of food." But, he continued, "The entire acreage of agricultural land is so small that individual holdings contain but few acres, the number ranging from 3 to 8; hence the productions of the farm must be supplemented largely by purchased supplies, which are paid for by the Indian's own earnings."[43]

Hupas earned money for necessary supplies or supplemented their family farm incomes in a variety of ways. Most sold their produce and livestock locally to the agency or through the Brizzard Trading Post, which extended credit to valley farmers and sold their produce regionally. Little produce from Hoopa Valley fields or orchards reached the coast because quarantines on insect infested fruit and "the lack of good roads makes it impossible to dispose of the products outside the valley." A second wagon road begun in 1908 raised hopes for better market access, but it was not completed until 1916. Seasonal work in the mines, fisheries, and forests of the region, work for the agency, and sales of finely woven baskets provided some families with small but needed cash incomes. Most subsisted on garden produce and traditional resources like acorns, venison, eels, and salmon, which, one agent noted, "form a considerable part of the diet of the older Indians." Only a few of the infirm received biweekly rations. George W. Nelson recalled that most of the people remained in Hoopa Valley on their small farms and that they "just figured on raising grain. They settled their bill once a year with Brizzard. They sell him hay and grain to settle their bills. And outside of that they never went out to work."[44]

The insurmountable problem of small field size was compounded by the physical exhaustion of the land, the result of fifty years of constant grain production without adequate field rotation or fertilization. In the first two decades of the twentieth century, wheat yields fell dramatically, and oats, oat hay, and alfalfa became the major Hupa crops. In 1900, several Hupa ranchers constructed private irrigation ditches from Hostler and Mill creeks to insure their alfalfa production through the dry summer months. Although others recognized the benefits such an irrigation system could have, the continuing feuds and village jealousies made cooperative ditch construction nearly impossible. By 1910, Hupa farmers irrigated only 40 acres from privately constructed ditches.[45]

Hupa agents believed that irrigation was the technological key to the agricultural problems of Hoopa Valley. Agency farmer Charles L. Davis tried to convince farmers to increase the irrigated area of valley fields in order to grow more alfalfa to feed beef and dairy cattle—transportable products with an outside market value. Irrigation would help mitigate the dry summer growing season while alfalfa, a nitrogen-fixing legume, would improve the quality of Hupa fields deleted by grain production. But Davis's plans ran into a wall of Hupa hesitation, the result of their insecurity about allotment patents. "The Indians do not feel willing to make the necessary improvements until they know better just what they have," wrote Davis. Superintendents and special agents visiting Hoopa Valley made similar assessments yet suggested pressing forward with plans to put 1,600 acres under ditch at an estimated cost of $30 per acre, financed by reimbursable federal loans.[46]

World War I interrupted these irrigation plans by limiting the availability of government loans. Nevertheless, encouraged by completion of the second wagon road and by higher wartime prices, Hupa farmers increased their production of oats, hay, alfalfa, wheat and vegetables to 1,600 acres in 1917. Still, high transportation costs ate up most of their profits and left Hupas out of the temporary prosperity enjoyed by the American farm industry. The real economic boom came for those young men who left Hoopa Valley to work seasonally in the area sawmills and lumber camps, ranches, fish canneries, and shipyards. Their wages and the war economy brought some needed capital into Hoopa Valley, but shortages and higher prices negated any real financial gain for those who stayed home to farm.[47]

In 1918, the Indian Bureau allotted Hoopa Valley Reservation for the second time. Since the original 1895 allotment, the Indian Bureau had made 395 individual allotments, but the interior secretary had issued none in trust patent. In the meantime, allottee deaths and an expanding population made it increasingly difficult to approve the 1895 schedule. The Hupa people through their elected Hupa Business Council (formed in 1911) petitioned for an investigation and redistribution of all reservation lands, provided they could keep their homesteads and part of their own improved fields. In 1915, Special Agent C. H. Asbury visited Hoopa Valley and agreed that the reservation be reallotted. His preliminary survey carved the valley floor into four-acre parcels by dividing the arable area (1,600 acres) by the estimated number of Hupas eligible for allotment (400). In allotment meetings that followed, Andrew Mesket and James Jackson, Sr., voiced the desires of their people for all land—valley, hill, timber—to be allotted equally. They argued that four acres was not enough to live on and "that they are afraid if the land is not allotted at this time that it will be thrown open to white settlers very soon and that they will lose it forever."[48]

It took nearly three more years for the interior secretary to cancel the 1895 allotment list and send an allotting team to Hoopa Valley. In October 1918, individual Hupas met with allotting agents to present claims on their improved lands. Using the 1895 list as a baseline, the agents attempted to allot each individual on that list (living or dead) and their children four acres of valley land and twenty acres of timber or grazing land on hillsides adjacent to the valley floor. In less than two months the agents made 374 allotments totalling 2,774 acres, with 40 more allotments pending additional surveys. The final allotment schedule, submitted in March of 1919, contained 414 Hupa allotments, and an Indian Competency Commission judged fully 50 percent of those allottees still living "competent" to receive their land in fee-patent immediately. Three years later, in July 1923, the interior secretary finally approved 365 allotments, all but 39 of them in 25-year trust-patent.[49]

Hupas accepted this allotment schedule with the same good faith and desire exhibited during the 1895 allotment. Since most families received their own houselots and fields, few real problems arose and disputes were amicably settled. In the case of a large landholder like James Jackson, Sr., his 35-acre farm on Norton Field was divided among immediate family members, so he did not lose much land. Even then, 55 allotments from the 1918 schedule never received approval, and with every passing year more eligible individuals applied for allotments. The Indian Bureau further complicated matters by reopening the valley to mineral exploration in 1919. Miners who leased gold and coal lands from the tribe added to the irritation and uncertainty when they encroached on patented or proposed allotments. Unresolved questions of land ownership and use resulting from allotment plagued Hupas until the 1930s, when the Indian Bureau suspended allotment entirely.[50]

Between 1890 and 1920 the pace of change in the physical and cultural structures of Hoopa Valley increased. Allotment brought about radical changes in residence patterns as families moved out of their villages and took up residence in white-style frame houses on their own allotments. *Xontas* gave way to frame houses, menstrual huts disappeared, and *taikyuws* (sweat houses) became almost exclusively ceremonial structures. Anglo clothing and material goods replaced Indian crafts; agency schools taught Hupa children English, housekeeping, and farming; white foods and subsistence pursuits coexisted with traditional staples and strategies; and Hupa men left the valley in search of wage work. Longstanding feuds faded as elders died and others recognized the necessity of communally purchasing and using expensive modern machinery. Mixed bloods made up more than one-third of the Hupa population, raising issues of tribal identity and rights to the limited land. Outbreaks of tuberculosis, pneumonia, typhoid, influenza, and venereal diseases replaced smallpox and cholera as the epidemic killers. New political mechanisms like the Hupa Business Council—emerging shortly before the last hereditary leader died in 1912, and based on agency support and election rather than traditional wealth—replaced older methods of Hupa decision-making.

More significant is the fact of how little basic aspects of Hupa culture changed. White agents found it difficult to explain how Hupas made such economic progress while continuing to observe group rituals and dances, marriage and burial customs, and to use Hupa shamans instead of agency doctors. They failed to realize how easy the economic changes were, given Hupa attitudes toward property and accumulation and the nature of their traditional harvest economy. Despite upstream mining, downstream commercial fishing, and restrictive California fish and game laws, people continued to build their annual fish weir and to dry salmon for winter use. Acorn harvests and consumption continued among older folks even as commercial operators logged valley oaks for the tannins in their bark. Superintendents like Jesse Mortsolf believed "that the dances are not particularly harmful, except as a waste of time, and that their suppression would result in such a wide-spread discontent that it would offset whatever advantages might result." Time and the passing of the older generation, he believed, would eventually end all of these lifeways, but as Byron Nelson, Jr., writes, "the people's quiet, persistent refusal to abandon ancient beliefs had itself become a way of life in Hoopa Valley."[51]

Prelude to Depression

"Well, during the twenties, everybody had a little farm here and that's how they made their living," recalled George Byron Nelson, Sr.:

> And we had the store . . . run by [Abe] Brizzard. He had a store here in Hoopa and the guys, the people, the farmers would charge there all winter and [say] "Charge book"—put it in their book and then they would put in their grain and raise their cattle and things like that and they would sell it in the fall of the year, and they would pay out their bills. And I can still remember in the twenties, because I used to go out there in the fields and work. . . . They would take all this wheat and pile it up in a big pile and then they would bring this threshing machine and they would put it through this machine and the corn, wheat, barley, or oats would come out and they would sack it up.

Nelson recalled how "they would start from one end of the valley and go right straight through and everybody would help one another. They would say, 'I'll help you next week and you can help me,' and that's the way they got by. There was no money involved, very little money." They used one of the few threshers in the valley owned by James Jackson, Sr., who "took grain in exchange for the use of the tractor." Most Hupa families owned a few cattle and harvested hay crops each year for winter feed using horse-drawn implements. Since hogs roamed the valley floor, families found it necessary to fence their fields and vegetable gardens. Joked Nelson, "if they got out well I guess it was . . . just some free meat there if they got in your garden."[52]

In the 1920s, Hupa alottees had most of their fields fenced and planted to oat hay, alfalfa, and wheat, and nearly every family maintained a home truck garden and some livestock. Hupas owned 620 head of cattle, 800 hogs, and 381 horses and mules, but prospects for a livestock industry remained poor. Hupa range land was overstocked, winter pasture in the valley was limited, and the hay produced barely served to subsist breeding stock over the winter. Dense chaparral growth took over valley margins and surrounding forest meadows after the 1913 Forest Service ban on brush burning, reducing the extent and quality of pasturage. Continued demand and high wages paid for labor in the timber industry outside Hoopa Valley drew more men away from their farms for seasonal labor. In 1923, Superintendent J. B. Mortsolf complained that this wage work was "absolutely pernicious," since it took many Hupas away from home during the growing season and placed them in camps where drunkenness and gambling corrupted their morals.[53]

Cultivated acreage in Hoopa Valley fluctuated between 1,600 and 2,000 acres during the 1920s, but Mortsolf reported that as dry-farmed grain and hay land, "it is growing poorer every year." Only a few Indians diverted water from the numerous streams flowing into the Trinity to their fields. "If we could be enabled to take advantage of this natural resource," wrote Mortsolf, "this little valley could be made into a garden, and at a comparatively small expense." Superintendent Charles W. Rastall reiterated the point that "the land in this valley has been cropped so continuously year after year that the land has been depleted and many fields are now in a worn out condition." Irrigation and rotated legume cropping was the only way to restore the soil and stimulate the stagnant cattle and dairy industry. In 1926, the Indian Irrigation Division constructed a modest ditch system to bring water from Mill Creek to 625 acres of Norton Field, not all of it arable. Hupas grumbled over the reimbursable cost of $60 per acre—double the 1915–16 irrigation survey estimates.[54]

With the help of a Bureau irrigation specialist, Hupas cultivated more alfalfa in the late 1920s, but maintenance problems plagued their irrigation system. Spring runoff waters from the source stream deposited thick layers of sediment in the shallow ditches. During the summer months, when natural stream flows declined, irrigation water disappeared in the porous ditch soil before reaching Hupa fields. The production of more alfalfa hay did not significantly increase the cattle and dairy industry as desired. Instead of investing in dairy cattle, Hupa families purchased and raised hogs, which could forage in the valley fruit orchards, oak groves, and chaparral-choked forest margins.[55]

Hupa farmers continued to command only a paltry outside market share for their agricultural produce. The completion of yet another graded road in 1924—linking Hoopa Valley with two major east-west highways on either end of the reservation—raised expectations of lower transportation costs and better access to coastal markets. But small lots of Hupa fruit, hay, and feed grains, raised on several combined four-acre allotments and marketed by individual families, found little acceptance in a marketplace glutted by commercial operators. The agency and Brizzard Trading Post continued to provide the main cash and credit markets for Hupa produce.

The roads also cut the costs of importing goods and allowed greater out-migration of Hupa men looking for seasonal wage labor. Likewise, improved access brought in whites who purchased what few fee-patent and inheritance allotments they could. By 1930, non-Hupas owned 496 acres and leased another 24 acres within the reservation.[56]

Commercial fishing on the Klamath River continued to provide some Indians with wage work but significantly reduced the number of spawning salmon returning to the Trinity River. By the mid-1920s, most of the fish passing through Hoopa Valley were smaller fish able to elude the commercial gill nets. Hupa fishermen constructed their annual fish dam despite state laws prohibiting closure of the river. In 1924, state game wardens, local fish and game associations, and Hupa fishermen worked out a mutually agreeable deal that allowed Hupas to construct and use their weir as long as it remained open twelve hours each day and all day Sunday. In return, the state stocked valley streams with trout to improve sport and subsistence fishing. This plan worked little hardship on Hupa fishermen, given their already diminished catches, and it preserved a traditional subsistence and ceremonial activity for future generations. It was a small victory in comparison to other threats to their environment and fisheries—such as upstream mining and plans to dam the Klamath and divert water from the upper Trinity to irrigate Sacramento Valley farms.[57]

As the importance of river resources declined, the importance of Hupa forests increased. During the first two decades of the twentieth century, Congress set aside the Trinity National Forest surrounding the reservation to protect it from corporate exploitation. The Forest Service limited Indian grazing rights in the Trinity and Klamath forest reserves to 100 animals per family at a rate of twenty-five cents per head—a ruling that placed an additional burden on the dozen Hupa families involved in stock raising. Finally, the Indian Bureau restricted timbering on Hupa trust allotments in an effort to prevent the clear-cutting that occurred on the Klamath Reservation when unscrupulous companies acquired both trust and fee-patented lands. These restrictions prevented the potential despoilation of the area from overgrazing and lumbering, but they locked up the single greatest potential cash resource of the Hupa people.[58]

In the 1920s, an increasing number of incendiary brush and forest fires on and around the Hoopa Valley Reservation worried state and fed-

eral officials. Superintendent Mortsolf complained of the large number
of fires set by Indians in 1922. "What their motive is I do not know,"
Mortsolf wrote after failing to catch the arsonists. Between 1927 and
1930, Bureau officials reported 102 incendiary fires on the reservation.[59]

The fires were symptomatic of a growing unrest. First, the Hupa
people set fires to reduce chaparral growth, promote useful plants, and
improve the grazing potential of the surrounding mountains for their
livestock. In effect, they reproduced an ecologically balanced activity
historically carried out to improve pasturage for deer, now for the benefit of cattle—a transformed but parallel food resource. In some cases
these fires blew out of control because of the dense undergrowth accu-
mulated since the 1913 burning ban. Second, people set fires to gain
some economic benefit from a resource they owned but could not control or exploit. Bureau regulations prohibiting the sale or lease of trust-
status timber allotments protected Hupa resources from rapacious
lumber companies but rendered them nearly valueless. Forest fires
became a way of benefiting from that "unusable" natural resource—a
native response to environmental and economic regulations. Fires created jobs close to home, and in the 1930s arson became "an established
community industry," an economic bonanza in an increasingly depressed regional economy. Government officials made efforts to halt the
growing frequency and intensity of forest fires, but the situation continued to escalate.[60]

Farming Decline and the 1930s

Despite their relative physical and economic isolation, the people of
Hoopa Valley felt the effects of the national depression. Hupa farmers
and stockmen, acclimated to modest markets for years, found it increasingly difficult to sell what little surplus they raised at a fair market
price. Making a living on four acres, or even the 12 to 20 acres some
families could put together, was never easy and became nearly impossible during the 1930s. Families depended on their vegetable gardens,
slaughtered their own pigs or cows, and supplemented their diets with
native foodstuffs. More serious for the economic health of the valley was
the precipitous decline of jobs in the surrounding region. The lumber
and fishing industries all but closed down, laying off Indian employees
first. The loss of outside income compounded the agricultural woes of
valley farmers, many of whom depended on the seasonal wages of
family members to make capital improvements or to pay off reimbursable loans on their livestock and farm equipment. In addition, the
depression made it nearly impossible for individuals owning fee-patent
or inheritance allotments to sell or lease their land at a fair price.[61]

In 1930, Hupa farmers cultivated 1,854 acres, irrigating only 41
acres. The next year cultivated acreage fell by half. In an effort to bol-
ster farm income and identity, agency farmer J. M. Walters organized

75 Hupas into the Hoopa Valley Farm Club. In 1932 he helped 20 farmers plant 6,000 strawberry plants on irrigated fields and tried to interest others in growing potatoes, but both experiments failed miserably. In meetings that fall with members of a Senate investigating committee, Hupa spokesmen complained that Walters and other agency employees "have not been of much use to us." Forty years later George W. Nelson recalled Walters as a "good guy," but as an ineffective farm agent. "They had some dandies in there," chuckled Nelson, "some dilly farmers." Despite the farm club, cultivation fell to 304 acres in 1934. Hupas tended their family gardens but allowed their fields to grow up in volunteer grains, grasses, and weeds, pasturage for their livestock. Superintendent Owen M. Boggess noted that "their farming activities alone would offer but a very meager living to Indian families."[62]

Environmental limitations and the loss of cash markets hurt Hupa farming, but a more important factor was the emergence of government jobs. As part of Franklin D. Roosevelt's "New Deal," Congress and the Indian Bureau approved funds for Indian Emergency Conservation Work jobs across the country. In Hoopa Valley, IECW projects (later subsumed by the Indian Division of the Civilian Conservation Corps) began in June 1933, employing 100 men paid $30 per month plus board. In 1934 the CCC-ID employed 460 Hupas, with 245 holding such jobs in any single month. By 1935, virtually everyone on the reservation had some form of federal employment. CCC-ID jobs included construction and maintenance of extensive horse and truck trails, forest lookout towers, telephone lines, and irrigation systems, as well as highway fencing, fire fighting, and reforestation projects. In addition to reservation work the CCC-ID used Hupas on projects in Oregon, Washington, and Nevada. Between 1933 and 1936, the CCC-ID spent $370,000 on Hoopa Valley, 36 percent of that in wages. In 1937, federal funding for Hupa projects fell to $50,000 and the program closed in 1939, but smaller CCC-ID and forestry programs continued into the early 1940s.[63]

Government officials believed the CCC-ID programs would ultimately help Indian farmers. CCC-ID camps were supposed to purchase supplies locally, but Hupa farmers received few contracts and felt left out of the general prosperity brought by government wage labor. Superintendent O. M. Boggess reported that he was trying to supply the camps with Indian produce but blamed Hupa farmers in general for demanding higher prices than those charged by white merchants. In one case, Boggess noted that a white man had bid 25 cents to Hupa James Marshall's 28 cents per gallon for milk. Boggess blamed Marshall while Marshall maintained that he could not make a profit at 25 cents because, given the limited pasturage, Hupa cattle were not heavy milk producers. By the late 1930s, area whites received a majority of supply contracts because Hupa farmers and ranchers with small operations and higher fixed costs could not match their low bids. Overall, CCC-ID funds improved Hupa fields through the construction and maintenance of ditches for "irrigating subsistence gardens" and through the eradication of noxious weeds and orchard pests. By 1938, Hupas irrigated 226 out of 520 cultivated acres. Alfalfa, clover, and feed grains made up production on all but 82 acres planted to family gardens. The remainder of the valley pastured a growing number of livestock.[64]

The CCC-ID proved to be a double-edged sword, stabilizing the economy of Hoopa Valley with jobs and cash while increasing the exodus of Hupa men from market agriculture as a way of life. Families maintained their house gardens, and some banded together to work larger irrigated fields, but few men chose to farm full-time for small returns when they could obtain work in or near the valley at decent wages plus room and board. By the late 1930s, the average annual family income from farming was $134 as opposed to over $700 from wage labor.[65]

Two related sources of economic development to emerge were forest fires and a changing Hupa livestock industry. In 1930, Forestry Assistant C. R. Patrie reported that "all the fires on the Hoopa are of incendiary origin and are presumably set by the Indians themselves principally to secure work, food and excitement." They set the fires, he observed, to stimulate the growth of basket materials, to clear brush areas for cattle grazing, and to obtain wage work close to home. His supervisor, Leonard Radtke, believed that Hupas fired their forests in order to benefit financially from this locked-up resource. He lamented that such fires took Hupas away from their farms, convincing many that fighting fires was more profitable than farming "with its drab toil, and frequent crop failures." Hupa elders understood the techniques and environmental benefits of controlled burning from long and intimate experience. They argued that government policies prohibiting selective burning both ruined reservation grazing lands and increased the intensity of brush fires that got started. Despite petitions for test burns and evidence that previously burned areas showed the benefits of fire, the Indian Bureau banned all range burning.[66]

When the ban failed to stop Hupa incendiarism, agency officials searched for economic causes and alternatives. They concluded that the reservation had neither enough grazing land nor forage crop production to support a viable dairy- or beef-cattle industry for every Hupa family. The range was already at peak grazing capacity with the 500 head of cattle, the majority owned by just a few families. Superintendent Boggess and Forest Supervisor Leonard Radtke blamed these big cattle owners for advocating forest burning, "since they believe that fire brings forth good grass." "We have never," Radtke lamented, "been able to convince the Indians of the fallacy of this theory." On the other hand, nearly every Hupa family owned some of the 1,500 hogs proliferating virtually untended in the hillside oak groves and overgrown orchards of Hoopa Valley. Radtke and Boggess hit upon the idea of creating a valley hog industry to circumvent the brush burning demanded by Hupa cattlemen.[67]

Radtke and Boggess set out to convince Hupas and the Indian Bureau that hogs were "the greatest asset that the Indians possess and the most natural way for them to earn a living." They proposed a Hupa stock association to market hogs collectively and linked the issue of a productive hog enterprise with the need to suppress forest fires and halt the commercial cutting of oak trees for their bark. "Save Your Hog Range" became the battle cry in attacking incendiary activities on the reservation in 1937. Hupas responded very favorably to the concept and requested $1,100 from the CCC-ID to fence valley fields and improve their breeding stock. Supervisors acknowledged that the program would "materially improve the economic condition of the Hoopa Valley Indians," but the CCC-ID director denied the request as falling outside his jurisdiction. Only one incendiary fire broke out during the 1937 campaign, but in 1938 and 1939, as plans for an association fizzled, incendiary fires once again swept the reservation—most limited to 25 acres and most in brush-choked grazing areas.[68]

During the economic and environmental problems of the early 1930s, Hupas organized a new tribal council to regulate the resources and people of Hoopa Valley. In 1933 they created a constitution and elected seven representatives, one from each of the six field councils and one from Bald Hill—reproducing an older village pattern of fields (*tlah ninnisan*, "one world") as units of Hupa political geography. As one of their first acts, the newly formed Hoopa Valley Business Council asked the Indian Bureau to complete Hupa allotment—what had been promised and denied them for so long. Between 1923 and 1932, Bureau officials estimated that there were an additional 600 people eligible for allotments, but little allottable land remaining. In 1934, the Indian Reorganization Act (IRA) prohibited further allotment or fee-patenting of reservations in order to stem the alienation of Indian lands. The act allowed tribal councils to "assign" individuals pieces of land from tribal holdings but did not allow them to convey title to those lands.

Unlike other tribes, Hupas desired an equitable allotment of their lands, in part because individual land and resource ownership reproduced pre-contact socioeconomic patterns. Given this desire for individual fee-patent allotments, the Hupa people rejected the IRA as a document for their tribal reorganization. The council continued to petition the government for allotments, but Commissioner John Collier ignored their wishes. Individual trust-patented lands reverted to the tribe, which reissued them as lifetime assignments. Usufruct rights replaced the security of ownership. Ultimately, people grew wary of improving fields to which they held no permanent title.[69]

During the depression, Hupa families fell back on traditional foodstuffs to supplement their diets. In 1934, Hupas harvested 11,750 pounds of acorns and chinquapin nuts. "I can remember, you know, we used some of it," said George B. Nelson, Sr., "but we didn't continue to depend on that." He recalled eating more venison and alder-smoked salmon, a staple for many families during the winter months. Hupas continued to recognize privately owned fishing places along the Trinity and to construct, both physically and ritually, their annual fish dam at Hostler or Campbell fields. As part of a strategy to protect and self-regulate tribal hunting and fishing rights, the business council negotiated with state and federal authorities over regulations prohibiting fish traps which blocked the Klamath or Trinity rivers. In the end, Hupas agreed to the ban and accepted instruction in alternative methods like gill netting, but continued to construct a modified version of their fish weir. By leaving both ends open to the current and keeping a central movable gate open 50 percent of the time, Hupa fishermen met the letter, if not the spirit, of the law and retained the right to construct and use their annual fish dam.[70]

In the late 1930s and early 1940s, the Hoopa Valley Business Council gained more authority to regulate reservation resources, subject always to Indian Bureau supervision. The council began to sell small quantities of tribal timber to provide employment and finance other tribal projects. They made leases to develop mineral resources and initiated an aggressive program to re-purchase alienated reservation allotments. In 1938 they organized a tribal cannery with funds provided by the Education Division of the Indian Bureau to put up vegetables, meat, and fish for local distribution. The council tried to provide more jobs and assistance as federal CCC-ID programs ended, but events of international import intervened to take up the slack in valley employment.[71]

Hoopa Valley in the Modern Age

"Yes, up until I say before World War II the people here they all had pigs, cows, hay fields, they had thrashers here, they raised wheat and thrashed it, and sold it," recalled seventy-year-old George B. Nelson, Sr., whose father owned a dairy in the 1930s.

> But that's what struck me so funny in my later years how the people survived in here because there was no social security and no what-you-call welfare or anything like that. You just have to survive some way, and that's how they did. They did their own butchering and gardens and things like that.

When asked what happened to this agrarian economy, he said:

> Well, when World War II came by most of the boys left and went in the service and everybody went off and worked in different places. There was very few people left in the valley. And I guess it just started to go down then. Then after World War II, well this mill, the Trinity River Lumber Company came in here and put a mill up . . . and they started to log the timber off the reservation here, put it through that mill, and then everybody went to work in the woods, in the mill. . . . Everybody had jobs and then they just—farms just went down.[72]

World War II touched off an economic boom in California that rattled even isolated Hoopa Valley. The war created new jobs and new opportunities, but all outside the valley. A number of Hupas joined the Armed Forces and fought with distinction. Many more took advantage of labor shortages and higher wages in the timber, fishing, shipbuilding, and war-related industries of California and the Pacific Northwest. Those who remained on the reservation finished work on the last CCC-ID projects and earned a modest living with their livestock and gardens. As Nelson put it, the war ended most agriculture in Hoopa Valley. "[T]hey just dropped out from farming altogether. And that's what it is today."[73]

The Indian Bureau and Hoopa Valley Business Council made some effort to revitalize valley agriculture in the 1940s, but with limited success. In 1941, they organized a Young Farmers' Club to encourage returning boarding school students to begin farming. After the Bureau abolished the position of agency farmer in 1943, the business council established the Hoopa Farm Enterprise to make loans from tribal industrial assistance funds to individuals wishing to procure modern agricultural equipment. The council purchased modern tractors and farm implements to rent out to valley farmers, but mismanagement and mechanical problems led the council to look for a way out of the equipment leasing business. The Hoopa Farm Enterprise with its revolving credit plan collapsed in 1954 under the weight of uncollected loans and the uneconomical equipment rental program. By 1960, the economic potential of farming the fragmented valley fields appeared too limited to warrant further tribal expenditures.[74]

The livestock industry in Hoopa Valley fared little better. In 1942, Hupa stock owners formed a loose association to improve profits by collectively marketing their hogs and cattle, but the continued individualism of Hupa families limited its effectiveness. By 1944, there were only 300 head of beef and dairy cattle compared to nearly 2,100 hogs. In the 1950s, the Hoopa Stockmen's Association tried to make Hoopa Valley an open range for their cattle. They petitioned the business council and Indian Bureau for cattle guards and fences to protect the highway, but ultimately failed to convince valley land holders to open or lease their four-acre fields for communal grazing. Periodic proposals to expand available public and reservation grazing land in the surrounding mountains by controlled burning received little support from federal agencies. Given range and market problems, both the number of cattle and families owning cattle declined through the 1960s. At the same time, free-ranging hogs became an increasing nuisance, digging up family gardens and raiding the sanitary landfill and cemeteries. By the early 1960s, wage work, tightening agricultural markets, and changing patterns of consumerism and food merchandising contributed to the virtually disappearance of valley hogs.[75]

An underlying factor in the collapse of Hupa agricultural enterprises was the instability of land tenure in the valley. The insecure nature of land assignments and unfulfilled desire for allotment, small farm size, and the continued sub-division of fee-patent and heirship allotments made farming more difficult and less productive. Throughout the 1940s and 1950s the Hoopa Valley Business Council continued to demand re-allotment and even drew up their own plans, arguing that their rejection of the IRA made such a division of land legal. The council even investigated the possibility of accepting governmental termination in 1954 if it would allow them to allot tribal land in fee-patent. The Indian Bureau, however, rejected council plans and ignored Hupas' fundamental desire for individual property ownership—an unusual twist on nineteenth-century assimilation and twentieth-century self-determination policy goals.[76]

Finally, the post-war economy and resource potential of Hoopa Valley left little room for a successful agricultural resurgence. Improved highway access to the valley and CCC-ID truck trails through the forests, regional over-cutting and a booming building industry combined to make isolated Hupa timber resources commercially viable. By 1948 the Hoopa Valley Business Council recognized that a sustained yield timber program was the best means of providing jobs at home for their people—a people who might venture out in search of work but who always came back to *Natinook*, "where trails return." Between 1950 and 1970, the Hoopa Timber Corporation leased valley mill sites to eleven outside firms and issues logging permits based on BIA sustained

Lumber yard and mill, Hoopa Valley. David R. Lewis, 1987.

yield estimates for between 11 and 40 million board feet of timber annually. Companies logged and processed pines and firs and stripped bark from the remaining oaks for use by the tanning industry. The timber industry employed hundreds of Hupas in the woods, and valley mills operated under quotas to employ 75 percent Indian workers. The new jobs, wages, and tribal per-capita payments from the millions in timber revenues brought an unprecedented degree of economic prosperity to Hoopa Valley.[77]

Despite the economic benefits, the mills permanently scarred hundreds of acres of valley farm land, polluting soil, air, and water. Logging trucks jammed the valley highway, making winding canyon roads even more hazardous. Logging clearcuts and area mining contributed to erosion and increased siltation in the Trinity drainage and may have contributed to two devastating valley floods in 1956 and 1965. Hupa elders described the 1956 flood as a punishment and act of purification, sweeping clean a sacred dance ground defiled by a white-owned lumber company. Between siltation above and commercial fisheries below, salmon runs up the Trinity declined from perhaps one million fish in 1850 to 500,000 fish in 1900 to barely 50,000 in the 1970s. California fishing regulations slowly eroded Hupa aboriginal rights, and the last fish dam in Hoopa Valley came down in 1956. With it ended the First Salmon Ceremony. By the time the timber boom went bust in the 1970s, 60 percent of Hupa timber—that closest and easiest to reach—had fallen to the saw. Many Hupas blame the Bureau of Indian Affairs for wildly miscalculating sustained yield figures—a mismanagement of precious resources that contributed to the economic and environmental degradation of Hoopa Valley.[78]

Aside from a few Hupa families who maintained livestock and some grass hay fields, valley farm land lay idle and irrigation works disintegrated. Wage labor and per-capita payments left little incentive to work land already overworked in an industry dominated by agribusiness with international marketing and transportation networks. Farming became too costly and difficult for all but a few families to pursue. While the floods destroyed mills and contributed to changes in valley residence patterns, they also hurt valley soils for gardening. The fields, neatly fenced into four-acre plots, became overgrown with brush and blackberry bushes and today provide garden spots or pasture for a few family horses. Complicated heirship cases—some in which more than 64 claimants share rights to one four-acre allotment—limit even tribal attempts to reorganize and use valley land in any collective agrarian enterprise.[79]

Natinook-Wā

"I understand that's just about the thing of the past is lumber," said George B. Nelson, Sr., in 1987. He went on to repeat a veritable litany of Hupa subsistence and economic changes:

Like I always said—I can still say it—that we have had our different eras—times in here—like what we had in here first is the gold rush days. Everybody rushing for gold. Next they came in as farmers. They raised wheat and natives that raised grain did fine. Cattle and hogs and that went out. Then came in the lumber industry. And that was a boom.

"Now which one will be the [next] one?" he wondered out loud, framing the question all Hupas are asking about their economic future.[80] While forest products and processing continue to be important for the economic future of the valley, the environment and recreational potential of the valley is becoming a recognized asset. Tourism may someday play a significant role in the valley's economy as outsiders discover the beauty and isolation that the region still provides.

The history of Hupa subsistence change is one of cultural reproduction and stubborn persistence, economic adaptation, and environmental limitations. Hupas reproduced their understanding of property and resource ownership, accumulation, individualism, and a "harvest" economy within the framework of contact and directed change. They played off civilian against military agents in order to mitigate change and retain some control of their world. They accepted wage work and farming as legitimate forms of trade and land use when their own harvest resources diminished. Farming began as a form of subsistence supplement or safety net and eventually became a staple, but Hupas never fully relinquished their traditional foodstuffs. Salmon, venison, and acorns in turn became the subsistence safety net, particularly during periods of farm crisis like the 1930s. Hupa individualism and continuing valley feuds made collective farming and marketing schemes ineffective. Hupa farming increased greatly when agents recognized this cultural predilection and offered them individual plots. Unlike other groups, Hupas desired but never received permanent allotments, and in the ensuing uncertainty people turned to other forms of land use and other resources for their tribal economy.

In the end the environmental realities of Hoopa Valley defined the progress of Hupa agriculture. The limited amount of arable land, its distribution in fields along the river, porous valley soils and seasonal rainfall, and the relative isolation of Hoopa Valley from coastal markets set the parameters for successful market agriculture. Inept agency administration and agricultural instruction compounded these problems. Continuous mono-cropping without adequate fallowing or rotation and the prohibition of native burning practices limited the land's ability to support crops and livestock. Despite efforts to alter this environment by irrigation, fertilization, cropping techniques, and road construction, the fundamental problem remained one of too many people and too little land for an individualistic, rather than a communal, farming enterprise.

The Hupa people understood their cosmological and natural world in terms of place, Hoopa Valley. They ordered the natural environment and their subsistence patterns around this place. They resisted removal that threatened to undermine the very basis of their culture, and attempted to control the pace of directed culture change in the nineteenth century. They adopted the methods and material trappings of white civilization they defined as advantageous and adapted these new structures in reproducing their own value system. Many aspects of Hupa culture have changed or been forgotten with time, but the most important ceremonies and beliefs continued despite periodic suppression and interference. To this day the Hupa people hold their White Deerskin Dance to renew the world for all people. In many ways life in Hoopa Valley closely resembles life in any isolated rural community suffering from economic underdevelopment, yet the people retain a fierce spirit and pride in their culture, which distinguishes them as *Natinook-wā*, "the people of where trails return."

6

TOHONO O'ODHAM, THE DESERT PEOPLE

When Jesuit missionaries made their *entradas* into the *Pimería Alta* of northern New Spain, they encountered a semi-nomadic desert people. Their riverine Piman neighbors called them *pavi au'autam*, the "bean-eating people," which Euro-Americans transformed into "Papabotas," or Papagos. The people called themselves *Tohono O'odham*, the "Desert" or "Country" or "Thirsty People" to distinguish themselves from their cultural relatives, the *'Akimel O'odham*, "River People," or Pimas. The O'odham are members of the Piman language family of the Sonoran division of the Uto-Aztecan language stock. They inhabited an area in southern Arizona and northern Sonora, Mexico bounded by the Gila River on the north, the Santa Cruz and San Pedro rivers on the east, the Colorado River and Gulf of California on the west, and the Magdalena and Altar rivers on the south. Today the majority of the approximately 16,000 Tohono O'odham live on one of three reservations in southern Arizona—the Papago (Sells), Gila Bend, and San Xavier reservations—incorporating 4,460 square miles (2,855,802 acres) called the American *Papaguería*.[1]

The Tohono O'odham have an elaborate origin cycle, told over four nights during the winter solstice, that explains the creation of the world and the appearance of the O'odham. In the beginning, Earth Maker made the world from the dirt and sweat on his skin. Darkness lay upon the water and they rubbed, producing *I'itoi*, the Papago's Elder Brother and culture hero. *I'itoi*, Earth Maker, and Coyote (*Ban*, the trickster, who came to life uncreated) finished the world, creating plants and animals and giving each a place and function. *I'itoi* and Earth Maker created people, but the tears from an abandoned baby flooded the world. *I'itoi*, Coyote, and Earth Maker sealed themselves in clay jars (*ollas*) and agreed that the first to emerge would become the leader. Once the water subsided Earth Maker emerged first, but *I'itoi* convinced the others that he had emerged first, thereby displacing Earth Maker as leader and culture hero.

I'itoi began making humans out of clay that came to life after four days. Coyote made different and deformed people that *I'itoi* threw to the other side of the world. *I'itoi* lived in a cave on Baboquivari Mountain, and from there he taught the people how to live and gave them all the practical and ceremonial knowledge they needed. One day Siwani, an important man living where the Pimas now live, became angry with *I'itoi* for singing at Siwani's daughter's puberty celebration and killed him; but *I'itoi* rose the next day. Four times Siwani killed *I'itoi*, and four times he rose, but finally he remained dead and decomposed.

Years later *I'itoi* came back to life as an old man and asked the chiefs of four villages (North, South, East, and West) to help him kill Siwani and his Apache-like people. The chief from the South agreed and went to the gopher boys, who guarded the doorway of the People Below. They told him to sing for four days to release the People Below. Siwani found out and sent Coyote to watch from Baboquivari Peak. Coyote saw the earth open up to the South and watched many Below People emerge and join *I'itoi* before Coyote could close up the hole. *I'itoi* invented war and promised land to his followers, who proceeded to defeat Siwani and displace the old people. Coyote escaped but to this day remains a solitary animal. Those of *I'itoi's* followers who were farmers chose land along the rivers (Pimas), and those who were hunters took lands below Baboquivari Peak, where game and food plants were abundant (Tohono O'odham). *I'itoi* completed his task of teaching the people and then went away, never to return.[2]

Archaeological reconstructions suggest many points of intersection with these accounts. Archaeologists posit three distinct culture periods prior to Piman occupation of southern Arizona and northern Sonora: Paleo-Indian big game hunters (by 9500 B.C.); a Desert Archaic tradition of hunter-gatherers who may have planted maize as part of their cyclical subsistence round (7000 B.C. to A.D. 300); and the Hohokam, who arrived in Sonora and southern Arizona by A.D. 300 after a rapid emigration from central Mexico. The Hohokam (*Huhugam O'odham*, "people who have vanished," or "exhausted people,") brought domesticated crops and an established irrigation technology with them. They lived in single-unit brush and adobe dwellings with excavated floors, organized in either scattered or concentrated village sites depending on the availability of water for farming. They made red-on-buff glazed pottery, practiced cremation, built large ball courts, and may have incorporated Desert Archaic peoples and hunting-gathering techniques in the arid margins.

By A.D. 1400, the Hohokam began to decentralize due to climatic fluctuations, the increasing salinity of their fields, and recurring attacks from Athapaskan or Piman peoples. By the 1520s, contagious European diseases reached Sonora and contributed to the Hohokam decline. Most archaeologists suggest that these decentralized Hohokam peoples were the ancestors of the historic O'odham, while others argue that Desert Archaic hunters, pushed into marginal upland areas by Hohokam expansion, moved back into lands vacated by the Hohokam and became the historic O'odham. Lexico-statistical studies do little to settle the debate or shed light on the origins of the Piman peoples.[3]

Environment

The greater part of the *Papaguería* lies in the Sonoran Desert of southern Arizona and northern Sonora, Mexico. The land appears stark and hostile but supports an astonishing variety of plant and animal life. In the clear desert air the eye sweeps across the vast panorama of broad valleys sparsely covered with burnt grasses, gray-green creosote, and dusty bursage. Dry red sand washes appear out of nowhere and disappear just as quickly into the tall brush. Stands of green mesquite and paloverde, cholla and prickly pear cactus break up the dry landscape with their color, especially during the early spring. Stately saguaro, their arms lifted skyward, march up the rocky hillsides. In the distance mountain ranges shimmer like blue shadows, distorted by waves of midday heat rising from the valley floor. Isolated storm clouds trailing gray curtains appear in the afternoon and threaten to soak the land, but the rain generally dissipates in the arid sunlit sky.

The *Papaguería* is a basin and range country of broad valleys and arid plains broken by steep, eroded-fault block mountains running generally northwest to southeast. The elevation of the country rises from 500 feet above sea level in the western Yuma Desert to 2,500 feet in the Santa Cruz Valley, and slopes off to the north in the Gila River drainage and in the far south in the Magdalena-Altar river drainage. Most of the valleys are between 1,370 and 3,000 feet. Soils are alluvial sand and clay with little humus content, changing to sand and coarser gravels on the bajada slopes and washes. Rugged and highly eroded mountains of granite, limestone, and volcanic conglomerates rise from the valley floors. Two major ranges—the Growler (3,029 feet) and Baboquivari (7,730 feet) mountains—trisect the *Papaguería*.

The *Papaguería* is arid, subject to extremes in temperature and moisture. There are no permanent streams and only a few ephemeral ones—the Gila, Santa Cruz, San Pedro, Sonita, and Altar rivers. Most water comes from mountain springs that collect in natural rock basins (*tinajas*), or from runoff that is captured in man-made earthen ponds (*charcos*). Evaporation from these sources can exceed nine feet per year. Precipitation increases locally with elevation but generally comes in intense and localized thunderstorms in July and August, and then again in more steady storms in December and January. Rainfall varies from zero to five inches annually in the extreme west up to fifteen inches in the east, and

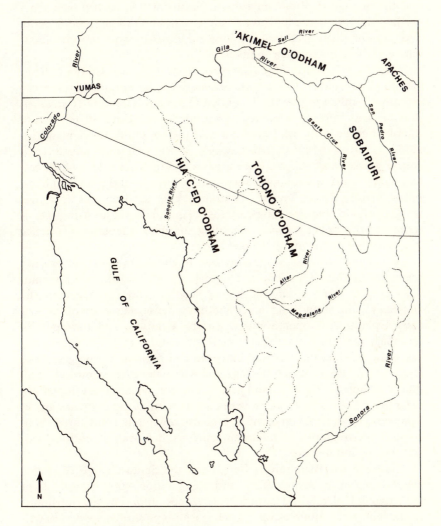

5. Pimería Alta and O'odham Territory

snow occasionally blankets the mountains and higher valleys. Valley tem-
peratures vary from a mean summer high of 101 degrees and a mean
winter low of 38 degrees, creating a 265- to 336-day growing season.[4]

The American *Papaguería* contains three physiographic regions—
western, central, and eastern—each exploited by a different group who
came to be known as Papago or Tohono O'odham—the *Areneños* or *Hia
C'ed O'odham* (Sand People), the Tohono O'odham (Desert People),
and the Sobaipuri. Biotic environments vary within each province according to elevation, exposure, precipitation, and human modification.
The O'odham survived by exploiting the diversity and periodic abundance of these micro-environments.[5]

The western third of the *Papaguería*, from the lower Colorado River
east to the Growler Mountains, is classic Lower Sonoran Desert environment, inhabited by the Hia C'ed O'odham. Creosote (*Larrea tridentata*) and bursage (*Ambrosia confertiflora*) make up 90 percent of
the plant cover in the valleys of this arid region. Other valley plants include sandroot (*Ammobroma sonorae*), covenas, lamb's-quarter, and
course grasses and lichens. Near washes and malpais fields, which collect more runoff water, appear mesquite, paloverde, and ironwood trees;
burro brush, desert broom, boxthorn, and catclaw; desert agave,
ocotillo, cholle, and organ pipe cactus. Plant life increases with precipitation on the upper *bajadas*, including the giant saguaros (*Carnegiea
gigantea*) that command the cooler slopes.

From the Growler Mountains east to the Baboquivari Range lies
the heart of the *Papaguería* and homeland of the Tohono O'odham.
This central third is slightly higher, cooler, and moister than the
western region, supporting larger and more dense vegetation of the Arizona Upland or Upper Sonoran variety. Creosote and bursage still
dominate the valley floors, but open grasslands appear in the southeast—the product of increased moisture and periodic burning. On the
lower *bajadas* creosote and bursage mix with paloverde, ironwood, mesquite, saltbush, amaranth, and lamb's-quarter, while on the upper *bajadas* more trees appear, along with cholla, ocotillo, prickly pear, agave,
beargrass, sotol, hackberry, yucca, saguaro, organ pipe, and barrel cacti.
In the upper regions and mountain canyons, oak, walnut, cottonwood,
and willow find a niche.

Between the Baboquivari Range and the Santa Cruz River valley
lies the area of highest elevation and precipitation, supporting biota of
the Arizona Uplands and Transition ecozones utilized by the Sobaipuri.
In the higher mountain elevations, chaparral-type shrubs appear, as well
as oak and piñon-juniper forests. The northern Santa Cruz valley supports the same Uplands vegetation found in the central zone, while the
intermittent flow of the Santa Cruz River sustains arrowweed, cattail,
willow, and cottonwood along the bottoms. The southern valley was a
vast desert grassland, supporting mainly bush muhly grass (*Muhlenbergia*) in the eighteenth century and later a variety of grama, blue, rice,
panic, June, wheat, bent, needle, Sacaton, rye, and curly mesquite

grasses. The Tohono O'odham used fire to destroy brush and mesquite and maintain this grass range for game animals.[6]

With the exception of the western deserts, the *Papaguería* supported a diverse if somewhat sparsely distributed fauna. Mountain sheep, bobcats, and some bear roamed the mountains. Mule and white-tailed deer, antelope, peccary (javelina), cottontail and jackrabbits, coyote, fox, badger, ground squirrel, and other desert rodents inhabited the hills and valleys along with various snakes, lizards, and gila monsters. Birds common to the region include the Gambel quail, western whitewinged and mourning doves, Merriam turkey, and some migratory waterfowl, as well as a number of raptors and scavengers.

Subsistence

The Tohono O'odham practiced a diversified subsistence system to utilize the periodic floral and faunal abundance scattered thinly across their territory. By exploiting a variety of resources they ensured against dependence on any single product which might fail in any given year. Their risk-spreading strategy, combining cyclical spatial movements for hunting and gathering with semi-sedentary agricultural village life and resource distribution mechanisms, provided for subsistence security rather than surplus.

Environmental differences modified subsistence strategies from west to east. The Hia C'ed O'odham were nomadic hunter-gatherers who planted few if any crops in the arid deserts. On the other hand, the eastern Sobaipuri lived in more permanent villages with flood-plain (*akchin*) and river-irrigated fields, venturing out to hunt and gather in the surrounding area. In the central zone the Tohono O'odham practiced a Two-Village residence system consisting of migrations between summer Field and winter Well villages, balancing their hunting and gathering rounds with the rhythms of *akchin* farming. Theirs is paradigmatic of the Tohono O'odham cultural system prior to Spanish contact.[7]

The Tohono O'odham "calendar" of seasons reflects their subsistence system and movements. Their ceremonial year began in July (Rain and Giant Cactus Ripe Moon) as the people moved into temporary cactus camps to gather saguaro fruits and then on to their Field villages to gather more foods and await the rains. They planted crops in July and August (Big Rain and Short Planting Moons) and continued to hunt and gather until the October harvest. The people returned to their foothill Well villages, where water was more readily available, and spent the relatively cold months of November and December (Pleasant Cold and Big Cold Moons) hunting and performing domestic manufactures. Hunting continued in January (Animals Thin Moon) but let up in February (Animals in Heat Moon) as the winter rains increased (Gray Moon). The people lived on stored foods during the early spring months, watching the desert bloom in March (Green Mesquite Moon), April (Yellow Flowers Moon), and May (Mesquite Buds Moon). They gathered early blossoms and buds but depended on what remained of their stored foods through the "Painful (no food yet) Moon" of May. In June, as the saguaro began to flower and fruit (Seeds Black Moon), they anticipated the move to their cactus camps and the renewal of their subsistence cycle.[8]

The basic unit of Tohono O'odham subsistence production was the extended family and the local kin-based residence group or village. Families worked individually yet traveled in concert with other related families to familiar gathering grounds or seasonally between Field and Well villages. All members of the family and community worked because laziness meant starvation. Women gathered and processed both wild and domesticated plants, cooked and stored foods, and made household items. Men hunted, assisted in gathering and the harvest when necessary, and tended their agricultural fields. Men pooled labor to construct runoff diversion dikes and banked earthen basins called *charcos* to catch and hold water for domestic purposes near the Field village. They traded labor in breaking and cultivating individually held plots within the village field system (*temporales*). Older people took over the more specialized crafts and manufactures and directed younger family members.[9]

Within the local kin group the Tohono O'odham practiced a form of reciprocal gift exchange (*niari*), usually of food, which had the latent effect of redistributing goods to less fortunate families and ensuring group solidarity. Recipients noted the gift equivalent and returned an equal measure immediately or when possible. The people considered it better to distribute fresh food during its abundance, thereby gaining immediate honor and a future reciprocal return, than to risk hoarding and losing the food to spoilage or seasonal migration. The Tohono O'odham also traded excess goods for equal measure with non-kin villagers or with other O'odham peoples, but true *niari* entailed a lasting obligation unlike equitable trade or pay for labor.[10]

Each local residence group possessed hunting and gathering grounds as well as formal Well and Field village locations. Villagers owned all land in common, but families held perpetual usufruct right to specific plots within the village *temporale* by virtue of their labor in farming that plot. Sons worked for their fathers and could inherit usufruct rights. Village councils decided on the distribution of plots within newly established *temporales* and organized the construction of water diversion works and *charcos*. Village councils also coordinated group movements and subsistence activities to maximize effective use of a subsistence area.[11]

Hunting was a male pursuit and, in some cases, an occupation for specialists. Village councils organized communal hunts or approved individual hunting plans. The Tohono O'odham believed that animals had special powers and could only be killed by their own consent. Animals offered their bodies to hunters who sang the proper songs and followed the proper rituals before and after the hunt. After death animals returned to their secret kingdoms to take new bodies and renew the cycle, but, if improperly treated, the animals could send disease or refuse to be recaptured.

Deer were the most important of these game animals, for *I'itoi* created deer from the desert mouse, gave it special gifts and senses, and endowed its flesh with curative power. Hunters prepared for the hunt by smoking tobacco and singing songs describing the deer's habits. Shamans or hunters could dream of deer or other game and arrange a rendezvous where the animal would allow itself to be taken. Individually or in small groups, hunters stalked deer with bows and arrows and used blinds, drives, or deer-head disguises. These disguised hunters, or "Head-Bearers" (*mó'opidam*), were hunting specialists who apprenticed from childhood and eventually obtained the deer's power song in dreams or visions. Tohono O'odham hunters also pursued antelope, mountain sheep, peccary, small mammals, turkeys, quail, and dove, and collected some insect larvae and caterpillars. Hunters used fire or worked around the borders of cultivated fields in communal rabbit drives, led by a hereditary hunt master or "Rabbiter" (*to'pidam*). In the western deserts the Hia C'ed O'odham added reptiles, fish, and shell fish from the Gulf of California to their diet.[12]

Tohono O'odham women provided the largest part of the family diet by gathering and preparing the wild fruits, roots, seeds, and greens of the *Papaguería* as each came into season. Women of related families traveled together to local gathering grounds, accompanied by their families only to the more distant areas. Villages rather than individuals held nonexclusive usufruct rights to these gathering areas, and they sponsored ceremonies to ensure the continued abundance of these wild food plants.[13]

In June, women led their families to cactus camps to gather and process the ripening saguaro fruits. Women used long saguaro-rib poles to knock the fruits from the tops of the saguaro. They made most of the fruits into a jam or thick syrup used in making *tiswin*, a ceremonial cactus wine, and they ground the dried black seeds into meal. During the spring and summer months, women gathered food plants as they matured around the Field Village. They collected greens from the bursage, lamb's-quarter, amaranth, cañaigre, and sotol; fruits from the organ pipe cactus, agave, and yucca; joints and buds of cholla and prickly pear; roots from the poverty weed, covenas, sandroot, agave, yucca, wild potato and onion; and nuts and berries from the squaw bush, mulberry, boxthorn, jojoba, walnut, and oak. Fall brought harvests of seeds from the paloverde, ironwood, tansy mustard, devil's claw, and numerous seed grasses. None was more important than the mesquite bean, which women gathered in large carrying baskets. After flailing the beans from their pods and drying or parching them with hot coals, women ground the beans into meal for making *pinole*, or baked dough cakes.

Tohono O'odham women and men gathered and stored a number of plants recognized for their medicinal and ritual value, including mesquite leaves and gum, cañaigre root, mistletoe, cereus, bucknut, and creosote leaves. Tobacco (*Nicotiana trigonophylla* and *N. attenuata*) was an important part of all male social and religious practices. Only older men cultivated and gathered the semi-domesticated tobacco, which they kept in secret patches away from the village *temporales*.[14]

Like the Hohokam before them, the Tohono O'odham cared for domesticated food and fiber plants in established fields. While the Hia C'ed O'odham did little farming due to the lack of water and mobility demanded by their subsistence quest, Tohono O'odham men cultivated fields where arroyos widened and runoff waters spread out and settled across the land (*akchin*, "mouth of the wash"). In the east, where rain and surface water was more abundant, Sobaipuri men practiced a more ambitious and intensive agriculture based on *akchin* and ditch irrigation. The Tohono O'odham cultivated the agricultural triumvirate of the Southwest—maize, beans, and squash—as well as cotton, tobacco, gourds, devil's claw, and a host of useful field-border "weeds." At contact, domesticated cultigens and cultivars provided between 17 percent of total subsistence needs in the central zone and 30 percent in the eastern zone. Most Tohono O'odham consumed vegetal foods in a ratio of four to one over meat.[15]

Stories tell how the O'odham farmed rich fields below Baboquivari Peak (*Waw kiwulik*, "rock drawn in the middle," referring to its original hourglass shape). Four men went to *I'itoi* and asked him to help them move the mountain to provide more land for fields. Following *I'itoi's* instructions, the men held a *tiswin* ceremony for four days and nights until the mountain moved back, causing the top half of the hourglass-shaped peak to break off. The people were very happy, but Wind Man (*Huh'wuhle O'odham*) and Cloud Man (*Chu'vahk O'odham*), who lived on the mountain, did not like having to travel farther to bring the rain and decided not to carry any more water than before. That is why, they explain, there is a large potentially cultivable area but only enough water for the original fields.[16]

Water, both its timing and amount, was indeed the limiting factor in Tohono O'odham agriculture. *Akchin* farming required a minimum of seven inches of rain to guarantee a crop—one good soaking and three or four milder soakings during the July and August rainy season. If summer rains came too hard or too late, seeds would wash away or not mature. Men constructed networks of diversion dikes, some up to a mile long, to concentrate and capture runoff rainwater on their alluvial *temporales* or *charcos*. In other instances they built low earthen dikes and brush structures that reduced erosion damage by slowing and spreading runoff, allowing it to settle on their fields. Runoff deposited nitrogen-rich detritus and organic matter, rejuvenating desert soils and creating "islands of fertility."[17]

Villagers chose field sites at the foot of a sloping catchment basin, on or near the alluvial fan of an arroyo. They looked for level land with dark soil and vigorous wild plant growth and then cleared it with fire. Tohono O'odham agriculture involved reciprocal—not communal—labor to clear and plant individually controlled field plots. Men worked the same one-quarter- to two-acre parcel until arroyo entrenchment, erosion, or soil depletion made the effort necessary to clear a new plot in the *temporale* practical. Village councils assigned new plots and relocated *temporales* or entire Field villages if extensive environmental changes or damage warranted.[18]

The Tohono O'odham waited for July rains before planting their fields. They watched the position of the Pleiades to determine if the rains had come in time for their crops to mature. In dry years they saved their seed. Their basic crops were a soft flour-type maize (*Zea mays*)—mainly white, yellow, or blue—tepary beans (*Phaseolus actifolius tenuifolius* and *P. a. latifolius*), and four varieties of squash or pumpkin (*Cucurbita pepo*, *C. mixta*, *C. moschata*, and *C. maxima*). They also cultivated and processed cotton, devil's claw, and tobacco. In a cleared field, Tohono O'odham men sowed up to four seeds at a depth of three to six inches in holes spaced thirty inches apart. They did not plant in rows, preferring alternate sowing to maximize water distribution and the soil-holding capacity of mature crops. Neither did they intercrop or rotate domesticated plants, relying instead on nutrient-rich flood waters to renew their fields.[19]

The Tohono O'odham believed that cultigens had to be taken care of in order to produce—that proper cultivation, not genetics, made for good seed and crops (although they chose seed from the best fruits). Men cultivated their plots two to four times during the season, allowing certain "useful weeds," or edible plants (*'oidag c-ed 'i:waki̇̆*, "in field herbs") to grow in their plots and field borders. These included wild tobacco, amaranth, lamb's-quarter, wild gourds and beans, spurge, chiltepin, bursage, cañaigre, poverty weed, peppergrass, and tansy mustard. These "in field herbs" added diversity to Tohono O'odham diets and, when eaten with other food crops and meat, provided enough overlap between amino acids to supply complete proteins and needed vitamins and minerals. The people recognized wild varieties of their domesticates but considered them retrogrades rather than progenitors of their seed stock. They called these plants *Ban*, meaning "Coyote's" (*Ban Bawi̇̆*, Coyote's beans, *Ban Toki̇̆*, Coyote's cotton, *Ban Wiw-ga*, Coyote's tobacco); and Coyote stories of degenerated plants served to warn farmers against laziness in tending their crops.[20]

Tohono O'odham men determined the proper time to harvest based on crop maturity, dryness, and the position of the Pleiades. Most domesticates took forty to sixty days to reach maturity, depending on the timing and amount of rain received. Their genetic history geared them for short season production and the ability to mimic wild summer ephemerals, which used both drought-escaping and drought-tolerating mechanisms. The variety and phenotypic plasticity of corn seed in particular allowed for higher yields during longer growing seasons. Estimates suggest average corn yields of twelve bushels per acre. Women took care of the harvest while men began their fall hunts. Women dried and stored the corn, beans, and squash for winter use in clay pots and coiled baskets.[21]

Not simply a physical activity, Tohono O'odham agriculture involved the observance of certain prescribed rituals to ensure adequate rain, plant growth, and a successful harvest. In July, as people gathered in their Field villages, they held their *Náwai't* ceremony ("to make liquor"). As they listened to ritual Mocking Bird speeches and songs taught them by *I'itoi* to "bring the clouds down," they drank *tiswin* to signify the saturation of the earth with rain. The consumption of large quantities of *tiswin* caused vomiting, a recognized ceremonial feature called "throwing up the clouds." After the rains, ritual speeches to ensure plant growth preceded and accompanied planting. Villagers placed fetishes and effigies of desired crops in their fields, sang to encourage their growth (called "singing up the crops"), or held Green Corn ceremonies and prayer stick ceremonies (*Wi:gida* or *Viikita*) in August. Prescribed songs and a ritual oratory of thanks preceded and accompanied the actual harvest. Attempting to raise crops without following these rituals would be futile, for nothing useful would grow or it would be inherently inferior, like the wild "Coyote" varieties of their domesticated plants.[22]

Society

The basic unit of Tohono O'odham society was the extended family, which traced kinship bilaterally. They recognized kin relations up to the fifth degree but owed reciprocal kin duties such as gift exchange only to those living in the immediate area. Marriages were generally village exogamous, since kinship in a single village could be very close. The Tohono O'odham divided themselves into two patrilineal moieties (Coyote and Buzzard with subsidiary totems of White Ant and Red Ant people). Moieties were nonexogamous and served simply to order people for group rituals. Each moiety contained between five and seven patrilineal sibs (clans), which at one time many have represented local residence groups.[23]

The typical Tohono O'odham village or dispersed ranchería consisted of families from one or more kin group living in dome-framed brush houses with earth roofs. Villages were semi-permanent, given the typical Well-to-Field-village movement the majority of people made each year. Well villages were smaller winter congregations that took advantage of the limited water available from small mountain springs or *tinajas*. Field villages, with their *charcos* and *temporales*, accommodated kin from several Well villages. As Field villages outgrew their resources they spun off Daughter villages, politically autonomous yet ceremonially and dialectically tied to the parent village. Linguists suggest the existence of eleven discrete Mother-Daughter village units in the American *Papaguería*. Village size for those practicing this Two Village system ranged from four to 60 households (up to 300 people). In the eastern zone, adequate water supplies allowed larger congregations to remain year-round in villages with simple adobe structures, while out in the arid west the Hia C'ed O'odham maintained no permanent villages. In the late seventeenth century there were perhaps 2,000 Sobaipuris living along the San Pedro and Santa Cruz rivers, several hundred Hia C'ed O'odham in the western deserts, and 10,000 Tohono O'odham in the central and eastern zones.[24]

Given the scattered nature of Tohono O'odham settlement, village councils were the largest units of political organization. Each village maintained a ceremonial Rain or Round House, a domed brush-and-earth shelter large enough to house all the men. The Keeper of the Smoke presided over council meetings, acted as ceremonial priest, patriarch, and adviser, and kept the village's sacred fetishes. Councils met nightly to decide or coordinate group activities. Women were not allowed inside but would gather outside to listen. Council members smoked ritual cane tube or corn husk cigarettes while listening to the Keeper's ritual speech of admonition. Councils based their actions on group discussion and consensus. The people prized oratorical ability, and council members blessed with this gift and a record of demonstrated experience and knowledge held particular sway. Consensus and group solidarity were important given their subsistence strategies and environmental realities. The people avoided open disputes or feuds and used gossip to maintain public order. Village councils verbally admonished offending individuals, threatening them with whipping, banishment, or, in the case of witchcraft, death.[25]

Warfare and intervillage games were two instances in which Mother-Daughter villages would band together. The Tohono O'odham were skilled and respected adversaries but had no formal warrior societies and considered war a "disagreeable necessity." Their enemies were usually Apachean groups (*Ohp*, "Enemy") who raided for slaves and food during the winter months. Villages took defensive precautions and banded together to avoid attack but also prepared measured responses. Councils sent out retaliatory war parties accompanied by shamans who helped locate and confound the enemy. Battles were short and furious. The Apache were considered "evil shamans," and any person or thing touching them became taboo and needed ritual purification. Therefore, Tohono O'odham raiders took little beyond scalps, which became powerful fetishes not for war but for curing, bringing rain and a good harvest.[26]

Intervillage games (*tcïrkona*) brought distant peoples together. Villages challenged each other to athletic contests including marathon kickball races, long distance runs, shorter sprints and relay races, double-ball shinny, as well as hand games. Gambling and trade were central parts of these athletic events and served to further redistribute food and material resources. Villagers and shamans sang power songs to aid their people in the competition, and group singing provided entertainment during the gathering. Success in the competitions brought with it luck for rain and good crops.[27]

Most Tohono O'odham customs centered around notable events in the lifecourse of an individual. Food taboos, segregation, and ritual purification requirements accompanied both parents and child at birth. Children received special shaman-given names at birth and took nicknames as they became adults. Grandparents often raised children, freeing parents for subsistence pursuits. At about age eight, children began learning their work roles and were segregated so that a male child would not accidentally come into contact with a girl suddenly starting her first menses. Girls underwent a puberty dance (*wuáka*) and ritual purification and joined the women in the four-day menstrual segregation and activity taboo they would observe until menopause.[28] Parents usually arranged exogamous marriages for their children to avoid relative taboos and to build kin ties with other villages. Following a ceremonial gift exchange, males stayed with their intended brides for four nights and then took up patrilocal residence. Both polygyny and divorce were possible.[29] Families attempted to remove sick persons from the house before death to avoid having to destroy the structure. Family members painted and dressed the corpse for burial, interred it in a rock cleft or shelter, and observed a ritual mourning period. They moved the family dwelling to evade the ghost before it went east to a land of plenty under the sunrise, accompanied by ancestors who came in the form of owls.[30]

Tohono O'odham cosmology revolves around stories of their Elder Brother *I'itoi*, an oral text for understanding the order of all things. Four is the ritual number, coinciding with the four directions and the death and renewal of their Elder Brother. Their "Man in the Maze" design represents a philosophy of life—the complicated, difficult, and often puzzling way a person must walk in order to find happiness and peace at the center.[31]

For the Tohono O'odham, all activities required ritual song, "the magic which called upon the powers of Nature and constrained them to man's will." The people sang to escape or prevent danger, to cure sickness, to confound enemies, to ensure a hunt, and to make crops grow. Songs or ritual oratory (*s'hámpatak*, "wise speeches")—set phrases originally created by *I'itoi* or given to a ceremonialist by a supernatural power—described a desired event in all its perfection. The Tohono O'odham believed that describing an event with "beautiful speech" made that event take place for all the people if the description was vivid and the singing or recitation done according to formula.[32]

These songs were central to each group ceremony, all of which focused on rainmaking, crop fertility, group unity, and health. In April or

May each year, people living around Santa Rosa renewed their Shrine of the Flood Children. They recounted how four children saved the earth when salty water flooded from a hole at that spot, and they sang to ensure a plentiful harvest. Other shrines, scattered throughout the *Papaguería*, required similar, although less regular and elaborate, treatment with songs and token offerings. During the *Náwai't* ceremony, ritual Mocking Bird speeches and songs accompanied the *tiswin* and described the coming of rain and the bounteous crops it would make possible. Group singing during the growing season aided crops, hunting songs ensured success, and gaming songs brought luck in intervillage competitions. The *Wi:gida* (*Viikita*, Harvest or Prayer-stick Festival) was the most important of all ceremonies, held every fourth year in the north and every year in the south. Initiated by *I'itoi* on his march of conquest, the purpose was to "keep the world in order"—to prevent floods, ensure good harvests, group unity, and health. Held during the summer or winter solstice period, the ten day festival brought Mother-Daughter villages together for ritual oratory, singing, and dancing by masked performers.[33]

Tohono O'odham men could obtain the power of special songs and become "ripe" in four different ways. First, they could experience a power dream of a supernatural force or animal that taught them a song to help them in a specialized endeavor. Second, men could gain power through warfare by becoming an Enemy-Slayer with a scalp fetish for curing. Third, an individual could gain heroic status and dream power by undertaking the hardships of four salt pilgrimages to the Gulf of California—an arduous journey surrounded by ritual oratory, taboos, and offerings. The fourth avenue to power came by eagle-killing, for the people considered eagles to be powerful shamans. Different eagle feathers held different properties or powers necessary for performing different rituals, from curing to rain making. During ritual purification, the eagle-killer could receive visions and songs. None of these avenues to dream power was open to women, but some post-menopausal women received recognized power songs for curing after repeated visions.[34]

Shamans (*mákai*) gained their specialized power to divine through extensive dreams of power animals or objects. They could foresee rain, the outcome of games, the location of enemies; and they could work their specialized songs to affect persons or events for good or evil. Their status as paid professionals came from their ability to diagnose diseases—to "see" the nature of an illness as it fit within the paradigm of Tohono O'odham disease theory. *Ká:cim múmkidag* ("staying sickness") was specific only to Piman peoples and resulted when a person made a ceremonial mistake or misbehaved toward a dangerous power animal or object (its "ways") and was afflicted by its "strengths." *'Óimmeddam múmkidag* ("wandering sickness") was a type of germ theory developed to explain the devastating epidemic diseases transmitted between different races. *Pi'áp'edag* ("afflictions") were nonsickness diseases resulting from accidents or sorcery. Shamans sent patients with "staying sickness" to the "ripe" men who possessed that specialized dream power. They sang their power songs to appease the offended supernatural power or sucked out the intruding "strength." In cases of "wandering sickness," shamans organized cleansing ceremonies to banish evil (*á'ata*). In other cases, people sought the help of herbalists—individuals with the knowledge of efficacious remedies gained through experience, instruction, or dream power.[35]

The O'odham inhabited their desert lands in southern Arizona and northern Sonora for years, secure in their mixed hunting-gathering-farming subsistence strategy and their adaptations to an environment of extremes. Their village organization and locations gave them the flexibility to adjust to environmental realities of limited water and scattered subsistence resources, as well as to raids by Apachean peoples. They actively modified their environment with fire and through the construction of water diversion and storage structures. They raised crops genetically adapted to the vagaries of the Sonoran Desert and observed elaborate ceremonial activities related to rain, subsistence, health, and group unity.

The Hohokam and O'odham of *Pimería Alta* felt the impact of the European invasion long before they experienced direct contact with Spanish *conquistadores* and missionaries. By 1524, contagious European diseases reached the area of the Sonoran Desert, carried along the trade routes from central Mexico. Smallpox and measles swept through the native populations, causing an estimated depopulation of 50 to 75 percent. By 1534, European diseases reduced the indigenous populations along the Gila River drainage system to one-quarter of their pre-1519 population density. This massive depopulation resulted in cultural disruptions of historic trade routes, subsistence systems, and religions based on curing.[36]

The first direct contacts between European and O'odham came in 1539, when Franciscan priest Fray Marcos de Niza and Estevan the Black led a party northward in search of the fabled Seven Cities of Cibola. The de Niza party encountered Sonoran Sobaipuri people as it made its way up the San Pedro River, but de Niza turned east for Cibola (Zuñi) before reaching the main Sobaipuri villages in southern Arizona. In 1540, Francisco Vasquez de Coronado may have met Sobaipuris as he followed a similar route on his way to Cibola. Coronado sent Melchior Díaz overland from the San Pedro Valley to find Hernando Ruiz de Alarcón, who was ascending the Colorado River by boat. Díaz never found the boats, but he made the first European transversal of the *Papaguería*. Spanish mission settlements pushed into the southern reaches of O'odham territory by the mid-seventeenth century, but did not penetrate the American *Papaguería* until the 1680s, when Fray Eusebio Francisco Kino and his Jesuit missionaries extended their missions into northern Sonora and southern Arizona.[37]

7

THE TOHONO O'ODHAM AND
AGRICULTURAL CHANGE

Spanish missionaries and Mexican soldiers asserted their colonial dominance over the land and native peoples of the *Papaguería* long before American officials arrived to dispense their own brand of "civilization." At first the Tohono O'odham continued to live much as they always had, selectively incorporating and interpreting the social, material, and subsistence resources offered by these foreigners. Their environment served as a buffer, allowing them a certain amount of cultural autonomy long after they were politically surrounded. Even after Americans acquired the *Papaguería* in 1854, the majority of Tohono O'odham remained beyond the control of government agents. The people continued as before but found themselves defending their land and water resources from intrusive miners and grazers. Their cattle herds grew and became an important symbol and economic resource, ultimately to the detriment of their fragile ecosystem and to farming itself. Environmental change chased changing subsistence patterns in a cycle ending with the loss of precious water resources and the abandonment of irrigated and *akchin* fields as people moved into the marketplace to sell their labor.

Colonials of Spain and Mexico, 1687–1854

In 1687, Jesuit Father Eusebio Francisco Kino received his calling to establish a mission at Dolores, Sonora. Between 1687 and 1711 he made fifty trips into the *Papaguería*, exploring for crown and Christ. Word of Kino preceded him, and native peoples reportedly welcomed him with crosses and arches—symbols of colonial authority. Kino found the

Piman Indians anxious for new food crops, the miracle cures offered by
his religion, and help in defense against their Apachean enemies. In the
1690s, Kino encountered the Sobaipuri of the San Pedro and Santa
Cruz river valleys cultivating Old World crops—wheat, flax, and water-
melons—obtained through trade with intermediary Sonoran tribes.
Their irrigated fields impressed him, and he established mission stations
among them. In 1697, Kino came to the village of Bac along the Santa
Cruz River. He found 800 Sobaipuris inhabiting 186 dwellings and an
extensive irrigated field system. Kino renamed the village San Xavier
after his own patron saint, and in 1700 he laid the foundation for the
mission church of San Xavier del Bac.[1]

Kino's *journadas* through the *Papaguería* brought him into contact
with numerous Piman and Yuman peoples of the lower Colorado. He
created mission stations to spread Christianity, but perhaps more importantly he spread Old World seed crops, livestock, and infectious diseases. By 1710 Kino had introduced wheat, barley, chick peas, lentils,
kidney beans, cabbage, onions, lettuce, garlic, anise, grapes, and other
Old World cultigens. Riverine Pimans readily incorporated wheat into
their subsistence cycle, planting it with the mid-winter rains and harvesting it in May or June before the saguaro ripened. Kino supplied
missions with cattle as well as horses, sheep, goats, and domestic fowl,
and distributed some two thousand cattle as gifts to Indians along the
Santa Cruz and San Pedro rivers.[2]

The Jesuits maintained nominal control of the *Papaguería* until
1767, when they were expelled from New Spain and replaced by Franciscans. Jesuit administration had been relatively quiet, with the exception of some Apache raiding, mission Indian resistance to weekly
labor requirements, and the Pima Revolt of 1750–51. Franciscans faced
a graver challenge as Apaches pushed Sobaipuris out of the San Pedro
Valley into mission settlements along the Santa Cruz. There they mixed
with Tohono O'odham expanding eastward from the interior valleys.
Construction of a series of Spanish garrisons along the frontier helped
until the Mexican Revolution of the 1820s, when Apache raiding went
virtually unchecked. Tohono O'odham villagers withdrew to larger
settlements along the Santa Cruz or retreated into the interior. The
revolution unleashed another invasion the Franciscans could not deal
with—the flood of Sonoran miners, cattle ranchers, and settlers with
Mexican land grants encroaching on the southern and eastern reaches
of Tohono O'odham territory.[3]

Jesuit and Franciscan administration of the *Papaguería* was relatively restrained. Missionary control fell most heavily on sedentary village peoples farming the riverine fringes of the Sonoran Desert. The
environment and scattered settlement of the vast interior precluded any
coercive administration, sheltering most of the Tohono O'odham from
directed culture change. Although missions in the *Pimería Alta* exacted
their own labor quotas and were focal points for violence and con-

tagious disease, they may have been less disruptive than missions and private land grants in other parts of northern New Spain. Both Jesuit and Franciscan missionaries were fairly successful at integrating their religious message and political authority into existing native structures, leaving community social organization essentially intact and able to respond to introduced elements. The Tohono O'odham found the miraculous aspects of Catholicism rather attractive and incorporated religious holidays, patron saints, and miracle cures into their own cosmology.[4]

Missions tended to reinforce the settled agricultural traditions of the O'odham without fundamentally altering their landholding patterns or diversified subsistence round. Native farmers incorporated wheat and other seed crops but continued to plant according to tradition in alternating hills rather than rows. Some adopted metal hoes and fashioned crude wooden plows to clear fields but continued to plant and cultivate with ironwood digging sticks. The addition of winter wheat and new seed varieties increased their total food supply and dependence on vegetal foods. The Tohono O'odham also incorporated cattle and horses within their cultural complex. Mission cattle allowed to run wild after Kino's death were hunted and butchered like deer, their meat divided in formal gift exchange (*niari*). Horses increased the prestige and mobility of their owners and allowed families to travel to the Gila River to harvest wheat for Pima farmers—expanding what may have been an aboriginal labor practice.[5]

Following the Mexican War and 1848 Treaty of Guadalupe Hidalgo, the United States took possession of the northern half of Mexico. Five years later they purchased an additional 30,000 square miles of Sonoran Desert for $10 million. The 1853 Gadsden Purchase unceremoniously divided the land and peoples of the *Papaguería* between two less-than-neighborly nations. Few Tohono O'odham knew or cared about these events of international import, for the treaty and purchase had little affect on their daily lives. Neither shows up on the village calendar sticks—ironwood or saguaro staffs with carved mnemonic symbols, annual notations of significant events inspired by the record keeping of Spanish priests. For the early territorial period, calendar sticks recount only prominent conflicts with Apaches and the increasing number of Mexican and American trespassers in the *Papaguería*, harbingers of things to come.[6]

Americans and the Tohono O'odham

In 1857, the Indian Bureau appointed John Walker agent for the Indians of the Gadsden Purchase area—the Pima and Papago or Tohono O'odham—and sent him to establish an agency at Tucson. Walker visited San Xavier del Bac and found the villagers farming an extensive area. Impressed by their irrigation system and surplus wheat production, he distributed some metal farm tools and arranged for a black-smith to care for their needs. In his reports he noted that a fair number of Tohono O'odham worked in Tucson or in the mines near Tubac and that they traded wheat, salt, pottery, and cordwood for cash and kind. Walker had little idea of the villages or numbers of Tohono O'odham living in the central and western reaches of the *Papaguería*, nor did he pursue that matter. By the time he arrived there were few if any Hia C'ed O'odham (Sand People) on the American side of the line. During the Mexican War they had been scattered by clashing Mexican and American armies and then exposed to an 1851 epidemic that killed all but a handful of families, who fled into northwestern Sonora.[7]

The American Civil War interrupted what little attention the government paid Indian affairs in the *Papaguería*, but it did create an agricultural market at Fort Breckenridge for the wheat, corn, and beans produced by the Gila River Pimas. The Tohono O'odham participated indirectly in this trade by traveling north to the Pima communities to harvest spring wheat in return for food to take back to their interior villages. The war also disrupted efforts by San Xavier leaders to obtain clear title to village lands in order to halt intruding Mexican and American settlers. In 1864, Charles D. Poston, superintendent of Indian affairs for New Mexico Territory, acquiesced and set aside a two-square-league area around the mission of San Xavier del Bac as a reserve for all the Tohono O'odham.[8]

While the reservation was never officially approved, Agent M. O. Davidson and the leaders at San Xavier opposed the idea of collecting all Tohono O'odham on that reserve. They argued that two square leagues was not nearly enough arable land for the estimated 6,300 Desert People inhabiting fifteen major villages scattered across the American *Papaguería*. Davidson thought it better to leave them where they were, farming "wherever there were lands susceptible of irrigation," and to confirm their ownership as guaranteed under Mexican law and the Treaty of Guadalupe Hidalgo. Later agents echoed Davidson's sentiments, recognizing the importance of the Tohono O'odham as allies in military campaigns against the Apaches. Despite pleas by agents and village leaders, the government did little either to recognize Tohono O'odham land and water rights or defend them against Mexican and American trespassers until 1874, when President Ulysses S. Grant signed an executive order setting apart 71,090 acres as the San Xavier Reservation. Even then the Indian Bureau established no agency or staff at San Xavier, preferring instead to administer the region from the Pima Indian Agency at Sacaton, over one hundred miles away.[9]

This benign neglect was a double-edged sword for the Tohono O'odham. During the 1860s and 1870s, they continued to pursue a diversified subsistence strategy, to hold their ceremonies, and to adapt to changing peoples and circumstances at their own pace, by choice and not by coercion. At the same time, they suffered the lack of material goods, protection against intruders, and the beneficial advocacy an on-site agent could afford them.

Despite periods of short rainfall and epidemic disease, the San Xavier O'odham planted two annual crops—their summer corn, bean, squash, and melons, and the introduced winter wheat crop. They diverted water from the Santa Cruz River through a system of canals to irrigate their fields. San Xavier villagers owned only two or three metal plows in 1875 and practiced cultivation techniques that Agent John W. Cornyn deemed "very destructive to the land and wasteful of labor." Cornyn and the other Pima agents knew relatively little about the agriculture practiced by Desert People in the central *Papaguería* except that their labors suffered from the severe lack of water. A few adopted winter wheat where water allowed, but the majority continued *akchin* farming and their Two-Village residence system. Agents did know that the Desert People provided valuable labor during the harvest at San Xavier and Gila River, that those in the south worked for Mexican ranchers, and that they were targets of Apache raiders.[10]

As the military began rounding up Apaches in the early 1870s, the Tohono O'odham returned to the southern and eastern territorial areas temporarily abandoned during the most active period of raiding (1810–70). Tohono O'odham and Mexican ranchers, once allies against the Apache, now found themselves at odds. Ranchers appropriated the best water and hunting and grazing lands by virtue of their Mexican land grants. Others simply made use of native resources without title. Peace enlarged the invasion as American ranchers imported large numbers of Texas cattle to graze in the *Papaguería*. Americans sank wells and let their cattle range through Tohono O'odham territory, an area they considered public domain. Local conflicts increased over the appropriation of land and water and the reported theft of livestock.[11]

When this trouble started, only a few Tohono O'odham families kept domestic cattle. The majority simply hunted feral cattle like they did deer. In the south and southeastern *Papaguería*, interest in building domestic herds increased as Tohono O'odham men began working for Mexican and American ranchers. Cattle hunting slowly gave way to cattle ranching, and domestic herds took over former hunting environs. As the number and size of family herds increased in the 1880s, Tohono O'odham village councils appointed stockmen to herd livestock collectively away from the village *temporale*. The position held a certain amount of social prestige, akin to that of traditional hunt leaders. In many cases hunt leaders (*tó'pidam* and *mó'opidam*) became village stockmen as cattle surpassed deer in subsistence and economic importance—thereby reproducing a traditional social position and subsistence occupation within a new economic framework.[12]

As Anglo and Hispanic settlers moved into the *Papaguería*, Tohono O'odham participation in the regional marketplace increased. San Xavier villagers sold pottery, mesquite cordwood, and their farm surplus in nearby Tucson. Men and women moved to Tucson to work as wage laborers and domestics, and men worked regionally during the agricultural off-season as cowboys and miners. Between 1877 and 1880 they worked construction on the Southern Pacific Railroad as it crossed the northern *Papaguería*. Some of those workers wintered along the Gila Bend at Burnt Saddle (*Sil Murk*), cultivating abandoned Pima fields and working for area farmers. In 1882 these residents secured an executive order reservation—the 25-square-mile Gila Bend Reservation, which served as both home and seasonal way-station for between eleven and six hundred Tohono O'odham farm laborers.[13]

This mobility for seasonal wage work was potentially disruptive of a stable village society, but not for the Tohono O'odham. Their seasonal subsistence migrations and Two-Village traditions made travel to distant jobs or temporary residence in towns like Tucson or Burnt Saddle a culturally acceptable option. They understood the concept of wage labor from long contact and differentiated between trade and *niari*. Tohono O'odham kinship bonds and identification with a Mother Village reduced the sense of cultural dislocation experienced by other Indian groups facing similar migrations.

Throughout the 1880s, the Tohono O'odham received little attention from the federal government or from their agents residing among the Gila River Pima at Sacaton. In 1883 Agent A. H. Jackson reported that while 500 people at San Xavier supported themselves by agriculture, the Indian appropriation of $1.10 per person for the estimated 7,300 Desert O'odham was totally insufficient. The next year Jackson did not even deem it necessary to report on the Desert O'odham, for nothing had been done for them in years. This neglect left O'odham territory open to trespassers, and agents repeatedly warned the Bureau that the Tohono O'odham could "not hope to hold the vast cattle ranges belonging to the public domain against the influx of white population that is constantly flowing into this Western country." The only protection agents could offer concerned villagers was the advice that they file for their land and water under the Homestead Act.[14]

Agents did not even have a clear idea of how the Desert People were living. After traveling through the interior *Papaguería* in 1887, Elmer A. Howard reported:

> A trip through their country is sufficient to fill a person with amazement that human beings are able to subsist in such a country. Place the same number of whites on the barren, sandy desert, such as they live on, and tell them to subsist there, the probability is that in two years they would become extinct. The country they occupy is a sandy desert, and they raise absolutely nothing from the soil, depending wholly for their support upon cactus fruit, mesquite beans, roots, and such game as they can kill, and raising such stock as they can with their limited facilities—the latter being their principal industry, and the one that has made it possible for them to live.

Although he was impressed by the Desert People's environmental adaptation, Howard's conception of proper farming and the timing of his spring trip led him to miss the reality of extensive *akchin* farming. Howard gazed across unplanted fields and desert valleys in one unbroken yet myopic glance.

Howard did point out two important trends. First, by supplying mesquite wood to regional mining camps and towns, the Tohono O'odham were clearing sensitive watersheds and slowly depriving themselves of mesquite beans, "one of their principal articles of food." Second, he noted that their increasing dependence on cattle had generated cultural changes and conflict. Tohono O'odham families had to move cattle regularly between water and distant pastures, straining established subsistence patterns. Even then, Howard reported, "This poor privilege is fast being wrested from them, for the country is fast filling up with cattlemen, and now at almost every spring or well some white man has a herd of cattle, and the inevitable result follows, the Indian is ordered to leave, and the 'superior race' usually enforces such orders."[15]

Between 1891 and 1893, the Tohono O'odham received help against Anglo and Hispanic ranchers from the weather. A three-year drought that caused ephemeral springs to dry up and well levels to fall reduced what remained of the vegetative cover on timbered and overgrazed sections of range, thus increasing the erosive force of subsequent storms. Between the drought, which killed 50 to 75 percent of the cattle in southern Arizona, and the general economic depression of 1893, many American ranchers abandoned what remained of their cattle herds. Native peoples took advantage of the withdrawal, appropriating cattle, wells, and range land. But Indian cattle suffered too as miners and ranchers abandoned their improvements and shut down pumps to wells once shared with native grazers. Competition for the land and resources returned with the rains. In 1897 and 1898, conflict between Tohono O'odham and Mexican ranchers reached the brink of open war when armed villagers crossed the international border to retrieve stolen cattle and horses. Confrontations increased as villagers took it upon themselves to defend their homeland against trespassers.[16]

In 1890, the Indian Bureau decided that in order to protect resources and speed Tohono O'odham assimilation, the San Xavier Reservation should undergo allotment. Agents allotted 41,600 acres to 291 male household heads. Each received 20 acres of farm land and 50 to 80 acres of mesquite timber land. The rest of the reservation—27,566 acres deemed worthless mesa land—was set aside for communal grazing. Allotting agent Stephen Whited reported that villagers kept 300 horses but only 50 head of cattle where there should have been 500. They had 300 to 400 acres under irrigation ditch, but the lack of water limited production to 100 acres of wheat and barley, making a "total remodeling of the ditches" necessary. The fields, he reported, were overgrown with weeds, and cultivation practices left much to be desired.

What they needed most, Whited wrote emphatically, was *"a good, industrious man to . . . teach them how to farm"*—farm in a white approved manner, he might have added, for he mistook the useful "in field herbs" and environmentally proven agricultural techniques for chaos.[17]

Water had long been a problem for San Xavier farmers. The community depended on two perpetual sources where subsurface geologic formations forced underground water to the surface in the bed of the ephemeral Santa Cruz River. The first, *Acequia de la Punta Agua*, surfaced upstream (south) from San Xavier. In the 1830s, José Martinez appropriated the spring by Mexican grant and dug an irrigation canal to water his fields. Floods in subsequent years eroded the canal into a barranca 60 to 100 feet wide and 6 to 20 feet deep. Later attempts to rehabilitate the barranca only increased erosion and lowered the surrounding water table. The second and more important source of water, *Agua de la Mision* near San Xavier del Bac, disappeared in 1883 when an earthquake disturbed the substrata, forcing water to the surface upstream from the San Xavier fields.

The drought of the early 1890s, the redistribution of land through allotment, and competition from area settlers aggravated the water problems at San Xavier. White farmers around Tucson dug trenches to intercept Santa Cruz water above San Xavier. Their efforts resulted in the creation of another eroded barranca that lowered the water table of the entire Santa Cruz Valley and diminished surrounding plant life, leading to ever greater erosion by seasonal runoff. By 1912 that barranca had consumed 150 acres of San Xavier farm land and forced the Indian Bureau to install expensive pumps to secure culinary and irrigation water from the river course.[18]

As water problems increased, the Indian Bureau appointed J. M. Berger as Farmer in Charge at San Xavier in 1894. Berger understood the situation better than most. Owner of the José Martinez land grant since the 1880s, Berger had been working with San Xavier farmers unofficially since 1891. Under his guidance they began reconstructing their irrigation system to meet the patterns of allotted land tenure and to counter the subsiding water table. Berger used his own farm as a demonstration plot and hounded the Indian Bureau and agent at Sacaton for a fair share of funds and agricultural equipment. There were no mechanical reapers or threshers at San Xavier, and plows were little more than forked mesquite limbs. Most serious was the wheat smut that had affected their crops and seed for years.[19]

With Berger's help, San Xavier O'odham expanded their fields to 1,000 cultivated acres in 1898 and 1,200 acres the following year. Harvests remained modest given insufficient water and tools, insect infestations, and late winter frosts. Those with a grain surplus faced discouragingly low prices, and families continued to earn cash by selling clay *ollas*, cordwood, or their labor in Tucson. Berger tried to convince families to move out of San Xavier del Bac and settle permanently on their own allotments because, in his estimation, traveling between village and field each day took too much time. The people knew better and resisted such an absolute move. Each year runoff from winter and summer storms flooded the fields, restoring their natural fertility. Flooding increased as villagers cut more cordwood from watershed timber allotments, making permanent field habitation precarious at best. Families maintained their adobe homes in San Xavier, while men used temporary brush shelters at the edge of their fields during the growing season.[20]

Neither Berger nor the agents at Sacaton paid much attention to the Tohono O'odham of the central *Papaguería*. They knew about their wage work, livestock interests, and *akchin* fields, and they were aware that the Desert People were nominally Sonoran Catholic yet continued to believe in their own Indian doctors and ceremonies. In 1890, the Indian Bureau considered allotting them land in the central *Papaguería* but found no land susceptible to "formal" irrigation or allotment. The Bureau considered moving them to the Pima and Maricopa reservations, where many worked as seasonal laborers, but Agent J. Roe Young downplayed that idea, calling them "ant-like" nomads who were "continually on the move," wandering with their livestock in a directionless search for water. The Tohono O'odham, Young reported, enjoyed their independence and "ask no help from the Government beyond the occasional issue of a spade or shovel." Later agents disagreed. Agent S. L. Taggart wrote:

> Nothing better than their precarious desert existence seems to have been offered them, and nothing better is in store for them unless . . . Congress is induced to pass some measure for providing them with land and water, on and with which by their labor a living more in keeping with their attempted civilization may be gained.

"Destitution," wrote Taggart, "has never yet proved a satisfactory civilizing influence."[21]

Tohono O'odham in a New Century

From the period of earliest Spanish contact through Mexican and then American control, the Tohono O'odham remained on the periphery of those expanding western societies. The people steadily lost land to all three but were never totally enclosed or controlled by these intruders. They retreated into unwanted lands and maintained their political organization and social customs. As people on the periphery of colonization, they were able selectively to adopt western innovations that contributed to their cultural and ecological well-being. But by the beginning of the twentieth century, increasing Indian Bureau programs designed to assimilate Indians threatened their cultural autonomy. In particular, the development of water resources for domestic, livestock, and agricultural use opened the door for more direct governmental intervention in the daily lives and political organization of the Tohono O'odham.[22]

In 1900, government farmer J. M. Berger felt pleased with the situation at San Xavier. "On the whole," he wrote, "there has been manifest a better appreciation of the value of the occupations pertaining to civilized life and a greater earnestness and persistence in pursuit of them." Berger sensed a pride in his allottees, who began to use the proceeds from sales of their improved grain harvests to make home improvements and to buy domestic and agricultural equipment. In 1901, San Xavier villagers received the first in a long string of appropriations designed to protect their water supply. Berger used the $3,000 to construct two new irrigation ditches, but late summer floods wiped out crops and filled the ditches with silt. Berger believed that more ditches would expand production at San Xavier and increase farmers' ability to purchase wagons and plows, but an 18-month drought in 1903–4 caused complete crop failures.[23]

In 1902, the Indian Bureau finally created a separate agency for the Tohono O'odham, making Berger agent at San Xavier. Berger knew the situation at San Xavier intimately but had little clear understanding of the people in the central interior. In 1902 he reported 533 San Xavier villagers, 344 O'odham living near Tucson, and several hundred more at Gila Bend, but counted only 1,639 Desert People—and this after living and working in the area for two decades. Three years later he conservatively estimated that they owned 3,500 cattle and 4,750 horses, mules, and burros. He reported that they received no rations and gained 80 percent of their subsistence from "civilized pursuits"—*akchin* farming, ranching, and wage work.[24]

San Xavier mission and village, looking west toward *Papagueria*, 1905.
Upham Collection, negative no. 65901, Arizona Historical Society, Tucson.

Wage work became an even more important seasonal activity and source of income for the Tohono O'odham in the twentieth century. The Desert People continued to harvest grain crops for the Gila River Pima, San Xavier O'odham, and area whites. Others moved nearer Tucson to perform domestic and unskilled wage labor or worked for the regional mines and railroads. In 1901, 180 Tohono O'odham men worked on railroad projects in California, Nevada, Arizona, and New Mexico, earning between $1.75 and $2.25 per day. "These Papago laborers gave satisfaction wherever they went," reported Berger, "and, in fact, several contractors informed me that they are preferable to white labor, principally for the reason that they are more peaceable and quiet and not troublesome as the white laborer. Probably the fact is that the Papago don't know yet how and when to strike for the purpose of bettering their conditions." The demand for "passive" nonunion Tohono O'odham workers continued through the first decade of the twentieth century as railroads expanded their coverage of the Southwest. The Indian Bureau even opened an Indian Employment office in Phoenix to place Indians in such jobs.[25]

By 1909, Indian Bureau officials realized they had to do something to protect Tohono O'odham lands in the central *Papagueria*—yet something short of establishing another reservation. Special agents visited the region and developed a plan to allot every adult 160 acres of grazing land or 80 acres of agricultural land, despite the fact that necessity and custom dictated a Two-Village lifestyle. They found the best agricultural land in the Baboquivari Valley and set about surveying that area first.[26]

The idea of allotment appealed particularly to those Tohono O'odham in the southern districts, where cattle ranching was becoming an established way of life. In May 1911, a group of Tohono O'odham men from the southern *Papagueria*—most of whom were Presbyterian, boarding school graduates, and considered to be "progressive" in their attitudes—established the Papago Good Government League to support educational efforts and the government allotment proposals. But opposition to allotment arose in the northern sections of the *Papagueria*, where people owned fewer cattle, practiced Sonoran Catholicism, and were more hesitant to accept the imposition of white rules and order. Superintendent Henry J. McQuigg reported that these people (along with a few families owning the largest cattle herds in the south) were "attached to the tribal system, and are much opposed to the allotment work done by the Government; as they prefer to hold the land in common as they have always done." Certain village councils feared that allotment and the withdrawal of school sections would attract more white settlers to compete for the limited resources of the *Papagueria*. But the program did not die until white cattlemen voiced their opposition to allotment, fearing that it would remove land from the public domain and give it to Indians.[27]

Water—its lack or periodic over-abundance—was the most critical issue facing the Tohono O'odham and Indian Bureau officials interested in protecting Indian resources and ensuring their self-sufficiency. At San Xavier, competition for water between Anglo, Hispanic, and O'odham farmers increased in the 1900s. Runoff erosion from overgrazed and logged water sheds widened and deepened the Santa Cruz River channel, lowering the valley water table. Each year San Xavier farmers and agency staff cleaned silt-filled ditches and constructed new canals to convey water to their allotments, but each year the water table fell further below their uptake canals. San Xavier council members petitioned the commissioner of Indian affairs to protect their water and prior appropriation rights.[28]

Between 1908 and 1912, the Irrigation Division of the Indian Bureau began serious study of water and flood plain erosion problems in the *Papaguería*. Along the Santa Cruz, irrigation officials proposed construction of an earthen dike four miles long across the river valley to slow erosion and divert flood waters into the eastern Santa Cruz River channel. From there water could be collected in underground infiltration galleries and delivered to San Xavier allotments through a closed-pipe gravity-feed system that would resist erosion, siltation, and evaporation. They argued that construction would create short-term jobs and that the finished project would provide water for 3,000 acres plus a surplus salable to non-Indian farmers, all at an estimated cost of $150,000.[29]

Superintendent McQuigg and farmer Charles A. Oertel strongly supported the water development and erosion control plan. Between 1909 and 1911, total cultivation at San Xavier fell by more than 50 percent. Oertel explained that the farmers were "very industrious and willing to undertake better methods of farming if they can be assured greater success by so doing," but that they refused to risk their precious seed after two seasons in which drought and then uncontrolled floods destroyed their summer plantings and buried their irrigation ditches. "Because of these floods," continued Oertel, "very few of the Indians attempt to grow any summer crop whatever, which if they could grow would double their income." In order to make up for lost crops, San Xavier allottees cut more cordwood from their timber allotments, ultimately increasing the intensity of storm runoffs, erosion, and flooding. McQuigg agreed "that unless something is speedily done to conserve and develop the present supply of water it will be necessary for these Indians to cease farming to any extent altogether, and there is no other occupation for them, who heretofore have always been farmers." The secretary of interior approved the irrigation project in 1911, but Congress never passed the needed appropriation.[30]

In 1912, summer floods once again destroyed earthen catchment dams hastily thrown up across the Santa Cruz channel, washed out irrigation ditches, and consumed planted fields at San Xavier. McQuigg blasted the Bureau: "It does not matter how many or how good implements you furnish them or how many employees are placed here to show them how to farm, unless they have sufficient water to irrigate their crops, they can not raise anything." He worried that if nothing was done about the irrigation system, "I am certain that they will have to give up farming altogether in a short time," leave the reservation in search of wage labor, and forfeit their prior appropriation water rights. As the situation grew worse, San Xavier councils decided a redistribution of the village *temporale* was in order to remedy flood damage and provide an equitable distribution of land and timber resources to those with none. But this time they found the decision was not theirs alone to make. The Indian Bureau refused to allow the land to be reallotted.[31]

A more serious threat to San Xavier land and water rights emerged in 1914 with the planned development of 20,000 acres to the north and south of the reservation. Tucson Farms Company had 22 wells drawing on the Santa Cruz valley water table upstream from the reservation and were preparing ditches to irrigate 4,000 acres. These wells lowered the water table substantially, leaving San Xavier high and dry. McQuigg and San Xavier leaders feared that the company would undermine water rights and then aggressively purchase fee-patent San Xavier allotments from discouraged villagers when the trust period ended in 1916. Under this threat, the Indian Bureau authorized an aggressive campaign of well drilling to maintain primary water rights and encourage farming, and honored village council requests that the trust period on San Xavier allotments be extended ten years.[32]

By 1918 the San Xavier Irrigation Unit consisted of four pumping stations with earthen dams on the Santa Cruz River and a mile long diversion dike to protect fields and bring runoff water into the main channel. Cultivated acreage leapt from 500 acres in 1915 to 1,800 acres in 1918. Superintendent Jewell D. Martin reported that water still limited their summer harvests by 30 percent. "[T]he amount of land they may put in depends more upon the water supply available for irrigation than upon getting the Indian to do it," wrote Martin who had just come from battling the intransigent Northern Utes, "for they are a very good bunch indeed to work with." San Xavier farmers donated much free labor to keep the system operating and, according to irrigation inspectors, were "entitled to a great deal of praise for the manner in which they are cultivating their lands, and utilizing the irrigation water provided."[33]

The lack of adequate agricultural equipment hampered San Xavier farming. Few individual farmers possessed the capital necessary to purchase modern power machinery on their meager earnings from hauling wheat, hay, and cordwood nine miles to Tucson. Others resisted taking out reimbursable loans for what they felt the government owed them outright. Instead, they made do with outdated hand equipment or borrowed and shared the few horse-drawn mechanical reapers, threshers, and hay presses available on the reservation. Patrick Johnny Franco recalled how they let horses trample the grain heads on a hardened dirt circuit; then men with baskets would "wait for a little wind to come and then we thresh it up in the air and let the straw blow away. . . ." Still, Peter Blaine, Sr., recalled that during this period, "You used to never see a spot on that San Xavier Reservation that wasn't cultivated. All year round we planted." Both Blaine and Theodore Rios remembered the people working their allotments together in groups, moving from one field to the next with the few agricultural implements they had, assisted by Desert People who traveled to San Xavier to help with the harvest in return for sacks of grain.[34]

As work went forward at San Xavier, the Bureau's Irrigation Division explored the development of water sources for the estimated five thousand Tohono O'odham living in the interior. John J. Granville surveyed the situation in 1911 and reported that livestock raising appeared to form their principal livelihood and that they, too, planted winter grain and summer vegetable crops, although on a much smaller scale than practiced at San Xavier. He observed that the costs of constructing and pumping deep wells (200 to 800 feet) would prove prohibitive and recommended instead that existing Tohono O'odham *akchin* farming techniques be fostered by upgrading their diversion dikes and ditches. *Charcos*, in his estimation, were still the best means for supplying adequate livestock and domestic water. Integrating these traditional techniques with strategic well drilling, instruction in dry farming, and the distribution of adequate tools would "give them more than a comfortable living." In 1912, Congress began appropriating annual reimbursable funds of up to $20,000 for developing domestic and stock water sources.[35]

Construction of these projects went forward as quickly as possible in the *Papaguería*. Irrigation crews sank wells at Santa Rosa, Topawa, and Indian Oasis (Sells). At Santa Rosa, the Keeper of the Smoke and conservative community members objected strongly to the well and pump. First, they objected to the location of the pump in the village center and got it moved. Second, they resented being asked to pay for a well they did not want. Third, the Keeper of the Smoke and other elders feared that it would put a halt to their old way of life and tie them to a dangerous single-village system. Finally, they believed that those drilling such holes ran the risk of unleashing terrible winds or salt water floods. Tribal oral traditions and shrines at Kaka and the Children's Shrine at Santa Rose warned of narrow escapes from such events. Even after the well went in, the Keeper of the Smoke warned that those who drank from it risked *ká:cim múmkidag*, "staying sickness," but nothing happened, and villagers began using the well against the Keeper's orders. Finally, late one night, villagers observed the Keeper himself using the well, and his general taboo lost force. Similar resistance and reactions accompanied well drilling in the northern *Papaguería* throughout the 1920s.[36]

As construction projects pressed into the interior *Papaguería*, the Indian Bureau gained its first clear picture of the lives and economies of the Desert People. Most of the Tohono O'odham continued their Field-to Well-Village movement and subsistence patterns, although where water permitted, some remained year round to plant winter wheat. In the south, those with large herds dispersed and moved more frequently, being unable to support their animals on the limited range around watering holes. Most families owned a few head and herded them collectively, a better ecological adaptation to scarce and scattered resources. Bureau of Plant Industry estimates at the time suggested that it took 120 acres of range to support each "cattle unit." Superintendent McQuigg recognized that environment and economic realities dictated a semi-nomadic life-style for the Desert People and that while allotment and water development might "anchor them more in one place," it would not change their basic "mode of life."[37]

In further surveys, irrigation officials estimated that the Tohono O'odham cultivated between nine and ten thousand acres in *akchin* fields—nearly two acres per person. Tohono O'odham farmers impressed agency personnel at the new subagency of Indian Oasis (Sells) by planting some 5,000 acres to winter grains in 1916, using the most basic agricultural implements—digging sticks and mesquite branch plows pulled by small horses. They reaped their crop with hand sickles, threshed it under horse hooves or with flails, and winnowed by hand, obtaining a low ten bushels per acre. But what worried officials most was overgrazed watersheds and the disappearance of heavy grass covers since 1870. Increased erosion and arroyo cutting in these areas made flood plain irrigation increasingly difficult and less thorough, as water moved too quickly across the *akchin* fields.[38]

In 1915, an Indian Bureau commission reported that 5,000 Tohono O'odham lived scattered across the *Papagueria* in 104 villages consisting of from 3 to 115 houses. They were impressed by the villagers' adaptation to the desert and recognized the limits of their own cultural assumptions:

> The Papago Indians by several hundred years of desert experience are thoroughly conversant with the conditions in their country, and with consummate judgment have so located their charcos and cultivated patches as to secure maximum results from the limited rainfall available. We cannot go into their country with the idea of teaching them farming or irrigation under conditions as we find them. Rather should we go to them to be taught.

Even experts from the Department of Agriculture learned much from the *akchin* techniques and crops like tepary beans. "Any attempt to introduce modern farming methods, as we understand them elsewhere," wrote the commission, "would result in disaster to the Papago Indians." Yet they could not resist recommending that the Indian Bureau provide "adaptable" modern farm equipment and seeds and teach the Tohono O'odham modern dry farming techniques.[39]

Commissioners praised the desert farmers but noted "that only those members of the tribe who have made any material progress at all are those who have given special attention to the cattle industry." In 1914, estimates placed Tohono O'odham livestock holdings at 30,000 to 50,000 cattle and 8,000 to 10,000 horses. While most owned small subsistence herds, several Tohono O'odham families in the southern grasslands had amassed herds on a commercial scale. In December 1914, a group of these "progressive" ranchers—many of them members of the Papago Good Government League—met at Indian Oasis (Sells) to organize the Papago Farmers Association. Their leaders, José Juan Pablo, Sam Cachora, and Richard Hendricks, discussed the continuing problem of Anglo and Hispanic ranchers and miners appropriating their range and water resources and the need to protect their rights. Sam Cachora called on his people to plant more grain on their farms and to raise more stock in order "to make better use of this desert land of ours, than our grand-fathers did." Over the next few years, the Papago Farmers Association helped sponsor Indian agricultural fairs and organized farm institutes in conjunction with the Extension Service to discuss livestock and farming techniques.[40]

By 1916, the importance of cattle was clear enough for the Indian Bureau to appoint José X. Pablo, a leading Tohono O'odham cattleman, as Stockman. Pablo faced several problems, among which was the growing conflict between Pancho Villa and the Mexican and United States armies. Border raiding and military activities made it difficult for Tohono O'odham ranchers to round up their livestock and retrieve cattle that drifted across the unfenced international boundary. As World War I heated up, so did tensions across the border. Under the guise of defending the border from "pro-German" attacks, Pablo and the Tohono O'odham requested and received arms, which they then used to "defend" their livestock and grazing lands.[41]

As part of their effort to protect Tohono O'odham resources in the *Papaguería*, the government finally set aside a reservation for the Desert People. On 14 January 1916, Woodrow Wilson established a 3.1-million-acre Papago Reservation. The Bureau transferred their agency from San Xavier to Indian Oasis, which the Tohono O'odham renamed Sells after Indian Commissioner Cato Sells. Wilson's executive order caught non-Indian citizens of Arizona by surprise. A coalition of ranchers, the Pima Farm Improvement Association, the state land commissioner, and the Tucson Chamber of Commerce joined forces to lobby for revocation of his order, hoping for a repeat of their success in getting William H. Taft to revoke four reservation orders in 1911 and 1912. Half a month later Wilson acquiesced, removing a jagged strip of 475,000 acres from the middle of the reservation. Tohono O'odham leaders demanded the return of the "strip," but the land remained tied up in litigation and white ownership for another twenty-one years.[42]

Reservation Agriculture and Ranching, 1917–1930

The Papago or "Sells" Reservation drew a great deal of attention, coming as the Indian Bureau was busy breaking up, not creating, reservations elsewhere. In 1919, Malcolm McDowell of the Board of Indian Commissioners reported that the 4,500 Tohono O'odham farmed 16,000 *akchin* acres while the San Xavier O'odham cultivated 1,500 acres in irrigated allotments. McDowell wrote of the Desert People, ". . . it is doubtful if agriculture is adventured under more adverse conditions than obtain in this land. With a persistence which years of repeated disappointment have failed to discourage the desert Indians continue to force the arid land to yield wheat, corn, beans, melons and other produce." In 1918, a light rain year, they harvested 300,000 pounds of corn and 1,800,000 pounds of beans, while the irrigated San Xavier farms produced 10,000 bushels of wheat and 350 tons of barley hay. McDowell noted that villagers continued to plant twice each season when there was any possibility of rain, but that the arid environment returned an adequate crop only once every three years.[43]

The Bureau's Irrigation Division kept busy trying to correct that perceived imbalance. Between 1917 and 1933 they developed 29 drilled wells, four shallow wells, and 31 *charcos* on the Papago and San Xavier reservations. Scattered resistance to well and dam construction continued in the northern *Papaguería*. At Big Fields village near Sells, the local residents opposed a planned well. They wanted neither the cost of the project nor the government school that seemed to pop up at every well. "They propose to be left alone and want nothing that tends toward civilization," reported Superintendent Thomas F. McCormick. In 1925, the same individuals opposed construction of an irrigation dam that they argued would ruin their *akchin* fields and attract more cattle to their already overgrazed range. The government allowed construction of the Menager dam despite local opposition, and when it failed as predicted, it left a large area of overgrazed and eroded land.[44]

The Irrigation Division met less resistance in the eastern and southern *Papaguería*. In 1919, at San Xavier, water from five wells reached 1,260 acres through 25 miles of irrigation canals and laterals. Villagers organized the San Xavier Farm Bureau and Water Users Association to improve their farming and irrigation methods through cooperative land improvement, cultivation, and water control. They received help from the Pima County Farm Bureau and the Arizona Agricultural College in Tucson. Southern ranchers welcomed the addition of *charcos* and government-operated wells. Cattle needed to be kept within three miles of water, causing large concentrations and overgrazing around existing sources. Carefully scattered wells and *charcos* opened up range heretofore beyond their reach but did not eliminate the problem of overgrazing. In 1919, officials estimated that 3,000 Tohono O'odham

owned 30,000 cattle and as many horses—five to six times the estimated carrying capacity of the range.[45]

"Livestock now is and ever will be the mainstay of the nomadic Papagoes [*sic*]," wrote Malcolm McDowell. He and others recognized that
the Tohono O'odham succeeded in their harsh environment where
others failed partly because their "scrub" stock proved better able to
survive on the scattered grasses, cactus, and even mesquite beans. But
concerned with overgrazing, the Indian Bureau in concert with Stockman José X. Pablo and the Papago Livestock Association began investigating ways to reduce the number of feral cattle and horses on the range
and to improve domestic cattle quality through selective breeding programs. The large number of cattle scattered across the *Papaguería* and
the Tohono O'odham love of horses as status symbols made the project
nearly impossible.[46]

What seemed beyond the means of human plans, nature accomplished in three straight years of drought (1921–1923). Livestock
browse disappeared, and natural *tinajas* and deep wells in the *Papaguería*
dried up. Tohono O'odham stockmen were unable to get reasonable
prices for their livestock in the glutted markets of Tucson and Mexico.
During the drought native ranchers lost over one-third of their cattle
and horse herds.

The drought affected farming as well. Without rain, *akchin* fields
remained unplanted, and families returned to their Well villages or left
the reservation to seek wage work. The drought was so severe that the
deep well at Sells dried up and the Indian Bureau considered moving
the agency back to San Xavier, until their irrigation wells went dry too.
The drought convinced officials at Sells that *akchin* agriculture was not
dependable more than once in five years and that "it is useless to plan
on any agricultural industries here."[47]

Villagers in the northern districts of the *Papaguería* responded to
the drought in very traditional ways—by moving to their Well villages,
increasing their reliance on gathered desert foods, and working through
their *Náwai't* ceremony to "bring down the clouds." But the *Náwai't*,
with its ritual consumption of *tiswin*, brought down the wrath of Bureau
officials already trying to stamp out native ceremonies and especially the
consumption of intoxicating beverages. At the height of the drought in
1922, agency police raided Big Fields and Santa Rosa, two villages
noted for their resistance to government wells and schools. There they
dispersed crowds of 200 to 300 celebrants and arrested "unprogressive"
leaders and Keepers of the Smoke for making *tiswin*. Superintendent
Thomas McCormick reported that the practice would be hard to stop
even after such arrests, for the people firmly believed that "if they gave
up the making of 'tiswin,' it would mean starvation for their wives and
children, as it would never rain again." Despite warnings and more arrests, Tohono O'odham throughout the northern *Papaguería* continued
to hold their ceremonies in secret, collecting an estimated 450,000

pounds of fruit annually through the 1930s and processing most of it into syrup for *tiswin*.[48]

In early 1924, the rains returned in sufficient quantities to fill *charcos* on the Papago Reservation and produce a winter wheat crop for the first time in three years. The 100,000 bushels sold for $1.60 per hundred pounds on the reservation and $2.15 in Tucson, and cattle prices rebounded to five cents per pound. The Bureau of Plant Industry planned to test new drought-resistant species on the reservation, and agency farmer A. M. Philipson attempted to organize Boys' and Girls' Clubs at San Xavier to demonstrate the potentials for "progressive employment" in agriculture. He set aside land on the 30-acre agency farm but never got more than a dozen boys interested in the program, because drought returned in the fall, destroying all summer crops and causing cattle prices to plummet again. Superintendent McCormick suggested eliminating the position of agency farmer altogether because "farming . . . is a losing proposition and their own system is the only system that can be used in this locality with any degree of success, and even with this system it means a crop only every four or five years." "The cattle industry," McCormick concluded, "is the only salvation of the Papagoes [*sic*], and I hope to see this developed in a short time to such an extent that the entire reservation will have nothing but white faced cattle."[49]

By the end of the 1920s there were nearly 5,000 full-blood Tohono O'odham. Superintendent Edward S. Steward reported that 850 people

Tohono O'odham Indians farming near Sells, 1920s. Negative no. 9979, Arizona Historical Society, Tucson.

(120 San Xavier and 730 Desert O'odham) "engage more or less in what we call farming operations," cultivating an average of ten acres. Despite instruction in deep plowing and planting techniques from University of Arizona instructors, observers noted that the Desert People continued to reproduce older methods in locating, irrigating, and cultivating their fields. Ascension Anton recalled that around Tecalote in the south, his father had an *akchin* farm, "and when they harvested their crop they gave it out to their relatives and when they did the planting they did it together." Across the reservation 700 individuals owned 25,000 head of cattle and even more horses "of little value," despite campaigns to "eliminate the inferior horses from the reservation and to encourage the increasing of cattle." In 1928, the Bureau reported an "annual average industrial return" of $700,000 for the Tohono O'odham: 20 percent from agriculture, 15 percent from firewood sales, 12 percent from livestock, 8 percent from basketry and other crafts, and a surprising 45 percent from wage work.[50]

Wage work became the chief source of income for the Tohono O'odham in the first two decades of the twentieth century. Some took agency jobs or worked for the Irrigation Division, drilling wells and maintaining pumps and ditches on the reservations. By the mid-1910s, 300 to 500 Tohono O'odham lived on the outskirts of Tucson performing domestic and wage labor in the city. The Indian Bureau appointed field matrons to reside in Tucson and oversee the employment of Indian women and the condition of family life in the urban setting. Tohono O'odham men worked in the Phelps-Dodge Corporation's New Cornelia mines at Ajo and performed seasonal labor for non-Indian ranchers and farmers.[51]

The demand for southwestern farm labor exploded in the 1910s when non-Indian farmers began raising commercial crops of long staple cotton. In 1914 the Indian Bureau assigned Pima superintendent Frank Thackery the task of overseeing Indian labor in the Salt River Valley cotton fields—to ensure that the growers had enough labor and that the Indians were treated fairly. When World War I cut access to Egyptian cotton and a simultaneous boll weevil infestation hit the Deep South, industries turned to southwestern cotton. By 1918 the Southwest Cotton Company, a subsidiary of Goodyear Tire and Rubber Company that needed cotton to make pneumatic tires, was the largest producer in the region. Even after the war, cotton growers needed 1,000 permanent workers and 5,000 to 6,000 seasonal workers to tend and harvest their crops and in 1925 could not find enough laborers to care for their 12,500 acres of cotton.[52]

Tohono O'odham families traveled to and from the cotton fields on a seasonal basis, earning between 2 and 3.5 cents per pound and gaining a reputation as "exceedingly competent and conscientious workers," favored by the growers over Mexican laborers. Growers did complain that they often came late following their pilgrimage to Magdalena,

Sonora in October for the Feast of Saint Francis, and then left early to plant their winter wheat crops. Superintendent McCormick replied:

> Regardless of the price for picking cotton, you cannot induce the Papago to remain away from the reservation and work for wages if the prospects of a crop are good on the reservation. In spite of the many crop failures these Indians will plant every year and have done so for generations, and it will be impossible, and I do not believe it would be practical, to give up this practice of planting crops on the reservation and go and establish homes off the reservation and become day laborers.

Even though the drought of the early 1920s encouraged more families to travel to the Salt River Valley to pick cotton, few settled permanently away from their reservation villages or gave up cultivating their *akchin* fields.[53]

The creation of the Papago Reservation, the work of the Irrigation Division of the Indian Bureau, and the expansion of off-reservation wage work opportunities increased Tohono O'odham participation in and dependency on government programs and the marketplace. But despite such changes, the people maintained central features of their cultural matrix. Most Desert People reproduced their Well-Field Village residence pattern and continued to plant their *akchin* fields and hunt and gather as they had always done. They received few if any government rations or supplies and prided themselves on their industrial self-sufficiency. Local village headmen and consensual decision-making councils remained the fundamental political unit. Despite government suppression, villagers continued to use Indian "doctors" and observe central group rituals, blending the old with the introduced in their own syncretic Sonoran Catholicism. Unlike other tribal groups, few O'odham intermarried with Anglos or Hispanics, and while many spoke Spanish, few learned English. As the physical and economic isolation of the *Papaguería* shrank in the 1920s, so did the people's ability to escape the momentous political, economic, and environmental changes of the 1930s.

Papaguería in the 1930s

In a meeting with San Xavier leaders in March 1930, E. H. Hammond, supervisor of Indian education, reported that the villagers complained of whites pumping water from the Santa Cruz River Valley. Antoni Moreno of San Xavier spoke for the farmers: "We don't have enough water to raise crops which we use ourselves. My land is lying idle because of lack of water. We have been promised many times these past few years but no water in sight yet; when we ask about it we are told to plant cotton, vegetables and more crops but we can't do it without water." That year the San Xavier O'odham watched 1,100 acres of crops wither for lack of moisture. The Indian Bureau demonstrated cotton farming as both a good cash crop and as an alternative for San Xavier farmers, whose fields were worn from continuous and unrotated wheat cropping. Despite depressed markets and the lack of water, two farmers, Frank Rios and Victor Bell, raised nine acres of cotton yielding 8.5 bales (4,600 lbs.) and seed worth $481. But this small success did little to convince other San Xavier farmers to alter their methods or crops without reassurance of more water.[54]

Later that year, San Xavier farmers and agency personnel told members of the Senate Subcommittee on Indian Affairs their familiar story. Harry H. Encanas described cultivating three acres of wheat and barley hay on his 50-acre farm. His case was not unusual among the 85 families farming at San Xavier because, as Agency Farmer Andrew Philipson explained, government cut-backs on expensive pumping plants left only enough water for 300 acres, one-fifth of the field area. Even worse, villagers were still paying off reimbursable loans on wells now abandoned by the government. Experts identified the source of the problem as Tucson. City wells developed on the Santa Cruz above San Xavier appropriated water to which the O'odham had historic prior rights, lowering the water table and leaving all but the deepest wells high and dry. But little had been done to remedy the situation.[55]

Water was also a concern for Tohono O'odham living in the central *Papaguería*, who farmed 18,000 acres of *akchin* fields and owned 20,000 head of cattle and 12,000 horses. According to Stockman José X. Pablo, the people planted every year but made only one crop in three because of the lack of water. They resisted farming their *temporales* communally, yet grazed family livestock in collective village herds. Pablo claimed that nearly every family owned some cattle. While the average herd size was 25 to 30 head, Pablo himself owned 250 cattle and the Toros family ran 2,000 head in the south. Pablo voiced his people's need for more wells and *charcos* to evenly distribute stock water throughout the *Papaguería* and remedy local overgrazing.[56]

Tohono O'odham concerns were symptomatic of larger problems looming on the national horizon. In the early 1930s, economic collapse and widespread environmental degradation ushered in a new activist philosophy in federal government called the New Deal. In 1934 Congress passed the Indian Reorganization Act, and Tohono O'odham leaders met to decide whether or not to adopt a central tribal government.

The issue was not a new one. In 1929, agency officials organized a Papago General Council to deal with issues surrounding a tentative claims case against the government. Two organizations vied for control of that council: the Papago Good Government League, whose members were mainly young, Protestant, boarding-school-educated Indians with "progressive" ideals from the southern Papago Reservation; and the League of Papago Chiefs, organized in 1925 by conservative Catholic leaders from San Xavier and the northern Papago Reservation, representing older Tohono O'odham ideals. They had locked horns earlier over the issue of whether to regain mineral rights excluded when the reservations were formed (Good Government) or to maintain the status quo and protect O'odham jobs in the mines at Ajo (Papago Chiefs). Both groups reemerged to debate the IRA and the form it should take on their reservations. Agency superintendents feared that the Papago Chiefs would undermine the proceedings, but league members merely desired full discussion and traditional consensus decision-making on the issue. Members of the Good Government League dominated the proceedings, ultimately influencing the character of the new tribal government.[57]

In preparation for organizing under the IRA, Superintendent T. B. Hall and the General Council divided the Papago Reservation into nine political and grazing districts, plus districts for San Xavier and Gila Bend, based as closely as possible on recognized dialectic and grazing use patterns. On 15 December 1934, Tohono O'odham voters approved the IRA 1,443 to 188 votes, with only 47.5 percent of those eligible participating. Stockman José X. Pablo became acting chairman of the provisional tribal council, which met to prepare a constitution and by-laws for the Papago Indian Tribe. To fund itself, the council voted a tax of 10 percent on wages derived from government relief jobs, not to exceed five dollars per month, and set aside 50 percent of that money for reimbursable development loans.

After voters approved the tribal constitution in January 1937, each district organized a formal council that elected two representatives to the Papago Tribal Council. Of the eleven district councils, Superintendent Hall noted that "the Indians in practically every instance coming to my attention to date have re-designated the men who have always served as leaders in the several villages." District councils made up of headmen and Keepers of the Smoke reproduced older patterns of local leadership and decision-making and until World War II maintained—along with village councils—more influence and control over Tohono O'odham affairs than did the tribal council.[58]

While these political changes were going on, the federal government instituted New Deal conservation programs to counter economic and environmental problems in the *Papaguería*. Between 1933 and 1942, the government funded Indian Emergency Conservation Work (IECW) projects on both the Papago and San Xavier reservations. Later subsumed under the Indian Division of the Civilian Conservation Corps, these projects included water development and erosion control works, livestock and range rehabilitation, and the construction of fences, roads, and telephone lines throughout the Papago Reservation. CCC-ID jobs became an important source of income for the Tohono O'odham, and fewer left the reservation to work in the mines at Ajo or in the cotton fields of the Salt River Valley once they found federal employment closer to home.[59]

The most important CCC-ID projects were those concerned with water development and erosion control. They included drilling wells, developing natural springs, building *charcos*, installing concrete and metal water tanks, and constructing diversion dikes and runoff channels to mitigate the problems of sheet erosion and to bring the runoff into productive use. Plans called for the development of such water projects at each village and scattered at three-mile intervals across the *Papaguería* to accommodate livestock. Between 1933 and 1938 the CCC-ID constructed 91 wells, 159 *charcos*, 2 masonry dams, and 41 storage tanks, and developed 36 natural springs.

In 1938, CCC-ID officials turned their attention from water development to flood-water farming projects. Under their direction, Tohono O'odham laborers constructed six *bolsas*, or "pockets," following a Mexican design. *Bolsas* differed from *charcos* in that they were banked fields up to several hundred acres, situated to catch and impound runoff from an arroyo. When the *bolsa* had a foot or more standing water, farmers sealed the field and allowed the water to percolate into the soil, which they then planted—a practice not compatible with the clay-bottomed *charco*, which was a culinary and stock watering pond, not an irrigation structure. Government officials expressed great hopes for this type of pre-irrigated field farming.[60]

While the Tohono O'odham benefited greatly from some of these projects, others failed to work as well as traditional methods of developing and storing water. In 1933, villagers of Pisinimo complained through Father Bonaventure Oblasser that the open masonry and metal surface storage tanks constructed by the local irrigation representative were unacceptable. "They state, they would rather die of thirst, than drink such water. Their own charcos do not have the steep sides of the ground tanks, and consequently Lizards, Desert Rats, Snakes, &c. do not drown in them. Furthermore the great surface of the Indian ponds gives them a large aeration space, which Mr. Richardson's ponds do not possess." Other villages voiced similar complaints, preferring the construction of *charcos* over open ground tanks.

Similarly, *bolsas* constructed to aid *akchin* farming proved ineffective and even detrimental. The *Papaguería* offered less water and a shorter growing season than *bolsa* sites in Mexico. Poor location and construction techniques left weak walls and uneven bottoms. One of the six washed out before completion and several others followed by 1950, accelerating flood plain erosion and leaving large areas denuded of vegetation. Finally, most *bolsas* were too big and too complicated in operation for one man or family to handle alone, and existing beliefs and economic attitudes continued to work against collective farming.[61]

Other CCC-ID projects revolved around the Tohono O'odham livestock industry. Early travelers in the *Papaguería* noted the extensive climax grasslands of bush muhly (*Muhlenbergia porteri*) and later grama and bunch grasses, but years of inadequate rainfall and an overabundance of cattle and horses resulted in the diminution of grass ranges. The suppression of natural and human-set fires in the nineteenth century inhibited grass regeneration and allowed woody shrubs to take over much of the grassland. Lower than normal precipitation, declining water tables, and heavy grazing diminished native ground cover in other areas and increased the frequency and severity of sheet erosion, gullying, and floods. The remaining soils absorbed more heat and less water, raising the average temperature of the region by as much as four degrees and setting the stage for further erosion and desertification. Between 1935 and 1939 the CCC-ID experimented with range reseeding projects, first on the San Xavier and then on the Papago Reservation. Range specialists tried a variety of exotic and native grasses using natural reseeding methods on closed ranges, but the lack of precipitation limited their success.[62]

In addition to range rehabilitation efforts, the CCC-ID began fencing the nine Papago Reservation grazing districts as the first step in an effective stock reduction and management program. In 1930, the Tohono O'odham owned 30,000 cattle and 12,000 horses. Drought, disease, and sales reduced their herds to 20,000 cattle and 8,000 horses by 1935, but the range remained overstocked. Agency officials, the Papago Tribal Council, and district councils approved limits on the number of animals any family could run and even considered mandatory reduction quotas for horses. But ranchers ignored district rules and countered by hiding or under reporting the size of their herds.[63]

Agency personnel encouraged ranchers to participate in the process by creating district livestock associations to coordinate grazing, breed-

Tohono O'odham cowboys, ca. 1920. Negative no. 21,395, Arizona Historical Society, Tucson.

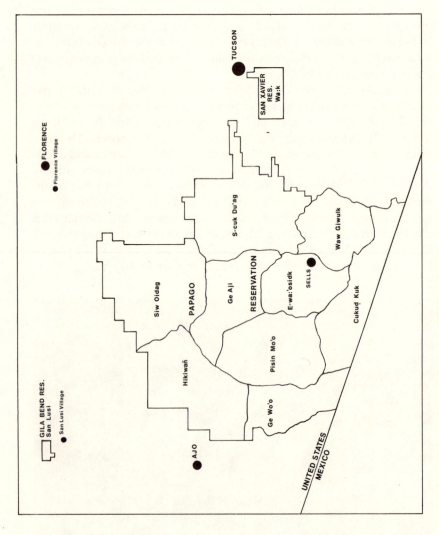

6. Papago Reservations and Grazing Districts, 1930s

ing, and sales. At a tribal meeting in 1935, Tohono O'odham headmen and ranchers universally spoke against the proposed regulations. Barnabe Lopez of San Pedro told the council, "While back, many years ago . . . we had our own ways of working our country and our cattle. . . . I don't see why anybody should try to put something over us like that [association], because I don't see anything wrong with how we are running our reservation." José Petero of San Lorenzo stressed that "I know my rules from way back here. I have been making my living and I believe in my rules. . . . We never had any trouble according to the rules we had." Tony Norris of Vamori decried the "White man's" way of sauntering in "to show what was to be done on this dry desert land," and then failing. "Now us Indians, what little help we get from our dry farms, we make a living. Our cattle is what we make our living." He feared association rules would take away individual initiative and control, basic Tohono O'odham economic values.[64]

By June 1936, CCC-ID crews had fenced nearly all of the grazing districts of the Papago Reservation. Many family ranchers disapproved of the arbitrary district boundaries and fences that kept them from moving herds between traditional ranges and water holes. Villagers distrusted stock programs and refused to cede the right to administer their own range and the number of livestock on it. They continued to appoint village hunt leaders as roundup bosses—reproducing local political rights and organization within a transformed political landscape. Such persistent village-level control allowed more livestock to graze than district rules permitted and created conflict between districts over trespass.[65]

Agency superintendents had little luck convincing Tohono O'odham ranchers to improve their livestock or to participate in group sales. Ranchers continued to judge their Spanish longhorn stock on the basis of horn size. In an effort to change their minds, the Indian Bureau imported 720 cattle from New Mexico to form a tribal herd and issued 845 Herefords to families on a reimbursable basis. But the demonstration was less than successful when only 12 of the New Mexican cattle survived the winter of 1935–36, and families failed to return sufficient Hereford yearlings to sustain a revolving fund. Likewise, attempts to convince Tohono O'odham ranchers to cull their herds of weak stock and participate in organized district or association sales fared poorly. While bulk sales improved the overall market price paid for each owner's livestock, ranchers resisted, suspecting agency motives and preferring the flexibility and autonomy of individual sales.[66]

To the Tohono O'odham, cattle were a "walking checkbook." In their minds, large herds represented wealth, which smaller herds, even of better quality stock, could not match. Whenever a person needed cash, he or she simply went out and sold as many cattle as required at that particular moment. Charles Whitfield, a range management specialist on the Papago Reservation during the 1930s, recalled that the people did not keep money in the bank. "His bank's walking out on that reservation, and therefore, as . . . he needs cash, he goes out and sells." These periodic, small-lot sales by individual ranchers reduced the price per pound they received but allowed them much greater freedom and control over their economic life. Cattle also served as a source of instant food for celebrations, barter, or for *níari*, the traditional gift exchange reproduced with an introduced foodstuff. Cattle had become a major subsistence resource, incorporating some of the symbolic meanings of older parallel activities and resources. For these reasons, many Tohono O'odham resisted anything that faintly resembled stock reduction, including district livestock associations, grazing rules, and cooperative sales.[67]

If cattle were a checkbook—a means to an end—horses remained prestige animals—an end in themselves. Often of little value in white economic terms, horses were prized more than cattle. Indian Bureau officials blamed horses for occupying range more productively used by cattle, eating grasses closer to the ground, and cutting up the land with their hooves, thereby contributing to erosion. In the early 1940s, dourine spread throughout the Southwest, and agency officials began testing and destroying Tohono O'odham horses in order to halt the epidemic. They tried to soothe disgruntled owners by convincing them that for years too many horses had hurt their range and cattle industry. But many people believed just the opposite—that the range was in bad condition because too many horses were being killed off. "The horse is endowed with magic powers," they told Alice Joseph and her investigating team, "and the white men are only asking for trouble when they slaughter sick animals."[68]

Agency Stockman José X. Pablo worried about livestock associations, the initiative and autonomy they would remove. In council he expressed Tohono O'odham pride in independence, their relationship to their animals and to the market place.

> Ever since I have been a small boy I have noticed that when an Indian cattleman gets out on his horse and goes through his herds of cattle, when the Indian gets on his horse he thinks he is in his glory when he is out among his cattle gathering them to sell. When the Indian gathers his cattle he sells them and collects his money for them, then he puts it in his pocket and he jingles it and his chest stands out as he rides among his own people.

The relationship of man, horse, cattle, and market was not lost on his listeners, who felt their control slipping away.[69]

Ultimately, stock reduction and improvement projects made some headway on the reservation, but the government consistently failed to convince Tohono O'odham ranchers that smaller herds of high-quality stock would bring the same economic return as larger poor-quality herds and allow overgrazed range to regenerate. The Tohono O'odham refused to believe that their range problems were a result of overgrazing. Peter Blaine, Sr., a Tohono O'odham assistant forester at the time, opposed formal stock reduction. He recalled:

I say that we never overgrazed! The thing that cut down our cattle was drought. If the drought hits, grass dies. We leave it up to the drought, he'll cut down on cattle. We didn't get rid of our cattle just because someone told us to. . . . We didn't see any sense in cutting our cattle down; we took our chances with the rain. If it rains, good. If not, then we are hurt. If cattle are going to die, let them die. But they will die right here on their reservation. Right here in their own country. That was the answer that we gave the white man and his Agency.

Blaine's response demonstrates the syncretic blending of Tohono O'odham values with white technical knowledge. Robert D. Holtz, Blaine's supervisor, agreed that drought was far more important than overgrazing in range depletion and erosion. Federal stock reduction programs did little to relieve overgrazing on the Papago Reservation. In 1939, the Tohono O'odham still owned 27,000 cattle and 18,000 horses. Livestock reduction efforts continued into the 1940s but, in the end, drought and animal diseases such as dourine, black leg, and hoof-and-mouth disease accomplished what government programs failed to achieve.[70]

The 1930s also spelled trouble for Tohono O'odham farmers as both the number of farmers and the acreage they cultivated began to decline. Water, the lack of it or the destructive force of flash floods, continued to limit field production. Reimbursable costs of irrigation projects weighed heavily on farmers despite governmental cancellation of large parts of that debt. Small field size and the lack of modern agricultural equipment kept their agriculture labor-intensive and subsistence oriented at the very time white farmers were expanding their field size to take advantage of modern machinery and market production. More and more Tohono O'odham neglected their irrigated farms and *akchin* fields in order to take government conservation jobs or find wage work in the neighboring mines and cotton fields.[71]

In 1935 and 1936, Superintendent Hall estimated that the Desert People farmed 12,000 acres in either winter or summer crops and that people in the north and west continued to follow a mobile subsistence round that included farming, hunting and gathering, herding, and seasonal wage labor. He reported one "commercial" farm of 640 acres at Chuichu in the north where 26 Tohono O'odham families cultivated 300 acres with the help of two electrically operated wells. Hall admitted that the $125,000 Chuichu Project was more "subsistence" than "commercial," despite subsidized irrigation and the proximity of a market in Casa Grande. At San Xavier, village farmers irrigated 600 acres of the 1,500-acre village field, producing "subsistence crops" with some wheat and grass hay for market in Tucson. The government canceled more than two-thirds of the $311,191 in reimbursable funds expended for irrigation at San Xavier, but farmers there still struggled under an enormous debt. Papago Agency staff paid little attention to the Gila Bend Reservation, which contained one village used as "a rendezvous for about forty Papago families who wander up and down the Gila and Salt River Valleys, supporting themselves largely by seasonal farm and ranch wages."[72]

By the end of the 1930s, family income for the 6,184 members of the Papago Tribe averaged $650: 41 percent from off-reservation wage work, 20 percent from government wage work, 18 percent from livestock, 12 percent from subsistence and market agriculture, and 19 percent from gathered foods and the sale of handicrafts and cordwood. Superintendent Hall worried about this growing dependence on wage labor, since government CCC-ID work was coming to an end and people were losing jobs in the mines and cotton fields to mechanization. Even cordwood sales were in jeopardy because of the installation of a natural gas pipeline in Tucson. Hall foresaw the need to expand Tohono O'odham agriculture and handicraft enterprises to cover these pending reductions in wage earnings.[73]

During the 1930s, Tohono O'odham ceremonialism underwent a period of modest renewal. Participation in the Feast of Saint Francis, held each October in Magdalena, Sonora, remained strong. Village Keepers of the Smoke renewed the open practice of *Náwai't* with the consumption of *tiswin* to bring rain to the land. Anthropologist Ruth Underhill reassured Indian commissioner John Collier that *tiswin* was harmless and that "the ceremony is dearer to the Papago heart than any other; they still feel that, without it, there would be no rain and an attempt to interfere with it would bring profound resentment." New ceremonies made their appearance among a people undergoing rapid change. In 1930 the 90-year-old Keeper of the Smoke at Santa Rosa village had visions directing him to compose songs for a ceremony to revitalize the old ways before whites overwhelmed them. In 1931 and 1933, the Keeper directed Santa Rosa villagers in songs and dances that made use of huge effigies representing places and things in his vision. This ceremony died with its originator, but older ceremonial traditions continue to the present day.[74]

Agricultural Decline, Post-1940

In 1940, 80 percent of the 1,200 Tohono O'odham families living on the three reservations continued to do some subsistence farming. Agricultural produce represented only one-sixth of the average family income, but nearly every farming family depended on that produce for their basic subsistence. As New Deal programs came to a close in the early 1940s, many men entered military service or returned to the cotton fields of the Gila and Salt River valleys in search of seasonal wage work. In 1943 a serious drought decimated both *akchin* and irrigated farms and the Tohono O'odham livestock industry. Up to 123 families applied for relief—the first ever large-scale distribution of rations. Nearly 3,500 Tohono O'odham left the reservation to pick cotton that fall. Most returned to harvest what subsistence crops they could and to plant winter wheat, but few farmers produced a marketable surplus of wheat or hay after 1940.[75]

The number of Tohono O'odham farmers and the extent of their cultivated acreage declined steadily in the 1940s. In 1944, Tohono O'odham on the Papago and San Xavier reservations worked nearly 5,000 acres of *akchin* and 2,125 acres of pump irrigated fields. Actual cultivation of the irrigated fields at San Xavier and Chuichu hovered around 50 per cent, and harvests of hay, wheat, corn, and beans on that land fell well below what non-Indian farmers in the area produced. Superintendent William Head emphasized that most Desert People possessed *akchin* fields but that many had fallen into disuse due to erosion from overgrazing. People from at least two villages—Santa Rosa (Gu Achi) and Big Fields (Gu Oidak)—continued their yearly migrations between Field and Well villages. Five years later farmers cultivated only 1,252 acres on both reservations, one-tenth of the approximately 12,900 acres cultivated in 1936.[76]

The cattle industry fared a little better. In 1940, 27,000 cattle and 18,000 horses shared a range with an estimated carrying capacity of 11,000 cattle and 1,000 horses per year. A dourine epidemic led to the wholesale destruction of horses in the early 1940s, and stockmen lost 5,000 cattle and sold another 15,000 at extremely low prices during the 1943 drought. The deep cattle reductions hit small herd owners hardest, driving many out of business and opening up the range for larger herd owners. By 1944, only 55 percent of the 1,200 Tohono O'odham families owned cattle, and fewer than 200 of those earned more than fifty dollars cash each year from sales. The Papago Tribal Council set stricter limits on the number of livestock each owner could keep on a grazing district. It also instituted a 3 percent tax on cattle sales to finance a revolving cattle program aimed at improving stock quality and restarting family enterprises decimated by the drought.

Just as herds and the number of families owning cattle began to rebound in the late 1940s, quarantines for black leg and hoof-and-mouth disease closed outside markets to Indian cattle. In 1947, 855 of 1,183 resident families owned 11,888 cattle, but the distribution remained skewed—69 percent of those families owned fewer than 10 cattle, and 96 percent owned fewer than 50. In 1948 the Papago Tribe terminated its debt-ridden revolving cattle program, and by 1949 only 673 families owned some of the 8,858 head of cattle. Five families, all but one from the southern grazing districts, continued to own the vast majority of livestock.[77]

The expenditure of one million dollars in the 1950s to develop and distribute deep wells and *charcos* throughout the grazing districts restimulated the Tohono O'odham livestock industry. Holdings rose from 13,000 cattle and 7,000 horses in 1950 to 15,000 cattle in 1960. Overgrazing remained a very real problem on range land with an estimated carrying capacity of 12,000 cattle units. Livestock remained unequally distributed. While 50 percent of Tohono O'odham families living on the reservations owned livestock in 1959, fewer than 5 percent of those owned 80 percent of the cattle. Gross livestock sales surpassed $750,000, but the majority of families used their few cattle for subsistence, not market sales. Ranchers lost some of their distrust of livestock associations and formed eight regional associations between 1951 and 1964. District associations allowed livestock management to be decided locally without undue tribal or federal supervision, reproducing local versus tribal forms of political and economic organization. The livestock industry remained strong in the 1960s and 1970s, but only a few families owned the majority of the 18,000 to 20,000 head of cattle. As recently as 1987, reports indicated that the range continued to be overstocked by 158 percent, with 26,300 head of livestock.[78]

In 1950, 800 tribal members lived permanently off the reservation, working year round in the cotton fields of the Gila and Santa Cruz river valleys. As many as 2,000 Tohono O'odham men joined them for seasonal work, taking as many as 4,500 people away from the reservation during the one-hundred-day cotton harvest. Others lived and worked in Tucson. The pattern was an old one, but, increasingly, wage workers and their families did not return to the reservation to plant or harvest their crops. Over half let their *akchin* fields grow wild, and others sold what few cattle they owned or left them in the care of relatives. Tohono O'odham workers earned $600,000 in gross wages picking Arizona cotton in the boom year of 1950, but as mechanization increased throughout the 1950s, they retained only the most intensive hand-labor jobs like thinning and weeding.[79]

In an attempt to maintain tradition and the agricultural viability of their land, the tribal council submitted a $23 million Papago Rehabilitation Program to Congress. Part of that program called for the expenditure of $5.25 million to bring water to 18,200 acres of land. Such development, they argued, would increase the agricultural self-sufficiency of the Tohono O'odham. In 1955, tribal chairman Mark Manuel testified that the bill was necessary to aid the 450 Tohono O'odham families earning a substandard living and the 600 families receiving tribal or federal relief. The Tohono O'odham, he explained, were about 25 years behind the more progressive non-Indian farmers and ranchers in equipment, farming techniques, and agricultural knowledge. Congress considered but never passed the request, in part out of fiscal conservatism, but also because the Arizona legislature opposed further reservation well-drilling in "critical" ground water areas being used by whites.[80]

In 1951, Tohono O'odham farmers reported 921 acres in *akchin* fields on the Papago Reservation, 615 irrigated acres at Chuichu, and 748 irrigated acres at San Xavier, but they actually cultivated only half that area. That year, 28 farmers at Chuichu banded together to form a cooperative association. They borrowed $9,000 from the Indian Bureau revolving credit program to purchase agricultural machinery and grossed $26,000 on 100 acres of cotton in 1952. Extension agents had great hopes for their continued success and made plans for the expansion of fields and irrigation works at Chuichu. Their hopes sank with the rehabilitation bill, but Chuichu farmers expanded their cultivation to 1,028 irrigated acres in cotton, grains, and vegetables by 1959.[81]

Although Congress ignored water and the economic rehabilitation on the reservations, it finally addressed the question of reservation mineral rights in 1955, returning those rights to the exclusive use of the Papago Tribe. Two years later the Papago Tribe and San Xavier allotment owners began leasing their lands. The American Smelting and Refining Company (Asarco) obtained exclusive prospecting rights to the San Xavier Reservation in 1957, paying over one million dollars in leases to individual landowners and the tribe for their mine and tailings sites. Other San Xavier farmers leased their allotments to non-Indian farmers. In 1957, San Xavier farmers worked 371 acres and leased 271 acres. Three years later they worked 88 acres and leased 876 acres, and by 1962 only 12 San Xavier farmers cultivated small garden patches amounting to 45 acres. Most San Xavier O'odham abandoned farming in the early 1960s because of the lack of water, content to live on the income from wage labor and their mineral and agricultural leases.[82]

One of the largest leases came in 1957 when the Papago Tribe signed a 25-year lease on 12,000 acres of land in the Chukut Kuk District of the southern Papago Reservation with two Phoenix firms, Freesh Land Ventures, Inc., and the James Stewart Company. In addition to an annual rental fee based on farm production, the Papago Farms lease called for development of 5,600 acres of irrigated farm land with 18 wells which would be turned over to the tribe in 1982. By 1960 the development companies reported 2,900 cleared acres with 1,920 acres under cultivation and 5.59 miles of concrete-lined irrigation canals. But in 1961 the Papago Agency superintendent canceled the lease when the company failed to produce promised results. Litigation resulting from the project was finally settled out of court in 1965, but the cleared land with its "improvements" went largely unused. The tribal council explored operating Papago Farms as a tribal enterprise and tried some experimental leases, but nothing came of the proposals or leases.[83]

The decline in Tohono O'odham farming continued through the 1960s. In 1962, investigators estimated that the Tohono O'odham planted about 1,000 acres in *akchin* fields, raising corn, beans, squash, watermelon, wheat, milo, and peas on a subsistence or dietary supplement basis. O'odham at Chuichu and San Xavier cultivated 80 and 45 acres respectively, leasing the rest of their irrigable lands to non-Indian farmers. Investigators blamed the decline of farming on the small size of individual fields, the lack of sufficient water, and the inability of Indian farmers to compete in the regional market place with non-Indians.

By 1970, no more than half of the over 9,000 Tohono O'odham lived on the three reservations. Many moved to the river valleys and mining towns in search of wage work. The bulk of Tohono O'odham income and subsistence came from wage work, cattle ranching, agricultural and mineral lease payments, a $27 million claims case settlement in 1964, handicraft sales, and tribal and government relief. On the reservations, the people averaged an annual income of $700, 67 percent of that coming from federal employment.[84]

In the last twenty years the Tohono O'odham Nation has made efforts to rehabilitate their land and water rights for native farming, ranching, and leasing. In 1971, farmers formed the San Xavier Cooperative Farm Association and received grants and loans to farm the 1,100 acres of land owned by 189 allottees, but the project failed to keep enough regular workers and to develop enough water to farm profitably. Landowners returned to leasing what land they could. Similar problems led Chuichu farmers to lease most of their land near Casa Grande, and the tribal council to lease all irrigable land at Gila Bend to non-Indian farmers. By 1981 the Applied Remote Sensing Program found that farmers on the Papago Reservation practiced *akchin* agriculture on less than 4 percent of the 9,177 acres cultivated in 1915. Today perhaps 100 acres of traditional *akchin* fields remain in crops, but the diversity in and around those fields continues, representing over 110 domesticates and 130 wild plant genera.[85]

In the beginning and the end, water has been a limiting factor in Tohono O'odham agriculture. When asked to explain the lack of farming today, Ascension Anton replied:

> It's due to the lack of rain and animals [horses] that they used then to plant. And I guess mainly because of the rains. . . . [T]hen when it rained a lot the water would flow evenly . . . and now it's just in the washes and it doesn't overflow like it used to and the soil is not good for farming anymore. It's too dry.

Ex-council member Patrick Johnny Franco put it more succinctly: "Ain't much water. . . . Tucson drinking it all up." This longtime struggle for water led federal officials to file suit in 1975 on behalf of the Tohono O'odham Nation against the City of Tucson. Tribal leaders hoped to regain enough water from the Central Arizona Project and City of Tucson to rehabilitate the agricultural potential of some land. In 1982 the government negotiated a favorable cash and water settlement to the suit. It remains to be seen whether that water will be used for agricultural development or whether the water will be sold to other water users. In 1988, Patrick Franco was hopeful that the water would reach San Xavier by 1992 but less hopeful that more than a handful of older folks who continue to farm small plots would be able to use it. "I don't know but I'm just going to sit back, get my pipe and smoke and see what's going to happen."[86]

O'odham

The Tohono O'odham were an agrarian people long before contact with Euro-Americans who viewed agriculture as the hallmark of civilization. The history of their subsistence change from farmers, hunters, and gatherers to farmers, herders, and wage earners is one of adaptation, cultural reproduction, and environmental degradation. The people rapidly but selectively adopted the subsistence offerings of early Spanish missionaries and incorporated them within their subsistence routine. They even accepted the mystical aspects of Catholicism, with its hierarchy of saints and miraculous cures that echoed Tohono O'odham mythology and concepts of curing, producing a syncretic version of Sonoran Catholicism.

For years the physical isolation of Tohono O'odham villages in the *Papaguería* kept them beyond the immediate control of colonial authority. American officials generally ignored these peaceful, self-sufficient village dwellers who continued to pursue their diversified subsistence system and social customs. They recognized their supreme adaptation to a difficult desert environment but could not stop themselves from trying to improve on years of Tohono O'odham adaptive experience. Over time settlers appropriated Indian land and water, exposing them to the livestock industry, seasonal wage work, and an economy based on barter and cash. Again, the Tohono O'odham demonstrated their adaptive nature by incorporating these changes within existing cultural patterns and norms, thereby mitigating the impact of sudden environmental or directed change.

In the twentieth century, their diversified subsistence strategy began to narrow. Tohono O'odham farmers faced environmental problems resulting from cyclical drought, overgrazing, erosion, and competition for precious ground water. They followed their old ceremonies despite suppression and reproduced elements of their village and regional identity in the transformation of tribal politics. *Akchin* farming gave way to cattle ranching and wage labor in the mines and cotton fields of the region, accelerating the pace of environmental change and increasing their dependence on outside markets and technologies. The 7,070 acres of San Xavier land leased to Asarco for mining and tailing piles has contaminated surrounding land and water sources with heavy metals that are now showing up in area vegetables, making even home gardening a risky proposition. All these changes in lifestyle and subsistence diets have resulted in increased health problems among the Tohono O'odham, particularly heart disease, obesity, and diabetes.[87]

Despite changes in their subsistence and social customs, members of the Tohono O'odham Nation maintain a strong sense of place and identity. The people continue to celebrate their connection with the land and each other through their language, traditional stories, crafts, and ceremonial life. Some continue to plant small gardens and *akchin* fields and to gather the native fruits of the *Papaguería*, but only as a ceremonial practice or subsistence supplement. Recent researchers note that if agriculture (and similarly, a healthier diet) is ever to make a comeback on the Papago Reservation, it will have to be through maintaining the traditional agricultural practices of *akchin* farming—practices little affected by modern technologies and the loss of ground water, practices refined over centuries of local adaptation.[88]

CONCLUSION

At the heart of the federal government's American Indian policy was the idea that Native Americans could be civilized and assimilated into the mainstream of American society as yeoman farmers and farm families. Government officials and assorted "friends of the Indians" believed that by turning Indians into farmers they could end their dependence on the vagaries of the chase and the starvation cycle of native subsistence systems and, at the same time, open more land for an expanding American populous. They saw reservation agriculture and allotment policies as the best first steps in accomplishing those goals.

On the early contact periphery, native groups like the Northern Utes, Hupas, and Tohono O'odham maintained productive subsistence economies geared towards subsistence security rather than the productive maximization of their environments. Each group utilized a diverse range of resources rather than concentrating on any single commodity or mode of production. This safety net approach insured against the periodic failure or scarcity of resources due to biological cycles or environmental phenomena beyond immediate human control.

This is not to say that natives did not experience periods of starvation or subsistence shortfall. Nor did they simply conform their strategies to the constraints of their physical environments or technologies. Each of these Indian groups actively altered its environments. They controlled fire and water to change the land, they encouraged useful plant and animal species, and they ordered their metaphysical world through stories and ritual speech. Cultural explanations were interwoven in their subsistence systems, regulating not only the amounts but the kinds of potential resources utilized. Likewise, these values encouraged a balance between periods of intense work and accumulation and the relative leisure time necessary for cultural continuity and elaboration—a balance often misinterpreted as laziness by Anglo-American observers.[1]

As directed change and the process of incorporation intensified, native subsistence systems underwent fundamental changes. Access to diverse resources narrowed as the government forced Indians onto ever smaller reserves, allotting them individual plots, teaching them the rudiments of western agriculture, and opening their land to white settlers. On this marginal periphery, Indian groups selectively adopted and adapted white items and beliefs as necessary or desirable. They resisted—passively or actively—other elements requiring more radical changes. Few groups were willing to completely abandon core elements like diversified subsistence approaches, especially after watching agency farmers fail on marginal reservation lands. Yet as native foodstuffs became more difficult to obtain, many tried farming and ranching to supplement their failing subsistence round. Others retreated to rations and wage work and, later, to leasing and per-capita payments as alternatives to farming. In either case, their importance as economic producers was minor even as their dependence on the core grew.

Culturally, few assimilated as they were incorporated into the American mainstream. Individuals and groups maintained their cultural identity by reproducing native subsistence practices and beliefs within the changing structures of reservation life. In the end, the integration of new elements and the reproduction of older patterns resulted not in the loss of but in the gradual transformation of Indian cultures. Living in rural areas, leasing or working small farms and livestock operations, Indians suffered the same reality as other small farmers caught by the corporate consolidation and environmental degradation of the early twentieth century.

By 1940, most groups had been fully incorporated on the periphery of American society and market economy. Those who continued to farm or run livestock operated somewhere between subsistence and market production, reproducing older ceremonial values or a newer turn-of-the-century tradition of agrarian self-sufficiency. Since the 1950s, western Indian tribes have leased a majority of their arable and grazing land to non-Indians. Few if any have established agricultural operations on a scale large enough to support their members, nor should they be expected to, given the realities of modern agriculture and the potential for other types of economic development. In effect they would be trading one dependent economy for another. Today, Indian farming has become a part-time operation for individuals supporting their families through wage work in the extractive resource industries that dot western reservations—resources and labor more valued than reservation agriculture by the urban-industrial core. The modern identity of Indian farmer or rancher or "cowboy" emerged as those occupations became more peripheral in a changing American society, offering less of a livelihood and more of an image than ever before.[2]

There were always a number of structural problems hindering the successful implementation of western-style agriculture on Indian reservations. The experiences of the Northern Utes, Hupas, and Tohono O'odham provide a collective portrait of the environmental, political, economic, and social reasons why reservation farming and ranching failed to fill the void left by the disappearance of contact economies. It is part of the larger story of how agrarian-based policies, environmental change, and native cultural responses contributed to the ultimate dependency of previously self-sufficient peoples.[3]

First, the government's agrarian program lacked consistency in direction, application, and support. Over time and under the direction of different commissioners and bureau personnel, Indian policy wavered between collectivism and individualism. Even the larger ideals of imminent civilization and assimilation faded.[4] Agents charged with implementing policy on the reservation level had to discover how to sell policies as absolute, yet explain their change. Collective fields and farming practices frustrated some groups, while the re-individualization of farming under allotment hurt those making progress in more communal operations. Some agents recognized and tried to work within existing native cultural preferences, while others, especially missionary agents, went so far as to subordinate such temporal matters for spiritual salvation. Likewise, the individual commitment and attitude of employees affected the translation and implementation of policy.

The government fell short in providing promised instruction and supplies early in the policy program and then in maintaining that commitment until a viable agricultural economy had been established. Experienced agency farmers familiar with the techniques of arid western agriculture were difficult to retain, given the low pay and isolation of reservations. Many farmers had to supervise several hundred Indian families, sometimes scattered over several hundred square miles. They worked without the best contemporary agricultural machinery and often made do with inadequate numbers of inferior quality implements for their budding Indian farmers. Even after the position became subject to civil service requirements, inept individuals slipped through, in some cases undoing in a single season the physical improvements and psychological goodwill built up over decades by competent farmers. Charged with teaching Indians to become self-supporting, agency farmers often ended up performing the work themselves to ensure that the agency had sufficient supplies for the coming winter. They hoped, by example, to stimulate Indian participation. Instead they reinforced the growing sense of paternalism and dependency.

Second, the physical realities of reservations and the environmental changes resulting from consolidation and directed subsistence change became major obstacles in the creation of self-sufficient agrarian communities. Tribal groups were removed to strange new environments or confined on small reservations with only a fraction of the biotic diversity of their original homelands. Consolidation contributed to the depletion of traditional resources as natives tried to reproduce their subsistence round. It also led to competition and conflict between groups on the same or adjoining reservations. Game animals and native vegetation gave way to invasive or introduced domesticants, changing the face of the land and narrowing native subsistence alternatives.

The pace of environmental change increased as government officials introduced field agriculture and livestock. They misunderstood or disapproved of native management techniques like controlled burns and water diversion structures. They remained unwilling to recognize that in some cases Indian farming techniques proved better adapted to the reservation environment than Anglo techniques. When forced to change methods or crops, both Indian farmers and the land suffered.

The fact is that reservations in the arid West were generally areas unwanted by nineteenth century Anglo-Americans. The lands, like the Indians put there, were deemed deficient at the time. Many reservations were relatively high in elevation, with shallow soils and short growing seasons. They lacked adequate water and timber, they were rocky and broken, or they were isolated from transportation and supply routes. Agents noted that even experienced white farmers found it difficult to farm the same lands successfully. Many of these reservations were environmentally better suited for grazing than farming, but policies like allotment divided arid lands into units too small for individuals to maintain adequate herds. Overgrazing by Indian ranchers and white lessees enlarged the scale of environmental change, denuding once-rich grasslands and increasing soil erosion and siltation in irrigation structures.

Water, or the lack of it at the right time in the growing season, was a deciding factor in Indian farming. To offset this environmental limitation, the government helped construct dozens of irrigation systems on western reservations, charging the costs against water users and the sale of unallotted reservation lands. However, the projects did not always solve the problems of aridity. Some irrigation systems were too small or poorly constructed or suffered the repeated effects of watershed erosion. Perhaps more importantly, the projects contributed to individual and tribal indebtedness, leading to the leasing and sale of additional allotments. Ultimately, white farmers benefited from irrigation systems paid for by Indian peoples or simply appropriated Indian water rights without compensation.

Environment is both a biological and cultural creation. People mold the land to meet their physical and cultural needs, and, in turn, the land shapes their social patterns. Environmental changes entailed in creating a settled agricultural landscape had profound impacts on native societies, trickling down through native social structures associated with regulating or utilizing land and resources. In turn, these changing patterns of use and thought precipitated further environmental changes as the dialectic continued.[5] In the case of Native Americans, the government was responsible for directing many of the larger environmental changes that affected their societies. But Indians contributed to the process by pursuing different responses and subsistence strategies. In clearing and plowing marginal lands, in cutting oaks that once afforded acorn harvests, in felling mesquite or pine timber from erosive watersheds, in burning or not burning grass or forest lands, in increasing the number of livestock on a limited range, each group made decisions that significantly altered their environments, their subsistence alternatives, and their societies.

Third, Indian farmers and ranchers grappled with the American market economy at different levels of intensity over time. Incorporated on the periphery, native communities were subject to the vagaries of the core's economy while having only limited access to it. Reservation farmers were physically isolated, lacking, first, marketable goods, and later, adequate outlets to regional or national markets. In the beginning, government officials geared Indian production for local consumption and self-sufficiency—vegetable, grain, and forage crops that had little outside market value given shipping costs and regional competition. But these local self-sufficient economies never developed as expected, nor could they insulate themselves from the need for imported goods forever. Without ready market access, Indian farmers could not accumulate the necessary capital for agricultural machinery or improvements without selling land that was their only real asset. Trust and heirship status complications arising from allotment limited their ability to sell or even expand their land base for farming or ranching operations. Those Indians who chose to take out reimbursable government loans ran the risk of failure, indebtedness, and the loss of yet more land. Others leased all or part of their land in return for a subsistence living.

Leasing frequently proved to be a more remunerative market strategy than actual farming for Indians who lacked capital, technical knowledge, and the drive to participate in the farm economy. Yet leasing broached the risk of further land alienation, increased the levels of Indian dependency, and proved a disincentive to Indian land use. Individuals came to rely on agency or tribal officials to arrange and supervise satisfactory leases—to find and keep lessees who could make productive use of the land or resources without ruining them and still meet their payments during both good and bad years. Leasing seemed to free individuals from the need to work by guaranteeing them a small but constant income, yet they remained tied through the lessee to the same market and environmental fluctuations. While they expended less capital and physical labor, they also had less control over the process and outcome. Because of individual need and the nature of tribal politics, tribal governments became what many remain today—entities that redistribute income per capita instead of accumulating capital for further economic development, reproducing traditional group functions and economic values in a transformed sociopolitical environment. Relegated to the market periphery, Indians found few incentives to farm when they could lease their land for a subsistence living.

In the nineteenth century, tribal herds represented one resource with the inherent mobility to overcome isolation and the potential economy of scale to find a market niche. But in their zeal to individualize Indian farmers and production, government officials disbanded many of the tribal herds, dividing them per capita into uneconomically small units where they became a subsistence rather than market resource. While some Indian families built up substantial private herds, they had to weather competition for range and markets from white ranchers, the jealousy of tribal members seeking to redistribute group assets, and environmental changes in their range lands. Even then, the reproduction of native socioeconomic values ranking quantity over quality and the problems of uncoordinated sales of small lots of livestock limited both the market share and cash return for Indian ranchers. Stock reduction programs in the 1930s and 1950s hit small-herd owners hardest, reducing the overall number of families able to support themselves by ranching. Cooperative livestock associations helped owners find markets, but they lost cohesion as more families gave up their livestock for livelihoods based on tribal wage work and per capita distributions.[6]

Over time, Indian farmers and ranchers did manage to find some local and regional markets for specialized agricultural products, but most were rather short lived. Agriculture as a national economic pursuit underwent periodic crises—boom and bust cycles resulting from environmental and market forces beyond the control of individual farmers, white or Indian. Federal Indian policies such as allotment launched Indians into farming small plots of land at the very time white farmers found it necessary to expand their farm size, increase the intensity of their cultivation with power equipment and irrigation, and cooperatively market their produce in order to survive. Since the depression of the 1930s, American agriculture in general has become increasingly corporate and, at the same time, increasingly dependent on government subsidies. Indian farming faded and wage labor increased as small family operations across the country struggled for a market share against integrated agribusinesses.[7]

Fourth, the government's Indian policy failed to take into consideration the cultural traditions and successful subsistence adaptations of each tribe before instituting wholesale change. They met functional systems and left them dysfunctional. By focusing on a prescribed type of row agriculture over shifting cultivation methods, on ditch irrigation over flood plain methods, and on farming over ranching, American officials ignored cultural and environmental realities that ultimately limited Indian participation. In societies where women farmed, government meddling with this gendered division of labor upset not only functional production but also the power structure of native societies. Forcing hunters and warriors to take on women's economic roles generated internal confusion and opposition as it transformed women's source of power.[8] The outcomes may not have been substantially different had the government paid closer attention to cultural features, but the process of change may have been more tolerable, group-directed, and less disruptive.

Finally, Indian peoples made certain choices—measured responses to incorporation and directed change that ultimately affected agrarian development. They adopted the more familiar or attractive features of Euro-American cultures, filtered through their own cultural values and ecological adaptations yet often carried to very different conclusions. Indians adopted but placed different use values on horses, cattle, and other livestock. They came to accept some idea of landownership yet ignored Euro-American concepts of primogeniture, resulting in the continual division of property and the emergence of complicated heirship arrangements that hindered farming.

Indians reproduced socioeconomic values balancing work with leisure, subsistence security against maximized production and accumulation. Even when incorporated and dependent, their expectations differed. Many refused to see subsistence as simply a market enterprise and chose a different approach and standard of living, one in line with more moderate material expectations. Others had that choice forced upon them by the nature of their land, their relationship with the government, and the cumulative weight of earlier strategies or choices. Still others chose to compete with white farmers, but few showed the persistence and skills necessary to succeed on marginal lands. In the process they became neither warrior nor farmer, wolf nor dog. Since the 1940s, Indian peoples and tribal governments have become incorporated and have adopted a more acquisitive American set of economic values. While they did not choose the poverty and underdevelopment that marks most reservation economies today, that situation is in part the result of both their choices and their lack of choice.[9]

The experiences of the Northern Utes, Hupas, and Tohono O'odham represent a range of choices, a continuum of nonexclusive strategies or responses to the federal government's agrarian civilization program. They chose from different culturally consistent responses along a continuum ranging from rejection and resistance, to adaptation and reproduction, to acceptance and culturally orchestrated modernization. They varied their strategies over time as the nature and intensity of incorporation shifted. While each situation was unique, other western Indian peoples experienced similar pressures and chose similar responses to incorporation and directed change.[10]

First, native communities chose to maintain their subsistence and social organization unchanged. They resisted, actively and passively, and sought alternatives to directed agrarian change. They pursued their subsistence round while they could and resisted wholesale agrarian change even after they could no longer survive in traditional ways. They fell back on rations, fled to remote areas to escape supervision, or retreated into nativistic movements like the Sun Dance, Ghost Dance, or Peyote Religion. Most groups, especially those without an established agricultural component, attempted this response. In the northern plains, Lakotas continued to hunt until buffalo herds gave way to waves of settlers and soldiers. Lakotas frustrated agents with their refusal to farm, their dependence on government annuities and rations, and their nativistic religions. Northern Cheyennes, Crows, Blackfeet, Gros Ventres, and Assiniboines all initially resisted a farming lifestyle. Shoshone Chief Washakie reputedly summed up his reaction to allotted farming by exclaiming to Bureau officials, "God Damn a potato!" On the southern plains and in Oklahoma, Cheyenne and Kiowa-Apache men rejected farming. Even those agricultural groups in the Southwest—Zunis, Hopis, and other pueblo peoples—resisted attempts to alter their agricultural techniques, ceremonial observances, and crops.[11]

Second, Indians chose to adopt and adapt new agrarian elements, reproducing native values in a transformed social and physical environment. Every native group attempted to protect core cultural elements and replicate valued political and social forms, diversified economies and land use, cyclical and gendered work patterns, language, and ritual observances within the imposed framework of reservation agriculture. They reproduced specific explanations for the cultural and environmental problems they faced on the reservations. Blackfeet reproduced their value for horses as prestige items by trading their cattle to mixed blood ranchers for horses. Navajos maintained large herds of horses despite the fact that they competed with sheep for overgrazed range. Cheyenne, Kiowa, Comanche, Kiowa-Apache, Shoshone, Crow, and Lakota bands reproduced traditional divisions of labor in which Indian women tended to the vegetal production while men hunted or adapted to domestic livestock production. Southern Cheyenne dog soldiers replicated their innovative leadership role and communal organization by leading their people into communal farming activities. Southwestern and pueblo agriculturalists maintained established methods and crops despite government attempts to alter those practices. Zunis accepted winter wheat crops and new irrigated fields but continued to use traditional lands and methods, reproducing communal labor and landholding patterns. Even after their reservation confinement, Western Apaches reproduced older patterns of field location, cultivation, ownership, and agricultural ritual.[12]

Finally, Indian individuals or whole groups chose to embrace agrarian change in an attempt at culturally orchestrated modernization. Such acceptance was rarely unconditional or unilateral but represented another strategy to retain group identity, political and economic control through conscious social transformation. Certain factions within a tribal group usually led the way—mixed bloods, Christians, boarding school graduates, or other "progressive" elements. They encouraged their people to accept the inevitable political and economic reorganization of their society in order to retain some control over the process of change and over their land and destiny. This internal change inevitably generated conflict as other group members countered this response in the same ways they resisted or manipulated externally directed change. As the level of incorporation increased following the Indian Reorganization Act of 1934, newly formed tribal governments adopted various modernization programs, seeking to legitimate themselves and preserve group identity by bettering the economic quality of reservation life. Many initiated revolving livestock programs, viewing ranching and livestock as a more acceptable and productive lifestyle choice for their people than farming. Most, however, looked to extractive natural resource economies rather than agriculture for the future.[13]

This continuum of Indian choices or responses to change is an ongoing process, one being played out every day by groups and individuals across the country. It is part of the process whereby American Indians survived the descendants of Columbus—the biological and acculturative assault—and remain separate and identifiable peoples.

The possibility always exists for Indian peoples to rebuild agricultural operations on their reservations, to enter the marketplace at some level of competitive production. In the Southwest, native farmers are preserving heritage crops, a storehouse of biodiversity in an increasing homogeneous world. Others are earning a living with their livestock. On a larger scale, western tribes are beginning to reclaim land and water rights, terminate leases, and use the latest technology to put land back under Indian production. An intertribal task force and agricultural council are exploring the needs of individual and tribal operators.[14] Many older generation Indians see the benefits of revitalizing such agricultural industries as a way to preserve valuable water rights and to keep the young people in touch with their land and heritage. But few young people today, Indian or white, desire such a lifestyle. Farming has become too hard, too capital intensive, too technical for many to make a start. A wholesale return to farming is a rather nostalgic vision for a future increasingly urban, increasingly dominated by agribusinesses. It is a vision that will be carried out, if at all, by the individual who finds cultural as well as economic value in working the land.

ABBREVIATIONS

ARCIA	*Annual Report of the Commissioner of Indian Affairs*
ASP:FR	*American State Papers: Foreign Affairs*
ASP:IA	*American State Papers: Indian Affairs*
BAE	Bureau of American Ethnology
BIA	Bureau of Indian Affairs
BIC	Board of Indian Commissioners
CCC-ID	Civilian Conservation Corps—Indian Division
CCF	Central Classified Files, BIA, 1907–39.
CIA	Commissioner of Indian Affairs
DDOHC-A	Doris Duke American Indian Oral History Project Collection, Arizona State Museum Archives, University of Arizona, Tucson, Ariz.
DDOHC-U	Doris Duke American Indian Oral History Project Collection, Western History Center, Marriott Library Manuscripts Collection, University of Utah, Salt Lake City
FARC-D	Federal Archive and Record Center, Denver
FARC-SB	Federal Archive and Record Center, San Bruno, Calif.
FARC-LN	Federal Archive and Record Center, Laguna Niguel, Calif.

GPO	Government Printing Office
GR	General Records, BIA, 1824–1907
HR	United States House of Representatives
HV	Hoopa Valley Agency, California
IECW	Indian Emergency Conservation Work
LMC	Lake Mohonk Conference, *Annual Proceedings*
LR	Letters Received
LS	Letters Sent
NA	National Archives, Washington, D.C.
OIA	Office of Indian Affairs
PL	Post Letterbook, Fort Gaston, Calif.
RG 75	Record Group 75, Bureau of Indian Affairs
RG 393	Record Group 393, U.S. Army Continental Command, Department of the Pacific
Sells	Sells Agency, Arizona
ser.	United States Serial Set
SI	Secretary of Interior
Stats.	*United States Statutes at Large*
Supt.	Superintendent
SW	Secretary of War
TOOHC	Tohono O'odham Oral History Collection, 1988, American West Center, University of Utah, and the Venito Garcia Library, Sells, Ariz.
U&O	Uintah and Ouray Agency, Utah
UCPAAE	University of California Publications, *American Archaeology and Ethnology*
UCPAR	University of California Publications, *Anthropological Records*
U.S.	*United States Supreme Court Reports*
USDA	United States Department of Agriculture
WR	U.S. War Department, *The War of the Rebellion* (1897)

NOTES

Preface

1. Richard White, *The Roots of Dependency: Subsistence, Environment, and Social Change among the Choctaws, Pawnees, and Navajos* (Lincoln: University of Nebraska Press, 1983); Mary Young, "Quakers, Wolves, and Make-Believe White Men: Assimilationist Indian Policy and Its Critics," *Journal of American Ethnic History*, 4 (Spring 1985), 97; Herbert T. Hoover, "American Indians from Prehistoric Times to the Civil War," in *Historians and the American West*, ed. Michael P. Malone (Lincoln: University of Nebraska Press, 1983), 28–29; Thomas R. Wessel, "Agriculture, Indians, and American History," *Agricultural History*, 50 (January 1976), 9–20; Robert McC. Netting, "Agrarian Ecology," *Annual Review of Anthropology*, 3 (1974), 21; Roy Ellen, *Environment, Subsistence and System: The Ecology of Small-Scale Social Formations* (Cambridge: Cambridge University Press, 1982), 123. For the growth of the field see R. Douglas Hurt, *Indian Agriculture in America: Prehistory to the Present* (Lawrence: University Press of Kansas, 1987); David Rich Lewis, "Plowing a Civilized Furrow: Subsistence, Environment, and Social Change among the Northern Ute, Hupa, and Papago Peoples" (Ph.D. diss., University of Wisconsin-Madison, 1988), 15 n.11.

2. James Axtell, *The European and the Indian: Essays in the Ethnohistory of Colonial North America* (New York: Oxford University Press, 1981), 5. See also William C. Sturtevant, "Anthropology, History, and Ethnohistory," *Ethnohistory*, 13 (Winter-Spring 1966), 1–55; Bruce G. Trigger, "Ethnohistory: Problems and Prospects," *Ethnohistory*, 29 (Winter 1982), 1–19.

3. See Clyde A. Milner II, "Off the White Road: Seven Nebraska Indian Societies in the 1870s: A Staistical Analysis of Assimilation, Population, and Prosperity," *Western Historical Quarterly*, 12 (January 1981), 38–39. Leonard Carlson's fine cliometric work, *Indians, Bureaucrats, and Land: The Dawes Act and the Decline of Indian Farming* (Westport, Conn.: Greenwood Press, 1981), struggles with this problem.

Introduction

1. Karl Marx and Friedrich Engles, *The German Ideology, Parts I & II* (New York: International Publishers, 1947), 7; Social Science Research Council, "Acculturation: An Exploratory Formulation," *American Anthropologist*, 56 (December 1954), 991; Julian H. Steward, *Theory of Culture Change: The Methodology of Multilinear Evolution* (Urbana: University of Illinois Press, 1955),

37; Roy Ellen, *Environment, Subsistence and System: The Ecology of Small-Scale Social Formations* (Cambridge: Cambridge University Press, 1982), 1–94; Benjamin Orlove, "Ecological Anthropology," *Annual Review of Anthropology,* 9 (1980), 235–73.

2. Marshall D. Sahlins, *Culture and Practical Reason* (Chicago: University of Chicago Press, 1976), vii–viii, 169–70, 205–10; Orlove, "Ecological Anthropology," 245–63; Loretta Fowler, *Shared Symbols, Contested Meanings: Gros Ventre Culture and History, 1778–1984* (Ithaca, N.Y.: Cornell University Press, 1987), 9–10.

3. Ellen, *Environment, Subsistence and System,* 236–51; Marshall D. Sahlins, "Culture and Environment: The Study of Cultural Ecology," in *Horizons of Anthropology,* ed. Sol Tax (Chicago: Aldine Publishing Co., 1964), 132–47; Alexander Alland, Jr., "Adaptation," *Annual Review of Anthropology,* 4 (1975), 59–73; Melvin J. Herskovits, "Introduction," in *Acculturation in the Americas: Proceedings and Selected Papers of the XXIXth International Congress of Americanists,* ed. Sol Tax (New York: Cooper Square Publishers, 1967), 53–57; John W. Berry, "Acculturation as Varieties of Adaptation," in *Acculturation: Theory, Models and Some New Findings,* ed. Amado M. Padilla (Boulder, Colo.: Westview Press, 1980), 9–25; Ralph Linton, ed., *Acculturation in Seven American Indian Tribes* (New York: D. Appleton-Century Co., 1940), 463–520; SSRC, "Acculturation," 973–1002; Clyde M. Woods, *Culture Change* (Dubuque, Ia.: Wm. C. Brown Co., 1975).

4. Ellen, *Environment, Subsistence and System,* 241–43; Alland, "Adaptation," 59–73.

5. Marshall D. Sahlins, *Historical Metaphors and Mythical Realities: Structure in the Early History of the Sandwich Island Kingdoms* (Ann Arbor: University of Michigan Press, 1981), 67–68.

6. Marshall D. Sahlins, *Islands of History* (Chicago: University of Chicago Press, 1985), vii–viii. See also William S. Simmons, "Culture Theory in Contemporary Ethnohistory," *Ethnohistory,* 35 (Winter 1988), 7; Woods, *Culture Change,* 11–49.

7. Sahlins, *Islands of History,* 144.

8. Thomas D. Hall, *Social Change in the Southwest, 1350–1880* (Lawrence: University Press of Kansas, 1989), 17–23.

9. Ellen, *Environment, Subsistence and System,* 252–73; Robert F. Berkhofer, Jr., "Protestants, Pagans, and Sequences Among the North American Indians, 1760–1860," *Ethnohistory,* 10 (Summer 1963), 201–202; Imre Sutton, *Indian Land Tenure: Bibliographical Essays and a Guide to the Literature* (New York: Clearwater Publishing Co., 1975), 182–83, 196–99.

Chapter 1

1. Paul H. Johnstone, "In Praise of Husbandry," *Agricultural History,* 11 (April 1937), 80–95; Johnstone, "Turnips and Romanticism," *Agricultural History,* 12 (July 1938), 224–55; Clark Emery, "The Poet and the Plough," *Agricultural History,* 16 (January 1942), 9–15; James A. Montmarquet, "Philosophical Foundations for Agrarianism," *Agriculture and Human Values,* 2 (Spring 1985), 5–14; Montmarquet, *The Idea of Agrarianism: From Hunter-Gatherer to Agrarian Radical in Western Culture* (Moscow: University of Idaho Press, 1989).

2. Elizabeth Fox-Genovese, *The Origins of Physiocracy: Economic Revolution and Social Order in Eighteenth-Century France* (Ithaca, N.Y.: Cornell University Press, 1976); Emrich de Vattel, *The Law of Nations; or, Principles of the Law of Nature, Applied to the Conduct and Affairs of Nations and Sovereigns*, trans. Joseph Chitty (Philadelphia: T. & J. W. Johnson & Co., 1883), Bk. I, Chap. 7, 34–35; Chester E. Eisinger, "The Influence of Natural Rights and Physiocratic Doctrines on American Agrarian Thought During the Revolutionary Period," *Agricultural History*, 21 (January 1947), 20–21.

3. J. Hector St. John de Crèvecoeur, *Letters from an American Farmer* (London, 1782; New York: E. P. Dutton & Co., 1957), 36, 12, 18, 20–21, 34; John Taylor, *Arator, Being a Series of Agricultural Essays, Practical and Political: In Sixty-four Numbers*, 6th ed. (Petersburg, Va.: J. M. Carter, 1818), 189–90; Alfred C. True, *A History of Agricultural Education in the United States*, USDA, Miscellaneous Publication 36 (Washington, D.C.: GPO, 1929), 7–18; Henry Nash Smith, *Virgin Land: The American West as Symbol and Myth* (Cambridge: Harvard University Press, 1950), 123.

4. Thomas Jefferson, *Notes on the State of Virginia* (New York: Harper Torchbooks, 1964), 157–58; Jefferson, *The Writings of Thomas Jefferson*, 10 vols., col. and ed. Paul L. Ford (New York: G. P. Putnam's Sons, 1892–1899), 4:87–90, 473–80; August C. Miller, Jr., "Jefferson as an Agriculturalist," *Agricultural History*, 16 (April 1942), 65–78.

5. Ronald L. Meek, *Social Science and the Ignoble Savage* (Cambridge: Cambridge University Press, 1976); Roy Harvey Pearce, *Savagism and Civilization: A Study of the Indian and the American Mind*, rev. ed. (Baltimore: Johns Hopkins University Press, 1965); Robert F. Berkhofer, Jr., *The White Man's Indian: Images of the American Indian From Columbus to the Present* (New York: Vintage Books, 1978), 44–49; Bernard W. Sheehan, *Savagism and Civility: Indians and Englishmen in Colonial Virginia* (Cambridge: Cambridge University Press, 1980); Smith, *Virgin Land*, 218–24.

6. See Jefferson's Second Inaugural Address, 4 March 1805, in *ASP:FR*, I:65; Jefferson to Wm. Ludlow, 6 September 1824, as quoted in Francis Paul Prucha, *The Great Father: The United States Government and the American Indians*, 2 vols. (Lincoln: University of Nebraska Press, 1984), I:138–39; Bernard W. Sheehan, *Seeds of Extinction: Jeffersonian Philanthropy and the American Indian* (New York: W. W. Norton & Co., 1974), 23–26; Stephen J. Kunitz, "Benjamin Rush on Savagism and Progress," *Ethnohistory*, 17 (Winter-Spring 1970), 31–42; Albert Gallatin, "A Synopsis of the Indian Tribes within the United States East of the Rocky Mountains, in the British and Russian Possessions in North America," *Transactions and Collections of the American Antiquarian Society*, vol. 2 (Cambridge, 1836), 6–7, 156–57; Lewis Cass, "Considerations on the Present State of Indians, and Their Removal to the West of the Mississippi," *North American Review*, 30 (1830), 64–66; William Clark to Secretary of War, 1 March 1826, *ASP:IA*, 2:653–54; Thomas L. McKenney to James Barbour, SW, 27 December 1826, *ASP:IA*, 2:701.

7. Nelson A. Miles, "The Indian Problem," *North American Review*, 128 (March 1879), 309; Henry Rowe Schoolcraft, *The American Indians, Their History, Condition and Prospects, from Original Notes and Manuscripts* (Buffalo: George H. Derby & Co., 1851), 367; Prucha, *Great Father*, I:128–29, ill. 15.

8. Lewis Henry Morgan, *League of the Ho-de'-no'sau'nee, or Iroquois* (Rochester, N.Y.: Sage & Brother, 1851), 141–43; Morgan, *Ancient Society; or, Re-*

searches in the Lines of Human Progress from Savagery through Barbarism to Civilization (New York: Henry Holt & Co., 1877), v–vii, 9–12, 18–27, 30–37, 40–41; Morgan, "The Indian Question," *The Nation*, 27 (28 November 1878), 332–33. See also George W. Stocking, Jr., *Race, Culture, and Evolution: Essays in the History of Anthropology*, rev. ed. (Chicago: University of Chicago Press, 1982), 69–132; Berkhofer, *White Man's Indian*, 49–61. Morgan's model even influenced Frederick Jackson Turner's analysis of national development and the significance of the frontier. For more details see David Rich Lewis, "Plowing a Civilized Furrow: Subsistence, Environment, and Social Change among the Northern Ute, Hupa, and Papago Peoples" (Ph.D. diss., University of Wisconsin-Madison, 1988), 24–25, 74 nn. 12, 13.

9. R. Douglas Hurt, *Indian Agriculture in America: Prehistory to the Present* (Lawrence: University Press of Kansas, 1987), 11–63; Jesse D. Jennings, *Ancient Native Americans* (San Francisco: W. H. Freeman & Co., 1978), 149–53, 203–13, 231–74, 293–94, 307–15, 337–38; Neal Salisbury, *Manitou and Providence: Indians, Europeans, and the Making of New England, 1500–1643* (New York: Oxford University Press, 1982), 18–19, 30–39; Peter Allen Thomas, "Contrastive Subsistence Strategies and Land Use as Factors for Understanding Indian–White Relations in New England," *Ethnohistory*, 23 (Winter 1976), 5–6, 12.

10. Harold E. Driver, *Indians of North America* (Chicago: University of Chicago Press, 1961), 38–56; William Cronon, *Changes in the Land: Indians, Colonists, and the Ecology of New England* (New York: Hill & Wang, 1983), 42–53, 116–19, 127–28; James Axtell, *The European and the Indian: Essays in the Ethnohistory of Colonial North America* (New York: Oxford University Press, 1981), 292–95; Richard I. Ford, "Gardening and Farming Before A.D. 1000: Patterns of Prehistoric Cultivation North of Mexico," *Journal of Ethnobiology*, 1, no. 1 (1981), 6–27; J. Donald Hughes, *American Indian Ecology*, (El Paso: Texas Western Press, University of Texas-El Paso, 1983), 65–67; Frederick Webb Hodge, *Handbook of American Indians, North of Mexico*, Smithsonian Institution, BAE Bulletin 30, 2 vols. (Washington D.C.: GPO, 1907–1910), I:24–27; Gary Paul Nabhan, *Enduring Seeds: Native American Agriculture and Wild Plant Conservation* (San Francisco: North Point Press, 1989), 49–52.

11. Hurt, *Indian Agriculture*, 27–40; Levi Chubbuck, "Indian Agriculture," *The Native American*, 14 (24 May 1913), 308; "American Indians in Agriculture," in *Agriculture In the United States: A Documentary History*, ed. Wayne D. Rasmussen, 4 vols. (New York: Random House, 1975), I:64–75; Salisbury, *Manitou*, 116–17, 185; Sheehan, *Savagism and Civility*, 5–6, 89–115; Thomas, "Contrastive Subsistence," 4–5; William Cronon and Richard White, "Indians in the Land," *American Heritage*, 37 (August–September 1986), 21.

12. Daniel Gookin, "Historical Collections of the Indians in New England . . . ," *Collections of the Massachusetts Historical Society*, I, series 1 (Boston, 1792), 149; Jedidiah Morse, *A Report to the Secretary of War of the United States on Indian Affairs, Compromising a Narrative of a Tour Performed in the Summer of 1820 . . .* (New Haven: Converse Press, 1822), 71; Gallatin, "Synopsis," 158. See also Joan M. Jensen, "Native American Women and Agriculture: A Seneca Case Study," *Sex Roles*, 3 (October 1977), 423–41.

13. John Winthrop, *Conclusions for the Plantation in New England*, quoted in Prucha, *Great Father*, I:14; Pearce, *Savagism and Civilization*, 20–21; Vattel, *Law of Nations*, Bk. I, Chap. 7, pp. 34–36, and Bk. I, Chap. 18, pp. 158–59.

14. Brackenridge, *Gazette Publications* (Carlisle, Pa., 1806), 94, as quoted in Eisinger, "Influences of Natural Rights," 18; Alexis De Tocqueville, *Democracy in America*, trans. George Lawrence, ed. J. P. Mayer (Garden City, N.Y.: Doubleday & Co., 1969), 30; Cass, "Considerations on the Present State," 95. See also Thomas Flanagan, "The Agricultural Argument and Original Appropriation: Indian Lands and Political Philosophy," *Canadian Journal of Political Science*, 22 (September 1989), 589–602.

15. Albert K. Weinberg, *Manifest Destiny: A Study of Nationalist Expansionism in American History* (Baltimore, Johns Hopkins Press, 1935), 72–99.

16. John Eliot, *A Brief Narrative of the Progress of the Gospel among the Indians of New England, 1670* (Boston: John K. Wiggin & Wm. Parsons, 1868); Neal Salisbury, "Red Puritans: The 'Praying Indians' of Massachusetts Bay and John Eliot," *William and Mary Quarterly*, 3d series, 31 (January 1974), 27–54; Eleazar Wheelock, *A Plain and Faithful Narrative of the Original Design, Rise, Progress and Present State of the Indian Charity-School at Lebanon, in Connecticut* (Boston: Richard and Samuel Draper, 1763), 24–25, 11–15, 33–35; Robert F. Berkhofer, Jr., "Model Zions for the American Indian," *American Quarterly*, 15 (Summer 1963), 176–78; Evelyn C. Adams, *American Indian Education: Government Schools and Economic Progress* (Morningside Heights, N.Y.: King's Crown Press, 1946), 18–19, 22–23; Frank J. Klingberg, "Sir William Johnson and the Society for the Propagation of the Gospel, 1749–1774," *Historical Magazine of the Protestant Episcopal Church*, 8 (March 1939), 4–37.

17. U.S. Continental Congress, "The Committee, Consisting of Mr. Dane, Mr. Hawkins, Mr. Kean, Mr. Irving and Mr. Carrington, . . . Relative to Indian Affairs in the Northern Department," 12 October 1787, Evans Imprints, 20768; Henry Knox, SW, to George Washington, 7 July 1789, *ASP:IA*, I:53–54; Speech of Cornplanter and Seneca Chiefs to Washington, 1 December 1790, *ASP:IA*, I:207; Speech of President George Washington to Cornplanter and Seneca Chiefs, 19 January 1791, *ASP:IA*, I:144; Speech of Henry Knox, SW, to Cornplanter and Seneca Chiefs, 8 February 1791, *ASP:IA*, I:145.

18. Charles J. Kappler, comp. and ed., *Indian Affairs: Laws and Treaties*, 2 vols. (Washington, D.C.: GPO, 1904), 2:28, 31, and passim; Act of 2 March 1793, 1 *Stats.* 329; Francis Paul Prucha, *American Indian Policy in the Formative Years: The Indian Trade and Intercourse Acts, 1790–1834* (Lincoln: University of Nebraska Press, 1973), 51, 53–54; "Report of Benjamin Hawkins to Congress about Southern Indian Affairs, 1801," *ASP:IA*, I:647; "Treaty Negotiations with the Creeks, June 8, 1802," *ASP:IA*, I:672. See also Hawkins, "Letters of Benjamin Hawkins, 1796–1806," in *Collections of the Georgia Historical Society*, vol. 9 (Savannah: Georgia Historical Society, 1916); Jack D. L. Holmes, "Benjamin Hawkins and United States Attempts to Teach Farming to Southeastern Indians," *Agricultural History*, 60 (Spring 1986), 216–32.

19. "Instructions from Henry Knox, SW, to Brigadier General Rufus Putman," 22 May 1792, *ASP:IA*, I:235; Knox, "Instructions to Colonel Timothy Pickering," 2 May 1791, *ASP:IA*, I:165–66; "Report to the President by the Indian Peace Commission, January 7, 1868," *House Executive Document* 97 (40–2), ser. 1337, 17–18. On treaty provisions see Kappler, *Indian Affairs*, for example, 2:31, 36, 70, 204–6, 403, 601–2, 772–73, 852, and passim. Of 386 treaties and agreements reproduced by Kappler, 46 percent contain provisions specifically related to the advancement of agriculture, with 22 percent specifically promising agricultural instructors or "white farmers." Of the roughly

115 different groups mentioned in those treaties, 94 percent were promised agricultural assistance in one or more treaties. On peace medal imagery see Bauman L. Belden, *Indian Peace Medals Issued in the United States, 1789–1889* (New Milford, Conn.: N. Flayderman & Co., 1966); Francis Paul Prucha, *Indian Peace Medals in American History* (Madison: State Historical Society of Wisconsin, 1971).

20. "Message of President Jefferson to Congress, December 8, 1801," *ASP:FR*, I:58; Act of 30 March 1802, 2 *Stats.* 139; "Regulating the Indian Department," 20 May 1834, *House Report* 474 (23–1), ser. 263, 4; Jefferson to Benjamin Hawkins, 18 February 1803, in Jefferson, *Writings*, 8:211–16; Jefferson, Message to Congress, 18 January 1803, *ASP:IA*, I:684.

21. Inaugural Speech of President Thomas Jefferson, 4 March 1805, *ASP:FR*, I:65.

22. Prucha, *Great Father*, I:129–30, 148–49; Act of 16 April 1818, 3 *Stats.* 428; Act of 20 April 1818, 3 *Stats.* 461; House Committee on Indian Affairs, Report, 22 January 1818, in *ASP:IA*, II:150–51; Act of 3 March 1819, 3 *Stats.* 516; Circular, John C. Calhoun, SW, 3 September 1819, in *ASP:IA*, II:201. See also Herman J. Viola, "Thomas L. McKenney, 1824–30," in *The Commissioners of Indian Affairs, 1824–1977*, ed. Robert M. Kvasnicka and Herman J. Viola (Lincoln: University of Nebraska Press, 1979), 1–7.

23. Robert F. Berkhofer, Jr., *Salvation and the Savage: An Analysis of Protestant Missions and American Indian Response, 1787–1862* (New York: Atheneum, 1976), 15, 70–88, 161–80; Berkhofer, "Model Zions," 178–190; Morse, *Report*, 78–79, 162–65, 188–91, 284–90; Cyrus Kingsbury, "Sketch of a Plan for Instructing the Indians," *Panoplist*, 12 (April 1816), 150–52; Ronald Rayman, "Joseph Lancaster's Monitorial System of Instruction and American Indian Education, 1815–1838," *History of Education Quarterly*, 21 (1981), 395–410; "Application of the Board of Commissioners for Foreign Missions for Pecuniary Aid in Civilizing the Indians, March 3, 1824," *ASP:IA*, II: 447. See also James P. Ronda and James Axtell, *Indian Missions: A Critical Bibliography* (Bloomington: Indiana University Press, 1978).

24. Morse, *Report*, 293, 392–96; Berkhofer, *Salvation*, 32; Report of Americus L. Hay, Creek Agency, 1 October 1849, *ARCIA* 1849, ser. 570, 1122; Ronald Satz, *American Indian Policy in the Jacksonian Era* (Lincoln: University of Nebraska Press, 1975), 257–71; Lewis, "Plowing a Civilized Furrow," 41–43; Adams, *Indian Education*, 35–37, 41; Berkhofer, "Protestants, Pagans, and Sequences among the North American Indians, 1760–1860," *Ethnohistory*, 10 (Summer 1963), 204.

25. John C. Calhoun, SW, to President James Madison, 24 January 1825, in Henry Rowe Schoolcraft, *Information Respecting the History, Condition, and Prospects of the Indian Tribes of the United States*, 6 vols. (Philadelphia: J. B. Lippincott & Co., 1853–1860), 3:575–80; William Clark, Supt., to Calhoun, 1 March 1826, *ASP:IA*, II:653–54; Report of Lewis Cass, SW, 21 November 1831, *House Executive Document* 2 (22–1), ser. 216, 27–34; Stokes Commission, "Report of Commissioners of Indian Affairs West," 10 February 1834, *House Report* 474 (23–1), ser. 263, 85.

26. Satz, *American Indian Policy*, 19, 253, 272; Weinberg, *Manifest Destiny*, 85–87; William T. Hagan, "Justifying the Dispossession of the Indian: The Land Utilization Argument," in *American Indian Environments: Ecological Issues in Native American History*, ed. Christopher Vecsey and Robert W. Venables (Syracuse: Sy-

racuse University Press, 1980), 71–72; Arrell M. Gibson, "The Great Plains as a Colonization Zone for Eastern Indians," in *Ethnicity on the Great Plains*, ed. Frederick C. Luebke (Lincoln: University of Nebraska Press, 1980), 26–27.

27. George Copway, *Organization of a New Indian Territory, East of the Missouri River* (New York: S. W. Benedict, 1850), 4–17; Luke Lea, CIA, *ARCIA* 1850, ser. 587, 35–44. See also Robert A. Trennert's sketches of commissioners William Medill, Orlando Brown, and Luke Lea in Kvasnicka and Viola, eds., *Commissioners of Indian Affairs*, 29–56; Robert A. Trennert, Jr., *Alternative to Extinction: Federal Indian Policy and the Beginnings of the Reservation System, 1846–51* (Philadelphia: Temple University Press, 1975) 60, 193–97, passim. For the duties of farmers see *House Report* 474 (23–1), ser. 263, 23–27. For an approximation of the number of agency farmers over time, see Lewis, "Plowing a Civilized Furrow," 70

28. Henry B. Whipple, "The Indian System," *North American Review*, 99 (October 1864), 452–54; Doolittle Committee, *Condition of the Indian Tribes* (Washington, D.C.: GPO, 1867), *Senate Report* 156 (39–2), ser. 1279; "Report to the President by the Indian Peace Commission," 7 January 1868, *House Executive Document* 97 (40–2), ser. 1337, 1–23. See also Robert H. Keller, Jr., *American Protestantism and United States Indian Policy, 1869–82* (Lincoln: University of Nebraska Press, 1983); Francis Paul Prucha, *American Indian Policy in Crisis: Christian Reformers and the Indian, 1865–1900* (Norman: University of Oklahoma Press, 1976).

29. Report of the Secretary of the Interior, 1879, *House Executive Document* no. 1, pt. 5 (46–2), ser. 1910, 5–6; Lawrie Tatum, *Our Red Brothers, and the Peace Policy of President Ulysses S. Grant* (Philadelphia: John C. Winston & Co., 1899), 23–24; Wilbur James, Agent, to CIA, as quoted in Keller, *American Protestantism*, 160, and also pp. 47–71, 189, 205–16, and 219–37.

30. Leonard A. Carlson, *Indians, Bureaucrats, and Land: The Dawes Act and the Decline of Indian Farming* (Westport, Conn.: Greenwood Press, 1981), and Carlson, "Learning to Farm: Indian Land Tenure and Farming Before the Dawes Act," in *Property Rights and Indian Economies: The Political Economy Forum*, ed. Terry L. Anderson (Lanham, Md.: Rowman & Littlefield, 1992), 67–83, presents an interesting cliometric analysis of Indian farming that indicates its growth prior to allotment. Problems emerge in assessing if Indians are in fact doing the farming, and in taking Indian Bureau statistics at face value.

31. William T. Hagan, "Private Property, the Indian's Door to Civilization," *Ethnohistory*, 3 (Spring 1956), 126–37; Paul W. Gates, "Indian Allotment Preceding the Dawes Act," in *The Frontier Challenge: Responses to the Trans-Mississippi West*, ed. John G. Clark (Lawrence: University of Kansas Press, 1971), 141–70; Lewis, "Plowing a Civilized Furrow," 49–51.

32. Henry L. Dawes, as quoted in Delos S. Otis, *The Dawes Act and the Allotment of Indian Lands*, ed. Francis P. Prucha (Norman: University of Oklahoma Press, 1973), 11; Kappler, *Indian Affairs*, I:33–36; Act of 8 February 1887, 24 *Stats.* 388. On allotment policy see Prucha, *Great Father*, II:659–916.

33. Frederick E. Hoxie, *A Final Promise: The Campaign to Assimilate the Indians, 1880–1920* (Lincoln: University of Nebraska Press, 1983), x–xi, 38–39, 112–13, 161–62, 183–87, 241–43, 284 n.74.

34. Otis, *The Dawes Act*, 78; Laurence F. Schmeckebier, *The Office of Indian Affairs: Its History, Activities and Organization*, (Baltimore: Johns Hopkins Press, 1927), 250, 414; "Pay of Farmers, Indian Service," 29 January 1910,

House Document 614 (61–2), ser. 5836; OIA, *Regulations of the Indian Office, with an Appendix Containing the Forms Used* (Washington, D.C.: GPO, 1894), 102–3; "Helping Indians to Understand Farming Better," *The Red Man*, 8 (December 1915), 126; OIA, "Demonstration Farms," U.S. Indian Service *Bulletin*, no. 2 (Washington, D.C.: GPO, 1910); Hoxie, *A Final Promise*, 168–74; Thomas J. Morgan, CIA, *ARCIA* 1890, ser. 2841, c–ci. For more information on Indian Bureau farmers, particularly the problems surrounding their tenure and performance, see Lewis, "Plowing a Civilized Furrow," 52–59.

35. Elsie E. Newton, "The Work of the Field Matron: A Letter to a Prospective Field Matron," *The Indian School Journal*, 14 (Nov. 1913), 107–9; "Letter from the Secretary of the Interior . . . Relative to the Employment of Matrons at Agencies," 18 April 1888, *Senate Executive Document* 160 (50–1), ser. 2513; Adams, *American Indian Education*, 55; Lida W. Quimby, "The Field Matron's Work," in Estelle Reel, *Report of the Superintendent of Indian Schools* (Washington, D.C.: GPO, 1900), 56–58. See also Lisa E. Emmerich, "'To Respect and Love and Seek the Ways of White Women': Field Matrons, The Office of Indian Affairs, and Civilization Policy, 1890–1938" (Ph.D diss., University of Maryland, 1987); Emmerich, "'Right in the Midst of My Own People': Native American Women and the Field Matron Program," *American Indian Quarterly*, 15 (Spring 1991), 201–16; Emmerich, "'Civilization' and Transculturation: The Field Matron Program and Cross-Cultural Contact," *American Indian Culture and Research Journal*, 15 no. 4 (1991), 33–47; Rebecca J. Herring, "The Creation of Indian Farm Women: Field Matrons and Acculturation on the Kiowa-Comanche Reservation, 1895–1906," in *At Home on the Range: Essays on the History of Western Social and Domestic Life*, ed. John R. Wunder (Westport, Conn.: Greenwood Press, 1985), 39–56.

36. OIA, "Indian Fairs," U.S. Indian Service *Bulletin* no. 1 (Washington, D.C.: GPO, 1909); OIA, "Progress in Indian Farming," U.S. Indian Service *Bulletin* no. 3 (Washington, D.C.: GPO, 1911); *ARCIA* 1913, ser. 6634, 10–12; *ARCIA* 1915, ser. 6992, 23; Special Agricultural Fair Number, *The Red Man*, 8 (December 1915), 109–146; "An Indian Farmers' Institute Organized," *Indian School Journal*, 15 (March 1915), 380; "Indians Called Agriculturalists to Get Help," *The Red Man*, 8 (December 1915), 130–31; J. F. Wojta, "Indian Farm Institutes in Wisconsin," *Wisconsin Magazine of History*, 29 (June 1946), 423–34.

37. Henry Teller, SI, quoted in *Regulations of the Indian Department, With an Appendix Containing the Forms Used* (Washington, D.C.: GPO, 1884), 91–92; House Committee on Indian Affairs, "Industrial Training Schools, Report," 14 June 1879, *House Report* 29 (46–1), ser. 1934; Estelle Reel, "Industrial Training for Indian Children," *Southern Workman*, 29 (April 1900), 199–202; Reel, *Report*, 6–13; Robert A. Trennert, *The Phoenix Indian School: Forced Assimilation in Arizona, 1891–1935* (Norman: University of Oklahoma Press, 1988). See also Francis Paul Prucha, *The Churches and the Indian Schools, 1888–1912* (Lincoln: University of Nebraska Press, 1979); Margaret Szasz, *Education and the American Indian: The Road to Self-Determination, 1928–1973* (Albuquerque: University of New Mexico Press, 1974).

38. OIA, *Course of Study for the Indian Schools of the United States, Industrial and Literary*, (Washington, D.C.: GPO, 1901); OIA, *Tentative Course of Study for United States Indian Schools* (Washington, D.C.: GPO, 1915); OIA, *Some Things That Girls Should Know How to Do and Hence Should Learn How to Do When in School* (Washington, D.C.: GPO, 1911); OIA, *Farm and Home Mechanics: Some*

Things That Every Boy Should Know How to Do and Hence Should Learn How to Do in School (Washington, D.C.: GPO, 1911); Ross L. Spalsbury, "Agricultural Instruction in Day Schools," *The Native American*, 14 (25 January 1913), 43–45, and (1 February 1913), 67–69; "Farmers Among Returned Indians," *Southern Workman*, 29 (March 1900), 172–73; Levi Chubbuck, "Indian Agriculture," *The Native American*, 14 (24 May 1913), 307–8; Alfred Jackson, "Agriculture and School Gardens," *The Native American*, 16 (22 May 1915), 251–52; Reel, *Report*, 18–21. For a less-than-favorable assessment of the results see Board of Indian Commissioners, "Returned Student Survey," *Bulletin*, nos. 24, 55, 57, and 59 (1916–18), Washington, D.C., typescripts, MS 909, Edward S. Ayer Collection, The Newberry Library.

39. Cato Sells, Circular Letter to Superintendents, *ARCIA* 1914, ser. 6815, 23; Hurt, *Indian Agriculture*, 139–40, 151, 157; Paul Stuart, *The Indian Office: Growth and Development of an American Institution, 1865–1900* (Ann Arbor, Mich.: UMI Research Press, 1979), 50–52. For problems, critiques, and regulation of government farmers see Lewis, "Plowing a Civilized Furrow," 55–58.

40. Jonathan Baxter Harrison, *The Latest Studies in Indian Reservations* (Philadelphia: Indian Rights Association, 1887), 19–24, 40–44, 75–79, 122–29, 181–82; Felix S. Cohen, *Handbook of Federal Indian Law, with Reference Tables and Index* (Washington, D.C.: GPO, 4th printing, 1945), 190–91, 204–5, 213–15; *Lake Mohonk Conference of Friends of the Indian and Other Dependent Peoples, Annual Proceedings*, 1899, pp. 19–20; 1900, pp. 20–21; and 1915, p. 65 (hereafter LMC, *Proceedings*). See also Orlan J. Svingen, "Reservation Self-Sufficiency: Stock Raising vs. Farming on the Northern Cheyenne Indian Reservation, 1900–1914," *Montana, The Magazine of Western History*, 31 (October 1981), 14–23; Peter Iverson, "Cowboys, Indians and the Modern West," *Arizona and the West* 28 (Summer 1986), 107–24.

41. Hoxie, *A Final Promise*, 158–87; Cohen, *Handbook*, 211–15, 325–32; Hurt, *Indian Agriculture*, 141–45, 158–59, 164; Schmeckebier, *Office of Indian Affairs*, 448–58; Act of 28 February 1891, 26 *Stats.* 794; Act of 25 June 1910, 36 *Stats.* 855; Janet A. McDonnell, *The Dispossession of the American Indian, 1887–1934* (Bloomington: Indiana University Press, 1991), 43–70.

42. John Wesley Powell, "Indians West of the Rocky Mountains," 22 January 1874, *House Miscellaneous Document* 86 (43–1), ser. 1618, 9; Cohen, *Handbook*, 248–52, 316–19; Hoxie, *A Final Promise*, 168–72; Prucha, *Great Father*, II:891–94; William A. DuPuy, "Giving the Indian an Irrigated Farm," *The Red Man*, 4 (September 1911), 17–24; Porter J. Preston and Charles A. Engle, "Report of Advisors on Irrigation on Indian Reservations," 8 June 1928, in *Survey of Conditions of the Indians in the United States: Hearings . . .* (Washington, D.C.: GPO, 1930), Part 6:2210–2673, particularly 6:2213–18.

43. Myrle Wright, "A Ritual for Citizenship," *National Magazine*, 45 (December 1916), 331–33; Janet A. McDonnell, "Competency Commissions and Indian Land Policy, 1913–1920," *South Dakota History*, 11 (Winter 1980), 21–34.

44. Meriam and Associates, *Problem of Indian Administration*, 5–8, 14–16, 21–23, 134–35, 382–90, 488–515, 591–98; Hurt, *Indian Agriculture*, 167–70.

45. Hurt, *Indian Agriculture*, 174–213; James E. Officer, "Arid Lands Agriculture and the Indians of the American Southwest," in *Food, Fiber, and the Arid Lands*, ed. William G. McGinnies, Bram J. Goldman, and Patricia Paylore (Tucson: University of Arizona Press, 1971), 74; Floyd A. O'Neil, "The Indian New Deal: An Overview," in *Indian Self-Rule: First-Hand Accounts of Indian-*

White Relations from Roosevelt to Reagan, ed. Kenneth R. Philp (Salt Lake City: Howe Brothers, 1986), 31; Prucha, *Great Father,* II:940–1110.

46. Sar A. Levitan and Barbara Hetrick, *Big Brother's Indian Programs— With Reservations* (New York: McGraw-Hill, 1971), 127–38; Terry L. Anderson and Dean Lueck, "Agricultural Development and Land Tenure in Indian Country," in Anderson, ed., *Property Rights,* 147–66; Tom Barry, "The Navajo Agricultural Products Industry: Subsistence Farming to Corporate Agribusiness," *American Indian Journal,* 5 (July 1979), 2–6; Henry W. Kipp, *Indians in Agriculture: A Historical Sketch,* prepared for the Task Force of the American Indian Agricultural Council, 7 August 1987; National Indian Agricultural Working Group, *Final Findings and Recommendations,* prepared for the Assistant Secretary of Indian Affairs and the Intertribal Agriculture Council, December 1987; Bunty Anquoe, "BIA Opposes Agriculture Bill," *Lakota Times* (Rapid City, S.Dak.), 30 September 1992, A-3. On the numbers and BIA inflation of numbers of Native Americans farming in the twentieth century see Nabhan, *Enduring Seeds,* 61–62.

47. Merrill E. Gates, president, BIC, in LMC, *Proceedings,* 1896, 11.

48. U.S. Bureau of the Census, "Agriculture on Indian Reservations," *Twelfth Census of the United States, 1900,* vols. 5 and 6 (Washington, D.C.: U.S. Census Office, 1902), 5:717–40; Carlson, *Indians, Bureaucrats, and Land,* 22–23, 130–44; Carlson, "Land Allotment and the Decline of American Indian Farming," *Explorations in Economic History,* 18 (April 1981), 128–54; Hurt, *Indian Agriculture,* 113–173.

Chapter 2

1. Sydney M. Lamb, "Linguistic Prehistory in the Great Basin," *International Journal of American Linguistics,* 24 no. 2 (1958), 95–100; Wick R. Miller, "Numic Languages," *Handbook of North American Indians,* vol. 11, *Great Basin,* ed. Warren L. D'Azevedo (Washington, D.C.: Smithsonian Institution, 1986), 11:98–106 (hereafter cited as D'Azevedo, ed., *Great Basin,* 11).

2. James A. Goss, "Ute Language, Kin, Myth, and Nature: A Demonstration of a Multi-Dimensional Folk Taxonomy," *Anthropological Linguistics,* 9 (December 1967), 1–11; Jay Miller, "Basin Religion and Theology: A Comparative Study of Power (Puha)," *Journal of California and Great Basin Anthropology,* 5, nos. 1 and 2 (1983), 66–86; John Wesley Powell, "Sketch of the Mythology of the North American Indians," *Annual Report of the Bureau of American Ethnology, 1879–1880,* no. 1 (Washington, D.C.: GPO, 1881), 17–56; Powell, "The Life and Culture of the Ute," National Anthropological Archives, no. 830, piece 10, Washington, D.C.; Joseph G. Jorgensen, "Functions of Ute Folklore" (Masters thesis, University of Utah, 1960).

3. Robert H. Lowie, "Shoshonean Tales," *Journal of American Folk-Lore,* 37 (January–June 1924), 3–4; Powell, "Sketch of the Mythology," 17–56; Powell, "Ute and Paiute Legends, 1873," National Anthropological Archives, no. 794–a, Washington, D.C.; Fred A. Conetah, *A History of the Northern Ute People,* ed. Kathryn L. MacKay and Floyd A. O'Neil (Salt Lake City: University of Utah Printing Service for the Uintah-Ouray Ute Tribe, 1982), 2.

4. Jesse D. Jennings, *Prehistory of Utah and the Eastern Great Basin,* University of Utah Anthropological Papers, no. 98 (Salt Lake City: University of Utah Press, 1978), 235, 245–46; C. Melvin Aikens and Younger T. Witherspoon,

"Great Basin Numic Prehistory: Linguistics, Archeology, and Environment," in *Anthropology of the Desert West: Essays in Honor of Jesse D. Jennings*, ed. Carol J. Condie and Don D. Fowler, University of Utah Anthropological Papers, no. 110 (Salt Lake City: University of Utah Press, 1986), 7–20; C. Melvin Aikens and David B. Madsen, "Prehistory of the Eastern Area," in D'Azevedo, ed., *Great Basin*, 11:149–60; Anne Milne Smith, *Ethnography of the Northern Utes*, Papers in Anthropology, no. 17 (Santa Fe: Museum of New Mexico Press, 1974), 10–17; Conetah, *History*, 23–26; Julian H. Steward, *Aboriginal and Historical Groups of the Ute Indians of Utah: An Analysis with Supplement* (New York: Garland Publishing Co., 1974), 62–93; Donald Callaway, Joel Janetski, and Omer C. Stewart, "Ute," in D'Azevedo, ed., *Great Basin*, 11:338–40, 364–67.

5. Powell, "Ute and Paiute Legends"; Uintah-Ouray Ute Tribe, *The Way It was Told* (Salt Lake City: University of Utah Printing Service for the Uintah-Ouray Ute Tribe, 1977), 5; Anne M. Cooke, "An Analysis of Basin Mythology," 2 vols. (Ph.D. diss., Yale University, 1940), 2:62–64, 85–86, 181–83.

6. The following descriptions of flora, fauna and biotic zones are found in: Ivar Tidestrom, "Flora of Utah and Nevada," *U.S. National Museum, National Herbarium Contributions*, 25 (Washington, D.C., 1925); Kimball T. Harper, "Historical Environments," in D'Azevedo, ed., *Great Basin*, 11:51–63; Elias Yanovsky, *Food Plants of the North American Indians*, USDA, Miscellaneous Publications no. 237 (Washington, D.C.: GPO, 1936); Walter Ebeling, *Handbook of Indian Foods and Fibers of Arid America* (Berkeley: University of California Press, 1986), 70–135 and passim; Julian H. Steward, *Basin-Plateau Aboriginal Sociopolitical Groups*, Smithsonian Institution, BAE Bulletin 120 (Washington, D.C.: GPO, 1938), 14–18, 33–44; Ralph V. Chamberlin, "Some Plant Names of the Ute Indians," *American Anthropologist*, 11 (January 1909), 27–40; Jennings, *Prehistory*, 9–15; Joseph G. Jorgensen, "The Ethnohistory and Acculturation of the Northern Ute" (Ph.D. diss., Indiana University, 1965), 168–74.

7. For Basin landscape see Jennings, *Prehistory*, 7; John McPhee, *Basin and Range* (New York: Farrar, Straus & Giroux, 1981); George D. Louderback, "Basin Range Structure in the Great Basin," University of California Publications, *Bulletin of the Department of Geological Sciences*, 14, no. 10 (8 November 1923), 329–76; Donald R. Currey and Steven R. James, "Paleoenvironments of the Northeastern Great Basin and Northeastern Basin Rim Region: A Review of Geological and Biological Evidence," in *Man and Environment in the Great Basin*, ed. David B. Madsen and James F. O'Connell, Society for American Archaeology Papers, no. 2 (Washington, D.C.: SAA, 1982), 27–52.

8. For Plateau landscape see Helen M. Wormington and Robert Lister, *Archaeological Investigations on the Uncompahgre Plateau in West Central Colorado*, Denver Museum of Natural History, Proceedings, no. 2 (Denver, 1956), 2–3; C. E. Dutton, *Report on the Geology of the High Plateaus of Utah*, U.S. Geographical and Geological Survey of the Rocky Mountain Region (Washington, D.C.: GPO, 1880); John Wesley Powell, *Report on the Lands of the Arid Region of the United States* (Washington, D.C.: GPO, 1878).

9. For Uinta Basin landscape see John Clark, "Geomorphology of the Uinta Basin," in *Guidebook to the Geology of the Uinta Basin*, ed. Otto G. Seal (Salt Lake City: Intermountain Assoc. of Petroleum Geologists, 1957), 17–20; G. E. Untermann and B. R. Untermann, *Geology of Uintah County*, Utah Geological and Mineralogical Survey, Bulletin 72 (Salt Lake City, 1964), 13–14; Powell, *Report on the Lands*, 150–64; Planning Support Group, Bureau of Indian

Affairs, *The Uintah and Ouray Indian Reservation: Its Resources & Development Potential*, Report no. 214 (Billings, Mont., February 1974), vii–x, 48, 52.

10. For Rockies landscape see Frederic M. Endlich, "Report on the Geology of the White River District," *U.S. Geological and Geographical Survey of the Territories*, 10 (Washington, D.C.: GPO, 1878), 66–69; Gustavus R. Bechler, "Topographical Report on the Yampa Division, 1876," Ibid., 365–75; Alice Hunt, *Archaeological Survey of the LaSal Mountain Area, Utah*, University of Utah Anthropological Papers, no. 14 (Salt Lake City: University of Utah Press, 1953), 2–4.

11. David B. Madsen, "Get It Where the Gettin's Good: A Variable Model of Great Basin Subsistence and Settlement Based on Data from the Eastern Great Basin," in Madsen and O'Connell, eds., *Man and Environment*, 207–26.

12. Marvin K. Opler, "The Ute and Paiute Indians of the Great Basin Southern Rim," in *North American Indians in Historical Perspective*, ed. Eleanor B. Leacock and Nancy O. Lurie (New York: Random House, 1971), 160–62; Opler, "The Southern Ute of Colorado," in *Acculturation in Seven American Indian Tribes*, ed. Ralph Linton (New York: D. Appleton-Century Co., 1940), 124–25; Jennings, *Prehistory*, 246–47; Steward, *Basin-Plateau*, 35–39.

13. Omer C. Stewart, *Culture Element Distributions XVIII: Ute-Southern Paiute*, University of California Publications, *Anthropological Records* (hereafter *UCPAR*), 6, no. 4 (Berkeley: University of California Press, 1942), 245–46, 298–99; Smith, *Ethnography*, 61–67; J. A. Jones, *The Sun Dance of the Northern Ute*, Smithsonian Institution, BAE Bulletin 157, Anthropological Paper no. 47 (Washington, D.C.: GPO, 1955), 255–56; Joseph G. Jorgensen, *Sun Dance Religion: Power for the Powerless* (Chicago: University of Chicago Press, 1972), 231–32.

14. Miller, "Basin Religion and Theology," 73–74; Smith *Ethnography*, 51–57; Powell, "Life and Culture of the Ute," piece 5; Omer C. Stewart, *Ute Peyotism: A Study of a Cultural Complex*, University of Colorado Studies, Series in Anthropology, no. 1 (Boulder: University of Colorado Press, 1948), 35.

15. Smith, *Ethnography*, 46–64, 268–69; Stewart, *Culture Element Distributions XVIII*, 240–54; Robert H. Lowie, "Notes on Shoshonean Ethnography," *American Museum of Natural History, Anthropological Papers*, 20, pt. 3 (New York: American Museum Press, 1924), 199–203; Steward, *Basin-Plateau*, 33–44; Powell, "Life and Culture of the Ute," piece 4; Robert F. Heizer, *Notes on the Utah Utes by Edward Palmer, 1866–1877*, University of Utah Anthropological Papers, no. 17 (Salt Lake City: University of Utah Press, 1954); Joel C. Janetski, "The Great Basin Lacustrine Subsistence Pattern: Insights from Utah Valley," in Condie and Fowler, eds., *Anthropology of the Desert West*, 145–67; Janetski, *The Ute of Utah Lake*, University of Utah Anthropological Papers, no. 116 (Salt Lake City: University of Utah Press, 1991).

16. Ralph V. Chamberlin, "Man and Nature in Early Utah," *Proceedings of the Utah Academy of Sciences, Arts and Letters*, 24 (1947), 3–11; Chamberlin, "Some Plant Names," 27–40; Smith, *Ethnography*, 64–67, 269–74; Stewart, *Culture Element Distributions XVIII*, 250–52; John Wesley Powell, *Anthropology of the Numa: John Wesley Powell's Manuscripts on the Numic Peoples of Western North America, 1868–1880*, ed. Don D. Fowler and Catherine S. Fowler (Washington, D.C.: Smithsonian Institution, 1971), 39; Florence Hawley et al., "Culture Process and Change in Ute Adaptation," *El Palacio*, 57 (October–November

1950), 324–25; Catherine S. Fowler, "Subsistence," in D'Azevedo, ed., *Great Basin*, 11:64–97.

17. Although John Wesley Powell and others noted that the Pahvant and Tumpanuwac Utes raised some maize, their shifting cultivation techniques were most probably a limited late-prehistoric diffusion or early contact phenomenon. Joseph C. Winter and Patrick F. Hogan, "Plant Husbandry in the Great Basin and Adjacent Northern Colorado Plateau," in Condie and Fowler, eds., *Anthropology of the Desert West*, 75–78, 117–144.

18. Smith, *Ethnography*, 46–47, 57–60, 67; Conetah, *History*, 9–11; Powell, "Life and Culture of the Ute," piece 4; Stewart, *Culture Element Distributions XVIII*, 244–45, 252–54. Utes called the months of February or March *miwi=pi kacuai*, "strip of buckskin," or "buckskin end," referring to the period when stored food ran low and they stewed buckskin bags for food.

19. Anne M. Smith, *Cultural Differences and Similarities Between Uintah and White River* (New York: Garland Publishing Co., 1974); Smith, *Ethnography*, 46–47; Stewart, *Culture Element Distributions XVIII*, 240–54; Callaway, Janetski, and Stewart, "Ute," 340–45; Madsen, "Get it Where the Gettin's Good," 207–26.

20. Jorgensen, "Ethnohistory and Acculturation," 11–15.

21. Smith, *Ethnography*, 121–28, 149–50; Jorgensen, "Ethnohistory and Acculturation," 25–33; Stewart, *Culture Element Distributions XVIII*, 296–303; Powell, "Life and Culture of the Ute," piece 7; Gottfried O. Lang, *A Study in Culture Contact and Culture Change: The Whiterock Utes in Transition*, University of Utah Anthropological Papers, no. 15 (Salt Lake City: University of Utah Press, 1953), 8–11; Steward, *Aboriginal and Historical Groups*, 33–35, 141–50; Hawley, "Culture Process and Change," 313; Calloway, Janetski, and Stewart, "Ute," 352–53.

22. Jorgensen, "Ethnohistory and Acculturation," 11–15, 20–22; S. Lyman Tyler, "The Yuta Before 1680," *Western Humanities Review*, 5 (Spring 1951), 162–63; Smith, *Ethnography*, 237–39. Others posit a more profound impact and radical change, including Jones, *Sun Dance*, 213–16, 236–37; Steward, "Native Cultures," 477, 482–87, 492; Opler, "Ute and Paiute Indians," 271–76. For more on Ute material culture see Smith, *Ethnography*, 33–46, 69–120, 228–37; Stewart, *Culture Element Distributions XVIII*, 256–95; Calloway, Janetski, and Stewart, "Ute," 345–50.

23. Jay Miller, "Numic Religion: An Overview of Power in the Great Basin of Native North America," *Anthropos*, 78, nos. 3–4 (1983), 337–54; Miller, "Basin Religion and Theology," 66–67; Jorgensen, "Ethnohistory and Acculturation," 328–29.

24. Miller, "Basin Religion and Theology," 77–78; Jorgensen, *Sun Dance Religion*, 206–16; Jorgensen, "Ethnohistory and Acculturation," 330–33; Joanna Lynne Endter, "Cultural Ideologies and the Political Economy of Water in the United States West: Northern Ute Indians and Rural Mormons in the Uintah Basin, Utah" (Ph.D. diss., University of California-Irvine, 1987), 92, 232–39; Stephanie Romero, "Concepts of Nature and Power: Environmental Ethics of the Northern Ute," *Environmental Review*, 9 (Summer 1985), 150–70.

25. Jorgensen, "Ethnohistory and Acculturation," 33–67, 328–61; Smith, *Ethnography*, 152–67; Stewart, *Culture Element Distributions XVIII*, 315–18; Hawley, "Culture Process and Change," 347–48; Densmore, *Northern Ute*

Music, Smithsonian Institution, BAE Bulletin 75 (Washington, D.C.: GPO, 1922), 127–30.

26. Smith, *Ethnography*, 137–52; Stewart, *Culture Element Distributions XVIII*, 303–15; Calloway, Janetski, and Stewart, "Utes," 350–52; Opler, "Southern Ute," 135–36.

27. Throughout the season, Utes held other social dances, some of which contained overtones of ritual health maintenance, but none as significant as the Bear Dance. See Verner Z. Reed, "The Ute Bear Dance," *American Anthropologist*, 9 (July 1896), 237–44; Julian H. Steward, "A Uintah Ute Bear Dance, March, 1931," *American Anthropologist*, 34 (April–June 1932), 263–73; Smith, *Ethnography*, 220–27; Stewart, *Culture Element Distributions XVIII*, 321–24.

28. Jorgensen, *Sun Dance Religion*, 5–12, 19–26, 39–40, 216, 219–20, 231–36; Marvin K. Opler, "The Integration of the Sun Dance in Ute Religion," *American Anthropologist*, 43 (October–December 1941), 550–72; Smith, *Ethnography*, 208, 216–20; Jones, *Sun Dance*, 227, 239–59; Robert H. Lowie, *Sun Dance of the Shoshoni, Ute, and Hidatsa*, American Museum of Natural History, Anthropological Papers, vol. 16, pt. 5 (New York, 1919), 405–10; James Mooney, *The Ghost-Dance Religion and the Sioux Outbreak of 1890*, ed. and abr. Anthony F. C. Wallace (Chicago: University of Chicago Press, 1965), 46, 49–50, passim; David F. Aberle and Omer C. Stewart, *Navaho and Ute Peyotism: A Chronological and Distributional Study*, University of Colorado Studies, Series in Anthropology, no. 6 (Boulder: University of Colorado, 1957); Stewart, *Ute Peyotism: A Study of a Cultural Complex*, University of Colorado Studies, Series in Anthropology, no. 1 (Boulder: University of Colorado, 1948).

29. S. Lyman Tyler, "Before Escalante, An Early History of the Yuta Indians and the Area North of New Mexico" (Ph.D. diss., University of Utah, 1951); Tyler, "The Spaniard and the Ute," *Utah Historical Quarterly*, 22 (October 1954), 343–61; Floyd A. O'Neil, "A History of the Ute Indians of Utah Until 1890" (Ph.D. diss., University of Utah, 1973), 7–24; Jorgensen, *Sun Dance Religion*, 29–31, 37–38; Conetah, *History*, 27–35; John R. Alley, Jr., "Prelude to Dispossession: The Fur Trade's Significance for the Northern Utes and Southern Paiutes," *Utah Historical Quarterly*, 50 (Spring 1982), 104–123.

Chapter 3

1. Howard A. Christy, "Open Hand and Mailed Fist: Mormon-Indian Relations in Utah, 1847–52," *Utah Historical Quarterly*, 46 (Summer 1978), 219–222; Richard Edmond Bennett, "Cousin Laman in the Wilderness: The Beginnings of Brigham Young's Indian Policy," *Nebraska History*, 67 (Spring 1986), 69–82.

2. John Wilson as quoted in Alban W. Hoopes, *Indian Affairs and Their Administration, with Special Reference to the Far West, 1849–1860* (Philadelphia: University of Pennsylvania Press, 1932), 131; Howard A. Christy, "'What Virtue There is in Stone' and Other Pungent Talk on the Early Utah Frontier," *Utah Historical Quarterly*, 59 (Summer 1991), 301–306; Floyd A. O'Neil, "A History of the Ute Indians of Utah Until 1890" (Ph.D. diss., University of Utah, 1973), 26–28; Gottfried O. Lang, *A Study in Culture Contact and Culture Change: The Whiterock Utes in Transition*, University of Utah Anthropological Papers, no. 15 (Salt Lake City: University of Utah Press, 1953), 12. For the importance of Utah Valley see Joel C. Janetski, *The Ute of Utah Lake*, University of Utah Anthropo-

logical Papers, no. 116 (Salt Lake City: University of Utah Press, 1991); Janetski, "Utah Lake: Its Role in the Prehistory of Utah Valley," *Utah Historical Quarterly*, 58 (Winter 1990), 5–31.

3. J. H. Holeman, Supt. of Indian Affairs, Utah, to CIA, 28 November 1851, NA, RG 75, microcopy 234, reel 897.

4. Brigham Young, Supt. of Indian Affairs, Utah, to CIA, 30 November 1851, NA, RG 75, microcopy 234, reel 897; Young to CIA, 20 May 1852, NA, RG 75, microcopy 234, reel 897; Young to CIA, 28 June 1853, NA, RG 75, microcopy 234, reel 897; Christy, "Open Hand," 232–33; Floyd A. O'Neil and Stanford J. Layton, "Of Pride and Politics: Brigham Young as Indian Superintendent," *Utah Historical Quarterly*, 46 (Summer 1978), 236–50; Beverly P. Smaby, "The Mormons and the Indians: Conflicting Ecological Systems in the Great Basin," *American Studies*, 16 (Spring 1975), 35–48.

5. Brigham Young, Supt. of Indian Affairs, Utah, to CIA, 30 September 1853, *ARCIA* 1853, ser. 710, 441–43; E. A. Bedell, Agent, to Young, 6 April 1854, NA, RG 75, microcopy 234, reel 897; O'Neil, "History," 28–34; Howard A. Christy, "The Walker War: Defense and Conciliation as Strategy," *Utah Historical Quarterly*, 47 (Fall 1979), 395–420.

6. George W. Armstrong, Agent, to Brigham Young, Supt. of Indian Affairs, Utah, 20 June 1855, NA, RG 75, microcopy 234, reel 897; Garland Hurt, Agent, to John Elliott, HR, 4 October 1856, NA, RG 75, microcopy 234, reel 897.

7. Garland Hurt, Agent, to CIA, 2 April 1855, NA, RG 75, microcopy 234, reel 897; Hurt to CIA, 30 June 1855, NA, RG 75, microcopy 234, reel 897.

8. Brigham Young, Supt. of Indian Affairs, Utah, to CIA, 30 June 1855, NA, RG 75, microcopy 234, reel 897; Garland Hurt, Agent, to Young, 31 December 1855, NA, RG 75, microcopy 234, reel 898; Joanna Lynne Endter, "Cultural Ideologies and the Political Economy of Water in the United States West: Northern Ute Indians and Rural Mormons in the Uintah Basin, Utah" (Ph.D. diss., University of California-Irvine, 1987), 108.

9. Brigham Young, Supt. of Indian Affairs, Utah, to CIA, 30 June 1856, and Garland Hurt, Agent, to Young, September 1856, *ARCIA* 1856, ser. 893, 775–83; Hurt to CIA, 30 June 1857, NA, RG 75, microcopy 234, reel 898; Hurt to Young, 29 November 1857, microcopy 234, reel 898; Hurt to Jacob Forney, Supt. of Indian Affairs, Utah, 14 September 1858, NA, RG 75, microcopy 234, reel 898. For general histories see Beverly Beeton, "Teach Them to Till the Soil: An Experiment with Indian Farms, 1850–1862," *American Indian Quarterly*, 3 (Winter 1977–78), 299–320; Richard H. Jackson, "The Mormon Indian Farms: An Attempt at Cultural Integration," in *Geographical Perspectives on Native Americans: Topics and Resources*, ed. Jerry N. McDonald and Tony Lazewski (Association of American Geographers, Associated Committee on Native Americans, Publication 1, 1976), 41–54.

10. John B. Floyd, SW, *Annual Report of the Secretary of War*, 5 December 1857, ser. 920, 6–9, 21–38; Garland Hurt, Agent, to Colonel A. S. Johnston, 24 October 1857, NA, RG 75, microcopy 234, reel 898; Jacob Forney, Supt. of Indian Affairs, Utah, to CIA, 6 September 1858, *ARCIA* 1858, ser. 997, 561–65; O'Neil, "History," 46–50; Beeton, "Teach Them," 306–15; Fred A. Conetah, *A History of the Northern Ute People*, ed. Kathryn L. MacKay and Floyd A. O'Neil (Salt Lake City: University of Utah Printing Service, for the Uintah-Ouray Ute Tribe, 1982), 41.

11. Joseph G. Jorgensen, *Sun Dance Religion: Power for the Powerless* (Chicago: University of Chicago Press, 1972), 34–35.

12. *Deseret News*, 25 September 1861, 172; Charles J. Kappler, ed., *Indian Affairs: Laws and Treaties*, 2 vols. (Washington, D.C.: GPO, 1904), 1:900.

13. Act of 5 May 1864, 13 *Stats.* 63, amended 18 June 1878, 20 *Stats.* 165; O'Neil, "History," 52–59, 87; Amos Reed, Agent, to CIA, 30 December 1862, *ARCIA* 1863, ser. 1182, 2–3; James D. Doty, Supt. of Indian Affairs, Utah, to CIA, July 1863, *ARCIA* 1863, ser. 1182, 513–14; Secretary of the Interior, 5 December 1864, *Annual Report of the Secretary of the Interior*, 1864, ser. 1219, 160–61; Edmund J. Danziger, Jr., *Indians and Bureaucrats: Administering the Reservation Policy during the Civil War* (Urbana: University of Illinois Press, 1974), 62.

14. Daniel W. Jones, *Forty Years Among the Indians* (Salt Lake City: Juvenile Instructor Office, 1890), 192; O'Neil, "History," 55–60, 70–85; Warren Metcalf, "A Precarious Balance: The Northern Utes and the Black Hawk War," *Utah Historical Quarterly*, 57 (Winter 1989), 24–35; Albert Winkler, "The Ute Mode of War in the Conflict of 1865–68," *Utah Historical Quarterly*, 60 (Fall 1992), 300–18.

15. O. H. Irish, Supt. of Indian Affairs, Utah, Council Proceedings, Spanish Fork Treaty, 7–8 June 1865, NA, RG 75, Unratified Treaty Files; O'Neil, "History," 60–68.

16. Parson Dodds, Agent, to F. H. Head, Supt. of Indian Affairs, Utah, 8 September 1868, *ARCIA* 1868, ser. 1366, 616; Conetah, *History*, 86–90; O'Neil, "History," 89–94; Floyd A. O'Neil and Kathryn L. MacKay, *A History of the Uintah-Ouray Ute Lands*, Occasional Papers, no. 10 (Salt Lake City: American West Center, University of Utah, 1979), 7–8; John Wesley Powell, *Exploration of the Colorado River of the West and its Tributaries* (Washington, D.C.: GPO, 1875), 42–43.

17. F. H. Head, Supt. of Indian Affairs, Utah, to CIA, 1 August 1869, *ARCIA* 1869, ser. 1414, 668–71; Almon H. Thompson, "Diary of Almon Harris Thompson," *Utah Historical Quarterly*, 7 (Jan., April, July, 1939), 28–31.

18. J. J. Critchlow, Agent, to CIA, 22 September 1871, *ARCIA* 1871, ser. 1505, 960–66; Conetah, *History*, 90.

19. J. J. Critchlow, Agent, to CIA, 1 September 1872, *ARCIA* 1872, ser. 1560, 673; Critchlow to CIA, 25 September 1873, *ARCIA* 1873, ser. 1601, 628–29; O'Neil, "History," 109–10. For an assessment of the Uintah Basin see John Wesley Powell, *Report on the Lands of the Arid Region of the United States* (Washington, D.C.: GPO, 1878), 33–34.

20. J. J. Critchlow, Agent, to CIA, 25 September 1873, *ARCIA* 1873, ser. 1601, 628–29; Critchlow to CIA, September 1875, *ARCIA* 1875, ser. 1689, 600; Thompson, "Diary," 28; Jones, *Forty Years*, 195–211.

21. Report of J. W. Powell and G. W. Ingalls, 18 December 1873, *ARCIA* 1873, ser. 1601, 415, 424–25; J. J. Critchlow, Agent, to H. R. Clum, 15 March 1873, NA, RG 75, microcopy 234, reel 904; Critchlow to CIA, 1 September 1876, *ARCIA* 1876, ser. 1749, 534.

22. J. J. Critchlow, Agent, to CIA, 1 September 1872, *ARCIA* 1872, ser. 1560, 676; Jorgensen, *Sun Dance Religion*, 38–40. This intertribal council, held near San Pete, Utah, was possibly an experiment with the first Ghost Dance movement.

23. Joseph Jorgensen, "The Ethnohistory and Acculturation of the Northern Ute" (Ph.D. diss., Indiana University, 1965), 63–64, 82–89.

24. J. J. Critchlow, Agent, to CIA, 1 September 1876, *ARCIA* 1876, ser. 1749, 533.

25. Kappler, *Indian Affairs*, 2:586; Act of 30 December 1849, 9 *Stats*. 984; O'Neil and MacKay, *History of the Uintah-Ouray*, 8–9; Conetah, *History*, 42–51; J. Donald Hughes, *American Indians in Colorado* (Boulder: Pruett Publishing Co., 1977), 41–56; Morris F. Taylor, "Action at Fort Massachusetts: The Indian Campaign of 1855," *Colorado Magazine*, 42 (Fall 1965), 292–310.

26. Kappler, *Indian Affairs*, 2:858; Act of 7 October 1863, 13 *Stats*. 673; James W. Covington, "Federal Relations with the Colorado Utes, 1861–65," *Colorado Magazine*, 28 (October 1951), 257–65; John Nicolay, Treaty Commissioner, to CIA, 10 November 1863, *ARCIA* 1863, ser. 1182, 265–69.

27. "Reply of Capt. Charles Kerber, 1st Colorado Cavalry, August 8, 1865," in Doolittle Committee, *Condition of the Indian Tribes . . .* (Washington, D.C.: GPO, 1867), appendix, 480.

28. James F. Rusling, *Across America: or, The Great West and the Pacific Coast* (New York: Sheldon & Co., 1874), 114, 125–27; O'Neil and MacKay, *History of the Uintah-Ouray*, 9–11.

29. Kappler, *Indian Affairs*, 2:990; Act of 2 March 1868, 15 *Stats*. 619; James W. Wardle, "Reluctant Immigrants of Utah, the Uncompahgre Utes" (Master's thesis, Utah State University, 1976), 58; Conetah, *History*, 56–59, 93–113.

30. J. E. Tourtellotte, Supt. of Indian Affairs, Utah, to CIA, 20 September 1870, *ARCIA* 1870, ser. 1449, 605–08; John S. Littlefield, Agent, to CIA, 30 September 1871, *ARCIA* 1871, ser. 1505, 967–70; James B. Thompson, Agent, to CIA, 1 September 1874, *ARCIA* 1874, ser. 1639, 579–81.

31. Report of the Commission to Negotiate with the Ute Tribe of Indians, 15 October 1873, *ARCIA* 1873, ser. 1601, 83–113; Kappler, *Indian Affairs*, 2:36–41; Act of 29 April 1874, 18 *Stats*. 36; Hafen, *Historical Summary of the Ute Indians and the San Juan Mining Region* (New York: Garland Publishing Co., 1974), 288–324; Conetah, *History*, 60–61, 107–09; Jorgensen, *Sun Dance Religion*, 42–44; Wardle, "Reluctant Immigrants," 65–77.

32. John W. Powell, "Statement of . . . as to the Condition of the Indian Tribes West of the Rocky Mountains," 13 January 1874, *House Misc. Doc.*, no. 86 (43–1), ser. 1618, 2–8; *ARCIA* 1875, ser. 1689, 600; Joseph B. Abbott, Agent, to CIA, 17 August 1878, *ARCIA* 1878, ser. 1851, 511.

33. HR, "Testimony in Relation to the Ute Indian Outbreak, Taken by the Committee on Indian Affairs of the House of Representatives, May 1, 1880," *House Misc. Doc.*, no. 38 (46–2), ser. 1931, 18–26, 32–38, 94–103, 136–39, 151; Conetah, *History*, 96–97; J. Donald Hughes, *American Indian Ecology* (El Paso: Texas Western Press, 1983), 56; Omer C. Stewart, "Forest and Grass Burning in the Mountain West," *Southwestern Lore*, 21 (1955), 5–9; Wardle, "Reluctant Immigrants," 90–106.

34. Marshall Sprague, *Massacre: The Tragedy at White River* (Boston, 1957; reprinted, Lincoln: University of Nebraska Press, 1980), 3–27, 39–60, 130–41; Thomas Dawson and F. J. V. Skiff, *The Ute War: A History of the White River Massacre* (Denver, 1879; reprinted, Boulder: Johnson Publishing Co., 1980), 151–56; Robert Emmitt, *The Last War Trail: The Utes and the Settlement of Colorado* (Norman: University of Oklahoma Press, 1954), 44–50. See also David Boyd, *History of Greeley and the Union Colony of Colorado* (Greeley, 1890); Charles Fourier, *Theory of Social Organization* (New York: C. P. Somerby, 1876).

35. Nathan C. Meeker, Agent, to CIA, 29 July 1878, *ARCIA* 1878, ser. 1851, 514–15; Meeker to Greeley *Tribune*, 2 October 1878, in Nathan Cook Meeker, "Papers of Nathan Cook Meeker, 1873–1879," microfilm, Marriott Library, University of Utah (hereafter Meeker Papers).

36. Nathan C. Meeker, "The Utes, of Colorado," *American Antiquarian*, 1, no. 4 (1879), 224–26; Meeker to Senator Henry Teller, 23 December 1878, quoted in Emmitt, *Last War Trail* 68–74.

37. N. C. Meeker, Agent, to CIA, 7 July 1879, NA, RG 75, GR, White River, LR; Emmitt, *Last War Trail*, 61–64, 85; HR, "Testimony in Relation to the Ute Indian Outbreak," 72–75.

38. N. C. Meeker, Agent, to CIA, 3 March 1879, Meeker Papers; Emmitt, *Last War Trail*, 121–25.

39. Dawson and Skiff, *Ute War*, 58–59, 176; HR, "Testimony in Relation to the Ute Indian Outbreak," 13, 71, 104–5, 198–203.

40. N. C. Meeker, Agent, to CIA, 8 September 1879, NA, RG 75, GR, White River, LR; Meeker to CIA, 10 September 1879, NA, RG 75, GR, White River, LR; Conetah, *History*, 97–100; Sprague, *Massacre*, 159–265; Emmitt, *Last War Trail*, 121–287.

41. HR, "Testimony in Relation to the Ute Indian Outbreak," 9–10, 13, 91–93, 128, 188, 190, 198–200, 203; "Letter from the Secretary of the Interior, transmitting . . . copy of report of Ute Commission, and copies of all correspondence . . . ," 2 February 1881, *Senate Ex. Doc.* no. 31, ser. 1913; Kappler, *Indian Affairs*, 1:834–35, 2:180, and 2:834–35; Act of 15 June 1880, 21 *Stats.* 199; O'Neil and MacKay, *History of the Uintah-Ouray*, 12–14; Wardle, "Reluctant Immigrants," 107–28.

42. A. B. Meacham, Ute Commission, to S. J. Kirkwood, 23 July 1881, NA, RG 75, GR, U&O, LR; J. J. Critchlow, Agent, to CIA, 15 January 1883, NA, RG 75, GR, U&O, LR; E. W. Davis, Agent, to Henry Teller, SI, 2 August 1883, NA, RG 75, GR, U&O, LR; Davis to CIA, 20 August 1885, *ARCIA* 1885, ser. 2379, 180–81; William Parsons, Special Agent, to CIA, 29 May 1886, NA, RG 75, GR, U&O, LR; Jorgensen, "Ethnohistory," 257–58; Jorgensen, *Sun Dance Religion*, 48–50; O'Neil, "History," 167–76; Floyd A. O'Neil, "The Reluctant Suzerainty: The Uintah and Ouray Reservation," *Utah Historical Quarterly*, 39 (Spring 1971) 129–44.

43. J. J. Critchlow, Agent, to CIA, 18 August 1881, *ARCIA* 1881, ser. 2018, 215; Critchlow to CIA, 30 January 1882, NA, RG 75, GR, U&O, LR; Major M. Bryant to Headquarters, Department of the Missouri, 28 March 1882, NA, RG 75, GR, U&O, LR; Critchlow to CIA, 12 September 1881, NA, RG 75, GR, U&O, LR; J. F. Minniss, Agent, to CIA, 30 August 1882, and Critchlow to CIA, 1 September 1882, *ARCIA* 1882, ser. 2100, 208–09 and 209–12.

44. Paris H. Folsom, Special Agent, Report on Uintah & Ouray Schools, to CIA, 7 August 1885, NA, RG 75, GR, U&O, LR; Folsom to CIA, 6 August 1885, NA, RG 75, GR, U&O, LR.

45. Elisha W. Davis, Agent, to CIA, 20 August 1885, *ARCIA* 1885, ser. 2379, 406–8, 616; Eugene E. White, *Experiences of a Special Indian Agent* (Norman: University of Oklahoma Press, 1965), 96; T. A. Byrnes, Agent, to CIA, 24 July 1888, NA, RG 75, GR, U&O, LR.

46. Major E. G. Bush to Asst. Adjutant General, Dept. of the Platte, 4 June 1886, NA, RG 75, GR, U&O, LR; J. F. Gardner, Agent, to CIA, 12 August 1885, *ARCIA* 1885, ser. 2379, 402–5; J. B. Kinney, Agent, to CIA,

6 April 1886, NA, RG 75, GR, U&O, LR; William A. McKewan, Clerk in Charge, Ouray Agency, to Eugene E. White, Agent, 14 August 1886, *ARCIA* 1886, ser. 2467, 447; Jorgensen, "Ethnohistory," 119.

47. J. F. Minniss, Agent, to CIA, 13 August 1883, and E. W. Davis, Agent, to CIA, 14 August 1883, *ARCIA* 1883, ser. 2191, 195–98; Davis to CIA, 21 August 1884, *ARCIA* 1884, ser. 2287, 200–201; Jorgensen, "Ethnohistory," 119; White, *Experiences*, 158–61.

48. George K. Burnett, Uintah Agency, to Adjutant General, Omaha, 10 September 1887, enclosed in T. A. Byrnes to CIA, 11 September 1887, NA, RG 75, GR, U&O, LR; William H. Beck, Agent, to CIA, 26 July 1897, NA, RG 75, GR, U&O, LR. See also Robert Waugh, Agent, to CIA, 14 November 1890, NA, RG 75, GR, U&O, LR; Meeting in Washington, D.C. with Delegation of Indians from Uintah Reservation, 24–26 November 1898, NA, RG 75, GR, U&O, LR; W. A. Jones, CIA, to Visiting Delegation of Indians from the Uintah Reservation, 24 November 1898, NA, RG 75, GR, U&O, LR; *Ward v. Race Horse* (1896), 163 *U.S.*, 504; David Rich Lewis, "Plowing a Civilized Furrow: Subsistence, Environment, and Social Change Among the Northern Ute, Hupa, and Papago Peoples" (Ph.D. diss., University of Wisconsin-Madison, 1988), 170–74.

49. T. A. Byrnes, Agent, to CIA, 13 March 1887, NA, RG 75, GR, U&O, LR; Byrnes to CIA, 1 November 1887, NA, RG 75, GR, U&O, LR; Robert Waugh, Agent, to CIA, 6 October 1890, NA, RG 75, GR, U&O, LR; Thomas J. Morgan, CIA, to Robert Waugh, Agent, 1 March 1892, NA, RG 75, GR, U&O, Special Case 191; CIA to SI, 23 April 1892, NA, RG 75, GR, U&O, Special Case 191; Waugh to CIA, 21 February 1893, NA, RG 75, GR, U&O, LR; O'Neil and MacKay, *History of the Uintah-Ouray*, 22–24; CIA to H. P. Myton, Agent, 21 December 1899, NA, RG 75, GR, U&O, LR.

50. J. F. Randlett, Agent, to CIA, 30 August 1895, Annual Statistics, NA, RG 75, GR, U&O, LR. Between 1880 and 1895, Northern Ute populations plummet 38 percent (2,825 to 1,770, or 2.5 percent annually) and continue to fall an average of 1.4 percent annually (48 percent total) before bottoming out at 917 in 1930. See Jorgensen, *Sun Dance Religion*, 91.

51. Robert Waugh, Agent, to CIA, 21 August 1891, *ARCIA* 1891, ser. 2134, 436; Waugh to Herbert Welsh, Indian Rights Association, 17 June 1891, NA, RG 75, GR, U&O, LR; George W. Parker, Special Agent, to CIA, 18 July 1891 and 21 July 1891, NA, RG 75, GR, U&O, LR.

52. George W. Parker, Special Agent, to CIA, 18 July 1891, NA, RG 75, GR, U&O, LR; Robert Waugh, Agent, to CIA, 12 August 1892, NA, RG 75, GR, U&O, LR; William W. Junkins, Indian Inspector, to SI, 10 October 1892, NA, RG 75, GR, U&O, LR.

53. T. A. Byrnes, Agent, to CIA, 18 February 1888, NA, RG 75, GR, U&O, LR; Ute Agreement to Cede Gilsonite Lands, 8 September 1888, FARC-D, RG 75, U&O; Act of 15 August 1894, 28 *Stats.* 337; O'Neil and MacKay, *History of the Uintah-Ouray*, 15–16. Ironically, the Gilsonite lands were not opened to leasing until the Presidential Proclamation of 6 June 1906, 34 *Stats.* 3214.

54. James F. Randlett, Agent, to SI, 12 December 1894, NA, RG 75, GR, U&O, LR; Randlett to President and Members of the Ute Commission, 24 December 1894, NA, RG 75, GR, U&O, LR; Act of 7 June 1897, 30 *Stats.* 87. See also Craig Wood Fuller, "Land Rush in Zion: Opening of the Uncompahgre and Uintah Indian Reservations" (Ph.D. diss., Brigham Young University, 1990).

55. William H. Beck, Agent, to CIA, 1 September 1897, NA, RG 75, GR, U&O, Special Case 147; Beck to CIA, 14 September 1897, NA, RG 75, GR, U&O, LR. Jorgensen, *Sun Dance Religion*, 231–36; Florence Hawley, et al., "Culture Process and Change in Ute Adaptation," *El Palacio*, 57 (October–November 1950), 324.

56. CIA to Ute Commission, 31 August 1897, NA, RG 75, GR, U&O, LR; Ute Allotting Commissioners to CIA, 10 May 1898, NA, RG 75, GR, U&O, LR; George Sutherland, Attorney, to CIA, 13 June 1903, NA, RG 75, GR, U&O, LR; D. M. Frost, Allotting Agent, to C. G. Hall, Agent, 31 August 1904, FARC-D, RG 75, U&O, Misc. Corr.; A. C. Tonner, Acting CIA, to SI, 30 April 1904, NA, RG 75, GR, U&O, LR; Jorgensen, "Ethnohistory," 122–28; Conetah, *History*, 120–22.

57. Act of 4 June 1898, 30 *Stats.* 429; CIA to Ross Guffin, Howell P. Myton, Erastus R. Harper, Uintah Commissioners, 6 August 1898, NA, RG 75, GR, U&O, LR; Myton to CIA, 21 August 1899, *ARCIA* 1899, ser. 3915, 351.

58. Ross Guffin and E.R. Harper, Uintah Commissioners, to CIA, 7 January 1899, NA, RG 75, GR, U&O, LR; Robert Waugh, Agent, to CIA, 21 August 1891, *ARCIA* 1891, ser. 2134, 438.

59. Act of 27 May 1902, 32 *Stats.* 263; Act of 19 June 1902, 32 *Stats.* 744; Act of 3 March 1903, 32 *Stats.* 997; CIA to James McLaughlin, Special Agent, 27 April 1903, NA, RG 75, GR, U&O, LR; O'Neil and MacKay, *History of the Uintah-Ouray*, 26–30.

60. James McLaughlin, Special Agent, to CIA, Minutes of Council held at Uinta Agency . . . 18–23 May 1903, NA, RG 75, GR, U&O, Special Case 147, p. 10; *Lone Wolf v. Hitchcock* (1903), 187 *U.S.*, 553. For more on McLaughlin, see Louis L. Pfaller, *James McLaughlin: The Man with an Indian Heart* (New York: Vantage Press, 1978); James McLaughlin, *My Friend the Indian* (Boston: Houghton Mifflin Co., 1910).

61. James McLaughlin, Special Agent, to CIA, Minutes of Council held at Uinta Agency . . . 18–23 May 1903, NA, RG 75, GR, U&O, Special Case 147, quotes in order, pp. 12–13, 20, 63, 20, 15, 62–63, 14, 66–67, 21, 68–69.

62. James McLaughlin, Special Agent, to CIA, Minutes of Council held at Uinta Agency . . . 18–23 May 1903, NA, RG 75, GR, U&O, Special Case 147, pp. 61, 48; McLaughlin to SI, 30 May 1903, NA, RG 75, GR, U&O, LR; CIA to SI, 18 July 1903, NA, RG 75, GR, U&O, LR; W. A. Mercer, Agent, to CIA, telegram, 8 September 1903, NA, RG 75, GR, U&O, LR.

63. W. H. Code, Chief Engineer, to SI, 4 May 1905, NA, RG 75, GR, Irrigation Div., Box 25; A. L. Hatch, Attorney, to Senator Reed Smoot, 5 December 1904, NA, RG 75, GR, U&O, LR; C. G. Hall, Agent, to CIA, 28 January 1905, NA, RG 75, GR, U&O, LR; CIA to Hall, 27 August 1904, NA, RG 75, GR, U&O, LS; Hall to CIA, 13 May 1905, NA, RG 75, GR, U&O, LR. See also Gregory D. Kendrick, ed., *Beyond the Wasatch: The History of Irrigation in the Uinta Basin and Upper Provo River Area of Utah* (Denver: Bureau of Reclamation, 1988).

64. Act of 3 March 1905, 33 *Stats.* 1069; CIA to C. G. Hall, W. H. Code, and C. S. Carter, Allotting Commissioners, 7 April 1905, NA, RG 75, GR, U&O, LS; Hall to CIA, 13 May 1905, NA, RG 75, GR, U&O, LR; Code to SI, 4 May 1905, NA, RG 75, GR, Irrigation Div., Box 25; Code to SI, 6 June 1905, NA, RG 75, GR, Irrigation Div., Box 25; Presidential Proclamations, 14 July 1905, 34 *Stats.* 3116, 3119, and 2 August 1905, 34 *Stats.* 3141.

65. C. G. Hall, Agent, to CIA, 23 August 1907, NA, RG 75, CCF, U&0, 31; Lewis, "Plowing a Civilized Furrow," 191–92, 235; Anne M. Smith, *Ethnography of the Northern Utes*, Papers in Anthropology, no. 17 (Santa Fe: Museum of New Mexico Press, 1974), 216–220; J. A. Jones, *The Sun Dance of the Northern Ute*, Smithsonian Institution, BAE Bulletin 157, Anthropological Paper no. 47 (Washington, D.C.: GPO, 1955), 227, 239–42; James Mooney, *The Ghost-Dance Religion and the Sioux Outbreak of 1890*, ed. Anthony F. C. Wallace (Chicago: University of Chicago Press, 1965), 46, 49–50.

66. Jorgensen, *Sun Dance Religion*, 5–12, 19–20, 216, 219–20, 231–36; Smith, *Ethnography*, 208–215; Marvin K. Opler, "The Integration of the Sun Dance in Ute Religion," *American Anthropologist*, 43 (October–December 1941), 568–72.

67. C. G. Hall to CIA, telegram, 22 May 1906, FARC-D, RG 75, U&O, Box 1; Floyd A. O'Neil, "An Anguished Odyssey: The Flight of the Utes, 1906–1908," *Utah Historical Quarterly*, 36 (Fall 1968), 315–27; Francis E. Leupp, *The Indian and His Problem* (New York: Charles Scribner's Sons, 1910), 170–256; Kenneth E. Batch-Elder, "Revelations from the Shadows of Thunderbutte" (Master's thesis, University of Colorado, 1993).

68. Act of 21 June 1906, 34 *Stats.* 375; A. W. Sewall to C. G. Hall, Agent, 28 May 1906, FARC-D, RG 75, U&O; *Winters v. U.S.* (1908), 207 *U.S.*, 564; *The Complied Laws of the State of Utah, 1907* (Salt Lake City, 1908), Ch.2, Sec. 1288, 549; William M. McCrea, Asst. U.S. Attorney, to C. G. Hall, Agent, 17 August 1910, NA, RG 75, CCF, U&O, 170; Albert H. Kneale, *Indian Agent* (Caldwell, Ida.: Caxton Printers, 1950), 268–70; Kendrick, ed., *Beyond the Wasatch*, 22–60; Endter, "Cultural Ideologies," 117–50.

69. Charles Larrabee, Acting CIA, to C. G. Hall, Agent, 11 February 1907, FARC-D, RG 75, U&O; Act of 30 April 1908, 35 *Stats.* 95; "Pioneers Wanted: Circular Relative to Leasing of Lands on the Uintah Reservation," 25 April 1907, FARC-D, RG 75, U&O, Box 6; Report of Proceedings of Council held with the Indians . . . , 13 April 1907, FARC-D, RG 75, U&O, Box 6; Hall to W. H. Code, Chief Engineer, 17 May 1910, NA, RG 75, CCF, U&O, 340; C. F. Hanke, 2nd Asst. CIA, to SI, 3 February 1912, FARC-D, RG 75, U&O, Box 6; H. J. Brees, Agent, to CIA, 25 October 1911, NA, RG 75, CCF, U&O, 310; Charles L. Davis, Agency Farmer, to CIA, 3 and 9 January 1912, NA, RG 75, CCF, U&O, 31.

70. Kneale, *Indian Agent*, 271, 295–97; Uintah, Whiteriver and Uncompahgre Allottees, Land Under Cultivation, 1914, NA, RG 75, CCF, U&O, 916; Albert H. Kneale, Supt., to CIA, 1 February 1915, NA, RG 75, CCF, U&O, 321; E. B. Meritt, Asst. CIA, to Kneale, 16 March 1915, NA, RG 75, CCF, U&O, 321; E. E. Paine, Save the Water: Report upon the Financial Operations of the Uintah & Ouray Indian Agency, to SI, 20 November 1916, NA, RG 75, CCF, U&O, 150.

71. Frank Knox, "Report on the Ute Indians, October 18, 1915," in Board Of Indian Commissioners, *Reports on Reservations and Schools*, vol. 1:1–30, MS 908, Edward E. Ayer Collection, The Newberry Library; Knox, "Conditions on the Three Ute Reservations," LMC *Proceedings*, 1914, 52–55; Albert H. Kneale, Supt., Annual Narrative Report 1915, NA, RG 75, CCF, U&O, 31; Kneale and Charles R. Olberg, Report on Crop Damage, to CIA, 20 July 1920, NA, RG 75, CCF, U&O, 31.

72. A. H. Kneale and C. R. Olberg, Report on Crop Damage, to CIA,

20 July 1920, NA, RG 75, CCF, U&O, 31; Kendrick, ed., *Beyond the Wasatch*, 48–52; Conetah, *History*, 128–29; Jones, *Sun Dance*, 233; Jorgensen, *Sun Dance Religion*, 147–48; Sarah Van Hackford, Interview, 31 January 1968, DDOHC-U, no. 297:27–28.

73. Agency Agricultural Roll, circa 1905, FARC-D, RG 75, U&O, Box 6; W. W. McLaughlin, *Agricultural Reconnaissance of the Uinta Indian Reservation*, Utah State Agricultural Experiment Station, Bulletin 93 (Logan, Utah, 1905), 4–5.

74. Harwood Hall, Inspection Report, 10 August 1909, NA, RG 75, CCF, U&O, 150; C. G. Hall, Agent, Report of Proceedings of Council Held with the Indians . . . 13 April 1907, and Hall, Council of the Uncompahgre Ute Indians . . . 20 April 1907, FARC-D, RG 75, U&O, Box 6; Hal Albert Daniels, Sr., Interview, 14 August 1967, DDOHC-U, no. 66:27–28; Kneale, *Indian Agent*, 284–86, 302, 323. Critics liked to blame rations for undermining Ute incentives to farm, but between 1913 and 1930 the government provided an average of $12,000 annually in rations to assist Ute families. In 1929, 19 percent of all Utes drew rations, but few could subsist solely on the meager issues, especially given Ute patterns of redistributing resources between relatives. See H. M. Tidwell, Supt., to CIA, 24 October 1929, NA, RG 75, CCF, U&O, 210; Jorgensen, *Sun Dance Religion*, 103; Hawley et al., "Culture Process and Change," 326, 329–31.

75. Hugh Owens, Agency Farmer, to D. S. Miller, Acting Agent, 16 March 1905, FARC-D, RG 75, U&O, Misc. Corr.; E. P. Holcombe, Inspector, to SI, 18 August 1910, NA, RG 75, CCF, U&O, 125; U.S. Bureau of the Census, 1909 Indian Census, Microcopy 595, Reel 610; Charles H. Davis, Agency Farmer, to CIA, 17 April 1912, NA, RG 75, CCF, U&O, 65; "Minutes of a Council Held August 28, 1913, at Washington, D.C. . . ." NA, RG 75, CCF, U&O, 56; Jewell D. Martin, "Address," *LMC Proceedings*, 1914, 70; U.S. Senate, *Survey of Conditions of the Indians in the United States: Hearings before a Subcommittee of the Committee on Indian Affairs* (Washington, D.C.: GPO, 1934), part 27:14,734–35; James Monaghan, "Report on the Uncompahgre Utes near Randlett, Utah," 1935, Civilian Work Administration Pamphlet 356/5, pp. 1–2, Colorado Historical Society, Denver; Wilson Johnson, Interview, 27 July 1967, DDOHC-U, no. 55:15; Oran F. Curry, Interview, 20 July 1967, DDOHC-U, no. 48:10.

76. Charles L. Davis, Agency Farmer, to CIA, 14 May 1912, NA, RG 75, CCF, U&O, 63; Jewell D. Martin, Agent, to CIA, 14 August 1912, NA, RG 75, CCF, U&O, 63; CIA to Martin, 11 August 1913, NA, RG 75, CCF, U&O, 63; William Wash to SI, 23 June 1914, NA, RG 75, CCF, U&O, 63; Kneale, *Indian Agent*, 156–58; Omer C. Stewart, *Peyote Religion: A History* (Norman: University of Oklahoma Press, 1987), 178–201; David F. Aberle and Omer C. Stewart, *Navaho and Ute Peyotism: A Chronological and Distributional Study*, University of Colorado Studies, Series in Anthropology, no. 6 (Boulder: University of Colorado Press, 1957), 5–24; David Rich Lewis, "Reservation Leadership and the Progressive-Traditional Dichotomy: William Wash and the Northern Utes, 1865–1928," *Ethnohistory*, 38 (Spring 1991), 131–37; Lewis, "Plowing a Civilized Furrow," 200–203.

77. O'Neil, "Reluctant Suzerainty," 140–41; Council of the Uncompahgre Ute Indians, 20 April 1907, FARC-D, RG 75, U&O, Box 6; E. E. Paine, "Save the Water: Report," to SI, 20 November 1916, NA, RG 75, CCF, U&O, 150; Sarah Van Hackford, Interview, 31 January 1968, DDOHC-U, no. 297:6–7.

78. Charles L. Davis, Agency Farmer, to CIA, 4 January 1912, NA, RG 75, CCF, U&O, 910; E. E. Paine, "Save the Water: Report", to SI, 20 November 1916, NA, RG 75, CCF, U&O, 150, pp. 70–75; Council Proceedings, Uintah & Ouray Agency, 25 January 1928, NA, RG 75, CCF, U&O, 54; U.S. Senate, *Survey of Conditions*, 27:14,778; CIA to C. G. Hall, Agent, 28 May 1907, FARC-D, RG 75, U&O, Box 6; Jewell D. Martin, Agent, to CIA, 12 October 1912, NA, RG 75, CCF, U&O, 160; Martin to H. C. Phillips, Secretary, LMC, 27 August 1914, FARC-D, RG 75, U&O, Misc. Corr. v.12; Martin, "Address," LMC, *Proceedings*, 1914, 40–41.

79. U.S. Senate, *Survey of Conditions*, 27:14,775–76, 14,778–79. Quotes from Hal Albert Daniels, Sr., Interview, 14 August 1967, DDOHC-U no. 66:28; Connor Chappose, Interview, 17 August 1960, DDOHC-U, no. 4:41. See also from the DDOHC-U, Connor Chapoose, Interview, September 1960, no. 10:7–21; Dewey Arapoo, Interview, 29 June 1967, no. 47:9–10; Lulu Wash Chapoose Brock, Interview, 23 February 1967, no. 14:16–17.

80. Albert H. Kneale and C. R. Olberg, Report on Crop Damage, to CIA, 20 July 1920, NA, RG 75, CCF, U&O, 916; Kneale, *Indian Agent*, 275–78, 295.

81. Charles Hunt, Quartermaster, Fort Duchesne, to W.A. Mercer, Agent, 3 December 1903, FARC-D, RG 75, U&O, Box 3; Charles L. Davis, Agency Farmer, to CIA, 4 January 1912, NA, RG 75, CCF, U&O, 910; H. W. Dick to Chief Engineer, U.S. Indian Service, June 1913, NA, RG 75, CCF, U&O, 341.

82. Jorgensen, *Sun Dance Religion*, 100–105; Conner Chapoose, Interview, 19 September 1960, DDOHC-U, no. 9:4; Oran F. Curry, Interview, 20 July 1967, DDOHC-U, no. 48:8–9; Porter J. Preston and Charles A. Engle, "Report of Advisors on Irrigation on Indian Reservations," 8 June 1928, in U.S. Senate, *Survey of Conditions*, part 6:2,217–18, 2,224.

83. Kathryn L. MacKay, "The Strawberry Valley Reclamation Project and the Opening of the Uintah Indian Reservation," *Utah Historical Quarterly*, 50 (Winter 1982), 68–89; C. C. Early, Agent, to CIA, 25 May 1912, NA, RG 75, CCF, U&O, 301; Jewell D. Martin, Supt., to CIA, 7 October 1913, FARC-D, RG 75, U&O; Crandall, Stockman, to Albert H. Kneale, Supt., 22 March 1923, FARC-D, RG 75, U&O; J. E. White, Credit Agent, "Social and Economic Report of the Uinta and Ouray Reservation," 2 March 1939, NA, RG 75, CCF, U&O, 31; Conner Chapoose, Interview, 17 August 1960, DDOHC-U, no. 4:40–41.

84. Jewell D. Martin, Agent, to CIA, 12 October 1912, NA, RG 75, CCF, U&O, 47; Martin to CIA, 8 October 1913, NA, RG 75, CCF, U&O, 47; Fred A. Gross, Annual Narrative Report 1925, FARC-D, RG 75, CCF, U&O, Annual Reports; Council Proceedings, 2 May 1927, Uintah & Ouray Indian Agency, Ft. Duchesne, Utah, NA, RG 75, CCF, U&O, 54; U.S. Senate, *Survey of Conditions*, 27:14,761–62, and Harris's quote, 27:14,777; O. D. Stanton, Asst. Agronomist, "Farm Management Plan, Uintah-Ouray Indian Reservation, Utah," 9 March 1937, NA, RG 75, CCF, U&O, 349; Coulsen Wright and Geneva Wright, "Indian-White Relations in the Uintah Basin," *Utah Humanities Review*, 2 (October 1948), 339–40.

85. Preston and Engle, "Report of Advisors," in U.S. Senate, *Survey of Conditions*, 6:2,218; Jasper Pike, Interview, August 1969, DDOHC-U, no. 267:11; Miscellaneous Statistics, 1936, FARC-D, RG 75, U&O, Hist. Notebook, 57504; Summary of the Results of Work on the Uintah Basin Land Utilization Study, 1 December 1937, FARC-D, RG 75, U&O, Misc. Corr.

86. E. J. Diehl, Extension Agent, Annual Report, 1 December 1934–30 November 1935, NA, RG 75, CCF, U&O, 31, pp. 7, 26; Henry F. Wershing, Asst. Range Examiner, Annual Forestry and Grazing Report, 1937, NA, RG 75, CCF, U&O, 31; J. E. White, Credit Agent, "Social and Economic Report of the Uinta and Ouray Resevrvation," 2 March 1939, NA, RG 75, CCF, U&O, 31; Resolution, U&O Tribal Business Committee, 12 May 1943, NA, RG 75, CCF, U&O, Accession 68A–4937, Box 61A, File 259; James B. Ring, Area Director, to Darrell Fleming, Supt., 3 September 1957, NA, RG 75, CCF, U&O, Accession 64A–528, Box 105, File 564.2; Jorgensen, *Sun Dance Religion*, 109, 122, 150; Jorgensen, "Ethnohistory," 220–24; Conetah, *History*, 140–53; Conner Chapoose, Interview, September 1960, DDOHC-U, no. 10:6–7, and Interview, 14 September 1960, no. 7:8–10.

87. Brian Q. Cannon, "Struggle Against Great Odds: Challenges in Utah's Marginal Agricultural Areas, 1925–39," *Utah Historical Quarterly*, 54 (Fall 1986), 308–27; B. O. Colton, Commissioner, "Report of Distribution of Water Supply, Lake Fork and Uintah Rivers, Year 1934," NA, RG 75, CCF, U&O, 341; E. J. Diehl, Extension Agent, Annual Report, 1 December 1934 to 30 November 1935, NA, RG 75, CCF, U&O, 31, p. 24; O. D. Stanton, Asst. Agronomist, "Farm Management Plan, Uintah-Ouray Indian Reservation, Utah," 9 March 1937, NA, RG 75, CCF, U&O, 349; Steering Committee of Uintah Basin Committee, Statement of Facts, 16 September 1937, NA, RG 75, CCF, U&O, 916.

88. Division of Extension and Industry, "1946 Program of Work and Project Outline, U&O Jurisdiction, Ft. Duchesne, Utah," NA, RG 75, CCF, U&O, Accession 56A–588, Box 318, File 919.1; U&O Tribal Planning Board, to Tribal Business Committee, 4 April 1951, "Ute Emergency Program," NA, RG 75, CCF, U&O, Accession 68A–4937, Box 62, File 71; Jones, *Sun Dance*, 233 (quote) and 229–36; Nielsen, Reeve & Maxwell, Inc., Consulting Engineers, "Report, Operation and Maintenance, Uintah and Ouray Indian Irrigation Project, Utah, 1960," NA, RG 75, CCF, Accession 64A–528, Box 105, File 341.4.

89. Lang, *A Study in Culture Contact*, 30–31; Jorgensen, *Sun Dance Religion*, 105–14, 150; Jorgensen, "Ethnohistory," 216–20, 228–33; Hawley et al., "Culture Process," 314, 322; Conner Chapoose, Interview, September 1960, DDOHC-U, no. 10:17 (quote) and 7–22; Chapoose, Interview, 14 September 1960, DDOHC-U, no. 7:6–14; Sarah Van Hackford, Interview, 31 January 1968, DDOHC-U, no. 297:25–28; Ute Ten Year Development Program, 1956, NA, RG 75, CCF, U&O, Accession 62A–523, Box 64, File 224.

90. Quotes from interviews in the DDOHC-U: Lulu Wash Chapoose Brock, 23 February 1967, no. 14:6; Conner Chapoose, 17 August 1960, no. 4:41; Chapoose, 19 September 1960, no. 9:4; Jasper Pike, August 1969, no. 267:12; Hal Albert Daniels, Sr., 14 August 1967, no. 66:39

91. Jorgensen, *Sun Dance Religion*, 97, 148; Conetah, *History*, 128, 135.

92. Conetah, *History*, 150–53; Jorgensen, *Sun Dance Religion*, 151–52; Act of 27 August 1954, 68 *Stats.* 868, Public Law 671, amended 70 *Stats.* 936.

93. Jorgensen, *Sun Dance Religion*, 9–12, 146–73; Jorgensen, "Sovereignty and the Structure of Dependency at Northern Ute," *American Indian Culture and Research Journal*, 10, no. 2 (1986), 75–94.

94. Endter, "Cultural Ideologies," 70–71, 80 n.20 (quote).

Chapter 4

1. Martin A. Baumhoff, *California Athabaskan Groups*, University of California Publications, *Anthropological Records* (hereafter *UCPAR*), 16, no. 5 (Berkeley: University of California Press, 1958), 157–65, 209; William F. Shipley, "Native Languages of California," *Handbook of North American Indians*, vol. 8, *California*, ed. Robert F. Heizer (Washington, D.C.: Smithsonian Institution Press, 1978), 8:87–88, 90 (hereafter Heizer, ed., *California*, 8); Byron Nelson, Jr., *Our Home Forever: A Hupa Tribal History* (Salt Lake City: University of Utah Printing Service for the Hupa Tribe, 1978), 3–5.

2. Pliny E. Goddard, *Hupa Texts*, University of California Publications, *American Archaeology and Ethnology* (hereafter *UCPAAE*), 1, no. 2 (Berkeley: University of California Press, 1904), 96–134, 215–26; Goddard, *Life and Culture of the Hupa*, *UCPAAE*, 1, no. 1 (Berkeley: University of California Press, 1903), 74–78; Lee Davis, "On This Earth: Hupa Land Domains, Images and Ecology on 'Deddeh Ninnisan'" (Ph.D. diss., University of California-Berkeley, 1988), 2–43; J. W. Hudson, "Ethnographic/Linguistic Notes on California Indians, 1901–1919", Anthropological Archives, MS A-11, p. 315, The Field Museum, Chicago, Ill.

3. Albert B. Elsasser, "Development of Regional Prehistoric Cultures," in Heizer, ed., *California*, 8:50–51; William J. Wallace, "Hupa, Chilula, and Whilkut," Ibid., 8:164; Victor Golla, "Coyote and Frog (Hupa)," *International Journal of American Linguistics, Native American Texts Series*, 2, no. 2 (1977), 17; Michael J. Moratto, *California Archaeology* (Orlando, FA: Academic Press, 1984), 484, 525, 540, 570; Nelson, *Our Home Forever*, 201 n. 1.

4. J. L. Poole, *Water-Resources Reconnaissance of Hoopa Valley, Humboldt County, California*, Water Supply of Indian Reservations, U.S. Geological Survey, Water Supply Paper 1576-C (Washington, D.C.: GPO, 1961), 1–6; Ralph L. Beals and Joseph A. Hester, Jr., *California Indians, I: Indian Land Use and Occupancy in California* (New York: Garland Publishing Co., 1974), 86, 90, 96–99, 261–62; Bradley C. Singer and Eugene L. Begg, *Soil Survey, Hoopa Valley, California*, Department of Land, Air and Water Resources, University of California-Davis, the BIA, U.S. Department of the Interior, and the Hoopa Valley Tribal Council (October 1975), 6–32; Wallace, "Hupa," in Heizer, ed., *California*, 8:164.

5. The following information is taken from Henry T. Lewis, *Patterns of Indian Burning in California: Ecology and Ethnohistory*, Ballena Press Anthropological Papers, no. 1 (Ramona, Calif.: Ballena Press, 1973), 17–36; Martin A. Baumhoff, "Environmental Background," in Heizer, ed., *California*, 8:18–19; Goddard, *Life and Culture*, 4–6; Beals and Hester, *California Indians, I*, 103–126; Elias Yanovsky, *Food Plants of the North American Indians*, U.S. Department of Agriculture, Miscellaneous Publication no. 237 (Washington, D.C.: GPO, 1936); Walter Ebeling, *Handbook of Indian Foods and Fibers of Arid America* (Berkeley: University of California Press, 1986), 186–274; Davis, "On This Earth," 74–75, 228–42.

6. For further information on the benefits of fire, see Lewis, *Patterns of Indian Burning*, 17–35, passim; Davis, "On This Earth," 228, 238–43.

7. Clinton Hart Merriam, "Ethnographic Notes on California Indian Tribes," com. and ed. Robert F. Heizer, in *Reports of the University of California Archaeological Survey*, no. 68, 3 parts (Berkeley: University of California Ar-

chaeology Research Facility, Department of Anthropology, 1966–67), 200–201; Merriam, *Indian Names for Plants and Animals among Californian and other Western North American Tribes*, assemb. and annot. Robert F. Heizer, Ballena Press Publications in Archaeology, Ethnology and History, no. 14 (Socorro, N. Mex.: Ballena Press, 1979), 24–28; Baumhoff, *California Athabaskan Groups*, 214–15.

8. Otis T. Mason, "The Ray Collection from Hupa Reservation," *Annual Report of the Smithsonian Institution, 1886*, in *House Miscelleneous Document* 11, no. 170, pt. 1 (49–2), ser. 2498, pp. 214–15; William J. Wallace, "Hupa Narrative Tales," *Journal of American Folklore*, 61 (1948), 352–53; Goddard, *Hupa Texts*, 157–61; Goddard, *Life and Culture*, 77; Davis, "On This Earth," 106–11, 248–49.

9. Goddard, *Life and Culture*, 22, 57–58; Nona C. Willoughby, *Division of Labor Among the Indians of California* (New York: Garland Publishing Co., 1974), 207–88; Davis, "On This Earth," 226–31, 266–67, 284–85, 310; Stephen Powers, *Tribes of California*, Contributions to North American Ethnology, vol. III (Washington, D.C.: GPO, 1877; reprinted, Berkeley: University of California Press, 1976), 74–75; Walter R. Goldschmidt, "Ethics and the Structure of Society: An Ethnological Contribution to the Sociology of Knowledge," *American Anthropologist*, 53 (October–December 1951), 506–23; Beals and Hester, *California Indians*, I, 281–90.

10. Goddard, *Life and Culture*, 23–26; Alfred L. Kroeber and S. A. Barrett, *Fishing among the Indians of Northwestern California*, UCPAR, 21, no. 1 (Berkeley: University of California Press, 1960), 18–22, 29–30, 76–79; Driver, *Culture Element Distributions, X: Northwest California*, UCPAR, 1, no.6 (Berkeley: University of California Press, 1939), 212–14, 379–80; J. O. Snyder, "Indian Methods of Fishing on the Trinity River," *California Fish and Game*, 10 (October 1924), 163–72; Robert F. Heizer and Albert B. Elasser, *The Natural World of the California Indians* (Berkeley: University of California Press, 1980), 64–66; Goddard, *Hupa Texts*, 252–70; Hudson, "Ethnographic/Linguistic Notes," 315–16; Davis, "On This Earth," 148–214.

11. Goddard, *Life and Culture*, 27–29, 77; Goddard, *Hupa Texts*, 157–61; Heizer and Elsasser, *Natural World*, 91–100; Driver, *Culture Element Distributions, X*, 314–16; Beals and Hester, *California Indians*, I, 308–13; Davis, "On This Earth," 252–68.

12. Goddard, *Life and Culture*, 29–32, 37; Hudson, "Ethnographic/Linguistic Notes," 303–25; Lewis, *Patterns of Indian Burning*, 62–63; Mason, "Ray Collection," 235–39; Merriam, *Indian Names*, 24–30, 33–35, 213–14; Heizer and Elsasser, *Natural World*, 239–52; Davis, "On This Earth," 101–103; George R. Mead, *The Ethnobotany of the California Indians: A Compendium of the Plants, Their Users, and Their Uses*, Occasional Publications in Anthropology, Ethnology Series, no. 30 (Greeley, Colo.: Museum of Anthropology, University of Northern Colorado, 1972).

13. Driver, *Culture Element Distributions, X*, 309–12, 315–16; Goddard, *Life and Culture*, 21–23; Goddard, *Hupa Texts*, 319–24; Davis, "On This Earth," 285–302; Alfred L. Kroeber and E. W. Gifford, *World Renewal: A Cult System of Native Northwest California*, UCPAR, 13, no. 1 (Berkeley: University of California Press, 1949), 56; George W. Nelson, Interview, 31 October 1975 (by permission of G. B. Nelson, Sr.).

14. Driver, *Culture Element Distributions, X*, 310–12, 375–76; Goddard, *Life and Culture*, 22–23; Wallace, "Hupa," in Heizer, ed., *California*, 8:165;

William J. Wallace, "Hupa Indian Dogs," *The Masterkey*, 25 (1951), 83–87; George W. Nelson, Interview, 29 January 1976.

15. Arthur F. McEvoy, *The Fisherman's Problem: Ecology and Law in the California Fisheries, 1850–1980* (Cambridge: Cambridge University Press, 1986), 13, 29, 38–39; Alan C. Zeigler, "Quasi-Agriculture in North Central California and its Effect on Aboriginal Social Structure," *Kroeber Anthropological Society Papers*, 38 (Spring 1968), 52–67; Lowell John Bean and Harry W. Lawton, "Some Explanations for the Rise of Cultural Complexity in Native California with Comments on Proto-Agriculture and Agriculture," in Lewis, *Patterns of Indian Burning*, viii–xxxviii; James T. Davis, "Trade Routes and Economic Exchange Among the Indians of California," *Reports of the University of California Archaeological Survey*, no. 54 (31 March 1961), 23.

16. Alfred L. Kroeber, *Handbook of the Indians of California*, Smithsonian Institution, BAE Bulletin 78 (Washington, D.C.: GPO, 1925), 130–33; Sherburne F. Cook, *The Aboriginal Population of the North Coast of California*, UCPAR, 16, no. 3 (Berkeley: University of California Press, 1956), 99–100; Baumhoff, *California Athabaskan Groups*, 216–24; Goddard *Life and Culture*, 7–8, 57–58; Wallace, "Hupa," in Heizer, ed., *California*, 8:168–69; Edward S. Curtis, *The North American Indian*, 20 vols. (Cambridge, Mass., 1907–30; reprinted, New York: Johnson Reprint Corp., 1970), 13:3–4, 10–13, 18–19.

17. Goddard, *Life and Culture*, 12–13, 58–59; Nelson, *Our Home Forever*, 5–12; Clinton Hart Merriam, "Ethnogeographic and Ethnosynonymic Data from Northern California Tribes," ed. Robert F. Heizer, *Contributions to Native California Ethnology from the C. Hart Merriam Collection*, no. 1 (Berkeley: Archaeological Research Facility, Department of Anthropology, University of California, 1976), 104–110; Hudson, "Ethnographic/Linguistic Notes," 301–2; Baumhoff, *California Athabaskan Groups*, 209–15; Kroeber, *Handbook*, 129–130, 133, 137–41; Davis, "On This Earth," 79–85.

18. Beals and Hester, *California Indians, I*, 274–78; Kroeber, *Handbook*, 20–52, 131–32; Goddard, *Life and Culture*, 59–60; Powers, *Tribes of California*, 74–75; Goldschmidt, "Ethics," 506–23.

19. William J. Wallace, *Hupa Warfare*, Southwest Museum Leaflets, no. 23 (Los Angeles: Southwest Museum, 1949); Goddard, *Life and Culture*, 62–63; Goddard, *Hupa Texts*, 332–36; Driver, *Culture Element Distributions, X*, 358–60; Nelson, *Our Home Forever*, 26–28.

20. Goddard, *Life and Culture*, 50–57, 69–74; Goddard, *Hupa Texts*, 275–305, 351–60; Nelson, *Our Home Forever*, 13–23; Driver, *Culture Element Distributions, X*, 344–57; Hudson, "Ethnographic/Linguistic Notes," 304–5, 310, 313, 318–21, 352–55; Kroeber, *Handbook*, 135–36, 864; Merriam, "Ethnographic Notes," 88, 197. In fact, it became a legal offense for anyone to speak or re-use the deceased's name. This habit of discarding personal names (which were often the names of plants or animals) and building new words to replace them faded in the nineteenth century, but over the centuries may have changed Hupa nouns completely. See Goddard, "Conscious Word-Making by the Hupa," *American Anthropologist*, 3 (January–March 1901), 208–9.

21. Pliny E. Goddard, "Wayside Shrines in Northwestern California," in *A Collection of Ethnographic Articles on the California Indians*, ed. Robert F. Heizer (Ramona, Calif.: Ballena Press, 1976), 3–4; Goddard, *Life and Culture*, 87–88; Edward Sapir, "Hupa Myths, Formulae and Ethnologic Narratives," MS, Bancroft Library, Berkeley, Calif.; E. W. Gifford, "Ethnographic Notes on the Folklore and Ceremonial Life of the Hupa, 1940–42," MS, Bancroft Library,

Berkeley, Calif.; Driver, *Culture Element Distributions, X*, 342–44; Davis, "On This Earth," 44–47, 57–58, 309–12; Kroeber and Gifford, *World Renewal*, 56; George W. Nelson, Interview, 31 October 1975.

22. William J. Wallace and Edith S. Taylor, "Hupa Sorcery," *Southwestern Journal of Anthropology*, 6 (Summer 1950), 188–96; Wallace, "Personality Variation in a Primitive Society," *Journal of Personality*, 15 (June 1947), 323–28; Goddard, *Life and Culture*, 63–69; Kroeber, *Handbook*, 136–37; Driver, *Culture Element Distributions, X*, 360–67; Wallace, "Hupa Narrative Tales," 345–46.

23. Davis, "On This Earth," 124–26; Goddard, *Life and Culture*, 67–69, 82, 85–87; Hudson, "Ethnographic/Linguistic Notes," 310, 314–15, 322–24; Kroeber and Gifford, *World Renewal*, 61–63; Samuel A. Barrett, "The Jump Dance at Hupa, 1962," *Kroeber Anthropological Society Papers*, 28 (Spring 1963), 73–85. The tale of the Scabby Young Man and the flowering of the Jump Dance as a health ritual might be connected with a smallpox epidemic that hit Hoopa Valley in the 1830s. See Goddard, *Hupa Texts*, 207–214, 226–52.

24. Kroeber and Gifford, *World Renewal*, 56–61; Goddard, *Hupa Texts*, 233, 252–69; Goddard, *Life and Culture*, 78–82; Nelson, *Our Home Forever*, 28–31; Hudson, "Ethnographic/Linguistic Notes," 321–22; Davis, "On This Earth," 124–25, 154, 181–90.

25. Kroeber and Gifford, *World Renewal*, 56, 61–65; Walter R. Goldschmidt and Harold E. Driver, *The Hupa White Deerskin Dance*, UCPAAE, 35, no. 8 (Berkeley: University of California Press, 1940), 103–141; Davis, "On This Earth," 36; Goddard, *Life and Culture*, 82–85; Goddard, "Hon-sitch-a-til-ya (A Hupa Dance)," University of Pennsylvania, Free Museum of Science and Art, *Bulletin*, 3, no. 2 (April 1901), 117–22; Kroeber, *Handbook*, 134–35; Driver, *Culture Element Distributions, X*, 364–67; E. W. Gifford, "Ethnographic Notes on Hupa Ceremonial and Rituals, 1940," MS, Bancroft Library, Berkeley, Calif.; Nelson, *Our Home Forever*, 31–34.

26. Nelson, *Our Home Forever*, 37–46; Goddard, *Hupa Texts*, 198–201; Wallace, "Hupa Narrative Tales," 352; Mahlon Marshall, "The Whites Come to Hoopa Valley," *Pacific Historian*, 15 (Spring 1971), 55–61; Lee Davis, "Tracking Jedediah Smith Through Hupa Territory," *American Indian Quarterly*, 13, no. 4 (Fall 1989), 369–90; Davis, "On This Earth," 39.

Chapter 5

1. A. J. Bledsoe, *Indian Wars of the Northwest* (1885; reprint, Oakland: Biobooks, 1956), 63–65; Byron Nelson, Jr., *Our Home Forever: A Hupa Tribal History* (Salt Lake City: University of Utah Printing Service for the Hupa Tribe, 1978), 39–41.

2. Nelson, *Our Home Forever*, 41–46; James J. Rawls, *Indians of California: The Changing Image* (Norman: University of Oklahoma Press, 1984), 175; Lee Davis, "On This Earth: Hupa Land Domains, Images and Ecology on 'Deddeh Ninnisan'" (Ph.D. diss., University of California-Berkeley, 1988), 250.

3. U.S. Department of the Interior, "Report of the Secretary of the Interior Communicating . . . a Copy of the Correspondence . . . Indian Agents and Commissioners of California," *Senate Executive Document*, no. 4 (33–SS), 17 March 1853, ser. 688, 8–9, 156–63; George Gibbs, "Journal of the Expedition of Colonel Redick McKee . . .", in Henry Rowe Schoolcraft, *Information Respecting the History, Condition, and Prospects of the Indian Tribes of the United States*, 6 vols.

(Philadelphia: J. B. Lippincott & Co., 1853–60), 3:106–73; Nelson, *Our Home Forever*, 47–57, 181–85; George E. Anderson, William H. Ellison, Robert F. Heizer, *Treaty Making and Treaty Rejection by the Federal Government in California, 1850–52*, Ballena Press Publications in Archaeology, Ethnology and History, no. 9 (Socorro, N. Mex.: Ballena Press, 1978), 1–36, 50–124; Chad L. Hoopes, "Redick McKee and the Humboldt Bay Region, 1851–1852," *California Historical Society Quarterly*, 49 (September 1970), 195–219.

4. William H. Ellison, "The Federal Indian Policy in California, 1846–60," *Mississippi Valley Historical Review*, 9 (June 1922), 59–67; Sherburne F. Cook, "Historical Demography," in *Handbook of North American Indians*, vol. 8, *California*, ed. Robert F. Heizer (Washington, D.C.: Smithsonian Institution Press, 1978), 8:91–98, (hereafter Heizer, ed., *California*, 8).

5. Nelson, *Our Home Forever*, 61–65.

6. Owen C. Coy, *The Humboldt Bay Region, 1850–1870: A Study in the American Colonization of California* (Los Angeles: California State Historical Association, 1929), 137–160; Bledsoe, *Indian Wars*, 84–139; Nelson, *Our Home Forever*, 59–77; Hubert Howe Bancroft, *The History of California*, 7 vols. (San Francisco: The History Company, 1888), 7:474; Arthur F. McEvoy, *The Fisherman's Problem: Ecology and Law in the California Fisheries, 1850–1980* (Cambridge: Cambridge University Press, 1986), 41–42, 46, 53, 56–58.

7. D. E. Buel[?], Klamath Agent, to Thomas J. Henley, 23 October 1858, NA, RG 75, GR, HV, LR; Lt. Col. James N. Olney to Asst. Adj. General, Ft. Humboldt, 15 August 1862, NA, RG 393, PL; Francis J. Lippitt, Commander, Humboldt Military Dist., to Lt. Col. R. C. Drum, 18 May 1863, *WR*, 445–46; Olney, Special Post Order No. 21, Ft. Gaston, 25 June 1863, NA, RG 393, PL; George W. Nelson, Interview, 26 April 1975 (by permission of G. B. Nelson, Sr.).

8. Lt. Col. S. G. Whipple, Commander, Humboldt Millitary Dist., to Lt. Col. R. C. Drum, 9 September 1863, *WR*, 611–12; Nelson, *Our Home Forever*, 79–84.

9. Nelson, *Our Home Forever*, 74, 84–86; Alfred L. Kroeber, *Handbook of the Indians of California*, Smithsonian Institution, BAE Bulletin 78 (Washington, D.C.: GPO, 1925),131–32; William S. R. Taylor, Commander, Ft. Gaston, to Capt. E. Sparrow Purdy, 10 December 1863, *WR*, 693–94; S. G. Whipple, Commander, Humboldt Military Dist., to Lt. Col. R. C. Drum, 23 December 1863, *WR*, 707–08; Coy, *Humboldt Region*, 164–191.

10. S. G. Whipple, Commander, Humboldt Military Dist., to Lt. Col. R. C. Drum, 12 January 1864, *WR*, 723–25; Whipple to Drum, 18 February 1864, *WR*, 758–9; Whipple to Lt. James Ulio, Ft. Gaston, 20 February 1864, NA, RG 393, PL; Whipple to Ulio, 28 April 1864, NA, RG 393, PL, 23; Whipple to Ulio, 24 May 1864, *WR*, 853; Nelson, *Our Home Forever*, 84–88.

11. Nelson, *Our Home Forever*, 88–91, 187–90; "Resolutions of the Legislature of California, in Relation to Indian Affairs in that State, April 20, 1863," *House Misc. Doc.* no. 29 (38–1), ser. 1200; Charles J. Kappler, comp. and ed., *Indian Affairs: Laws and Treaties*, 2 vols. (Washington, D.C.: GPO, 1904), 1:815; Act of 8 April 1864, 13 *Stats.* 39.

12. McEvoy, *Fisherman's Problem*, 46, 53–58; Martin A. Baumhoff, *California Athabaskan Groups*, University of California Publications, *Anthropological Records* (hereafter *UCPAR*), 16, no. 5 (Berkeley: University of California Press, 1958), 216–24; Davis, "On This Earth," 148–50, 235, 250–51.

13. Charles Maltby, Supt. of California Indian Affairs, to CIA, *ARCIA* 1866, ser. 1284, 92; Robert J. Stevens, Special Commissioner, to CIA, 1 January 1867, *ARCIA* 1867, ser. 1326, 123–25; U.S. Army Subsistence Office to Commander, Ft. Gaston, 17 May 1865, NA, RG 393, PL, 79; Doolittle Committee, *Condition of the Indian Tribes* (Washington, D.C.: GPO, 1867), 509–10.

14. Charles Westmorland, Eureka, to CIA, 7 February 1866, NA, RG 75, GR, HV, LR; Robert L. Stockton, Agent, to Charles Maltby, Supt. of California Indian Affairs, 20 August 1866, *ARCIA* 1866, ser. 1284, 95–96; Maltby to CIA, Ibid., 92.

15. Peter Moffatt, Physician, Ft. Gaston, to Maj. A. W. Bowman, 2 April 1867, NA, RG 393, PL; *ARCIA* 1867, ser. 1326, 106–107; William H. Pratt, Agent, to CIA, 20 July 1868, *ARCIA* 1868, ser. 1366, 592; Pratt to Capt. William E. Appleton, Ft. Gaston, 4 August 1868, NA, RG 75, GR, HV, LR; Edward S. Curtis, *The North American Indian*, 20 vols. (Cambridge, Mass., 1907–30; reprint, New York: Johnson Reprint Corp., 1970), 13:6; William J. Wallace, "Hupa Narrative Tales," *Journal of American Folklore*, 61 (1948), 346–51; Nelson, *Our Home Forever*, 99–101.

16. W. H. Pratt, Agent, to [Major] Henry R. Mizner, Commander, Ft. Gaston, 2 June 1869, NA, RG 75, GR, HV, LR; Mizner to Lt. Col. Roger Jones, Asst. Inspector General, 3 August 1869, NA, RG 393, PL.

17. Maj. Henry R. Mizner, Commander, Ft. Gaston, to Lt. Col. Roger Jones, Asst. Inspector General, 3 August 1869, NA, RG 393, PL; Capt. R. G. Parker, Ft. Gaston, to Asst. Adj. General, 31 March 1872, NA, RG 393, PL; D. H. Lowry, Agent, to B. C. Whiting, Supt. of California Indian Affairs, 10 August 1872, *ARCIA* 1872, ser. 1560, 764; J. L. Broaddus, Agent, to CIA, 1 September 1875, *ARCIA* 1875, ser. 1680, 220–21; George W. Nelson, Interview, 31 October 1975.

18. Capt. S. G. Whipple, Agent, to CIA, 1 September 1870, *ARCIA* 1870, ser. 1449, 548; Whipple to CIA, 20 March 1871, *ARCIA* 1871, ser. 1505, 333; Nelson, *Our Home Forever*, 101–3; Francis A. Walker, *The Indian Question* (Boston: James B. Osgood and Co., 1874), 265–66.

19. Capt. S. G. Whipple, Agent, to CIA, 20 March 1871, *ARCIA* 1871, ser. 1505, 332–35; D. H. Lowry, Agent, to CIA, 1 September 1871, Ibid., 329–32; E. K. Dodge, Agent, to CIA, 3 November 1873, NA, RG 75, GR, HV, LR; Dodge to CIA, 31 August 1874, *ARCIA* 1874, ser. 1639, 311–12; Nelson, *Our Home Forever*, 103.

20. Maj. Henry R. Mizner, Commander, Ft. Gaston, Testimonial, 9 April 1875, NA, RG 75, GR, HV, LR; Mizner to Col. Nelson H. Davis, Inspector General, 16 September 1874, NA, RG 393, PL.

21. W. H. Pratt, Agent, to Maj. Mack, Ft. Gaston, 29 December 1868, NA; RG 75, GR, HV, LR; A. D. Nelson, Commander, Ft. Gaston, to Asst. Adj. General, 22 September 1873, NA, RG 393, PL; E. K. Dodge, Agent, to Gen. Schofield, Commander, Military Division of the Pacific, 20 July 1874, NA, RG 75, GR, HV, LR; Maj. Henry R. Mizner, Commander, Ft. Gaston, to Asst. Adj. General, 25 July 1874, NA, RG 393, PL. For Hupa populations, see Otis T. Mason, "The Ray Collection from Hupa Reservation," *Annual Report of the Smithsonian Institution, 1886*, in *House Ex. Doc.* 11, no. 170, pt. 1 (49–2), ser. 2498, 207.

22. J. L. Broaddus, Agent, to CIA, 1 September 1875, *ARCIA* 1875, ser. 1680, 220–22; Broaddus to CIA, 7 January 1876, NA, RG 75, GR, HV, LR;

Broaddus to CIA, 1 March 1876, NA, RG 75, GR, HV, LR; Broaddus to CIA, 21 August 1876, *ARCIA* 1876, ser. 1749, 12–14.

23. Capt. Rich G. Parker, acting commander, Ft. Gaston, to Asst. Adj. General, 4 December 1875, NA, RG 393, PL; J. L. Broaddus, Agent, to CIA, 18 March 1876, NA, RG 75, GR, HV, LR; Broaddus to CIA, 15 April 1876, NA, RG 75, GR, HV, LR.

24. Kappler, *Indian Affairs*, 1:815; Lt. James Halloran, acting commander, Ft. Gaston, to Asst. Adj. General, 30 September 1876, NA, RG 393, PL.

25. J. D. Cameron, SW, to SI, 26 January 1877, NA, RG 393, PL; Nelson, *Our Home Forever*, 106–13; Davis, "On This Earth," 126.

26. E. C. Watkins, Indian Inspector, to Capt. Rich C. Parker, acting commander, Ft. Gaston, 9 May 1877, NA, RG 393, PL; Parker to Asst. Adj. General, 14 May 1877, NA, RG 393, PL; Parker, Agent, to CIA, 24 August 1877, *ARCIA* 1877, ser. 1800, 431; Maj. Henry R. Mizner, Agent, to CIA, 4 November 1878, NA, RG 75, GR, HV, LR. For estimates of Hupa subsistence, see Sherburne F. Cook, *The Conflict Between the California Indian and White Civilization* (Berkeley: University of California Press, 1976), 461.

27. Maj. Henry R. Mizner, Agent, to CIA, 31 July 1880, *ARCIA* 1880, ser. 1959, 7–8, 238–39; Lt. Gordon Winslow, Agent, to CIA, 8 August 1881, *ARCIA* 1881, ser. 2018, 11–12; Winslow to CIA, 31 July 1882, *ARCIA* 1882, ser. 2100, 9–10; Capt. Charles Porter, Agent, to CIA, 1 August 1883, *ARCIA* 1883, ser. 2191, 10–14.

28. Capt. William E. Dougherty, Agent, to CIA, 21 December 1887, NA, RG 75, GR, HV, LR; Dougherty to CIA, 20 September 1888, *ARCIA* 1888, ser. 2637, 9–10; Dougherty to I. H. Albro, Supt. of Indian Schools, 26 December 1888, NA, RG 75, GR, HV, LR; Dougherty to CIA, 25 August 1889, *ARCIA* 1889, ser. 2725, 123–24; Cook, *Conflict*, 460–61; Nelson, *Our Home Forever*, 120–26.

29. McEvoy, *Fisherman's Problem*, 58–61; CIA to Capt. Charles Porter, Agent, 7 January 1885, NA, RG 75, GR, HV, LS; J. H. Blair to CIA, 25 February 1887, NA, RG 75, GR, HV, LR; CIA to SI, 21 June 1887, NA, RG 75, GR, HV, LS; Capt. William E. Dougherty, Agent, to Asst. Adj. General, 19 September 1889, NA, RG 393, PL; Cook, Conflict, 461.

30. Capt. Charles Porter, Agent, to CIA, 1 August 1885, *ARCIA* 1885, ser. 2379, 4–7.

31. Capt. William E. Dougherty, Agent, to CIA, 29 January 1887, NA, RG 393, PL.

32. J. D. C. Atkins, CIA, to SI, 2 April 1887, NA, RG 75, GR, HV, LS; Capt. William E. Dougherty, Agent, to CIA, 26 February 1887, NA, RG 75, GR, HV, LR; Dougherty to CIA, 28 June 1887, NA, RG 75, GR, HV, LR; Dougherty to CIA, 23 August 1887, NA, RG 75, GR, HV, LR.

33. Capt. William E. Dougherty, Agent, to CIA, 26 February 1887, NA, RG 75, GR, HV, LR; G. R. Stanley to General C. B. Fisk, BIC, 11 December 1888, NA, RG 75, GR, HV, LR; Nelson, *Our Home Forever*, 136; John H. Bushnell, "From American Indian to Indian American: The Changing Identity of the Hupa," *American Anthropologist*, 70 (December 1968), 1110; C. Hart Merriam, "Ethnographic Notes on California Indian Tribes," comp. and ed. Robert F. Heizer, *Reports of the University of California Archaeological Survey*, no. 68, 3 parts (Berkeley: University of California Archaeology Research Facility, Department of Anthropology, 1966–67), 199–200.

34. G. R. Stanley to Gen. C. B. Fisk, BIC, 11 December 1888, NA, RG 75, GR, HV, LR; Mrs. M. E. Duigan to Herbert Welsh, Indian Rights Assoc., 29 July 1889, NA, RG 75, GR, HV, LR; Mrs. Doreas L. Spencer, California Women's Christian Temperance Union, to Reverend M. E. Strieby, American Missionary Assoc., 29 October 1889, in Strieby to CIA, 14 November 1889, NA, RG 75, GR, HV, LR; Frank Armstrong, Indian Inspector, to SI, 3 October 1889, NA, RG 75, GR, HV, LR; Petition, Hoopa Agency, 2 October 1889, enclosed in Thomas J. Morgan, CIA, to SI, 16 November 1889, NA, RG 75, GR, HV, LS.

35. Capt. William E. Dougherty, Agent, to Asst. Adj. General, 8 February 1890, NA, RG 393, PL; Dougherty to CIA, 8 February 1890, NA, RG 75, GR, HV, LR; Isaac A. Beers, Agent, to CIA, 20 August 1891, *ARCIA* 1891, ser. 2934, 219–21.

36. Isaac Beers, Agent, to CIA, 20 August 1891, *ARCIA* 1891, ser. 2934, 219–21.

37: Kappler, *Indian Affairs*, 1:815; Nelson, *Our Home Forever*, 130–31.

38. Isaac A. Beers, Agent, to CIA, 23 November 1891, NA, RG 75, GR, HV, LR; Beers to CIA, 19 March 1892, NA, RG 75, GR, HV, LR; Beers to CIA, 15 August 1892, *ARCIA* 1892, ser. 3088, 228–30; William E. Dougherty, Agent, to CIA, 20 August 1894, *ARCIA* 1894, ser. 3306, 115–17; Nelson, *Our Home Forever*, 131.

39. Isaac A. Beers, Agent, to CIA, 23 November 1891, NA, RG 75, GR, HV, LR.

40. F. C. Armstrong, Acting CIA, to Charles W. Turpin, Special Agent, 21 February 1894, NA, RG 75, GR, HV, LS; William E. Dougherty, Agent, to CIA, 20 September 1894, NA, RG 75, GR, HV, LR; Dougherty to CIA, 1 December 1894, NA, RG 75, GR, HV, LR.

41. Charles W. Turpin, Special Agent, to CIA, 7 December 1895, NA, RG 75, GR, HV, LR; Nelson, *Our Home Forever*, 133.

42. William B. Freer, Supt., to CIA, Annual Statistics 1900, NA, RG 75, GR, HV, LR; U.S. Bureau of the Census, "Agriculture on Indian Reservations," *Twelfth Census of the United States, 1900*, vols. 5–6 (Washington, D.C.: U.S. Census Office, 1902), 5:64–65, 269, 422–23, and 6:155, 232, 363, 544, 624–25; Cook, *Conflict*, 461.

43. William B. Freer, Supt., to CIA, 15 August 1900, *ARCIA* 1900, ser. 4101, 204–7.

44. Frank Kyselka, Supt., to CIA, 22 August 1902, *ARCIA* 1902, ser. 4458, 171–72; Jesse B. Mortsolf, Supt., to CIA, 30 July 1909, FARC-SB, RG 75, Box 151; George Byron Nelson, Sr., Interview, 14 January 1987 (by permission of G. B. Nelson, Sr.); George W. Nelson, Interview, 26 April 1975 (quote). George W. Nelson, also known as Nelson Billy, was the grandson of Ene-nuck, one of the original signers of the Treaty of 1851. He was also the father of George Byron Nelson, Sr. and the grandfather of Hupa historian Byron Nelson, Jr.

45. William B. Freer, Supt., to CIA, 8 January 1900, NA, RG 75, GR, HV, LR; Freer to CIA, 15 August 1900, *ARCIA* 1900, ser. 4101, 206; M. T. Holland, Supervisor, Hoopa School, to CIA, 24 December 1901, NA, RG 75, GR, HV, LR; Frank Kyselka, Supt., to CIA, 22 August 1902, *ARCIA* 1902, ser. 4458, 170–74; Kyselka to CIA, Annual Narrative Report 1905, 31 August 1905, NA, RG 75, GR, HV, LR; Jesse B. Mortsolf, Supt., to CIA, 18 October 1910, NA, RG 75, CCF, HV, 031.

46. Charles L. Davis, Farming Supervisor, to CIA, 4 September 1911, NA, RG 75, CCF, HV, 916; Jesse B. Morsolf, Supt., to CIA, Annual Narrative Report 1912, FARC-SB, RG 75, HV, Box 151; C. H. Asbury, Special Agent, to CIA, 15 January 1915, NA, RG 75, CCF, HV, 150; Mortsolf to CIA, Annual Narrative Report 1916, FARC-SB, RG 75, HV, Box 151; Malcolm McDowell, "Report on the Hoopa Valley Indian Reservation, California, October 8, 1919," BIC, *Bulletin*, no. 97, 4 December 1919, in BIC, *Reports on Reservations and Schools*, 2:405–27, Edward E. Ayer Collection, MS 908, The Newberry Library, Chicago, Ill.

47. Jesse B. Mortsolf, Supt., 7 May 1917, NA, RG 75, CCF, HV, 920; Mortsolf to CIA, Annual Narrative Report 1917, 18 August 1917, FARC-SB, RG 75, Box 151; Nelson, *Our Home Forever*, 156.

48. Joe H. Norris, Inspector, to CIA, 27 September 1910, NA, RG 75, CCF, HV, 150; Charles L. Davis, Farming Supervisor, to CIA, 4 September 1911, NA, RG 75, CCF, HV, 54; C. H. Asbury, Special Agent, to CIA, 15 January 1915, NA, RG 75, CCF, HV, 150; Andrew Mesket to CIA, 5 November 1915, NA, RG 75, CCF, 54; Petition for Allotment, 20 November 1915, NA, RG 75, CCF, HV, 54; J. B. Mortsolf, Supt., to CIA, 24 November 1915, NA, RG 75, CCF, HV, 54; Mortsolf to CIA, 6 December 1915, NA, RG 75, CCF, HV, 54.

49. Jesse B. Mortsolf, Supt., to CIA, Annual Narrative Report 1919, NA, RG 75, CCF, HV, 31; Mortsolf, Annual Narrative Report 1923, NA, RG 75, CCF, HV, 31.

50. Jesse B. Mortsolf, Supt., to CIA, Annual Narrative Report 1919, NA, RG 75, CCF, HV, 31; Charles W. Rastall, Supt., Annual Narrative Report 1925, NA, RG 75, CCF, HV, 31; Act of 30 June 1919, 41 *Stats.*, 3; Nelson, *Our Home Forever*, 149–58, 163–64, 195–97.

51. Jesse B. Mortsolf, Supt., to CIA, Annual Narrative Report 1912, FARC-SB, RG 75, HV, Box 151; Nelson, *Our Home Forever*, 162; Davis, "On This Earth," 79–80, 250–51. For examples of the above, see William B. Freer, Supt., to CIA, 15 August 1900, NA, RG 75, GR, HV, LR; Mortsolf to CIA, 16 August 1911, NA, RG 75, CCF, HV, 31; Mortsolf to CIA, 12 April 1916, FARC-SB, RG 75, HV, Box 133; Mortsolf to CIA, Annual Narrative Report 1916, NA, RG 75, CCF, HV, 31; Malcolm McDowell, "Report on Hoopa," 409–412, 422; Charles W. Rastall, Supt., to CIA, 7 April 1924, FARC-SB, RG 75, HV, Box 264; Ales Hrdlicka, *Tuberculosis among Certain Tribes of the United States*, Smithsonian Institution, BAE Bulletin 42 (Washington, D.C.: GPO, 1909), 4–8, 20–27.

52. George Byron Nelson, Sr., Interview, 14 January 1987, and 25 August 1988.

53. Jesse B. Mortsolf, Supt., to CIA, Annual Narrative Report 1920, NA, RG 75, CCF, HV, 31; Mortsolf to CIA, Annual Narrative Report 1913, FARC-SB, RG 75, HV, Box 151; Curtis, *North American Indian*, 13:3; Mortsolf, to CIA, Annual Narrative Report 1923, NA, RG 75, CCF, HV, 31; John D. Keeley, Supt., to CIA, Annual Narrative Report 1927, NA, RG 75, CCF, HV, 31.

54. Jesse B. Mortsolf, Supt., to CIA, Annual Narrative Report 1923, NA, RG 75, CCF, HV, 31; Charles W. Rastall, Supt., to Herbert Clotts, Supervising Engineer, 5 February 1925, FARC-SB, RG 75, HV, Box 273; Charles H. Burke, CIA, *ARCIA* 1926, 24; George Byron Nelson, Sr., Interview, 25 August 1988.

55. John D. Keeley, Supt., to CIA, 21 April 1926, FARC-SB, RG 75, HV, Box 121; Keeley, Annual Narrative Report 1927, FARC-SB, RG 75, HV, Box 154-A; Keeley to CIA, 9 April 1930, NA, RG 75, CCF, HV, 54.

56. Jesse B. Mortsolf, Supt., to CIA, Annual Narrative Report 1923, NA, RG 75, CCF, HV, 31; Leonard B. Radtke, Forest Supervisor, to Lee Muck, Associate Forester, 6 December 1930, FARC-SB, RG 75, HV, 218.

57. L. A. Dorrington, Special Agent, to CIA, 20–27 October 1916, NA, RG 75, CCF, HV, 150; J. O. Snyder, "Indian Methods of Fishing on the Trinity River," *California Fish and Game*, 10 (October 1924), 166–72; Charles W. Rastall, Supt., to C. I. Clay, Humboldt Fish & Game Association, 23 May 1924, FARC-SB, RG 75, HV, Box 273; Rastall to R. J. Wade, Eureka Chamber of Commerce, 11 August 1925, FARC-SB, RG 75, HV, Box 273.

58. Kappler, *Indian Affairs*, 1:646–49, 674; Act of 4 June 1897, 30 *Stats.*, 34–36; CIA to William B. Freer, Supt., 13 February 1901, NA, RG 75, GR, HV, LS; Frank Kyselka, Supt., to CIA, 28 December 1905, FARC-SB, RG 75, HV, Box 151; Kyselka to CIA, 29 January 1908, NA, RG 75, CCF, HV, 339; Nelson, *Our Home Forever*, 190–92.

59. J. B. Mortsolf, Supt., to CIA, 16 February 1923, NA, RG 75, CCF, HV, 339; C. R. Patrie, Forest Asst., Report on Fire Protection on the Hoopa Indian Reservation, 22 August 1930, NA, RG 75, CCF, HV, 339.

60. J. B. Mortsolf, Supt., to CIA, 29 January 1919, NA, RG 75, CCF, HV, 339; C. R. Patrie, Forest Asst., Report on Fire Protection on the Hoopa Indian Reservation, 22 August 1930, NA, RG 75, CCF, HV, 339; Leonard B. Radtke, Forest Supervisor, to CIA, 8 September 1930, NA, RG 75, CCF, HV 339; Nelson, *Our Home Forever*, 165–66; Davis, "On This Earth," 238–42.

61. Nelson, *Our Home Forever*, 166–67; George Byron Nelson, Sr., Interview, 14 January 1987, and 25 August 1988.

62. Leonard B. Radtke, Forest Supervisor, to Lee Muck, Associate Forester, 6 December 1930, FARC-SB, RG 75 HV, Box 218; Memo, Hoopa Valley Farm Club, 16 February 1932, FARC-SB, RG 75, HV, Box 209; J. M. Walters, Farmer, District Farmer Reports 1932, FARC-SB, RG 75, HV, Box 209; George W. Nelson, Interview, 26 April 1975; O. M. Boggess, Supt., Annual Narrative Report 1933, FARC-SB, RG 75, HV, Box 151; Bradley C. Singer and Eugene L. Begg, *Soil Survey, Hoopa Valley, California*, Department of Land, Air and Water Resources, University of California-Davis, the BIA, U.S. Department of the Interior, and the Hoopa Valley Tribal Council (October 1975), 9.

63. Nelson, *Our Home Forever*, 173–74; John Collier, CIA, to O. M. Boggess, Supt., telegram, 1 June 1933, FARC-SB, RG 75, HV, Box 218; Collier to Boggess, 17 May 1935, FARC-SB, RG 75, HV, Box 218; Leonard B. Radtke, Forest Supervisor, Conservation Working Plan Report, 11 April 1935, FARC-SB, RG 75, HV, Box 218; Patrick I. Rogers, Asst. Clerk, IECW, Report: Distribution of IEWC Expenditures, Hoopa Valley Agency, 1 July 1933–31 March 1936, FARC-SB, RG 75, HV, Box 219; Boggess to CIA, 2 September 1937, NA, RG 75, CCF, HV, 344.

64. O. M. Boggess, Supt., to CIA, 24 October 1933, FARC-SB, RG 75, HV, Box 218; Boggess to CIA, 30 July 1934, FARC-SB, RG 75, HV, Box 218; John Collier, CIA, to Boggess, 24 September 1935, FARC-SB, RG 75, HV, Box 219; Collier to Boggess, 19 November 1935, FARC-SB, RG 75, HV, Box 219; Boggess to CIA, 19 April 1937, FARC-SB, RG 75, HV, Box 219; J. M. Walters, Farmer, Annual Report of Extension Workers, 1938, FARC-SB, RG 75, HV, Box 209; USDA, Soil Conservation Service, *Reconnaissance Survey of the Hoopa Valley Indian Reservation, California* (Denver, October 1938), FARC-SB, RG 75, HV, Box 224.

65. J. M. Walters, Farmer, to O. M. Boggess, Supt., 22 January 1935, FARC-SB, RG 75, HV, Box 218.

66. C. R. Patrie, Forest Asst., Report on Fire Protection on the Hoopa Indian Reservation, 22 August 1930, NA, RG 75, CCF, HV, 339; Leonard B. Radtke, Forest Supervisor, to CIA, 8 September 1930, NA, RG 75, CCF, HV, 339; U.S. Senate, *Survey of Conditions of the Indians in the United States*, Hearings before a Subcommittee of the Committee on Indian Affairs (72–1), (Washington, D.C.: GPO, 1934), Part 29:15,552–53; O. M. Boggess, Supt., to CIA, 21 November 1933, FARC-SB, RG 75, HV, Box 218; John Collier, CIA, to Boggess, 18 June 1934, FARC-SB, RG 75, HV, Box 218.

67. O. M. Boggess, Supt., to CIA, 2 September 1937, NA, RG 75, CCF, HV, 344; Leonard B. Radtke, Forest Supervisor, to CIA, 7 December 1937, FARC-SB, RG 75, HV, Box 219.

68. J. Harold Thompson, CCC-ID Supervisor, to CIA, 15 October 1937, FARC-SB, RG 75, HV, Box 219; L. W. Page, CCC-ID Supervisor, to CIA, 16 December 1937, FARC-SB, RG 75, HV, Box 219; D. E. Murphy, CCC-ID Director, to Boggess, 23 December 1937, FARC-SB, RG 75, HV, Box 219; Leonard B. Radtke, *Shall We Destroy the Tan Oaks on the Hoopa Indian Reservation in Northern California* (n.p., 1937); Radtke, Forest Supervisor, to Frank B. Lenzie, Regional Director, 21 October 1938, FARC-SB, RG 75, HV, Box 220; Hoopa Agency, Fire Reports, 1938–39, FARC-SB, RG 75, HV, Box 210; Radtke to CIA, 25 January 1940, NA, RG 75, CCF, HV, 339; American Indian Technical Services, *Indian Land and Forest Resources: An Issue of Federal Trust. A Forest History of the Hoopa Valley Indian Reservation of Northwestern California* (Broomfield, Colo.: AITS for the USDI and BIA, September 1983), Appendix C.

69. Nelson, *Our Home Forever*, 163–64, 169, 174–75, 196–97; Davis, "On This Earth," 79–80; Act of 18 June 1934, 48 *Stats.*, 984; O. M. Boggess, Supt., to CIA, 19 June 1933, NA, RG 75, CCF, HV, 54; Boggess to CIA, 10 July 1933, NA, RG 75, CCF, HV, 54; Boggess to CIA, 20 August 1934, NA, RG 75, CCF, HV, 54.

70. O. M. Boggess, Supt., Annual Narrative Report, 1933, FARC-SB, RG 75, HV, Box 151; Singer and Begg, *Soil Survey*, 9; George Byron Nelson, Sr., Interview, 25 August 1988; Boggess, to Men Having Fish Traps in the Trinity River, 20 January 1932, FARC-SB, RG 75 HV, Box 273; Boggess to CIA, 22 November 1939, NA, RG 75, CCF, HV, 931; George W. Nelson, Interview, 31 October 1975.

71. Nelson, *Our Home Forever*, 175–78; Henry J. Morin, Asst. Land Negotiator, to CIA, 26 January 1936, NA, RG 75, CCF, HV, 308; O. M. Boggess, Supt., to CIA, 12 January 1939, NA, RG 75, CCF, HV, 910; J. M. Walters, Farmer, Hoopa Valley Extension Cannery, 1940, FARC-SB, RG 75, HV, Box 210.

72. George Byron Nelson, Sr., Interview, 25 August 1988.

73. Nelson, *Our Home Forever*, 178; Bushnell, "From American Indian," 1112–13; George Byron Nelson, Sr., Interview, 14 January 1987.

74. O. M. Boggess, Supt., to CIA, 13 May 1941, FARC-SB, RG 75, HV, 210; Boggess to CIA, Hoopa Valley Jurisdiction, California, Ten Year Program, Office Circular 3514, 18 January 1944, NA, RG 75, CCF, HV, 112; Boggess to CIA, 4 March 196, NA, RG 75, CCF, HV, 916; Walter V. Woehike, Asst. CIA, to Hoopa Tribe, 10 January 1947, NA, RG 75, CCF, HV, 916.

75. O. M. Boggess, Supt., to A.C. Cooley, Director of Extension and Industry, 6 April 1942, FARC-SB, RG 75, HV, Box 210; Boggess to CIA, Hoopa Valley Jurisdiction, California, Ten Year Program, Office Circular 3514, 18 January 1944, NA, RG 75, CCF, HV, 112.

76. "Minutes of a Regular Meeting of the Hoopa Valley Business Council," 8 January 1948, NA, RG 75, CCF, HV, 57; "Resolution of the Hoopa Valley Business Council," 1 June 1950, NA, RG 75, CCF, HV, 57; "Minutes of a Regular Meeting of the Hoopa Valley Business Council," 18 March 1954, NA, RG 75, CCF, HV, 57; "Minutes of a Special Meeting of the Hoopa Valley Business Council," 23 July 1959, NA, RG 75, CCF, HV, 57.

77. AITS, *Indian Land and Forest Resources*; Nelson, *Our Home Forever*, 178; George Byron Nelson, Sr., Interviews, 14 January 1987 and 25 August 1988.

78. Davis, "On This Earth," 148–50; John H. Bushnell, "Hupa Reaction to the Trinity River Floods: Post-Hoc Recourse to Aboriginal Belief," *Anthropological Quarterly*, 42 (October 1969), 318–19; Singer and Begg, *Soil Survey*, 9–10. There are indications that both the First Salmon and First Acorn ceremonies are making a comeback in Hoopa Valley.

79. Davis, "On This Earth," 348–49; George Byron Nelson, Sr., Interview, 25 August 1988 and 14 January 1987.

80. George Byron Nelson, Sr., Interview, 14 January 1987.

Chapter 6

1. Bernard L. Fontana, *Of Earth and Little Rain: The Papago Indians* (Flagstaff, Ariz.: Northland Press, 1981), 35; Alice Joseph, Rosamond B. Spicer, and Jane Chesky, *The Desert People: A Study of the Papago Indians* (Chicago: University of Chicago Press, 1949), 3; Wick R. Miller, "Uto-Aztecan Languages," in *Handbook of North American Indians*, vol. 10, *Southwest*, ed. Alfonzo Ortiz (Washington, D.C.: Smithsonian Institution Press, 1983), 10:113–24 (hereafter cited as Ortiz, ed., *Southwest*, 10); Bernard L. Fontana, "History of the Papago," Ibid., 10:146.

2. Donald M. Bahr, *Pima and Papago Ritual Oratory: A Study of Three Texts* (San Francisco: Indian Historian Press, 1975); Dean Saxon and Lucille Saxon, *O'othham Hoho'ok A'agitha: Legends and Lore of the Papago and Pima Indians* (Tucson: University of Arizona Press, 1973), 1–9, 45–61, 147–68; Ruth M. Underhill, *Singing for Power: The Song Magic of the Papago Indians of Southern Arizona* (Berkeley: University of California Press, 1938) 13–14; Harold B. Wright, *Long Ago Told (Huh-kew ah-kah): Legends of the Papago Indians* (New York: D. C. Appleton, 1929), 7–34.

3. Linda M. Gregonis and Karl J. Reinhard, *Hohokam Indians of the Tucson Basin* (Tucson: University of Arizona Press, 1979), 1–27; Emil W. Haury, *The Hohokam: Desert Farmers and Craftsmen* (Tucson: University of Arizona Press, 1978), 351–57; Henry F. Dobyns, *From Fire to Flood: Historic Human Destruction of Sonoran Desert Riverine Oases*, Ballena Press Anthropological Papers, no. 20 (Socorro, N. Mex.: Ballena Press, 1981), 48–56; George J. Gumerman and Emil W. Haury, "Prehistory: Hohokam," in *Handbook of North American Indians*, vol. 9, *Southwest*, ed. Alfonzo Ortiz, (Washington, D.C.: Smithsonian Institution Press, 1979), 9:75–90 (hereafter cited as Ortiz, ed., *Southwest*, 9); Charles C. Di Peso, "Prehistory: O'otam," Ibid., 9:91–99; Kenneth Hale and David Harris, "Historical Linguistics and Archeology," Ibid., 9:170–71.

4. Robert A. Hackenberg, *Aboriginal Land Use and Occupancy of the Papago Indians* (New York: Garland Publishing Co., 1974), 41–48, 133–42, 193–208, 264–70; Edward F. Castetter and Willis H. Bell, *Pima and Papago Indian Agriculture* (Albuquerque: University of New Mexico Press, 1942), 12–21; Kirk Bryan, *Erosion and Sedimentation in the Papago Country, Arizona, with a Sketch of the Geology*, U.S. Geological Survey, Bulletin 730-B (Washington, D.C.: GPO, 1923), 19–90; Henry F. Dobyns, *The Papago People* (Phoenix: Indian Tribal Series, 1972), 70; Fontana, *Of Earth and Little Rain*, 12–15.

5. The following comes from Hackenberg, *Aboriginal Land Use*, 50–97, 133–42, 193–208, 264–70; Forrest Shreve and Ira L. Wiggins, *Vegetation and Flora of the Sonoran Desert*, 2 vols. (Stanford: Stanford University Press, 1964); Walter Ebeling, *Handbook of Indian Foods and Fibers of Arid America* (Berkeley: University of California Press, 1986), 461–533, 588–96; Edward F. Castetter and Ruth M. Underhill, *Ethnobiology of the Papago Indians*, University of New Mexico Bulletin, Biological Series, vol. 40, no. 3 (Albuquerque: University of New Mexico Press, 1935), 13–28; Castetter and Bell, *Pima and Papago Indian Agriculture*, 21–27, 64–72; Elias Yanovsky, *Food Plants of the North American Indians*, U.S. Department of Agriculture, Miscellaneous Publications, no. 237 (Washington, D.C.: GPO, 1936); Fontana, *Of Earth and Little Rain*, 15–19; Gary Paul Nabhan, Wendy Hodgson, and Francis Fellows, " A Meager Living on Lava and Sand? Hia Ced O'odham Food Resources and Habitat Diversity in Oral and Documentary Histories," *Journal of the Southwest*, 31, (Winter 1989), 508–33.

6. See especially Dobyns, *From Fire to Flood*, 39–40.

7. Hackenberg, *Aboriginal Land Use*, 69–77, 89–90; Hackenberg, "Pima and Papago Ecological Adaptations," in Ortiz, ed., *Southwest*, 10:163–64; Bernard L. Fontana, "Pima and Papago: Introduction," in Ibid., 10:126–33; Fontana, *Of Earth and Little Rain*, 36–40; Joseph, Spicer, and Chesky, *Desert People*, 28–29; Ebeling, *Handbook*, 644–45; *Tohono O'odham: History of the Desert People* (Salt Lake City: Printed for the Papago Tribe by University of Utah Printing Services, 1985), 3–4.

8. Ruth M. Underhill, *Social Organization of the Papago Indians*, Columbia University Contributions to Anthropology, vol. 30 (New York: Columbia University Press, 1939), 124; Karl S. Lumholtz, *New Trails in Mexico: An Account of One Year's Exploration in North-western Sonora, Mexico, and South-western Arizona, 1901–1910* (New York: Scribner and Sons, 1912), 76; Charles Bowden, *Killing the Hidden Waters* (Austin: University of Texas Press, 1977), 46, 51–54.

9. Underhill, *Social Organization*, 90–92; Bernard L. Fontana, "Assimilative Change: A Papago Indian Case Study" (Ph.D. diss., University of Arizona, 1960), 120–21.

10. Underhill, *Social Organization*, 90–106, 211–34; Lumholtz, *New Trails*, 164–65; Castetter and Bell, *Pima and Papago Indian Agriculture*, 45–46; Donald M. Bahr, "Pima and Papago Social Organization," in Ortiz, ed., *Southwest*, 10:187–92.

11. Underhill, *Social Organization*, 94–100; Castetter and Bell, *Pima and Papago Indian Agriculture*, 124–33.

12. Underhill, *Singing for Power*, 49–61; Underhill, *Papago Indian Religion*, Columbia University Contributions to Anthropology, vol. 33 (New York: Columbia University Press, 1946), 85–115; Castetter and Bell, *Pima and Papago Indian Agriculture*, 64–72; Castetter and Underhill, *Ethnobiology*, 40–44;

Amadeo M. Rea, "Hunting Lexemic Categories of the Pima Indians," *The Kiva*, 44 (Winter–Spring, 1979), 113–19; Ebeling, *Handbook*, 594–96; Ralph L. Beals, *Material Culture of the Pima, Papago, and Western Apache, with Suggestions for Museum Displays* (Berkeley: Department of the Interior, National Park Service, 1934), 13–14; Philip Drucker, *Culture Element Distributions, XVII: Yuman-Piman*, University of California Publications, *Anthropological Records*, vol. 6, no. 3 (Berkeley: University of California Press, 1941), 98–104; Hackenberg, *Aboriginal Land Use*, 56–62.

13. Castetter and Underhill, *Ethnobiology*, 13–14; Bowden, *Killing the Hidden Waters*, 51–54; Joseph, Spicer, and Chesky, *Desert People*, 28–29.

14. Ebeling, *Handbook*, 588–90, 628–31; Nabhan, *The Desert Smells Like Rain: A Naturalist in Papago Indian Country* (San Francisco: North Point Press, 1982), 101–7; Nabhan, *Gathering the Desert* (Tucson: University of Arizona Press, 1985); Nabhan, "Papago Fields: Arid Lands Ethnobotany and Agricultural Ecology" (Ph.D. diss., University of Arizona, 1983), 208–217; Drucker, *Culture Element Distributions, XVII*, 96–102; Castetter and Bell, *Pima and Papago Indian Agriculture*, 59–63; Castetter and Underhill, *Ethnobiology*, 13–28, 45–47, 64–65; Willis H. Bell and Edward F. Castetter, *The Utilization of Mesquite and Screwbean by the Aborigines in the American Southwest*, University of New Mexico Bulletin, Biological Series, vol. 5, no. 2 (Albuquerque: University of New Mexico Press, 1937), 21–47.

15. Castetter and Bell, *Pima and Papago Indian Agriculture*, 55–58; Hackenberg, "Pima and Papago Ecological Adaptations," in Ortiz, ed., *Southwest*, 10:163; Bahr, "Pima and Papago Social Organization," in Ibid., 10:187; Richard B. Woodbury and Ezra B. W. Zubrow, "Agricultural Beginnings, 2000 B.C.–A.D. 500," in Ibid., 9:43–60; Joseph Charles Winter, "Aboriginal Agriculture in the Southwest and Great Basin" (Ph.D. diss., University of Utah, 1974), 34–41; Fontana, *Of Earth and Little Rain*, 36–40.

16. Wright, *Long Ago Told*, 135–40.

17. Hackenberg, *Aboriginal Land Use*, 48–50; Nabhan, "Papago Fields," 155–93; Nabhan, *Desert Smells*, 125–28; Bahr, "Pima and Papago Social Organization," in Ortiz, ed., Southwest, 10:187–89; Dobyns, *Fire to Flood*, 47; Castetter and Bell, *Pima and Papago Indian Agriculture*, 44, 156–169.

18. Dobyns, *Fire to Flood*, 47; Ebeling, *Handbook*, 631–33; Castetter and Bell, *Pima and Papago Indian Agriculture*, 124–33; Nabhan, "Papago Fields," 55–66; Nabhan, "The Ecology of Floodwater Farming in Arid Southwestern North America," *Agro-Ecosystems*, 5 (July 1979), 245–55.

19. Castetter and Bell, *Pima and Papago Indian Agriculture*, 79–221; Ebeling, *Handbook*, 603–34; Russell, *Pima Indians*, 86–92; Castetter and Underhill, *Ethnobiology*, 29–39; George F. Carter, *Plant Geography and Culture History in the American Southwest*, Viking Fund Publications in Anthropology, no. 5 (New York: Viking Fund, 1945), 18–83; Underhill, *Social Organization*, 125; Nabhan and Richard S. Felger, "Teparies in Southwestern North America: A Biogeographical and Ethnohistorical Study of *Phaseolus acutifolius*," *Economic Botany*, 32, no. 1 (1978), 2–19.

20. Nabhan, *Desert Smells*, 77–86; Nabhan, "Papago Fields," 119–54, 200–206; Frank S. Crosswhite, "Desert Plants, Habitat, and Agriculture in Relation to the Major Pattern of Cultural Differentiation in the O'odham People of the Sonoran Desert," *Desert Plants*, 3, no. 2 (1981), 47–76; Ebeling, *Handbook*, 591, 644–45; Castetter and Bell, *Pima and Papago Indian Agriculture*, 172–76; Saxon and Saxon, *O'othham*, 20–23, 27–44.

21. Nabhan, "Papago Fields," 67–118; Castetter and Bell, *Pima and Papago Indian Agriculture*, 55–56, 179–221; Drucker, *Culture Element Distributions, XVII*, 95–96, 100–102.

22. Castetter and Bell, *Pima and Papago Indian Agriculture*, 222–30; Underhill, *Singing for Power*, 21–47; Underhill, *Papago Indian Religion*, 41–67, 75–84, 135–61; Underhill, Donald M. Bahr, Baptisto Lopez, José Pancho, and David Lopez, *Rainhouse and Ocean: Speeches for the Papago Year* (Flagstaff: Museum of Northern Arizona Press, 1979), 17–35; Nabhan, *Desert Smells*, 25–38; Frank S. Crosswhite, "The Annual Saguaro Harvest and Crop Cycle of the Papago, with Reference to Ecology and Symbolism," *Desert Plants*, 2, no. 1 (1980), 2–61; Lumholtz, *New Trails*, 45–61; Edward H. Davis, *The Papago Ceremony of Vikita*, Museum of the American Indian, Heye Foundation, vol. 3, no. 4 (New York, 1920), 153–79; John Alden Mason, "The Papago Harvest Festival," *American Anthropologist*, 22 (January–March 1920), 13–25.

23. Underhill, *Social Organization*, 31–56, 90–92; Fred Eggan, "Comparative Social Organization," in Ortiz, ed., *Southwest*, 10:735–36; Bahr, "Pima and Papago Social Organization," in Ibid., 10:187; Lumholtz, *New Trails*, 354–55; Joseph, Spicer, and Chesky, *Desert People*, 45–46, 54–57.

24. Underhill, *Social Organization*, 57–69; Bahr, "Pima and Papago Social Organization," in Ortiz, ed., *Southwest*, 10: 179–80, 186–87; Joseph, Spicer, and Chesky, *Desert People*, 4, 66–71; Dobyns, *Papago People*, 10–16; J. W. Hoover, "Generic Descent of the Papago Villages," *American Anthropologist*, 37 (April–June 1935), 257–64; William S. King and Delmos J. Jones, *Papago Population Studies* (New York: Garland Publishing Co., 1974); Edward H. Spicer, *Cycles of Conquest: The Impact of Spain, Mexico, and the United States on the Indians of the Southwest, 1533–1960* (Tucson: University of Arizona Press, 1962), 119; Hackenberg, *Aboriginal Land Use*, 69–77.

25. Underhill, *Social Organization*, 70–83, 113–21; Hackenberg, *Aboriginal Land Use*, 126–29; Bahr, "Pima and Papago Social Organization," in Ortiz, ed., *Southwest*, 10:182–86.

26. Underhill, *Social Organization*, 128–38; Lumholtz, *New Trails*, 9–10, 41, 140–43, 359–63; José Lewis Brennan, "Papago Material of José Lewis Brennan, 1897," 3 vols., MSS 1744, National Anthropological Archives, Washington, D.C., 2:16–28; Underhill, *Singing for Power*, 63–103; Drucker, *Culture Element Distributions, XVII*, 134–37; Underhill, "The Autobiography of a Papago Woman," *Memoirs of the American Anthropological Association*, no. 46 (Menasha, Wis.: AAA, 1936), 11–18.

27. Underhill, *Social Organization*, 102–10, 139–55; Drucker, *Culture Element Distributions, XVII*, 125–31; Underhill, "Autobiography," 40–41; Underhill, *Singing for Power*, 151–56; Underhill, *Papago Indian Religion*, 116–34.

28. Underhill *Social Organization*, 156–67, 174–78; Drucker, *Culture Element Distributions, XVII*, 139–46; Joseph, Spicer, and Chesky, *Desert People*, 53; Underhill, "Autobiography," 27–36, 41–42; Underhill, *Papago Indian Religion*, 252–60; Russell, *Pima Indians*, 182–92; Underhill, *Singing for Power*, 135–40.

29. Underhill, *Social Organization*, 179–87, 197; Joseph, Spicer, and Chesky, *Desert People*, 48–53; Drucker, *Culture Element Distributions, XVII*, 137–38, 163; Underhill, "Autobiography," 36–39; Russell, *Pima Indians*, 183–85; Brennan, "Papago Material," 2:9–15.

30. Underhill, *Social Organization*, 188–93; Underhill, "Autobiography," 50–51; Drucker, *Culture Element Distributions, XVII*, 146–48; Brennan, "Papago Material," 2:16–20.

31. *Tohono O'odham: Lives of the Desert People* (Salt Lake City: For the Papago Tribe by University of Utah Printing Services, 1984), 1; Underhill, *Papago Indian Religion*, 27–29; Underhill, *Social Organization*, 123–24.

32. Underhill, *Singing for Power*, 5–8; Underhill, *Papago Indian Religion*, 31–37; Underhill, *Rainhouse and Ocean.*

33. Underhill, *Papago Indian Religion*, 23, 41–161, 327–36; Underhill, *Singing for Power*, 21–40; Drucker, *Culture Element Distributions, XVII*, 150–57, 164; Davis, *Papago Ceremony*, 153–79; Nabhan, *Desert Smells*, 25–38; Lumholtz, *New Trails*, 45–61; Underhill, *Rainhouse and Ocean*, 17–35, 71–82, 141–46; Underhill, "Autobiography," 45–47; Louise Lamphere, "Southwestern Ceremonialism," in Ortiz, ed., *Southwest*, 10:758–62; Julian D. Hayden, "The Vikita Ceremony of the Papago," *Journal of the Southwest*, 29 (Autumn 1987), 273–324; Jacques Galinier, "From Montezuma to San Francisco: The Wi:gita Ritual in Papago (Tohono O'odham) Religion," *Journal of the Southwest*, 33 (Winter 1991), 486–538; Donald M. Bahr, "Papago Ocean Songs and Wi:gita," *Journal of the Southwest*, 33 (Winter 1991), 539–56; Mason, "Papago Harvest Festival," 13–25; David Kozak and Camillus Lopez, "The Tohono O'odham Shrine Complex: Memorializing the Locations of Violent Death," *New York Folklore*, 17 (Winter–Spring 1991), 1–20; Frances Densmore, *Papago Music*, Smithsonian Institution, BAE Bulletin 90 (Washington, D.C.: GPO, 1929), 135–218.

34. Underhill, *Papago Indian Religion*, 165–252; Underhill, *Singing for Power*, 105–140; Lumholtz, *New Trails*, 268–73; Lamphere, "Southwestern Ceremonialism," in Ortiz, ed., *Southwest*, 10:759–60; Brennan, "Papago Material," vol. 1, "Custom in Going for Salt;" Underhill, *Social Organization*, 167–74; Underhill, *Rainhouse and Ocean*, 37–69.

35. Underhill, *Papago Indian Religion*, 263–301; Donald M. Bahr, Juan Gregorio, David I. Lopez, and Albert Alvarez, *Piman Shamanism and Staying Sickness (Ká:cim Múmkidag)* (Tucson: University of Arizona Press, 1974), 19–289; Brennan, "Papago Material," 2:3–6; Drucker, *Culture Element Distributions, XVII*, 157–61; Lumholtz, *New Trails*, 35–37; Densmore, *Papago Music*, 82–134; Donald M. Bahr, "Pima and Papago Medicine and Philosophy," in Ortiz, ed., *Southwest*, 10:193–99; Underhill, *Singing for Power*, 141–50; Underhill, "Autobiography," 18–25, 47–50, 57–58; Underhill, *Rainhouse and Ocean*, 83–88.

36. Dobyns, *Fire to Flood*, 48–56.

37. Underhill, *Social Organization*, 13–23; Bryan, *The Papago Country*, 3–7; Herbert E. Bolton, *The Spanish Borderlands: A Chronicle of Old Florida and the Southwest* (New Haven: Yale University Press, 1921), 79–119; John F. Bannon, *The Mission Frontier in Sonora, 1620–1687*, United States Catholic Historical Society, Monograph Series 26 (New York, 1955); Bannon, *The Spanish Borderlands Frontier, 1513–1821* (New York: Holt, Rinehart and Winston, 1970); James E. Officer, *Hispanic Arizona, 1536–1856* (Tucson: University of Arizona Press, 1987), 25–31.

Chapter 7

1. Henry F. Dobyns, *The Papago People* (Phoenix: Indian Tribal Series, 1972), 17–21; Dobyns, *From Fire to Flood: Historic Human Destruction of Sonoran Desert Riverine Oases*, Ballena Press Anthropological Papers, no. 20 (Socorro, N. Mex.: Ballena Press, 1981), 60–62; Herbert E. Bolton, *Rim of*

Christendom: A Biography of Eusebio Francisco Kino, Pacific Coast Pioneer (New York: Macmillan Co., 1936), 247–48, 268, 356, 502–10; James E. Officer, *Hispanic Arizona, 1536–1856* (Tucson: University of Arizona Press, 1987), 28–31; *Tohono O'odham: History of the Desert People* (Salt Lake City: Printed for the Papago Tribe by University of Utah Printing Services, 1985), 7–9.

2. Robert W. Delaney, "The Modification of Land Use by Plant Introduction: The Spanish Experience," *Journal of the West*, 26 (July 1987), 32; Edward F. Castetter and Willis H. Bell, *Pima and Papago Indian Agriculture* (Albuquerque: University of New Mexico Press, 1942), 49–51, 73–75; Gwyneth H. Xavier, *The Cattle Industry of the Southern Papago Districts, With Some Information on the Reservation Cattle Industry as a Whole* (New York: Garland Publishing Co., 1974), 353–54; Rolf W. Bauer, "The Papago Cattle Economy: Implications for Economic and Community Development in Arid Lands," in *Food, Fiber, and the Arid Lands*, ed. William G. McGinnies, Bram J. Goldman, and Patricia Paylore (Tucson: University of Arizona Press, 1971), 86–87; Alice Joseph, Rosamond B. Spicer, and Jane Chesky, *The Desert People: A Study of the Papago Indians* (Chicago: University of Chicago Press, 1949), 29–30.

3. Edward H. Spicer, *Cycles of Conquest: The Impact of Spain, Mexico, and the United States on the Indians of the Southwest, 1533–1960* (Tucson: University of Arizona Press, 1962), 119–34, 279–342; Officer, *Hispanic Arizona*, 25–218; Dobyns, *Papago People*, 21–39; Ruth M. Underhill, *Social Organization of the Papago Indians*, Columbia University Contributions to Anthropology, vol. 30 (New York: Columbia University Press, 1939), 25; Bernard L. Fontana, *The Papago Tribe of Arizona* (New York: Garland Publishing Co., 1974), 182–83; John L. Kessell, "Friars verses Bureaucrats: The Mission as a Threatened Institution on the Arizona-Sonora Frontier, 1767–1842," *Western Historical Quarterly*, 5 (April 1974), 151–62.

4. *Tohono O'odham: History*, 10–12; Bauer, "Papago Cattle Economy," 82–83; Joseph, Spicer, and Chesky, *Desert People*, 27; Gary P. Nabhan, *The Desert Smells Like Rain: A Naturalist in Papago Indian Country* (San Francisco: North Point Press, 1982), 113–119; Ruth M. Underhill, *Papago Indian Religion*, Columbia University Contributions to Anthropology, vol. 33 (New York: Columbia University Press, 1946), 312–24; Dobyns, *From Fire to Flood*, 48–56; Donald M. Bahr, "Pima-Papago Christianity," *Journal of the Southwest*, 30 (Summer 1988), 133–67. Sonoran Catholicism developed as a syncretic blend of Christianity and native tradition, demonstrated most graphically in the combination of a native harvest and trade festival with the Feast of Saint Francis (itself a blend of the Jesuits' Saint Francis Xavier and the Franciscans' Saint Francis of Assisi) held in Magdalena, Sonora, each October.

5. Spicer, *Cycles of Conquest*, 541–42; Bernard L. Fontana, "Assimilative Change: A Papago Indian Case Study" (Ph.D. diss., University of Arizona, 1960), 10, 119, 122–23; Fontana, *Papago Tribe*, 180, 199–204; Xavier, *Cattle Industry*, 353–54; Joseph, Spicer, and Chesky, *Desert People*, 29–30, 58–59; Bauer, "Papago Cattle Economy," 87; Daniel McCool, "Federal Indian Policy and the Sacred Mountains of the Papago Indians," *Journal of Ethnic Studies*, 9 (Fall 1981), 58–59; Joseph C. Winter, "Cultural Modifications of the Gila Pima: AD 1697–AD 1846," *Ethnohistory*, 20 (Winter 1973), 67–77.

6. *Tohono O'odham: History*, 14–15; Spicer, *Cycles of Conquest*, 133–34, 343–67; Dobyns, *Papago People*, 40–41; Ruth M. Underhill, *A Papago Calendar Record*, University of New Mexico Bulletin, Anthropological Series, vol. 2, no. 5 (Albuquerque: University of New Mexico Press, 1938); A. T. Kilcrease,

"Ninety Five Years of History of the Papago Indians," *Southwestern Monuments*, Random Papers Supplement (April 1939), 297–310.

7. John Walker, Agent, to James L. Collins, Supt. of Indian Affairs, New Mexico, 28 September 1859, *ARCIA* 1859, ser. 1023, 719–21; Walker to Collins, 6 September 1860, *ARCIA* 1860, ser. 1078, 391–93; Karl S. Lumholtz, *New Trails in Mexico: An Account of One Year's Exploration in North-western Sonora, Mexico, and South-western Arizona, 1901–1910* (New York: Scribner and Sons, 1912), 329–32; Robert A. Hackenberg, *Aboriginal Land Use and Occupancy of the Papago Indians* (New York: Garland Publishing Co., 1974), 69–70; Kilcrease, "Ninety Five Years," 299–300, 302; Robert K. Thomas, "Papago Land Use West of the Papago Indian Reservation, South of the Gila River, and the Problem of Sand Papago Identity" (typescript, Ithaca, N.Y., 1963).

8. Castetter and Bell, *Pima and Papago Indian Agriculture*, 38–39, 47; Charles D. Poston, Supt. of Indian Affairs, New Mexico, to CIA, 29 February 1864, *ARCIA* 1864, ser. 1220, 165–66.

9. Fontana, *Papago Tribe*, 188–90; M. O. Davidson, Special Agent, to CIA, 12 August 1865, *ARCIA* 1865, ser. 1249, 131–36; Levi Buggles, Special Agent, to G. W. Dent, Supt. of Indian Affairs, Arizona, 20 June 1867, *ARCIA* 1867, ser. 1326, 161–65; R. A. Wilbur, Agent, to H. Bendell, Supt. of Indian Affairs, Arizona, 31 August 1872, *ARCIA* 1872, ser. 1560, 704–6; Edward Smith, CIA, to Wilbur, 7 July 1874, FARC-LN, RG 75, Sells, Box 1; Charles Hudson, Agent, to CIA, 31 August 1876, *ARCIA* 1876, ser. 1749, 6–9; Charles J. Kappler, comp. and ed., *Indian Affairs: Laws and Treaties*, 2 vols. (Washington, D.C.: GPO, 1904), 1:805, Executive Order, 1 July 1874.

10. M. O. Davidson, Special Agent, to CIA, 12 August 1865, *ARCIA* 1865, ser. 1249, 131–36; R. A. Wilbur, Agent, to H. Bendell, Supt. of Indian Affairs, Arizona, 31 August 1872, *ARCIA* 1872, ser. 1560, 704–06; John W. Cornyn, Agent, to CIA, 14 September 1875, *ARCIA* 1875, ser. 1680, 212–13; J. H. Stout, Agent, to CIA, 31 August 1877, *ARCIA* 1877, ser. 1800, 429–30; Gary P. Nabhan, "Papago Fields: Arid Lands Ethnobotany and Agricultural Ecology" (Ph.D. diss., University of Arizona, 1983), 21–23.

11. T. M. Beckwith to CIA, August 1872, FARC-LN, RG 75, Sells, Box 1; Charles Hudson, Agent, to CIA, 31 August 1876, *ARCIA* 1876, ser. 1749, 6–9; J. H. Stout, Agent, to CIA, 31 August 1877, *ARCIA* 1877, ser. 1800, 429–30; Underhill, *Papago Calendar*, 25–44, 52; Hackenberg, *Aboriginal Land Use*, 76, 290–308; Dobyns, *Papago People*, 45–46.

12. J. H. Stout, Agent, to CIA, 31 August 1877, *ARCIA* 1877, ser. 1800, 429–30; Bernard L. Fontana, "Desertification of Papagueria: Cattle and the Papago," in *Desertification: Process, Problems, Perspectives*, ed. Patricia Paylore and Richard A. Haney, Jr. (Tucson: University of Arizona, Office of Arizona Land Studies, 1976), 62–63; Bauer, "Papago Cattle Economy," 83, 87; Xavier, *Cattle Industry*, 354–58; Henry F. Manuel, Juliann Ramon, and Bernard L. Fontana, "Dressing for the Window: Papago Indians and Economic Development," in *American Indian Economic Development*, ed. Sam Stanley (The Hague: Mouton Publishers, 1978), 523–26; Hackenberg, *Aboriginal Land Use*, 76, 290–308; Bernard L. Fontana and D. Matson, "Papago Seminar, 1970," University of Arizona, Arizona State Museum Archives, A537, Tucson, Ariz., 16 February 1970, 3–4, and 23 February 1970, 2–3; Walter Ebeling, *Handbook of Indian Food and Fibers of Arid America* (Berkeley: University of California Press, 1986), 633; Amadeo M. Rea, "Hunting Lexemic Categories of the Pima Indians," *The Kiva*, 44 (Winter–Spring 1979), 118.

13. John W. Cornyn, Agent, to CIA, 14 September 1875, *ARCIA* 1875, ser. 1680, 212–13; Underhill, *Papago Calendar*, 43–45; Elizabeth J. Tooker, "Papagos in Tucson: An Introduction to Their History, Community Life, and Acculturation" (Master's thesis, University of Arizona, 1952), 1–11, 33; Fontana, *Papago Tribe*, 199–204; Dobyns, *Papago People*, 42–45; *Tohono O'odham: History*, 26–27; Hackenberg, *Aboriginal Land Use*, 185–90; Kappler, ed., *Indian Affairs*, 1:804, Executive Order, 12 December 1882.

14. A. H. Jackson, Agent, to CIA, 24 August 1883, *ARCIA* 1883, ser. 2191, 63–65; Jackson to CIA, 14 August 1884, *ARCIA* 1884, ser. 2287, 51; Roswell G. Wheeler, Agent, to CIA, 29 August 1885, *ARCIA* 1885, ser. 2379, 229–30; Wheeler to CIA, 2 August 1886, *ARCIA* 1886, ser. 2467, 257; Fontana, *Papago Tribe*, 213.

15. Elmer A. Howard, Agent, to CIA, 1887, *ARCIA* 1887, ser. 2542, 88; Fontana, *Papago Tribe*, 212.

16. Manuel, Ramon, and Fontana, "Dressing," 525–26; Dobyns, *Papago People*, 46–48; Nabhan, "Papago Fields," 24; Underhill, *Papago Calendar*, 55–59; WJ McGee, "The Beginning of Zooculture," *American Anthropologist*, 10 (July 1897), 221–22; Cornelius W. Crouse, Agent, to CIA, 25 March 1891, NA, RG 75, GR, LR; J. Roe Young, Agent, to CIA, 7 May 1895, NA, RG 75, GR, LR; Minutes of a Meeting Held at the District Court Room, Tucson, Pima County, Arizona, 4 May 1895, NA, RG 75, GR, LR; J. M. Berger, Farmer in Charge, San Xavier, to Elwood Hadley, Agent, 3 September 1898, *ARCIA* 1898, ser. 3757, 129.

17. Stephen Whited, Allotting Agent, to CIA, 26 October 1890, NA, RG 75, GR, LR; J. M. Berger, Farmer in Charge, to J. Roe Young, Agent, 28 August 1894, *ARCIA* 1894, ser. 3309, 108; Nabhan, "Papago Fields," 119–154.

18. Dobyns, *From Fire to Flood*, 62–64; Dobyns, *Papago People*, 52; Hackenberg, *Aboriginal Land Use*, 65–68, 76; Lee F. Brown and Helen M. Ingram, *Water and Poverty in the Southwest* (Tucson: University of Arizona Press, 1987), 110–12; Underhill, *Papago Calendar*, 52; Charles Olberg, Supt. of Irrigation, to W. H. Code, Chief Engineer, 20 June 1908, and John J. Granville, Supt. of Irrigation, to Code, 1 April 1911, NA, RG 75, CCF, Sells, 341.

19. J. M. Berger, Farmer in Charge, to J. Roe Young, Agent, 28 August 1894, *ARCIA* 1894, ser. 3309, 108–11; Young to CIA, 27 August 1895, *ARCIA* 1895, ser. 3382, 121–22; Berger to H. J. Cleveland, Agent, 10 September 1897, *ARCIA* 1897, ser. 3641, 109–10; Fontana, "Assimilative Change," 16–17.

20. J. M. Berger, Farmer in Charge, to J. Roe Young, Agent, 28 August 1894, *ARCIA* 1894, ser. 3309, 109–11; Berger to H. J. Cleveland, Agent, 10 September 1897, *ARCIA* 1897, ser. 3641, 109–10; Berger to Elwood Hadley, Agent, 3 September 1898, *ARCIA* 1898, ser. 3757, 128–29; U.S. Bureau of the Census, "Agriculture on Indian Reservations," *Twelfth Census of the United States, 1900*, vol. 5–6 (Washington, D.C.: U.S. Census Office, 1902), 5:60–61, 267, 418–19, 732–33; 6:154, 230, 361, 542, 622–23; Fontana, "Assimilative Change," 33.

21. Cornelius W. Crouse, Agent, to CIA, 18 August 1890, *ARCIA* 1890, ser. 2841, 5–9; John K. Rankin, Special Agent, to CIA, 27 June 1890, NA, RG 75, GR, LR; J. Roe Young, Agent, to CIA, 1 September 1894, *ARCIA* 1894, ser. 3309, 104; S. L. Taggart, Special Agent in Charge, to CIA, 13 August 1898, *ARCIA* 1898, ser. 3757, 126.

22. Bauer, "Papago Cattle Economy," 84–85; Henry F. Dobyns, *Pagogos [i.e. Papagos] in the Cotton Fields, 1950* (Tucson, 1951), 76–77.

23. J. M. Berger, Farmer in Charge, to CIA, *ARCIA* 1900, ser. 4101, 199–200; Berger to Elwood Hadley, Agent, 17 August 1901, *ARCIA* 1901, ser. 4290, 188–90; Hadley to CIA, Annual Statistical Report, 1901, NA, RG 75, GR, LR; Nabhan, "Papago Fields," 29.

24. J. M. Berger, Farmer in Charge, to CIA, 28 August 1902, *ARCIA* 1902, ser. 4458, 167–69; Berger to CIA, 24 September 1904, *ARCIA* 1904, ser. 4798, 148–50; Berger, Statistics Accompanying Annual Report, 1905, FARC-LN, RG 75, Sells, Box 7.

25. J. M. Berger, Farmer in Charge, to Elwood Hadley, Agent, 17 August 1901, *ARCIA* 1901, ser. 4290, 189; Berger to CIA, 28 August 1902, *ARCIA* 1902, ser. 4458, 167, 169; Losson L. Odle, Asst. Supervisor, Indian Employment, to Henry J. McQuigg, Supt., 15 July 1910, and Odel to McQuigg, 20 July 1910, FARC-LN, RG 75, Sells, Box 2.

26. Ralph Aspaas, Allotting Agent, to CIA, 22 November 1909, and CIA to Aspaas, 13 January 1910, NA, RG 75, CCF, Sells, 313.

27. Henry J. McQuigg, Supt., to CIA, 3 July 1912, FARC-LN, RG 75, Sells, Box 19; McQuigg to CIA, 3 September 1913, NA, RG 75, CCF, Sells, 313; McQuigg, Annual Narrative Report, 1916, FARC-LN, RG 75, Sells, Box 7; Ruth M. Underhill, *Acculturation at the Papago Village of Santa Rosa* (New York: Garland Publishing Co., 1974), 315–16. On the Papago Good Government League, see Bernard L. Fontana, "History of the Papago," in *Handbook of North American Indians*, vol. 10, *Southwest*, ed. Alfonzo Ortiz (Washington, D.C.: Smithsonian Institution Press, 1979), 10:143 (hereafter Ortiz, ed., *Southwest*, 10); Spicer, *Cycles of Conquest*, 141–42; Peter Blaine, Sr., with Michael S. Adams, *Papagos and Politics* (Tucson: Arizona Historical Society, 1981), 45–64.

28. Carlos Rios, Pablo Rios, Nunca Siembra, and Little Chico, to CIA, 3 August 1900, FARC-LN, RG 75, Sells, Box 1; Dobyns, *From Fire to Flood*, 62–64; John Granville, Supt. of Irrigation, to CIA, 7 April 1911, NA, RG 75, CCF, Sells, 341.

29. Charles Olberg, Supt. of Irrigation, to W. H. Code, Chief Engineer, 20 June 1908, Code to SI, 17 July 1909, and John J. Granville, Supt. of Irrigation, to Code, 1 April 1911, NA, RG 75, CCF, Sells, 341; C. R. Olberg and F. R. Schanck, Supts. of Irrigation, "Special Report on Irrigation and Flood Protection, Papago Indian Reservation," 14 November 1912, *Senate Document* no. 973 (62–3), pp. 5–25.

30. Charles A. Oertel, Expert Farmer, to Henry J. McQuigg, Supt., 1 May 1911, McQuigg to CIA, 9 May 1911, and F. H. Abbott, Asst. CIA, to SI, 9 December 1911, NA, RG 75, CCF, Sells, 916.

31. Henry J. McQuigg, Supt., to CIA, 30 July, 2 October, and 17 September 1912, NA, RG 75, CCF, Sells, 916. On reallotment see, McQuigg to CIA, 13 September 1913, C. F. Hanke, 2nd Asst. CIA, to McQuigg, 3 October 1913, and McQuigg to CIA, 5 January 1915, NA, RG 75, CCF, Sells, 313.

32. Henry J. McQuigg, Supt., to CIA, 7 February 1913, NA, RG 75, CCF, Sells, 341; McQuigg to John F. Armstrong, Supt. of Allotting Agents, 14 April 1913, NA, RG 75, CCF, Sells, 304; McQuigg to CIA, 16 September 1913, FARC-LN, RG 75, Sells, Box 2; McQuigg to J. F. Truesdell, Asst. Attorney General, 1 September 1914, NA, RG 75, CCF, Sells. On extension of the San Xavier trust period, see McQuigg to CIA, 4 June 1913, NA, RG 75, CCF, Sells, 312.

33. Jewell D. Martin, Supt., to Roscoe Rice, 13 August 1917, FARC-LN, RG 75, Sells, Box 3; E. B. Linnen, H. Brown, and W. West, Irrigation In-

spectors, to CIA, 18 March 1918, NA, RG 75, CCF, Sells, 341.

34. Henry J. McQuigg, Supt., to CIA, 2 August 1911, FARC-LN, RG 75, Sells, Box 2; Charles Oertel, Expert Farmer, to McQuigg, 1 May 1911, NA, RG 75, CCF, Sells, 914; Patrick Johnny Franco, San Xavier, Interview, 9 September 1988, Tohono O'odham Oral History Collection, 1988, American West Center, University of Utah, and the Venito Garcia Library, Sells, Ariz. (hereafter TOOHC), typescript, 9–10; Blaine, *Papagos and Politics*, 25–26; Theodore Rios, Autobiography, recorded by Timothy Dunnigan, Summer 1969, Doris Duke American Indian Oral History Project Collection, Papago No. A-0527, Arizona State Museum, University of Arizona, Tucson, pp. 7–9, 11 (hereafter DDOHC-A); Rufina Morris, San Xavier, Interview, 10 September 1988, TOOHC, typescript, 8–14.

35. John J. Granville, Supt. of Irrigation, to W. H. Code, Chief Engineer, 18 May 1911, NA, RG 75, CCF, Sells, 341. See the following Indian Appropriation Acts: 1912, 37 *Stats.* 522; 1913, 38 *Stats.* 85; 1916, 39 *Stats.* 130; 1917, 39 *Stats.* 974; 1918, 40 *Stats.* 568.

36. Charles Bowden, *Killing the Hidden Waters* (Austin: University of Texas Press, 1977), 5–6; Kilcrease, "Ninety Five Years," 307–8; Henry J. McQuigg, Supt., to CIA, 10 April 1915, FARC-LN, RG 75, Sells, Box 2; McQuigg to Charles R. Olberg, Supt. of Irrigation, 20 May 1916, FARC-LN, RG 75, Sells, Box 19; Underhill, *Papago Indian Religion*, 23, 68–75; J. W. Hoover, "The Indian Country of Southern Arizona," *Geographical Review*, 19 (January 1929), 54; Spicer, *Cycles of Conquest*, 140; Bauer, "Papago Cattle Economy," 85–86.

37. Henry J. McQuigg, Supt., to CIA, 28 October 1914, FARC-LN, RG 75, Sells, Box 11; McQuigg to CIA, 17 March 1914, FARC-LN, RG 75, Sells, Box 15. A "cattle unit" (or animal unit) is a range management measurement which draws grazing equivalents between different animals. In this case, two sheep or one horse or one cow/steer equals one animal unit.

38. Herbert V. Clotts, "Nomadic Papago Surveys," unpublished report, U.S. Indian Service, Los Angeles, Calif., 1915, and Clotts, comp., "History of the Papago Indians and History of Irrigation, Papago Indian Reservations, Arizona," unpublished report, U.S. Indian Service, Los Angeles, Calif., 1917, FARC-LN, RG 75, Sells; E. M. Sweet, Jr., Inspector, to CIA, 7 June 1916, NA, RG 75, CCF, Sells, 150; Nabhan, "Papago Fields," 34–36.

39. Frank A. Thackery et al., to CIA, Committee Report on Conditions and Needs of the Papago Indians, 18 August 1915, FARC-LN, RG 75, Sells, Box 23.

40. Frank A. Thackery et al., to CIA, Committee Report on Conditions and Needs of the Papago Indians, 18 August 1915, FARC-LN, RG 75, Sells, Box 23; Manuel, Ramon, and Fontana, "Dressing," 526–27; Fontana, "Desertification," 63, 66; Bauer, "Papago Cattle Economy," 87–88; Underhill, *Acculturation*, 315–16; Xavier, *Cattle Industry*, 355–58. On the Papago Farmers Association, see Minutes of the Meeting of the Papago Farmers Association held on 15 December 1914, in Henry J. McQuigg, Supt., to CIA, 19 March 1915, FARC-LN, RG 75, Sells, Box 1; Thomas F. McCormick, Supt., 27 March 1919, FARC-LN, RG 75, Sells, Box 4.

41. Jewell D. Martin, Supt., to CIA, 22 December 1916, and Cato Sells, CIA, to José X. Pablo, 29 January 1917, FARC-LN, RG 75, Sells, Box 4. On the border conflicts, see Henry J. McQuigg, Supt., to CIA, 16 March 1916, FARC-LN, RG 75, Sells, Box 2; McQuigg to Commanding Officer, U.S. Army, Nogales, 13 May 1916, FARC-LN, RG 75, Sells, Box 21; McQuigg to CIA, 8

May 1916, FARC-LN, RG 75, Sells, Box 21; McQuigg to J. H. Delgado, Mexican Consul, Nogales, 20 May 1916, FARC-LN, RG 75, Sells, Box 21; E. B. Meritt, Asst. CIA, to J. D. Martin, Supt., 8 February 1917, FARC-LN, RG 75, Sells, Box 21; SW to SI, 3 December 1918, NA, RG 75, CCF, Sells, 122.

42. Woodrow Wilson, Executive Order No. 2300, 14 January 1916; Wilson, Executive Order No. 2524, 1 February 1917; *Tohono O'odham: History*, 30–34; McCool, "Federal Indian Policy," 62–63; Henry J. McQuigg, Supt., to CIA, 15 May 1916, Reverend F. S. Herndon to CIA, n.d. [May 1916], and José X. Pablo, Stockman, to CIA, 15 July 1916, NA, RG 75, CCF, Sells, 130. On the Hunter-Martin claims case, see Charles A. Cook, "The Hunter Claim: A Colossal Land Scheme in the Papagueria," *Arizona and the West*, 15 (Summer 1973), 213–44.

43. Malcolm McDowell, "Report on the Papago Indians, Arizona, April 8, 1919," BIC *Bulletin*, no. 83, 27 May 1919, in BIC, *Reports on Reservations and Schools*, vol. 2:312–47, MS 908, Edward E. Ayer Collection, The Newberry Library. See especially pp. 316–17, 323, 334–37, 340–41.

44. McDowell, "Report," 2:317–21, 341; T. B. Hall et al., Proposed Range Management Program for the Papago Indian Reservation, 28 June 1938, NA, RG 75, CCF, Sells, 344; Thomas F. McCormick, Supt., to CIA, 23 October 1919, FARC–LN, RG 75, Sells, 4; Report of Meeting in Office of Superintendent T. F. McCormick, 11 December 1925, NA, RG 75, CCF, Sells, 54; Tribal Meeting of the Papago Indians on 12 October 1935 at Sells, Ariz., NA, RG 75, CCF, Sells, 54, pp.13; Bauer, "Papago Cattle Economy," 85–86; James E. Officer, "Arid Lands Agriculture and the Indians of the American Southwest," in *Food, Fiber, and the Arid Lands*, ed. McGinnies et al., 56.

45. McDowell, "Report," 2:339, 341–47; Constitution and By-Laws of the San Xavier Farm Bureau & Water Users Association of Pima County, Arizona, 10 April 1919, FARC-LN, RG 75, Sells, Box 4; Bauer, "Papago Cattle Economy," 87–88; William H. Kelly, *The Papago Indians of Arizona: A Population and Economic Study* (New York: Garland Publishing Co., 1974), 107–9;

46. Jewell D. Martin, Supt., to CIA, 1 August 1917, FARC-LN, RG 75, Sells, Box 3; McDowell, "Report," 2:334–39; Cato Sells, CIA, to Thomas F. McCormick, Supt., 18 October 1919, FARC-LN, RG 75, Sells, Box 4; McCormick, Annual Narrative Report, 1920, FARC-LN, RG 75, Sells, Box 8; Bauer, "Papago Cattle Economy," 87–88.

47. Herbert V. Clotts, Supervising Engineer, to Tucson Chamber of Commerce, 21 March 1921, and Thomas McCormick, Supt., to CIA, 3 June 1921, FARC-LN, RG 75, Sells, Box 19; McCormick to CIA, 8 March 1922, FARC-LN, RG 75, Sells, Box 6; Charles E. Dagenett, Supervisor, to CIA, 14 April 1922, NA, RG 75, CCF, Sells, 150; McCormick to CIA, 25 October 1922 and 12 February 1923, NA, RG 75, CCF, Sells, 916; Rios, Autobiography, DDOHC-A, 9–11.

48. Thomas F. McCormick, Supt., to CIA, 18 September 1922, FARC-LN, RG 75, Sells, Box 19; McCormick to CIA, 28 February 1923, FARC-LN, RG 75, Sells, Box 6; McCormick to CIA, 9 February 1924, FARC-LN, RG 75, Sells, Box 50; McCormick to CIA, 17 August 1924, NA, RG 75, CCF, 126; Underhill, *Papago Calendar*, 62; Rios, Autobiography, DDOHC-A, 45–54; Bernard L. Fontana, *Of Earth and Little Rain: The Papago Indians* (Flagstaff, Ariz.: Northland Press, 1981), 37–40.

49. Frank A. Thackery, Bureau of Plant Industry, to Thomas McCormick, Supt., 16 January 1924, FARC-LN, RG 75, Sells, Box 103; McCormick to

CIA, 16 March 1924, and 21 June 1924, NA, RG 75, CCF, Sells, 916; McCormick to CIA, 30 September 1924 and 5 November 1924, FARC-LN, RG 75, Sells, Box 6. On clubs, see A. M. Philipson, Farmer, to McCormick, 27 September 1924, and McCormick to CIA, 21 November 1924, FARC-LN, RG 75, Sells, Box 101.

50. Edward S. Stewart, Supt., to F. A. McKenzie, Survey of Indian Affairs, 8 August 1927, FARC-LN, RG 75, Sells, Box 32; A. M. Philipson, Farmer, Farmer's Report, 29 October 1927, NA, RG 75, CCF, 916; W. J. Spillman, "Extra-Dry Farming," *Farm Journal*, 52 (March 1928), 22; Ascension Anton, Sells, Interview, 10 September 1988, TOOHC, typescript, 1–3; Chester E. Faris, District Supt., to CIA, 1 November 1928, NA, RG 75, CCF, Sells, 150.

51. Henry J. McQuigg, Supt., to CIA, 7 January 1915, NA, RG 75, CCF, 920; McQuigg to CIA, 27 April 1916, FARC-LN, RG 75, Sells, Box 2; E. B. Meritt, Asst. CIA, to R. A. Ward, Acting Supt., Pima Agency, 17 July 1916, FARC-LN, RG 75, Sells, Box 23; McDowell, "Report," 2:329, 340–41; Janette Woodruff, Field Matron, to Thomas F. McCormick, Supt., 1 July 1919 and 31 December 1919, FARC-LN, RG 75, Sells, Box 4; McCormick to CIA, 28 February 1923, FARC-LN, RG 75, Sells, Box 6; Tooker, "Papagos in Tucson," 9–17; *Tohono O'odham: History*, 45–46; Rios, Autobiography, DDOHC-A, 16.

52. Fontana, "Assimilative Change," 126–29; Manuel, Ramon, and Fontana, "Dressing," 533–34; Jack O. Waddell, *Papago Indians at Work*, Anthropological Papers of the University of Arizona, no. 12 (Tucson: University of Arizona Press, 1969), 39–41; Dobyns, *Pagogos*, passim; Cato Sells, CIA, to Frank A. Thackery, Supt., 6 February 1914, FARC–LN, RG 75, Sells, Box 23; Thackery to Papago Missionaries, 12 May 1916, FARC-LN, RG 75, Sells, Box 2; W. H. Knox, Arizona Cotton Growers Association, to CIA, 14 June 1922, and Charles H. Burke, CIA, to Knox, 19 June 1922, FARC-LN, RG 75,   Sells, Box 6.

53. L. V. W. Brown, Salt River Valley Cotton Company, to Thomas F. McCormick, Supt., 5 August 1919, FARC-LN, RG 75, Sells, Box 4; Charles H. Burke, CIA, to McCormick, 10 February 1923, FARC-LN, RG 75, Sells, Box 6. The block quote is from McCormick to CIA, 29 August 1922, FARC-LN, RG 75, Sells, Box 6.

54. E. H. Hammond, Supervisor, to CIA, 8 April 1930, NA, RG 75, CCF, 54; J. W. Elliot, Supt., Annual Narrative Report, 1930, FARC-LN, RG 75, Sells, Box 44; A. M. Philipson, Farmer, Project No. 1, Cotton Growing Demonstration, 27 December 1930, FARC-LN, RG 75, Sells, Box 103; Division of Extension and Industry, Diversified Farming Project, San Xavier Reservation, 31 January 1931, FARC-LN, RG 75, Sells, Box 14; Rios, Autobiography, DDOHC-A, 170–71.

55. U.S. Senate, *Survey of Conditions of the Indians in the United States*, Hearings before a Subcommittee of the Committee on Indian Affairs, U.S. Senate (72–1), (Washington, D.C.: GPO, 1934), Part 17:8,370–82, 8,350–61, 8,382–86; Brown and Ingram, *Water and Poverty*, 114–15.

56. U.S. Senate, *Survey of Conditions*, 17:8,395–432, 8,446–456.

57. Act of 18 June 1934, 48 *Stats.* 984; Blaine, *Papagos and Politics*, 45–64; Peter Blaine, Tucson, Interview, 11 September 1988, TOOHC, typescript, 17–20; Fontana, *Papago Tribe*, 199–204; Spicer, *Cycles of Conquest*, 141–42; Constitution, Papago Good Government League, 15 November 1924, NA, RG 75, CCF, Sells, 100; J. W. Elliott, Supt., to CIA, 20 March 1931, NA, RG 75, CCF, Sells, 100; Underhill, *Acculturation*, 315–16.

58. *Tohono O'odham: History*, 59–60; Kilcrease, "Ninety Five Years," 310; T. B. Hall, Supt., Report of Referendum Vote, Act of 18 June 1934, Public No. 383, December 1934, FARC–LN, RG 75, Sells, Box 50; Hall, Papago Indian Reservation, District Organization Plans, 13 February 1935, FARC-LN, RG 75, Sells, Box 50; Stipulation of the Papago Tribe, 18 May 1935, FARC-LN, RG 75, Sells, Box 29; Hall to CIA, 11 March 1937, NA, RG 75, CCF, Sells, 54; Bauer, "Papago Cattle Economy," 96–97; Dobyns, *Papago People*, 62–63; Joseph, Spicer, and Chesky, *Desert People*, 4.

59. Dobyns, *Papago People*, 58–65; Fontana, "History of the Papago," in Ortiz, ed., *Southwest*, 10:145–46; Donald L. Parman, "New Deal Indian Agricultural Policy and the Environment: The Papagos as a Case Study," *Agricultural History*, 66 (Spring 1992), 23–33; Eric W. Allstrom, "In Papago Land," *Indians at Work*, 6, no. 8 (1939), 11–13; B. A. Sanders, Disbursing Agent, to CIA, 5 August 1935, FARC-LN, RG 75, Sells, Box 90; T. B. Hall, Supt., Annual Narrative Report, 21 November 1936, NA, RG 75, CCF, Sells, 031, pp. 48–52; Rios, Autobiography, DDOHC-A, 37–39, 44, 70, 103, 117–32.

60. J. W. Elliott, Supt., to CIA, 7 May 1934, FARC-LN, RG 75, Sells, Box 51; E. A. Johnson, Associate Silviculturalist, to CIA, 9 March 1934, FARC-LN, RG 75, Sells, Box 42; T. B. Hall, Supt., et al., Proposed Range Management Program for the Papago Indian Reservation, 28 June 1938, NA, RG 75, CCF, Sells, 340; R. D. Holtz, Production Supervisor, to W. J. Keays, Senior Conservationist, 14 April 1938, FARC-LN, RG 75, Sells, Box 52; Bauer, "Papago Cattle Economy," 93; Dobyns, *Papago People*, 62; Castetter and Bell, *Pima and Papago Indian Agriculture*, 169–70; Xavier, *Cattle Industry*, 386–88.

61. Father Bonaventure Oblasser, Pisinemo Village, to CIA, 26 September 1933 and 24 October 1933, NA, RG 75, CCF, Sells, 341; Henry F. Dobyns, "Report on Investigations on the Papago Reservation" (Cornell University, Department of Sociology-Anthropology, October 1949), NA, RG 75, CCF, assession #57a-185, Sells, 31, pp. 29–31; Dobyns, *From Fire to Flood*, 70; Brown and Ingram, *Water and Poverty*, 153–54.

62. Hackenberg, *Aboriginal Land Use*, 62–68; McCool, "Federal Indian Policy," 64; "Roasting the Range," *High Country News*, 21, no. 14 (31 July 1989), 6; T. B. Hall et al., Proposed Range Management Program for the Papago Indian Reservation, 28 June 1938, NA, RG 75, CCF, Sells, 340; Robert D. Holtz, Forest Supervisor, Notes on Experimental Range Planting on the Papago Reservation, Arizona, March 1939, and Hall to Lee Muck, Director, Forestry and Grazing, OIA, 30 June 1939, NA, RG 75, CCF, Sells, 32.

63. Fontana, "Desertification," 66; Bauer, "Papago Cattle Economy," 87–90; Xavier, *Cattle Industry*, 360–61, 368–69; Manuel, Ramon, and Fontana, "Dressing," 529–31; Fontana and Matson, "Papago Seminar," 23 February 1970, 8–13; T. B. Hall, Supt., Annual Narrative Reports, 1935 and 1936, FARC-LN, RG 75, Sells, Box 50.

64. Tribal Meeting of the Papago Indians, 12 October 1935 at Sells, Ariz., typescript, NA, RG 75, CCF, Sells, 54.

65. T. B. Hall, Supt., Papago Indian Reservation, District Organization Plans, 13 February 1935, FARC-LN, RG 75, Sells, Box 50; Hall, Annual Narrative Report, 21 November 1936, NA, RG 75, CCF, Sells, 31; Xavier, *Cattle Industry*, 384–88; Bauer, "Papago Cattle Economy," 96–97; Manuel, Ramon, and Fontana, "Dressing," 529–30; Rea, "Hunting," 118; Ebeling, *Handbook*, 633.

66. J. W. Elliott, Supt., to CIA, 15 April 1932, NA, RG 75, CCF, Sells, 916; T. B Hall, Supt., Annual Narrative Reports, 1935 and 1936, FARC-LN,

RG 75, Sells, Box 50; Hall, Annual Narrative Report, 1939, FARC-LN, RG 75, Sells, Box 47; Joseph, Spicer, and Chesky, *Desert People*, 33; Bauer, "Papago Cattle Economy," 91–93; Xavier, *Cattle Industry*, 370–72; Manuel, Ramon, and Fontana, "Dressing," 530–31.

67. Charles Whitfield, Lecture, in Fontana and Matson, "Papago Seminar," 16 February 1970, 23 and passim, also quoted in Fontana, "Desertification," 63–64; Bauer, "Papago Cattle Economy," 88–90; Xavier, *Cattle Industry*, 359, 367, 373–75; Joseph, Spicer, and Chesky, *Desert People*, 33, 58–59; Manuel, Ramon, and Fontana, "Dressing," 528–29.

68. Bauer, "Papago Cattle Economy," 90; Blaine, *Papagos and Politics*, 97; T. B. Hall, Annual Narrative Report, 1935, FARC-LN, RG 75, Sells, Box 50; Joseph, Spicer, and Chesky, *Desert People*, 31–33, 58–59. On dourine epidemic and horse reductions 1944–46, see NA, RG 75, CCF accession #53a–367, Sells, 566.

69. Tribal Meeting of the Papago Indians on 12 October 1935 at Sells, Ariz., NA, RG 75, CCF, Sells, 54, p.6.

70. Blaine, *Papagos and Politics*, 75–77; Robert D. Holtz, Forest Supervisor, Notes on Experimental Range Planting on the Papago Reservation, Arizona, March 1939, FARC-LN, RG 75, Sells, Box 78; Bauer, "Papago Cattle Economy," 88–90; Xavier, *Cattle Industry*, 359; Fontana, "Assimilative Change," 126–29; Fontana, "Desertification," 66; Rios, Autobiography, DDOHC-A, 26–29.

71. Fontana, "Assimilative Change," 126–29.

72. T. B. Hall, Supt., Annual Narrative Reports, 1935 and 1936, FARC-LN, RG 75, Sells, Box 50; Dobyns, *Report*, 34–37.

73. T. B. Hall, Supt., to X. Vigeant, Director, Rehabilitation Division, 1 August 1939, FARC-LN, RG 75, Sells, Box 93; Hall to Mrs. Welford C. Rupkey, 8 December 1938, FARC-LN, RG 75, Sells, Box 44; Spicer, *Cycles of Conquest*, 142.

74. T. B. Hall, Supt., Interview with Bernabe Lopez, Chief, San Pedro, 2 November 1936, to CIA, 7 November 1936, FARC-LN, RG 75, Sells, Box 50; Hall to CIA, 4 August 1937, FARC-LN, RG 75, Sells, Box 50; Ruth Underhill to John Collier, CIA, 19 February 1936, NA, RG 75, CCF, Sells, 62; Underhill, *Papago Indian Religion*, 305–10; Underhill, *Acculturation*, 311–48.

75. William Wade Head, Supt., to CIA, Program, Papago Reservations, Arizona, Sells Agency, 15 April 1944, FARC-LN, RG 75, Sells, Box 56; Beulah L. Head, to Dear Friends in the Armed Services, 1 November 1943, FARC-LN, RG 75, Box 4; Dobyns, *Papago People*, 65–68; Waddell, *Papagos at Work*, 41; Joseph, Spicer, and Chesky, *Desert People*, 33–37.

76. William Wade Head, Supt., to CIA, Program, Papago Reservation, Arizona, Sells Agency, 15 April 1944, FARC-LN, RG 75, Sells, Box 56; Burton A. Ladd, Supt., Summary of Important Accomplishments Relating to Extension Work, 1949, NA, RG 75, CCF, Sells, 32.

77. William Wade Head, Supt., to CIA, Program, Papago Reservation, Arizona, Sells Agency, 15 April 1944, FARC-LN, RG 75, Sells, Box 56; Head to CIA, 22 May 1944, FARC-LN, RG 75, Sells, Box 78; Moris Burge, Supt., to CIA, 28 January 1946, FARC-LN, RG 75, Sells, Box 31; Burge to CIA, 24 June 1946, FARC-LN, RG 75, Sells, Box 31; E. H. Walker, Extension Agent, and Burton A. Ladd, Supt., Annual Report of Extension Work, 23 December 1947, and Ladd, Summary of Important Accomplishments Relating to Extension Work, 1949, NA, RG 75, CCF, Sells, 32; Bauer, "Papago Cattle

Economy," 90, 93; Manuel, Ramon, and Fontana, "Dressing," 529–30.

78. Bauer, "Papago Cattle Economy," 88–90, 97; Manuel, Ramon, and Fontana, "Dressing," 527–32; Fontana and Matson, "Papago Seminar," 16 February 1970, 21–30, and 23 February 1970, 8–13; Fontana, "Desertification," 66; Department of Interior, Bureau of Indian Affairs, News Release, 12 August 1987.

79. Dobyns, *Pagogos*, passim; Peter Blaine, Tucson, Interview, 11 September 1988, TOOHC, typescript, 8–9; Rufina Morris, San Xavier, Interview, 10 September 1988, TOOHC, typescript, 15–17.

80. John H. Provinse, Asst. CIA, to Papago Tribal Delegates, 10 March 1948, NA, RG 75, CCF, Sells, 54; U.S. Senate, *Rehabilitation of the Papago Tribe of Indian, Arizona*, Hearings before a Subcommittee of the Committee on Interior and Insular Affairs, U.S. Senate (81–1), 16 July 1951 (Washington, D.C.: GPO, 1952); W. L. Miller, Chief, Branch of Irrigation, to CIA, 12 July 1951, NA, RG 75, CCF, Sells, 341; U.S. House of Representatives, *Papago Rehabilitation Legislation*, Hearings before the Subcommittee on Indian Affairs of the Committee on Interior and Insular Affairs, HR (84–1), 29–30 August 1955 (Washington, D.C.: GPO, 1955); Thomas A. Segundo, Chairman, Papago Council, to CIA, 28 April 1953, NA, RG 75, CCF, Sells, accession #57a–185, 304; Officer, "Arid Lands Agriculture," 56; Dobyns, *Papago People*, 69–70.

81. Chue Chu Farmers Cooperative Association, Articles of Association and By-Laws, 19 February 1951 and 5 April 1951, NA, RG 75, CCF, Sells, accession #57a–185, 257; Dobyns, *Report*, 34–37; Stephen Bingham, Credit Examiner, to Ralph M. Gelvin, Area Director, 19 September 1951, and Will R. Bolen, Supt. of Extension Credit, to Harry L. Stevens, Supt., 13 February 1952, NA, RG 75, CCF, Sells, 259; Officer, "Arid Lands Agriculture," 56; Kelly, *Papago Indians*, 108–9.

82. U.S. Senate, *To Restore Lands of the Papago Indian Reservation in Arizona to Exploration and Location Under the Public Land Mining Laws*, Hearing before the Committee on Indian Affairs, Senate (73–2), 24 April 1934 (Washington, D.C.: GPO, 1934); Act of 27 May 1955, 69 *Stats*. 67; Blaine, *Papagos and Politics*, 115–16, 122–24; Fontana, "Assimilative Change," 137–39; Fontana, *Papago Tribe*, 106, 199–204; Manuel, Ramon, and Fontana, "Dressing," 539, 551–56; Kelly, *Papago Indians*, 107–8.

83. Manuel, Ramon, and Fontana, "Dressing," 564–65; Kelly, *Papago Indians*, 109–110; Officer, "Arid Lands Agriculture," 56. For the original contract and letters see NA, RG 75, CCF, Sells, accession #64a–528, 320.

84. Kelly, *Papago Indians*, 4–5, 98–117; Officer, "Arid Lands Agriculture," 64, 69, 71, 74; Fontana, "Assimilative Change," 53–57; Nabhan, "Papago Fields," 16; Nabhan, *Desert Smells*, 47, 107–10; Dobyns, *Papago People*, 70–75; Manuel, Ramon, and Fontana, "Dressing," 529–30, 532–35.

85. Manuel, Ramon, and Fontana, "Dressing," 526–64; Applied Remote Sensing Program, *Application of Remote Sensing in Evaluating Floodwater Farming on the Papago Indian Reservation* (Tucson: Office of Arid Land Studies, University of Arizona, 1982), 9, 35; Nabhan, *Enduring Seeds*, 38.

86. Brown and Ingram, *Water and Poverty*, 117–77; U.S. Senate, *Water Claims of the Papago Tribe*, Hearing before the Select Committee on Indian Affairs, Senate (97–2), 31 March 1982 (Washington, D.C.: GPO, 1982); U.S. Congress, Senate Committee of Conference, *Conference Report to S. 1409*, Senate Report 97–568, Title III (Washington, D.C.: GPO, 1982); Ascension Anton, Sells, Interview, 10 September 1988, TOOHC, typescript, 11; Patrick

Johnny Franco, San Xavier, Interview, 9 September 1988, TOOHC, typescript, 15, 44.

87. "Tohono O'odham Faced with Mine Contamination," *Lakota Times* (Rapid City, S. Dak.), 19 August 1992, B-11; Nabhan, *Desert Smells*, 107–10; Ebeling, *Handbook*, 644–45.

88. ARSP, *Application of Remote Sensing*, 35; William Stolzenburg, "Sacred Peaks, Common Grounds," *Nature Conservancy*, (September/October 1992), 17–23.

Conclusion

1. Richard White, *The Roots of Dependency: Subsistence, Environment, and Social Change among the Choctaws, Pawnees, and Navajos* (Lincoln: University of Nebraska Press, 1983), 315–8; William Cronon and Richard White, "Indians in the Land," *American Heritage*, 37 (August–September 1986), 21; Marshall D. Sahlins, *Stone Age Economics* (New York and Chicago: Aldine-Atherton, 1972), 1–39; Sahlins, *Culture and Practical Reason* (Chicago: University of Chicago Press, 1976), 168–79.

2. Peter Iverson, "Cowboys, Indians and the Modern West," *Arizona and the West*, 28 (Summer 1986), 107–24; Theodore E. Downing, "The Crisis in American Indian and non-Indian Farming," *Agriculture and Human Values*, 2 (Summer 1985), 18–24; Sar A. Levitan and Barbara Hetrick, *Big Brother's Indian Programs—With Reservations* (New York: McGraw-Hill, 1971), 127–38.

3. See also R. Douglas Hurt, *Indian Agriculture in America: Prehistory to the Present* (Lawrence: University Press of Kansas, 1987), 154–73, 195–213; James E. Officer, "Arid Lands Agriculture and the Indians of the American Southwest," in *Food, Fiber, and the Arid Lands*, ed. William G. McGinnies, Bram J. Goldman, and Patricia Paylore (Tucson: University of Arizona Press, 1971), 47, 72–75.

4. Joseph G. Jorgensen, "Federal Policies, American Indian Polities and the 'New Federalism,'" *American Indian Culture and Research Journal*, 10, no. 2 (1986), 2–9; Frederick E. Hoxie, *A Final Promise: The Campaign to Assimilate the Indians, 1880–1920* (Lincoln: University of Nebraska Press, 1983).

5. Sahlins, *Culture and Practical Reason*, vii–viii, 169–79, 205–10; White, *Roots of Dependency*, 323; Benjamin Orlove, "Ecological Anthropology," *Annual Review of Anthropology*, 9 (1980), 245–62.

6. Russel L. Barsh, "The Substitution of Cattle for Bison on the Great Plains," in *The Struggle for the Land: Indigenous Insight and Industrial Empire in the Semiarid World*, ed. Paul A. Olson (Lincoln: University of Nebraska Press, 1990), 101–26; Barsh, "Plains Indian Agrarianism and Class Conflict," *Great Plains Quarterly*, 7 (Spring 1987), 83–90; Iverson, "Cowboys, Indians," 107–24; Ronald L. Trosper, "American Indian Relative Ranching Efficiency," *American Economic Review*, 68 (September 1978), 503–16.

7. Floyd A. O'Neil, "The Indian New Deal: An Overview," in *Indian Self-Rule: First-Hand Accounts of Indian-White Relations from Roosevelt to Reagan*, ed. Kenneth R. Philp (Salt Lake City: Howe Brothers, 1986), 31; Hurt, *Indian Agriculture*, 233–34; John L. Shover, *First Majority, Last Minority: The Transforming of Rural Life in America* (DeKalb: Northern Illinois University Press, 1976).

8. Joan M. Jensen, "Native American Women and Agriculture: A Seneca Case Study," *Sex Roles*, 3 (October 1977), 423–41; Alex F. Ricciardelli, "The Adoption of White Agriculture by the Oneida Indians," *Ethnohistory*, 10 (Fall

1963), 309–28; Carolyn G. Pool, "Reservation Policy and the Economic Position of Wichita Women," *Great Plains Quarterly*, 8 (Summer 1988), 158–71.

9. Gary C. Anders, "Theories of Underdevelopment and the American Indian," *Journal of Economic Studies*, 14 (September 1980), 681–701.

10. White, *Roots of Dependency*, 320–21; John W. Berry, "Acculturation as Varieties of Adaptation," in *Acculturation: Theory, Models and Some New Findings*, ed. Amado M. Padilla (Boulder, Colo.: Westview Press, 1980)," 9–17. For a general overview of responses, see Hurt, *Indian Agriculture.*

11. Herbert T. Hoover, "Arikara, Sioux, and Government Farmers: Three American Indian Agricultural Legacies," *South Dakota History*, 13, nos. 1 & 2 (1983), 22–48; Raymond J. DeMallie, "Pine Ridge Economy: Cultural and Historical Perspectives," in *American Indian Economic Development*, ed. Sam Stanley (The Hague: Mouton Publishers, 1978), 237–312; Thomas R. Wessel, "Agent of Acculturation: Farming on the Northern Plains Reservations, 1880–1910," *Agricultural History*, 60 (Spring 1986), 233–45; Wessell, "Agriculture on the Reservations: The Case of the Blackfeet, 1885–1935," *Journal of the West*, 18 (October 1979), 17–24; William D. Pennington, "Government Agricultural Policy on the Kiowa Reservation, 1869–1901," *Indian Historian*, 11 (Winter 1978), 11–16. Washakie's quote comes from Oliver La Farge, *A Pictorial History of the American Indian* (New York: Crown Publishers, 1956), 191.

12. Wessel, "Agriculture on the Reservations," 17–24; Wessel, "Phantom Experiment Station: Government Agriculture on the Zuni Reservation," *Agricultural History*, 61 (Fall 1987), 1–12; Hoover, "Arikara, Sioux, and Government Farmers," 22–48; Orlan J. Svingen, "Reservation Self-Sufficiency: Stock Raising vs. Farming on the Northern Cheyenne Indian Reservation," *Montana, The Magazine of Western History*, 31 (October 1981), 14–23; Robert P. Nespor, "From War Lance to Plow Share: The Cheyenne Dog Soldier as Farmers, 1879–1930s," *Chronicles of Oklahoma*, 65 (Spring 1987), 42–75; William D. Pennington, "Government Policy and Indian Farming on the Cheyenne and Arapaho Reservation, 1869–1880," *Chronicles of Oklahoma*, 57 (Summer 1979), 171–89; Pennington, "Government Agriculture," 11–16; Paul B. Wilson, "Farming and Ranching on the Wind River Indian Reservation, Wyoming" (Ph.D. diss., University of Nebraska, 1972); Winfred Buskirk, *The Western Apache: Living With the Land Before 1950* (Norman: University of Oklahoma Press, 1986).

13. Donald L. Parman, "New Deal Indian Agricultural Policy and the Environment: The Papagos as a Case Study," *Agricultural History*, 66 (Spring 1992), 23–33; C. Matthew Snipp, "American Indians and Natural Resource Development," *American Journal of Economics and Sociology*, 45 (October 1986), 457–74; Sam Stanley, ed., *American Indian Economic Development* (The Hague: Mouton Publishers, 1978); Peter Iverson, ed., *The Plains Indians of the Twentieth Century* (Norman: University of Oklahoma Press, 1985).

14. Gary Paul Nabhan, *Enduring Seeds: Native American Agriculture and Wild Plant Conservation* (San Francisco: North Point Press, 1989); National Indian Agricultural Working Group, *Final Findings and Recommendations*, Prepared for the Assistant Secretary of Indian Affairs and the Intertribal Agricultural Council, December 1987; Henry W. Kipp, *Indians in Agriculture: A Historical Sketch*, Prepared for the Task Force of the American Indian Agricultural Council, 7 August 1987, esp. 64–84.

INDEX